RELATIONAL PRACTICE

A clear and compelling text written by teachers, psychologists, and educationalists, *Relational Practice: New Approaches to Mental Health and Wellbeing in Schools* proposes a dynamic and relational approach to supporting the mental health needs of children and young people within education. Contributing authors advocate a movement away from the deficit, medicalised model of mental health and instead encourage readers to embrace a relational approach, considering philosophical and spiritual dimensions, as well as the wider everyday contexts that shape the mental health of individuals, groups, and school communities.

Filled with case studies, intervention strategies, and CPD activities, this essential guide bridges the gap between theory, research, and practice to offer evidence-based resources for practical application within schools.

Areas covered include, but are not limited to:

- Supporting neurodivergent and LGBT+ students to thrive
- Creating and actioning an anti-racist approach
- Multi-agency interventions
- Relationships in SEND settings
- Creating a supportive culture to enhance staff wellbeing
- Appreciative inquiry
- Staff perceptions of Building Relational Schools (BRS)
- The role of intersubjective processes and the impact they have on relationships in educational settings

Providing a comprehensive introduction to relational practice within education, this is an indispensable resource for anyone working in education who wishes to support the mental health and wellbeing of their school community.

Sahaja Timothy Davis is a practitioner, teacher, and researcher of mindfulness and non-duality who has contributed to national and international research projects, conferences, and publications in these areas. He is also the co-director for the doctorate in child and educational psychology at the University of Sheffield.

Tom Billington is Emeritus Professor of educational and child psychology at the University of Sheffield (UK) and is a fellow of the British Psychological Society. His work as a practitioner has driven his research, utilising critical approaches to developmental psychology that accord with principles of equality, diversity, and social inclusion.

Mary Chilokoa is a practising educational psychologist working in Leeds Educational Psychology Service. She is an academic tutor on the doctoral course in child and educational psychology at the University of Sheffield and has published in the areas of peer supervision and pupil 'voice'.

Claire-Marie Whiting is a specialist educational psychologist for participation and engagement at Rotherham Educational Psychology Service. She is the co-lead for 'Genuine Partnerships', a group of practitioners, parent carers, and young people who model and support co-production and inclusive practice. Claire is also the director of placements and a course tutor for the educational psychology doctorate at the University of Sheffield.

RELATIONAL PRACTICE

New Approaches to Mental Health and Wellbeing in Schools

Edited by Sahaja Timothy Davis,
Tom Billington, Mary Chilokoa, and
Claire-Marie Whiting

Routledge
Taylor & Francis Group

LONDON AND NEW YORK

Designed cover image: © Getty Images

First published 2025
by Routledge
4 Park Square, Milton Park, Abingdon, Oxon OX14 4RN

and by Routledge
605 Third Avenue, New York, NY 10158

Routledge is an imprint of the Taylor & Francis Group, an informa business

British Library Cataloguing-in-Publication Data
A catalogue record for this book is available from the British Library

ISBN: 978-1-032-58873-5 (hbk)
ISBN: 978-1-032-58872-8 (pbk)
ISBN: 978-1-003-45190-7 (ebk)

DOI: 10.4324/9781003451907

Typeset in Interstate
by Apex CoVantage, LLC

CONTENTS

CONTRIBUTORS

Dr Amy Bamford (Rotherham Educational Psychology Service)

Dr Catherine Beal (Leeds Educational Psychology Service)

Emeritus Professor Tom Billington (University of Sheffield)

Dr Mary Chilokoa (University of Sheffield, Leeds Educational Psychology Service)

Pauline Clarke (Educational Psychologist, Nottinghamshire County Council)

Dr Julie Connor (Doncaster Educational Psychology Service)

Dr Rachel Cooper (Wakefield Educational Psychology Service)

Associate Professor Tim Corcoran (Deakin University, Australia)

Chris Davey (Blessed Sacrament Catholic Primary School, Liverpool)

Dr Sahaja Timothy Davis (University of Sheffield)

Dr Laura de Cabo Serón (Doncaster Educational Psychology Service)

Dr Emily Forde (Educational Psychologist, University of Sheffield)

Carol Fordham (SAYiT – Sheena Amos Youth Trust, LGBTQ+ Youth Charity)

Dr Laura Griffiths (Wakefield Educational Psychology Service)

Dr Lucy Hatton (Wakefield Educational Psychology Service)

Jacqueline Hunter (St Brigid's Catholic Primary School, Liverpool)

Dr Emily Jackson (Leeds Educational Psychology Service)

Dr Scott Johnson (University of Sheffield, Rotherham Educational Psychology Service, Genuine Partnerships)

Dr Jayne Manning (Doncaster Educational Psychology Service)

Dr Jo Marriott (Nottinghamshire Educational Psychology Service)

Professor Sheila McManee (University of New Hampshire/TAOS Institute United States of America)

Dr Changjie Meng (Relational Practitioner, Researcher, and Mindfulness Teacher)

Kelly Moran (Blessed Sacrament Primary School, Liverpool)

Tom Mullen (Practice Development Lead at EMERGE Leeds, Leeds and York Partnership NHS Foundation Trust)

Dr Natalie Neal (Trainee Educational Psychologist, University of Sheffield)

Heather Paterson (SAYiT (Sheena Amos Youth Trust, LGBTQ+ Youth Charity)

Sharon Richards (St Brigid's Catholic Primary School, Liverpool)

Mary Scorer (Assistant Educational Psychologist, Nottinghamshire)

Dr Kate Taylor (Nottinghamshire Educational Psychology Service)

Dr Helen Waters (Leeds Educational Psychology Service)

Dr Claire-Marie Whiting (University of Sheffield, Rotherham Educational Psychology Service, Genuine Partnerships)

Dr Emily Williams (Doncaster Educational Psychology Service)

Dr Angela Wright (Wakefield Educational Psychology Service)

1 Working *relationally*

A paradigm choice

Tom Billington, Sahaja Timothy Davis, Mary Chilokoa, and Claire-Marie Whiting

We live at a time in which a generation of children and young people is commonly thought to be afflicted by a mental health crisis, with anxieties fuelled by stories of global financial pressures, pandemics, climate change, wars, and the vagaries of fast-changing social media. The challenge for adults working with children and young people can be daunting, and our responses can feel superficial, often inviting us to tackle symptoms in individual children and young people without addressing what might lie at the heart of any crisis. Rather than despair at the scale of the challenge, however, in this book we locate solutions which, through demonstrations of our practice and research, are to be found in the *relational* networks we inhabit with the children and young people, parents, our colleagues, and other practitioners.

This original publication brings the developing paradigm of the *relational* to the field of children and young people's mental health in education. We are psychologists, teachers, and educationalists (and, in some instances, parents, children, and young people) who, through our lived experiences, feel compelled to find better ways of attending to the mental health needs of the children and young people who are the focus of our working lives. We aim to explore how the *relational* can be performed in ways that achieve a sense of partnership, ownership, and wellbeing.

In setting out our case, we draw primarily upon the pedagogical, developmental, and psychological, but at times also the biological, cultural, philosophical, political, sociological, and even the spiritual, in order to find better ways of representing the children and young people and the situations we share. In performing the *relational*, therefore, we move beyond the individual but also, at times, beyond a narrow conceptualisation of mental health and propose, as a scientific first principle, that the young person can neither be conceptualised nor represented outside the conditions of our collective histories and experiences.

Over the years, we have become acutely aware of the limitations of the prevalent within-child, medicalised model in meeting the needs of children and young people, families, and schools, and especially aware that the language of deficit can itself be problematic, fixing and oppressing service users in discursive practices from which there is little escape. As intrinsically *relational beings* (Gergen, 2009), we offer an alternative lens through which to conceptualise, respond, and ultimately even change positions and lives. Whilst we highlight children and young people's mental health as an area of contemporary research and practice, our work in this book has a particular history that demonstrates our long-standing commitment to *relational* approaches.

DOI: 10.4324/9781003451907-1

Origins of the book

Examples of the *relational* in this book are drawn from contemporary practice and research situations, but it is important to acknowledge both our history and also a context in which changing global epistemologies, as well as national and local priorities, have influenced the direction of our work.

The professional training programme for educational and child psychologists at the University of Sheffield (DEdCPsy) has, for many years, been developing a distinctive approach to practice. We have drawn not only on empirical research and good practice models but also older traditions within psychology, education, and the social sciences that look to challenge assumptions in key aspects of knowledge and experience.

In the decades either side of the millennium, global and national policy changes created new contexts for all those in the UK who work with children and young people, for example, invoking children's rights, disability rights, and the 'voice of the child' (UNICEF, 1989; Department of Health, 1989; DfES, 2001; Every Child Matters, 2003). However, despite the emancipatory and inclusive thrust of such initiatives, we found that our work with schools and families continued to implicate us in the language and processes of social marginalisation. In particular, we could not but remain suspicious as to the nature of 'governmentality', through which too often we were invited to act in ways that served to subject individual children and young people to various forms of social exclusion (Foucault, 1977). We have been persistent in our efforts to create and develop alternative practices as acts of resistance (Burman et al., 1996), and our book is a contribution to that resistance.

The Sheffield programme has a history of concern for children and young people and social issues (Thompson et al., 1994; Desforges et al., 1995), and for the last 25 years or so, teaching, research, and approaches to professional practice have focused on the ways in which children and young people are too easily marginalised and excluded (Billington & Pomerantz, 2004; Pomerantz et al., 2007; Mercieca, 2011). In order to ground our resistance to unnecessary exclusions, we began to draw increasingly on a rich methodological and theoretical palette, including narrative psychology (Bruner, 1991; Reissman, 2008), critical psychology (Fox & Prilleltensky, 1997; Parker, 2016), and social constructionist approaches to both practice and research (Shotter, 1994; Burr, 2015). These developing paradigms have enabled us to challenge the inexorable drift towards social exclusion, to identify and confront awkward ethical dilemmas, and to work with trainees, psychology services, and schools to find alternative ways of working (Billington, 2006).

One strand of our work has been to examine and gain an understanding of the various dimensions involved in the creation of individual differences (Billington, 2000) which embrace both political – 'children with a persistent mental health problem face unequal chances in life. This is one of the burning injustices of our time' (DfE, 2017, p. 6) – and empirical – 'much of the variation between people stems from the synergistic combinations of nature and nurture. What really matters is not the relative strength of genetic and environmental effects but the mechanisms by which they exert their effects' (Rutter, 2002) influences.

It is through our willingness to remain curious in respect of all the possible forms of 'evidence' that we have looked to remain sensitive to human diversity and difference.

The 'medical model' and children and young people's mental health

Since the emergence of the antipsychiatry movement and Szaz's seminal work *The Myth of Mental Illness* (1974), there has been a critical gaze turned towards what has been termed the 'medical model' of mental health (Brissenden, 1986; Cromby et al., 2013; Hogan, 2019). In education, too, there has been a growing sense of unease as to the appropriateness of medicalised representations of the distress children and young people experience (Children's Commissioner, 2017). The distinctive application of the *relational* in this book reflects our continuing engagement with critical approaches to both psychology and education (Williams et al., 2017).

We maintain, therefore, that the medical model of problem identification, diagnosis, and treatment at the level of the individual can obscure the complex aetiology of situations in which both children and young people and practitioners experience their lives and in which psychopathologies can incubate. We have found that the narrow focus of the pathologising tendency constrains psychologists, schools, and education institutions, rendering us ill-equipped to respond to the distress of children and children and young people. Many practitioners can become overwhelmed by the larger contextual issues which seem out of their control, while the *relational* gives permission to aspire to small changes which can impact on an individual's wellbeing but also on the wider school community. The relational then extends beyond mental health to affect people's life chances in the face of problems which can play out as discriminatory or oppressive.

We argue that the framing of children and children and young people's mental health through the narrative of psychopathology (disorder) as opposed to distress (Parker, 2005) isolates both the blame and the focus of intervention within the individual child and, in so doing, fails to acknowledge the complexity of the *relational* conditions in which the young person and their distress are created, that is, in specific locations of time and place. Our resistance is not just ideological but scientific, for we suggest that many existing practices fail to acknowledge either the impact of complex variables or the opportunities that *relational* work can provide for more durable analyses of human differences and, ultimately, sustainable solutions in schools.

Social models of developmental psychology and mental health have, for some time, challenged the appropriateness and efficacy of the medical model (Burman, 1994/2017; Corcoran, 2014; Allan, 2018). In this book, we build on such work and offer alternative perspectives arising from a paradigm shift away from a medicalised, diagnostic perspective and towards a dynamic, social constructionist, and specifically *relational* understanding of children and young people, and their wellbeing and mental health. We will illustrate our positions by introducing the reader to ways in which psychologists, teachers, and other members of the school staff are already working tirelessly and effectively, often successfully, with parents and children and young people themselves, to enhance children and young people's sense of wellbeing and to both reduce and alleviate potential mental health difficulties.

From relationships to the *relational* in practice

Positivist methodologies have been strident in their authoritative over-simplifications of educational and psychological processes and have often ignored the importance of the social and environmental circumstances for human development foregrounded by key figures in psychology and education, for example, James (1890/2010), Vygotsky (1934/1962), Dewey (1938), Clark and Clark (1939), Fanon (2008), Freire (1972), Henriques et al. (1984), and Holl-way (1989). We follow in this tradition, and the ontological premise of this book conceives the child or young person's selfhood as existing within a multi-layered weft of shifting conditions and not as a completely autonomous entity acting in a vacuum (Sugarman & Martin, 2020). We argue for, and demonstrate, a more dynamic, contemporary social constructionist stance (McNamee et al., 2020) in which we focus our efforts on an understanding of the fluidity of *relational* conditions and processes that shape the wellbeing of individuals, groups, and whole school communities. For schools are communities, places of relationships, socialisa-tion, and lived experiences shared by children and young people and school staff at every juncture in the school day.

Cornelius-White's (2007) meta-analysis concluded that healthy teacher–student relation-ships could account for a range of positive outcomes, including attainment, critical thinking, self-esteem, motivation, and a reduction in disruptive behaviour. A more recent resurgence of interest in the significance of relationships in schools has led to a range of school-wide models being implemented based on trauma-informed approaches, adopted by local authori-ties and individual schools (Avery et al., 2020).

Whilst having a strong emphasis on the *relational*, however, these approaches, too, can, if we are not careful, still drift towards medicalised and pathologising narratives surrounding children and children and young people. It can be easy in practice to ignore the complex-ity of the power relations involved (Johnstone et al., 2018), and opportunities to empower the children and young people, and practitioners can be missed. We have sought to develop research and practice partnerships that, in their performance, demonstrate the effectiveness of the *relational*.

Alongside our evolving approaches to professional practice at Sheffield, we have similarly been looking to adopt the same ethical and scientific principles in our research, conducted both by staff and by trainees in the last year of their training programme.

The partnership network: Service users, practice, and research

At Sheffield, we had been encouraging our trainee educational psychologists to create pro-jects that pay attention to human relationships and *relational* contexts and, specifically, to conduct research *with*, not *on*, participants. In practical terms, we think these methodologies enable our trainees to become better listeners, more able to reflect on themselves and others, and better prepared to engage in a range of future practice situations. In the performance of our various research projects in the Yorkshire and Humber region, we became increasingly confident that our approaches would lead to more productive interventions and outcomes, for example, in the *relational* models they developed with services and service users.

At the same time, academic staff had been looking to contribute directly to city and regional communities and undertook commissions to evaluate initiatives to support the wellbeing and mental health of children and young people in schools (Billington et al., 2015). One of our projects, in accord with social constructionist principles, led to a phased process that was informed at each stage by the research participants themselves (Billington et al.,

2019). A thematic list of 20 factors was empirically identified from interviews with service managers, clinicians, school leaders, specialist teachers. The factors formed part of the questionnaire which asked respondents to select which factors they felt had the most impact on a young person's wellbeing and mental health.

Respondents (*n* = 875; parents and school staff, 14 primary and 1 secondary) selected the following four factors from the longer thematic list presented to them in order of approximate frequency:

Relational factors

- Family circumstances (i.e. including finances and relationships)
- Parental wellbeing and mental health
- Safeguarding issues (e.g. substance misuse, domestic abuse)
- School culture (including school climate, peer, and all other school-based relationships)

(Billington et al., 2022)

As a result of this phased empirical process, practitioners, parents, and school staff had mapped out themes in which we can see not individual children and young people but the *relational*; circumstances and networks in which a young person's wellbeing and mental health are forged. It seemed to us that these *relational* factors could be used as the basis to create more effective service responses and initiatives, involving groups of people, and working together to address their own *relational* circumstances. These factors were the conclusions, not of researchers or clinicians, but of the project participants, from commissioners to parents and school staff.

The results of our various empirical projects emboldened us to strengthen our partnerships with local services, and in collaboration with regional principal educational psychologists, we devised CPD days and further funded research, all based on social constructionist principles and increasingly focusing on the *relational* (e.g. Yorkshire & Humberside, 2020; Cameron & Billington, 2020). In consultation with the principal educational psychologists, we decided to disseminate our *relational* work across the region, and in the development days, we realised the extent of the interest being shown by practitioners. This book is just one facet of the process in which we catalogue and celebrate the *relational* work that is already being conducted in our educational communities.

The book process: Themes and chapter descriptors

In this book, we offer alternative perspectives, based initially on our history of practice and research and founded on the premise that relationships, arising in particular *relational* situations, are at the heart of children and young people's development and wellbeing. By seeing children and children and young people as essentially *relational*, teaching as a *relational* act, and schools as the site for *relational* experiences, this book offers a rationale for practice and acts as a guide, and hopefully an inspiration, for members of the education community working together to address the mental health and wellbeing of children and young people working to address the mental health and wellbeing of children and young people.

In the actual writing and constructing of this book, we have similarly endeavoured to embody *relational* principles, in the manner of its inception, from the aforementioned empirical research and practice, and in the manner of its production, with psychologists, teachers, academics, mental health practitioners, parents, children, and young people.

Our aim is to build on existing research and professional practice to demonstrate the potential of *relationally* oriented approaches to addressing mental health issues in education, through practice-based research and supported by a coherent theoretical framework. While some chapters have a theoretical focus, all chapters have implications for educational practice, for classroom teachers, as well as for both senior and support staff. At the end of many chapters, you will find a box summary, a checklist of successful strategies, and additional references to facilitate practice and CPD activities.

The book is presented in three parts: 'understanding relations', 'working together', and 'working for and with children'.

Understanding relations involves chapters that identify some of the key theoretical premises of the relational as a paradigm which inevitably offers a challenge to some of the current dominant narratives surrounding children and young people. Both Sheila and Tim offer a compelling argument for the transformative power of thinking and working relationally. In Sahaja's and Mary Chilokoa's chapters, they draw on paradigms outside of the dominant psychological narratives of the geopolitical 'West' as well as new and emergent thinking within psychological literature to orientate the reader towards a more relational way of being and practising. Emily Jackson and Mary Chilokoa offer a very personal account of practice in which they suggest that meaningful, engaged educational practice is essentially relational and therefore deeply personal, encompassing the emotional, social, and political.

Working together encompasses a range of research and practice-based chapters that present ways in which practitioners can work together for, and with, children, young people, and their parents and carers, through a relational lens. The four cornerstones approach, through Rotherham's Genuine Partnerships, emerged from a co-productive project work that is deeply rooted in relationships. Exploring the team's four cornerstones principles for co-production and inclusive practice, Claire and Scott have co-created their chapter with children/young people, parent/carers, and schools/settings. Jo and Pauline also take us on their collaborative journey, focusing on the development of antiracist practice within their local authority. Their *The Shimmer* story was a result of a collective endeavour that, in its creation, provided a rich source of reflection and learning.

Appreciative inquiry (AI), a social constructionist, collaborative, strengths-based approach, was utilised by both Natalie and Laura and Amy in their chapters to create systemic change in a number of complex contexts. Using three case studies, Natalie and Laura give a refreshingly frank and honest account of educational psychologists using AI with practitioners to support systemic change in local authority settings. Amy describes the development of a relational culture in a specialist setting through a focus on the wellbeing of their staff. Action research also provides a structure or set of principles that can guide professionals and practitioners to collaboratively work towards systemic change within organisations. Kate and Mary

Taylor use these principles to introduce and work with schools to develop relational-based practice in their settings.

Whilst relational-based practice is important for whole communities, there are a number of groups that, in particular, might benefit from this orientation. Tom Billington and his co-authors highlight the importance the relational plays for children in care proceedings who arguably might be said to have experienced some of the biggest disruptions in their relational networks. The authors demonstrate the vital role that schools can play in providing a safe place of care and stability within lives that might feel full of uncertainty. They explore the challenge for school staff to respond to the needs of these children and young people. Neurodiverse LGBTQ+ students, too, are another group that could potentially benefit greatly from relationally informed approaches. Many of the challenges that young LGBTQ+ people who are described as neurodiverse face are of a relational nature, for example, being bullied and feeling isolated. Rooted in the voices of the young people with whom they have worked, Carol and Heather explore what schools can do to support these young people. A particularly challenging stage of development for any young person highlighted by Tom Mullen is the transition to adulthood; this is markedly so for those with complex emotional needs. EMERGE Leeds is an NHS-led multi-agency service that works collaboratively with young people and partners from a wide range of services across the city to support young people through this period in their lives.

Working for and with children relationally can involve thinking differently about how we understand and respond to their needs. The REFLECT approach was conceived by a group of practising psychologists in Rotherham who were frustrated with dominant discourses in education involving notions of progress being applied to the social, emotional, and mental health of children. Drawing upon developmental, social constructionist, psychodynamic, and systemic theories, REFLECT (Claire) offers ways of working with partners to identify the conditions for our children and young people to flourish.

Through her interviews, Emily Forde offers us an insight into what young people value and find difficult in their relationships with their teachers. Through theory and the powerful voices of young people, she highlights the crucial role these relationships play in their lives. Rachel and her fellow authors in their chapter identify a specific approach to responding to the relational needs highlighted in Emily's work. They have adopted the concept of 'special time' found in parenting literature and applied it to work with school staff and young people. They provide a strong argument for 'special time' as an alternative to more behaviourally oriented approaches as we are encouraged to place more of our attention on relationships in school rather than just on the behaviours.

Changjie explores how concepts of transitional objects and transitional space can enable us to contemplate the relational space between child and adult. Through exploring play between a father (Mathew) and his child, we see how these concepts can provide an opportunity for creativity, growth, and a fundamental bridge between self and other.

In our final chapter, Catherine and Helen take us into the lives of young people transitioning to high school by exploring the stories that surround them. They also pay attention to the stories that surround themselves as education practitioners. Drawing on key practices and concepts within narrative therapy, specifically 'beads of life', they reveal the value of being listened to and of listening with curiosity.

It is our hope that through this collage of theories, practices, and research, which includes a diverse range of contexts involving different practitioners, we are able to illuminate from different positions the same value afforded to relational practice.

Importantly, our book has given all of us, as contributors, the opportunity to develop and participate in a community of academics, practitioners, and in some instances, parents, children, and young people that has inspired, informed, and emboldened each of us to allow the relational to become more figural in our work. The aspiration of this book is to expand this community across different disciplines and settings.

References

Allan, C. (2018, October 16). The mental health crisis is down to government policy, not stigma. *The Guardian*. Retrieved February 20, 2019, from www.theguardian.com/society/2018/oct/16/mental-health-crisis-government-policy-not-stigma

Avery, J. C., Morris, H., Galvin, E., Misso, M., Savalglio, M., & Skouteris, H. (2020). Systematic review of school-wide trauma-informed approaches. *Journal of Child and Adolescent Trauma, 14*(3), 381-397.

Billington, T. (2000). *Separating, losing and excluding children: Narratives of difference*. Routledge Falmer.

Billington, T. (2006). *Working with children: Assessment, representation and intervention*. Sage.

Billington, T., Fogg, P., Lahmar, J., & Gibson, S. (2019). *Evaluation of the Sheffield Healthy Minds Framework (HMF) for schools*. Sheffield City Council and Sheffield NHS Children's Trust.

Billington, T., Gibson, S., Fogg, P., Lahmar, J., & Cameron, H. (2022). Conditions for mental health in education: Towards relational practice. *British Educational Research Journal, 48*(1), 95-119.

Billington, T., & Pomerantz, M. (Eds.). (2004). *Children at the margins: Supporting children, supporting schools*. Stoke-on-Trent, Trentham Books.

Billington, T., Williams, A., Abdi, M., & Lahmar, J. (2015). *Evaluation of the emotional wellbeing mental health service for schools*. Sheffield City Council.

Brissenden, S. (1986). Independent living and the medical model of disability. *Disability and Society, 1*(2), 173-178.

Bruner, J. (1991). The narrative construction of reality. *Critical Inquiry, 18*(1), 1-21.

Burman, E. (2017). *Deconstructing developmental psychology* (4th ed.). Routledge. (Original work published 1994)

Burman, E., Aitken, G., Alldred, P., Allwood, R., Author, Goldberg, B., Gordo Lopez, A. J., Heenan, C., Marks, D., & Warner, S. (Eds.). (1996). *Psychology discourse practice: Regulation and resistance*. Taylor & Francis.

Burr, V. (2015). *Social constructionism*. Routledge.

Cameron, H., & Billington, T. (2020). *Developing a psychosocial model of mental health for schools: Perspectives from educational psychologists*. Research England.

Children's Commissioner. (2017). *Children's voices: A review of evidence on the subjective wellbeing of children with mental health needs in England*. www.childrenscommissioner.gov.uk/wp-content/uploads/2017/10/Voices-Mental-health-needs-1_0.pdf

Clark, K., & Clark, M. (1939). The development of consciousness of self and the emergence of racial identification in Negro pre-school children. *Journal of Social Psychology, 10*(4), 591-599.

Corcoran, T. (Ed.). (2014). *Psychology in education: Critical theory-practice*. Sense.

Cornelius-White, J. (2007). Learner-centered teacher-student relationships are effective: A meta-analysis. *Review of Educational Research, 77*(1), 113-143.

Cromby, J., Harper, D., & Reavey, P. (Eds.). (2013). *Psychology, mental health and distress*. Palgrave Macmillan.

Department for Education. (2017). *DfE mental health services and schools link pilots: Evaluation report (February 2017)* (DFE-RR640). Department for Education. Retrieved September 2, 2018, from https://assets.publishing.service.gov.uk/government/uploads/system/uploads/attachment_data/file/590242/Evaluation_of_the_MH_services_and_schools_link_pilots-RR.pdf

Department of Health. (1989). *The children act*. The Stationery Office.

Desforges, M. F., Desforges, G. S., & Desforges, L. C. (1995). On becoming a bicycle. *Educational Psychology in Practice*, *11*(1), 49–52.

Dewey, J. (1938). *Experience and education*. Macmillan.

DfES. (2001). *Special needs and disability rights Act*. Department for Education and Skills.

Every Child Matters. (2003). *Every child matters. Green paper presented to parliament by the chief secretary to the treasury by command of her majesty, September 2003*. The Stationery Office.

Fanon, F. (2008). *Black skin, white masks* (C. L. Markmann, Trans.). Pluto. (Original work published 1952)

Foucault, M. (1977). *Discipline and punish: The birth of the prison*. Pantheon Books.

Fox, D., & Prilleltensky, I. (Eds.). (1997). *Critical psychology: An introduction*. Sage Publications.

Freire, P. (1972). *Pedagogy of the oppressed*. Continuum.

Gergen, K. J. (2009). *Relational being*. Oxford University Press.

Henriques, J., Hollway, W., Urwin, C., Venn, C., & Walkerdine, V. (1984). *Changing the subject: Psychology, social regulation and subjectivity*. Routledge.

Hogan, A. J. (2019). Social and medical models of disability and mental health: Evolution and renewal. *Canadian Medical Journal*, *191*(1), E16–E18.

Hollway, W. (1989). *Subjectivity and method in psychology*. Sage.

James, W. (2010). *Principles of psychology* (Vols. 1&2). Dover Publications. (Original work published 1890)

Johnstone, L., & Boyle, M. with Cromby, J., Dillon, J., Harper, D., Kinderman, P., Longden, E., Pilgrim, D., & Read, J. (2018). *The power threat meaning framework: Towards the identification of patterns in emotional distress, unusual experiences and troubled or troubling behaviour, as an alternative to functional psychiatric diagnosis*. British Psychological Society. Retrieved September 2, 2018, from www.bps.org.uk/sites/bps.org.uk/files/Policy%20-%20Files/PTM%20Main.pdf

McNamee, S., Gergen, M. M., Camargo-Borres, C., & Rasera, E. F. (Eds.). (2020). *The Sage handbook of social constructionist practice*. Sage.

Mercieca, D. (2011). *Beyond conventional boundaries: Uncertainty in research and practice with children*. Sense Publishers.

Parker, I. (2005). *Qualitative psychology: Introducing radical research*. Open University Press.

Parker, I. (Ed.). (2016). *Handbook of critical psychology*. Routledge.

Pomerantz, K., Hughes, M., & Thompson, D. (Eds.). (2007). *How to reach 'hard to reach' children: Improving access, participation and outcomes*. John Wiley.

Reissman, C. K. (2008). *Narrative methods for the human sciences*. Sage.

Rutter, M. (2002). Nature, nurture and development: From evangelism through science toward policy and practice. *Child Development*, *73*(1), 1–21.

Shotter, J. (1994). *Social construction: Knowledge, self and others: Continuing the conversation*. Taylor and Francis.

Sugarman, J., & Martin, J. (Ed.). (2020). *A humanities approach to the psychology of personhood*. Routledge.

Szasz, T. (1974). *The myth of mental illness: Foundations for a theory of personal conduct*. Harper & Row.

Thompson, D., Whitney, I., & Smith, P. K. (1994). Bullying of children with special needs in mainstream schools. *Support for Learning*, *9*(3), 103–106.

UNICEF. (1989). *Children's rights: The United Nations Convention on the Rights of the Child*.

Vygotsky, L. (1962). *Thought and language*. MIT Press. (Original work published 1934)

Williams, A., Billington, T., Goodley, D., & Corcoran, T. (Eds.). (2017). *Critical educational psychology*. BPS Books/Wiley Blackwell.

Yorkshire and Humberside Principal Educational Psychologists. (2020, June 24). *Educational psychology CPD event*.

2 Humanising our practice

The radical possibilities of a relational approach

Sheila McNamee

Introduction

We face several challenges in our lives today. Articulating these challenges can inform how we - as educators, mental health professionals, and policymakers - can be of help in attending to the educational and mental health needs of the young people who populate our schools. Educational professionals are trained to educate and assess in specific ways. These techniques and methods are quickly naturalised: 'this is the way it is done.' We see this in mental health, where one's choice of model or theory is expertly utilised 'on' the client. We see this in education, where standardised tests require educators to deliver information in a specific manner and 'best practices' dictate how information should be taught. As Biesta (2020) notes, most believe that education is successful when what is expected of you is what you do (referring to both teacher and student). But are our current standards for education useful? Are they addressing the challenges we face in today's world? Are they tending to the wellbeing of students? And are our educational standards preparing youth for the world of tomorrow? Two significant and related cultural shifts call our attention to our need to question our current practices. The first is a shift from a presumption of community homogeneity to daily emersion in heterogeneity. The second follows from the first. It is a shift from presumed social and global stability to all-encompassing and constant instability.

From homogeneity/stability to heterogeneity/instability

There was a time when families, teachers, and school administrators could be fairly certain that the population attending school was more homogeneous than not. This is because, prior to instantaneous connection via technology, communities confronted less cultural, socioeconomic, religious, and even political differences. Certainly, those differences existed prior to technological advances, but they often remained invisible due to geographic barriers (even if those barriers were physically absent). Christians lived in one community, Jews in another, and Muslims in yet another. We might refer to this as homogeneity by location.

However, today - and for the past several decades - a wide range of worldviews and beliefs are available at our fingertips via social media and the internet. Add to this the increasing migration of people seeking improved employment opportunities, better education, a more forgiving climate, or freedom from religious persecution. Homogeneity in schools today

DOI: 10.4324/9781003451907-2

seems aligned with the privilege of private educational institutions. With our access to global mobility, we are more likely to encounter a wide range of diversity in communities and, thus, in education as well.

In addition, we must consider that globally, politics are in a state of instability that we have not seen since the Cold War. Where we once enjoyed a sense of hemispheric (if not national) dominance, a decline in ideological struggle, and a high degree of global cooperation, we are now living in a moment of contestation, where competition has replaced cooperation and opposition of ideologies dominates. Additionally, we have front-row viewing and around-the-clock commentary on coups d'Ètat, school shootings, airport bombings, and other violent crimes around the world. Our access to personal suffering is proliferating, thereby inviting an all-encompassing narrative of danger, distrust, and fear.

If we look at the state of affairs globally, it might be less surprising that psychopharmaceutical 'solutions' to our distress are (and have been) in rapid ascent. There are anti-depressants for those unable to find joy in life. We have anti-anxiety medications for those who find the world too much to handle. And we have a wide array of drugs for those who suffer from inattention, hyperactivity, and impulsivity. The belief is that the problem lies within the person, and therefore the responsible and acceptable recourse is to seek diagnosis and treatment. Doing so will provide us with the resources to make our way through a chaotic, divisive, and challenging world. Like all other institutions, schools today are ill-suited to respond to these challenges in humanising ways.

In the clutch of modernism

Our very conception of education, born out of a modernist tradition, is focused on the individual. It is the individual mind that is the target of learning. The teacher is responsible for providing the 'right' information, in the 'right' manner, so that students can learn and succeed. But given the multiplicity of beliefs, values, customs, and priorities that we now live amongst, what would count as the right information, the right method, and how could we possibly know that what is effective with one group would be equally effective with another?

Herein lies the conundrum we face in schools today. If we rely on our tradition of education where a standardised curriculum and form of delivery – acquired through context-independent guidelines – is employed, then the cultural diversity we live amongst today remains invisible. Those with diverse values and beliefs will inevitably be viewed as deficient, perhaps mentally unstable, and failures. All this to say that, for the most part, the discourse of the helping professions – a category in which I include education and mental health – emerges within the tradition of modernist science, where social problems or challenges become the problem of the individual because expert professionals know what standards should apply to all. The presumption is that education should eliminate diverse knowledges. And if the complexity and diversity of the world (or of your community, school, family, or intimate relationship) become too much to bear, *you*, the individual, must find a way to 'cope', to 'deal with', and to 'manage' *your* discomfort, irritation, feelings of being overwhelmed, etc. The focus is always on the individual.

The ideology of liberal humanism, very much an individualist stance, privileges the pathologising and subsequent treatment of persons over deconstructing and transforming social and cultural institutions. We must admit, it is far easier to prescribe therapy and medication for students who are overwhelmed with deadlines and exams and who struggle to pay attention than to examine how we educate and who benefits and who loses by virtue of our policies and practices. In a world saturated with social media that informs, entertains, and often confers social status, why should a young person endure the dry lessons offered in the sterile context of the classroom? It is easier to medicalise/psychologise a person's experience than to critically examine our ways of living. Given all that has changed in our world, is it not time we reconstruct how we educate?

Today's educational institutions have been crafted within the neoliberal, individualist paradigm. As Sir Kenneth Robinson (2010) aptly demonstrates, we educate children in 'batches', as if age were the most important thing about them. Also noted by Robinson is the 'factory-like' organisation of education, with bells to organise the start and end of classes and compartmentalisation of 'subjects'. Learners are expected to work individually, either succeeding or failing their tests and assignments. It is important to acknowledge that, by imposing this individualist discourse on the interactions that challenge one's sense of presence in the world and ability to cope, we ignore the larger political and social issues that contribute to the eroding mental health and wellbeing of youth as they participate in contemporary education.

The rise of disciplinary knowledge

Foucault (1977) argues that our sense of self, very much situated within the 20th century ideology of individuality, autonomy, free choice, and liberty, has been constructed by the rise in stature of the social and 'psy' disciplines (Rose, 1990). These disciplines (psychology, psychiatry, psychotherapy, psychoanalysis, and even sociology and anthropology) have emerged as dominant discourses that regulate our lives. Specifically, what a culture or society comes to believe is 'normal' is regulated by the psy-disciplines, including normal education and all that we take to be rational, reasonable, and right.

No matter what professional domain we encounter, we offer ourselves to the surveillance of experts – expert teachers, expert doctors, expert therapists, expert politicians, expert managers. Foucault's argument makes clear that the construction of dominant discourses (generated within what he refers to as 'disciplinary regimes' – or professional domains, we might say) guides our actions, and recursively, as we act in concert with the dominant discourse, we unwittingly ensure that this dominant (unquestioned) way of acting is maintained. Again, as Biesta (2020) says, we do what we are expected to do. The standards from which what is expected to emerge are never questioned. As we abide by the taken-for-granted practices perpetuated by educators and mental health professionals, we are not only acting in ways that are simply taken-for-granted as the proper way to be in an educational institution but also, in so doing, keeping these unquestioned beliefs and practices alive. In other words, it is time we recognise that as we 'follow the rules', we are the ones who keep them alive.

Pathologising discourses

Foucault (1972) makes clear that the disciplinary discourses (of psychotherapy, education, etc.) are just that, discourses. They are ways of talking, ways of being in the world. And to put it that way is to suggest that there are, or could be, other ways of talking and being in the world available to us. This suggests that, when engaged in any sort of professional encounter, we should ask ourselves how useful the associated vocabulary and practices are. How useful is it to view an adolescent's difficulties in school as a sign of inferior intellect rather than a sign of repeated oppression or utter boredom amidst a cultural backdrop of enticing social media options?

The concentrated focus on the individual in contemporary society is the by-product of these emergent and eventually dominating discourses. And when understood in historical, cultural, and social context, it becomes possible to recognise that all of us are active participants in the power and dominance of pathologising discourses. Pathologising discourses are ways of talking that cast a person, family, or group as abnormal, lacking in some way, or unable to meet social expectations. And every time we draw upon these dominant discourses, we participate in maintaining their very dominance.

Recognising our own part in maintaining the dominance of individualist practices is critical. It is critical because it shows us the by-product of this internal, individualist focus. If one is not perpetually satisfied, fulfilled, and emotionally and behaviourally 'adjusted' in school, there must be something wrong. Inability to 'do what is expected' is a personal failure, not a systemic one. Even admitted contextual problems in the way in which school and everyday life are structured, or in the physical constraints of these environments, are viewed in terms of how these problems affect the individual. In other words, the dominance of psychological discourse actually shapes the contours of our day-to-day lives. Since the individual is always the unit of analysis, focus remains on individual performance at the cost of creating collaborative and communal environments. Thus, competition and comparison to others become the norm, and constant surveillance (by self and others) leaves one feeling incompetent, inadequate, and – most importantly – the cause of one's own hardships. And most unfortunate is the fact that the very professions and their practices that are designed to help people connect with each other and their environments (e.g. education and mental health) actually further separate and divide, making success in life a private pursuit.

What individualism ignores is that we live in community. We engage in relations with each other and with the material world that surrounds us. The challenge that confronts us as we examine the pervasive problem of living in contemporary culture is the challenge to move beyond the neoliberal, individualist ideology, where it remains the purview of the individual to resolve their problems and where homogeneity and stability are favoured. We should be, instead, questioning the larger social orders – the very institutions and taken-for-granted ways of relating – that invite divisiveness, conflict, and human suffering. In doing so, we shift from enticing people into a self-focused practice (treatment for my learning disability, for my hyperactivity, for my educational failures) to a future-forming ritual, that is, our attention focuses on creating more inclusive, diverse, humanising, and welcoming institutions.

Where is the community to support one who is falling behind in school or who is feeling ostracised by repeated bullying? Who – if anyone – might be able to offer alternative descriptions of what one is experiencing, descriptions that are not based on personal deficiencies? Are an adolescent's problems really due to their inability to 'cope', or might 'inability to cope' be a rational response to institutional systems of discipline? Should a student engage in therapy because she finds the competition in the classroom unbearable, or might an invitation to work collaboratively add excitement and energy to her school day? A concentrated effort to attend to the wellbeing of all requires a shift in focus from unquestioned techniques to an active attentiveness to *processes of relating*.

The central challenges we face as we confront mental health and wellbeing in schools can be summarised as:

- Adherence to the neoliberal, individualist discourse that focuses our attention on isolated individuals
- Codification of theories and practices into competing models, movements, and techniques
- Formulaic practice (strategies) by professionals
- Lack of awareness of the inseparable connection between how we relate (micro-interactions) and the institutions, beliefs, and values that guide us (macro-discourses)
- The construction of normalcy, which gives birth to pathologising individuals

These challenges, in turn, generate what Shotter (2010) calls 'aboutness thinking' as opposed to (what is needed) 'withness thinking'. For example, we are concerned *about* the adolescent's poor attention rather than exploring *with* the adolescent when and where their attention is distracted and comparing that to where and when their attention is laser-focused. Also generated by these challenges is the aim for professionals to focus on *knowing that* as opposed to *knowing how*. In other words, the educator or mental health professional is quick to evaluate, diagnose, and propose remedies to a student's problems and pays little – if any – attention to *how* such problems emerge and are sustained by contextual and relational elements. Additionally, there is a focus on 'getting it right' as opposed to 'finding a way', where getting it right suggests employing one's well-learned tools of the trade, while finding a way – attention to unfolding processes of interaction – implies a stance of uncertainty, thereby initiating an exploration of options and entertaining diverse values, beliefs, and understandings.

Challenging the tradition: The relational alternative

Focusing on unfolding processes of relating acknowledges and assigns primacy to relations and how people in the present co-construct meaning and socially construct a local reality (Gergen, 2009). A more relational and processual perspective to learning prioritises the 'how' of teaching over the 'what' of teaching. In other words, there is more attention given to the processual, relational, and identity constructing aspects that transpire in the educational context. The notion that our understandings of the world are given birth in social processes challenges traditional assumptions about the nature of truth, objectivity, knowledge, and the place of human values. Released from the burden of expert knowledge, professionals are now free to question taken-for-granted understandings by adopting a self-reflexive curiosity about all that is assumed to be real, rational, and good. Questioning one's own worldview invites an acknowledgement of the vast array of alternative worldviews, thereby embracing curiosity in others' beliefs and ways of life. To view understandings as emerging in our processes of coordinated action offers an optimistic sense that together, more viable futures can be crafted. Such a focus – on unfolding processes of coordination – releases us from the

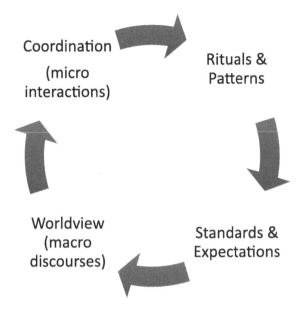

Figure 2.1 Recursivity of micro and macro in creating a worldview.

modernist emphasis on technique, where the assumption is that the right technique will yield desired and predicted results.

The recursivity of the micro and macro

Figure 2.1 offers a visualisation of interactive processes (micro-interactions) and how the responsiveness of persons to one another and to their environment comes to create what we 'know', what we 'understand', and what we believe to be 'real' (macro-discourses). Let us consider how specific ways of understanding the world emerge. Meaning emerges as communities of people coordinate their activities with one another. These meanings, in turn, create a sense of social order. The continual coordination required in any relationship or community eventually generates a sense of taken-for-granted, common practices otherwise known as dominant (and largely unquestioned) discourses.

As people coordinate their activities with others in their daily interactions (e.g. teacher directs and corrects, students respond accordingly), patterns quickly emerge (e.g. active teacher, passive students). These rituals generate a sense of standards and expectations that we use to assess our own and others' actions (e.g. the student who questions the teacher is seen as violating the classroom norm). Once these standardising modes are in place, the generation of values and beliefs (a worldview or dominant discourse) is initiated (e.g. in education, it is always important that the teacher be in control and the students do as they are told). *Thus, from the very simple process of coordinating our activities with each other, we develop entire belief systems, moralities, and values (macro-discourses).* Of course, the starting point for analysis of any given worldview (reality) is not restricted to our relational coordinations.

We can equally explore patterns of interaction or the sense of obligation (standards and expectations) that participants report in any given moment. We can also start with the emergent worldviews themselves (dominant discourses, as many would call them) and engage in a Foucauldian archaeology of knowledge (1972),[1] where we examine how certain beliefs, values, and practices originally emerged (which returns us to the simple coordinations of people and environments in specific historical, cultural, and local moments). This is the relational process of creating a worldview which, in turn, informs our very local interactions (coordinations).

What is important to consider is that, within any family, group, community, or culture, these micro-processes are not only ongoing and multiple but also diverse. We all have dozens of interactions each day. And as we can see in the simple figure earlier, it is the very interactions we engage in that create what we take to be real. But different families, different communities, different cultures engage in different forms of coordinated action, and thus, the diversity of worldviews (dominant discourses) is not only inevitable but also plentiful. This observation makes it difficult to hold on to the modernist/individualist view that, with the right tools, questions, and context, we could discover a universal truth (e.g. best practices for educational wellbeing). This also raises an important question for us: How can we recognise our own participation in maintaining these dehumanising ways of living? To Foucault, if we question these taken-for-granted practices, we come to question the truth value of these practices and free ourselves to construct alternatives. To question taken-for-granted practices and assumptions is to engage in self-reflexive inquiry.

Self-reflexivity

In simplest terms, *reflexivity* involves questioning our own assumptions and beliefs. It means entertaining doubt about our own certainties. It is a way of being in the world, and not a technique. According to Pollner (1991), reflexivity can be understood as '[a]n "unsettling" i.e., an insecurity regarding the basic assumptions, discourse, and practices used in describing reality' (p. 407). By thinking more critically about our own assumptions and actions, we can develop more collaborative, responsive, and ethical ways of acting.

To be reflexive is to call into question our taken-for-granted assumptions and meanings regarding a specific situation. Once called into question, we are invited to think in different ways and entertain alternative understandings. It is important to note that, within a modernist/individualist orientation, there is certainty about what we know and how we know it. Thus, there is no impulse to adopt a self-reflexive stance. When we are self-reflexive, we are acknowledging how the situations we encounter are socially and relationally enacted into being (Gergen, 2009). Reflexivity might best be understood as the way we position ourselves; it is an invitation to embrace our own role in co-creating the realities of which we are a part.

This relational focus, with its emphasis on self-reflexivity, offers an alternative to the neoliberal ways of describing social life, elevating our attention to processes of relating as opposed to objects or entities (such as an individual person, an individual's thoughts, feelings, or bodily sensations). It is a humanising approach calling attention to how all participants create understanding together. This relational sensibility offers us a very different path for living in today's complex world and points us beyond the (often) pathologising discourses of contemporary life. From a relational orientation, our attention is on how we position ourselves in the interactive moment rather than attend to how well we are employing the prescribed techniques. To that extent, the relational approach entails a form of radical presence (McNamee, 2020).

Radical presence

The writings of both Bateson (1972) and Sampson (1993) contribute to our understanding of the relational stance of radical presence. Bateson talked about human interaction as the pattern that connects, and to that end, he described mind or mental states as social – not bound by the skull but, rather, as 'immanent also in pathways and messages outside the body . . . still immanent in the total interconnected social system and planetary ecology' (p. 461). This more expansive view of mind – mind as released from the confines of the body into our relational patterns of engagement – provides fertile ground for a relational reconstruction of our professional practice as educators and mental health providers.

In a similar vein, Sampson (1993) describes

> people's lives are characterized by the ongoing conversations and dialogues they carry out in the course of their everyday activities, and therefore *the most important thing about people is not what is contained with them, but what transpires between them* (emphasis in the original).
>
> (p. 20)

The term *radical presence* is a deliberate attempt to avoid drawing upon the discourse of mind. If we can avoid mental language, our attention is more readily drawn towards *relational processes* and away from self-contained individuals. Where contemporary professional discourses guide one to attend to oneself in the sense of bodily feelings, sensations, and thoughts, radical presence places our attention on relational (interactive) processes. There is an active attentiveness to the process of relating itself. This is distinguished from consideration of 'what I am doing' or 'what is going on inside me' (not to imply that attention to these aspects of our relational being should be ignored); rather, radical presence orients our concern towards what *we* are creating together as our interaction unfolds within specific local circumstances, histories, and cultural patterns. Rather than solely scrutinising the integrity of our own actions, we recognise how our actions and the actions of others – as well as the material conditions within which our engagements transpire – invite certain responses. And in inviting certain responses, we pause to consider (i.e. engage in self-reflexive inquiry) what other responses we might offer and what sorts of alternative supplements they might invite. The significance of this attention to unfolding, interactive patterns is that we recognise that our wellbeing and the wellbeing of the other are intricately connected. They cannot be separated and evaluated independently.

The relational focus of radical presence offers us a way out of the self-contained focus offered by our neoliberal tradition. That tradition, while not intended to ignore broader social issues of inequality, injustice, and oppression, inadvertently informs us that attending to your short fallings will help you cope in a chaotic, challenging world. But is this the message (or the practice) that we want to perpetuate? It is akin to giving sedative drugs to someone who is suffering from poverty and oppression. If they are sedated, they will be less likely to attend to the ever-emerging features of their poverty or oppression; they will be less likely to engage in social activism to change the injustices in the system. The response to 'the problem' is imposed by a professional, otherwise known as an expert. The vision of normality offered by individualist discourse is one where the solution to one's problems is remediation of the self. By individualising problems, we ensure that the larger discursively constituted realities and structures that are the main contributors to our present angst are ignored.

Radical presence, on the other hand, directs our attention to relational processes, to the ways in which we are all connected to – and part of constructing – all that we love and enjoy as well as all that disturbs and worries us. Radical presence can take many forms. It is the administrator, policymaker, teacher, or mental health professional who adopts an unknowing, ready-to-learn-from-others stance. It is the invitation to collaborate that a teacher offers her students. It means adopting the assumption that we are, if even in some small way, part of the larger problems we confront.

Humanising our practice

Radical presence positions us to appreciate a relational understanding of the social world. Amidst all the diversity and complexity of our daily lives, how could a practice that advocates attention to and centring of oneself be responsive to the need to collaboratively deconstruct and reconstruct our ways of going on together? The world is complex, not simple. It is time that we embrace this complexity and develop ways of *coordinating* our diversity rather than eliminating it. When we orient ourselves to the other, to the complexity and difference, with curiosity and a desire to 'know differently', we are radically present. Our respectful attempts to understand might foster new forms of coordinated activity, and this coordination might be focused on embracing the diversity among which we live.

We need to widen the lens; we need to see and assess what is happening within our communities, our institutions, and our culture. It is important to ask how our present practices assist in challenging oppressive and unjust social orders or encourage engagement with others to create social transformation. As long as we shelter ourselves within an individualist ideology, we avoid confronting some of the most vexing challenges of today. When problems are individual problems, we remain locked in patterns of first-order change (Watzlawick et al., 1974), where we substitute our usual action with an action that we think will produce different outcomes. However, the overall pattern remains the same because the new action serves the same function as the original. This simple substitution does not change the entire scenario. If, instead, we ask ourselves how our broader social structures and our ways of maintaining those social structures contribute to alienation, disengagement, humiliation, degradation, and negative evaluation, we recognise our own participation in the perpetuation of individualised pathology. By adopting a radical presence, we can move beyond the focus on individuals and harness the vast resources available when multiple communities coordinate together to create ways of 'going on together' (Wittgenstein, 1953).

If the central question of modernist discourse is 'How can I learn to control myself – and cope – in the face of complexity, diversity, and chaos?' our radically relational approach takes the form of four questions:

1. What are we making together?
2. How are we making this?

3. Who are we becoming as we make this?
4. How might we make a more liveable future?

(Pearce, 2007, p. 53)

Knowing the challenges we face in promoting mental health and wellbeing in schools can inform how we relate to being of help and use to youth. First, we can acknowledge that there is a wide diversity of beliefs, values, and understandings and that each worldview (or dominant discourse) is coherent for those who coordinate their micro-interactions in particular ways. This does not mean that 'anything goes'. But it does mean that we should never be too quick to presume we *know that* (e.g. *about* another). Acknowledging the way in which dominant discourses (worldviews) guide our actions and how our interactions, in turn, can support, maintain, or transform those discourses positions us as active participants in creating the possibilities and constraints that we live amongst.

Understanding how relational processes create meaning tempts us to examine how alternative relational processes might yield alternative understandings. Recognising the multiplicity of understandings ignites curiosity about diverse beliefs, values, and understandings. And our curiosity, in turn, tempts us to embrace difference rather than attempt to reduce it. In the face of such multiplicity, we are reminded to remain poised – ready to move in many directions – as opposed to following a well-rehearsed technique. We are also reminded to embrace our discomfort with the diversity we face. Discomfort removes us from the comfort of the 'expert' position, reminding us to be radically present in the moment.

Once we imagine a relational understanding of our world, a dramatic shift ensues. This shift is best described as a shift from a form of police-state-existence, where we all act and make sense as we do because 'that is the way it is' to a fully reflective form of existence, where attention is directed to what we are making together as we engage. This is radical presence: recognising our own fingerprints on the forms of life we view as 'right' or 'natural'. A relational approach turns our gaze toward our actions *in relation to others and to our environments*.

In adopting a relational approach, we are invited to entertain fluid and flexible conversational resources. There are many ways in which any of the following can be achieved, thus privileging local, situated contexts. The following resources are not mutually exclusive; they are overlapping possibilities one might use to invite possible futures.

- **Avoid abstraction.** Try to avoid global statements about good/bad, right/wrong, etc. and invite people to speak from their lived stories, culture, and values.
- **Suspend the tendency to judge and evaluate and the propensity to problem-solve.** Speak instead from a desire to understand and from a position of curiosity about differences.
- **Engage in self-reflexive inquiry.** Question your assumptions, your understandings. Ask yourself how else things might be described and understood. Do not be too quick to 'know'.
- **Engage in relational reflexivity** (Burnham, 2005). Check in with those you are in conversation with concerning how the interaction is going for them. Are there other topics all of you should be discussing? Are there questions they were hoping you would ask or details you would provide? Are there other issues to be addressed?
- **Coordinate multiplicity.** Rather than search for unity, appreciate difference. Avoid the move toward consensus (a small overlap in agreement). Can we open a space where we

can talk about our differences without trying to persuade or prove that one position is superior to another. Our focus should not be on agreement but on creating new forms of understanding.

- **Use the familiar in unfamiliar contexts.** Invite yourself and others to draw on conversational/action resources that they use in other contexts, in other relations. We spend too much time trying to teach people how to do things in a different way. What if we invite them, instead, to draw upon their familiar ways of interacting in contexts that seem to call for something else. For example, might it be useful to use the voice you harbour as a caring friend when you are confronted with a differing opinion from a colleague or superior?

- **Imagine the future.** We spend too much of our time trying to figure out what in the past has caused the present conflict. What if we focused, instead, on what we might construct together in the future? How would we like to see ourselves four months from now? A year from now? In ten years? Once we engage in this conversation, we have already initiated the possibility of co-creating that future together.

- **Create the conversational space.** It is not always possible, but if we can invite conversations about difficult topics in contexts, spaces, atmospheres that are more conducive to human care and consideration, we might be surprised at what might unfold. Living rooms and lounges invite human contact, and food also helps bring people together.

- **Search for local coherence.** Rather than judge a person's stance on an issue, can we try to understand how that stance has evolved from that person's history of interactions? No ideas, beliefs, or values emerge in a vacuum; they emerge within communities where participants negotiate together what counts as true, right, and wrong.

- **Suspend the desire for agreement and seek new forms of understanding.** If we maintain our disagreement on an issue but we come to understand the rationale for the other's position, we have already moved away from framing an issue as true or false, black or white, to grey (that is, complex and diverse).

Summary box

Relational resources for humanising contemporary education

- Avoid abstraction.
- Suspend the tendency to judge and evaluate and the propensity to problem-solve.
- Engage in self-reflexive inquiry.
- Engage in relational reflexivity.
- Coordinate multiplicity.
- Use the familiar in unfamiliar contexts.
- Imagine the future.
- Create the conversational space.
- Search for local coherence.
- Suspend the desire for agreement, and seek new forms of understanding.

Note

1   To engage in an archeology of knowledge (Foucault, 1972) is to trace a certain social practice or way of talking back to its origins. For example, when did health professionals first start diagnosing workers with trauma, and (most important) what else was going on at that time, in that context and historical/cultural moment? The assumption is that social practices emerge as "sensible" within the communities that construct them. Yet over time, a particular practice might lose its utility.

References

Bateson, G. (1972). *Steps to an ecology of mind*. Ballentine.

Biesta, G. (2020). Can the prevailing description of educational reality be considered complete? On the Parks-Eichmann paradox, spooky action at a distance and a missing dimension in the theory of education. *Policy Futures in Education, 18*(8), 1011-1025. https://doi.org/10.1177/1478210320910312

Burnham, J. (2005). Relational reflexivity: A tool for socially constructing therapeutic relationships. In C. Flaskas, B. Mason, & A. Perlesz (Eds.), *The space between: Experience, context, and process in the therapeutic relationship* (pp. 1-17). Karnac.

Foucault, M. (1972). *Archeology of knowledge* (A. M. Sheridan Smith, Trans.). Pantheon.

Foucault, M. (1977). *Discipline and punish* (A. Sheridan, Trans.). Pantheon.

Gergen, K. J. (2009). *Relational being: Beyond self and community*. Oxford University Press.

McNamee, S. (2020). Radical presence: Alternatives to the therapeutic state. In D. Loewenthal, O. Ness, & B. Hardy (Eds.), *Beyond the therapeutic state* (pp. 55-65). Routledge.

Pearce, W. B. (2007). *Making social worlds: A communication perspective*. Blackwell Publishing.

Pollner, M. (1991). Left of ethnomethodology: The rise and decline of radical reflexivity. *American Sociological Review, 56*, 370-380.

Robinson, K. (2010). Retrieved June 18, 2023, from www.ted.com/talks/sir_ken_robinson_changing_education_paradigms

Rose, N. (1990). *Governing the soul: The shaping of the private self*. Routledge.

Sampson, E. E. (1993). *Celebrating the other*. Westview Press.

Shotter, J. (2010). *Social construction on the edge: Withness thinking & embodiment*. Taos Institute Publications.

Watzlawick, P., Weakland, J., & Fisch, R. (1974). *Change: Principles of problem formation and problem resolution*. W. W. Norton.

Wittgenstein, L. (1953). *Philosophical investigations*. Blackwell.

3 Psychosocial justice
A matter of ecologics
Tim Corcoran

Introduction

This chapter belongs to a line of critically informed argument seeking to acknowledge life as always-both an ontological (i.e. involving ways of being) and epistemological (i.e. involving ways of knowing) enterprise (Barad, 2007; Jackson & Mazzei, 2023; Shotter, 2016). What I mean by that is, practices like education, here represented by formal, institutionally run primary, secondary, and tertiary levels of teaching and learning, carry with them unique responsibilities in our societies. I will outline some of these responsibilities in the following discussion. But from the get-go, let us not presuppose that responsibilities for social practices like education or mental health care rest in the hands of our institutions or solely in the agency of the individual. If responsibilities are to be accounted, these should be primarily understood in relational terms. I believe Giroux is speaking to all practicing professionals when he says:

> Educators need to cast a critical eye on those forms of knowledge and social relations that define them through a conceptual purity and political innocence that not only cloud *how they come into being* but also ignore that the alleged neutrality on which they stand is already grounded in ethico-political choices.
>
> (2011, p. 75; my emphasis)

As ethical, moral, and political practice, education must be about the pursuit of justice (i.e. fairness and equity), and those involved cannot ignore the obligations intrinsic to responsible action. But – and here I direct the question primarily to educational psychologists – how should we understand the possibilities entailed in treating education as an enabler of justice? I ask because I am concerned that psychology, via traditional theory ~ practice, actively supports a kind of impersonality to education more often than not promoting the epistemological aspect of learning and ability to the detriment of relationally sustained ontological opportunities like supporting mental health.

In this chapter, I extend arguments previously made (see Corcoran & Billington, 2015). If accepted as an ontological opportunity, education can invite the pursuit of a particular kind of justice – psychosocial justice (Corcoran et al., 2019; Corcoran & Vassallo, 2021). My concern – and I believe here is one place where responsibility involving educational psychologists endures – is that such opportunity continues to be restrained when considered solely in social

DOI: 10.4324/9781003451907-3

justice terms. What is required is a more nuanced understanding of justice in educational practice (and it could be argued, in socio-political practices more broadly), one informed by a critical account of psychology Corcoran, 2022; Williams et al., 2017). To this end, this chapter outlines the concept of psychosocial justice. First, I consider how the concept of social justice has been appropriated in education by psychological theory. I will explore what different justice theories potentially stand for and how these may or may not establish ontological opportunity, particularly as these pertain to mental health. Running alongside this discussion, I look to consider what psychosocial justice might mean and how the idea could play out in practice – specifically in the practice of educational psychologists. In the final section of the chapter, I review the five prospective conditions of ecologics, offered to guide those working in schools to more ethical engagements with mental health (Corcoran, 2023a). The five conditions are (1) explicating orientation, (2) affirming relationality, (3) respecting unfinalisability, (4) accepting not knowing, and (5) working transparadigmatically. These conditions are considered necessary for the pursuit of psychosocial justice.

Trying to untie the knot

In this opening section, I need to cover some theoretical ground. To begin, I will briefly explain what I mean when referring to dualism in psychology and do so by employing what is probably the dominant paradigm in contemporary psychological discourse, social cognition or constructivism (Piaget, 1953). What I am referring to as dualist accounts of personhood purposively separate the individual from the world or context in which they live. It was as an undergraduate that I first studied psychological theory and was formally introduced to the constructivist model – some 30 years ago now. As I progressed through the program, I could sense growing discomfort with the seemingly unquestioned detachment of the person from relational action. My intention in undertaking the qualification was to work with people, and I could clearly foresee an impending conflict between the program's espoused expert scientist-practitioner model premised on dualism and what I believed was possible, namely, a more just kind of practice striving to understand lives lived without needing to reduce entangled events to normative explanation.

In relation to the present discussion, the so-called justice motive is a case in point that highlights psychological dualistic approaches. One account of the justice motive states that 'individuals strive to maximise rewards for themselves. However, in the pursuit of this end, individuals learn that they must conform to certain norms of justice in their dealings with others' (Taylor & Moghaddam, 1987, p. 85). See how, within the flux of relational action, the psychology of the individual is positioned as the unit of analysis or locus of control? Also, seen as intrinsic to human being in this account is the contention that a primary reason for the way people act is to maximise benefits (material or psychological) for themselves. But as we are a person-in-the-world (Kelly, 1955), limits are placed on us in the guise of norms operating as rules enacted in our relationships. Such norms are often operationalised in behavioural terms and speak directly to standards involving mental health.

Moral discourse is central to living psychosocial lives (Harre, 1998). This could be as basic as making meaning of what is 'good' and what is 'bad'. Having graduated from my undergraduate psychology program, I then practiced for about ten years, first in an adult prison, and later in government P–12 schools. In my time as a school psychologist, the majority of my caseload was boys who were either in the process of being excluded from their present school or who had recently enrolled at a new school, having either been formally excluded or informally moved on. One student I met during this time was a 13-year-old named Adam. This conversation took place shortly after Adam moved to a new school:

Adam:	Well, um, just, I couldn't think of being good hopefully. I don't know why.
TC:	Wha-what was the problem with being good?
Adam:	It was boring.
TC:	Hu-huh, it was boring? Um, what was it –
Adam:	But really, when you'd be good, you'd get reward for it.
TC:	Yeah. Seems like, um, from what you were saying to me, seems like, um, wha-what instead of being good, what was the other one? What were you doing?
Adam:	Being bad.
TC:	Being bad, okay. Seems like when you're being bad, all the good stuff seems to get, um, covered up or, you know, um, you don't see what's good about being good. Is – would that be right?
Adam:	Oh, I do.
TC:	No, I meant before. Not, not now, before.
Adam:	Well, I-I did.
TC:	Oh, you did?
Adam:	I know what's right and wrong and . . . but I just do it anyway.

We will return to Adam's situation shortly. For now, let us consider how the justice motive is evidenced in two more well-known psychological theories. Describing distributive justice, it has been suggested that '[w]hen the normative expectations of the person making social comparison are violated, when he [sic] finds the outcomes and inputs are not in balance in relation to those of others, feelings of inequity result' (Adams, 1965, p. 280). Here there are actions taking place in a relational world, but the psychological work being done occurs in 'outcomes and inputs' or, more formally, cognitive expectations or attributions and feelings. There is acknowledgement that the psychology of the functional individual does not occur in a vacuum, that is, it is learnt via norm-based rules guiding social engagement. However, the metaphor of inputs and outcomes seems akin to a mathematical equation or manufacturing production line. So too does the parameter of the 'norm' remain largely uncomplicated. Psycho-scientific preferences regarding rationality figure dominantly here.

Also, from the area of distributive justice, we can consider Reis's (1987) self-regulatory model of just behaviour. Herein the justice motive is described as 'an internalised mechanism that induces people to delay immediate gratification for the long-term good of the individual, his or her group, and the society at large' (p. 140). Or 'justice, as a motive, is a form of self-control to which people actively aspire so that they may interact effectively with others' (p. 148-49). For a moment, consider the metaphors in play and the ontological opportunities or ways of being these make possible. Motives, it is claimed, are the sparks that fire a powerful engine. From these examples we can see a model of distributive justice suggesting a resource-based or self-control model of psychology again focused on the internal rational machinations of the individual as they go about the business of relating to their world. How is it that motives need be so circumscribed?

Searching for a more process-oriented account of justice, we can look at the area of procedural justice. Let us take two examples. Thibaut and Walker's (1975) research focuses on the individual's evaluation of process (i.e. an ability to control presentation of evidence) and decision control (i.e. an ability to effect decisions). They claim that distribution of control is the most significant factor affecting views about fairness and desirability of procedures. Further in this regard, Tyler's work has been suggested to be a more relationally oriented version of the justice motive. Accordingly, in cognitively processing aspects of social justice, individuals are concerned with their own positioning within social groups. For example, Boeckmann and Tyler's (1997, pp. 365–366) relational concerns hypothesis asserts that 'judgements about the quality of relationships in a community and the symbolic impact that deviance is expected to have on the community are related to attitudes toward abandoning procedural protections'. Psychological research dedicated to explaining attitudes has previously been criticised for downplaying the intimate connection between psychosocial action and personal cognition (see Corcoran, 2023b or Danziger, 1997).

The issue of procedural protections directly takes us to an application of justice that I have previously engaged in relation to education (Corcoran, 2007, 2016). In considering the practice of school exclusion as a punishment for reported student infractions, retributive justice comes into play. Retribution is said to aim directly at the moral value of the offending action specifically looking to impact the individual's belief system via sanction. As Vidmar and Miller (1980, p. 581) claim, 'the offence confronts essential belief systems – an impersonal, objective order has been disturbed'. Recourse to an 'objective order' is significantly problematic, for such rhetoric ignores cultural, historical, and socio-political conditions and highlights previous concerns raised regarding the uncomplicated invocation of societal norms influencing behaviour. They go on to suggest that 'internalised beliefs are derived from the socialisation process and are the psychological representations of more overt social and social psychological processes' (p. 581). Against such normativity, what chance is there of any divergence from dominant belief systems, and in doing so, how would the person attempting to voice opposition be understood? What ontological opportunity is being enabled here? So far, I have been highlighting how a dualist model of psychology separates the individual from their context. Let us now bring an acknowledgement of the constitutive potentials of language into the discussion.

According to the *Education Act* (the legislation guiding relational action in Queensland government schools at the time of my engagement with Adam), grounds for exclusion from an educational institution included 'disobedience' and 'misconduct'. Added to these,

> other conduct of the student that is prejudicial to the good order and management of the State educational institution' and where 'the student's disobedience, misconduct or other conduct is so serious that suspension of the student is inadequate to deal with the behaviour.
>
> (Queensland Government, 1989, p. 26)

As in Adam's narrative, there is a textual invitation to consider the antonym of each as the preferred way of being. In this example, disobedience becomes obedience as the ideal mode of student conduct. The antonymic process holds ontological implications in that any student acting against the good order of the school must be of bad moral character. According to this onto-epistemological process, exclusion is seemingly a straightforward outcome, given the student's behaviour. Such action is also supported by a liberal discourse involving the rights and responsibilities of the individual. If education is the right of the obedient, then those deemed disobedient automatically suspend their rights when they choose to act against the good order of the institution. They, the students of bad moral character, forego their rights when behaving irresponsibly.

Let us return to Adam's circumstance to take stock of what has been discussed thus far. Recall from the outset I highlighted the necessity for practices within education to be considered for their potential as ontological opportunities, particularly as these potentially support or subvert mental health. In accord with Gergen and McNamee (1999), there are always relational responsibilities present in social practices, like education. In our conversation, Adam said his previous school had tried to help change his behaviour, but he admitted he did not accept the help. In terms of the justice motive, it could be said that Adam's 'disobedience' or 'misconduct' was an attempt to maximise rewards for himself that did not take into account the norms of his school community. It could also be argued that there was an issue with distributive justice here, as he suggested that school was 'boring'. In Adam's case, somehow the educational 'inputs' did not guarantee the kind of 'outputs' expected (e.g. compliant and/or responsible behaviour). Those in authority would probably argue that Adam did not exhibit appropriate self-regulatory behaviour, hence the sanctions enacted under a rationale of retributive justice. In sum – and this is a matter every educational psychologist should recognise – it is a simple move to individual accountability and exclusion when that is what the theory~practice demands.

Always-both

Before proceeding to discuss the concept of psychosocial justice, I think it is important to consider how certain positions which, at first, might not intentionally align with more dominant psychologies are hampered by inadvertently employing dualist discourse. As Prilleltensky (2012) recognises, issues of fairness and equity or justice are inextricably linked to our health and wellbeing. Admirably, he is looking for an integrated way of understanding wellness as simultaneously personal, relational, organisational, and communal. Thus, as he sees it, the challenge psychologists and other social researchers have faced 'lies in the inability to disentangle motivational factors from the environment in which the person grows up' (p. 3). The examples I have discussed so far highlight this very point, that is, concern with the justice motive understood as an intrapsychic process capable of being disentangled from relational action. Put simply, scientific attempts to untie the psychosocial knot.

Prilleltensky suggests that empirical research showing environmental impacts on health and wellbeing should go some way to challenging the dominance of intrapsychic or motivational accounts. But what concerns me is that he does so retaining a subjective/objective dichotomy. He suggests that whilst subjective accounts (e.g. self-reports) will remain as standard data in psychological research, attention should also be drawn to assessments of settings to identify aspects that promote health. As he states:

> By measuring wellbeing with objective and subjective measures at the personal, inter-personal, organisational, and communal levels, we can obtain a richer picture of human and social wellbeing. Paradoxically, the exclusive focus on the individual as both the unit of analysis and the source of information precludes us from exploring how changes at multiple levels can benefit the same individual with which psychology is so concerned.
>
> (p. 4)

Certainly, a comprehensive approach to theorising being human is preferred, but I suggest that the continued dualism inherent in dichotomies like the subjective/objective split only sustain the kind of intrapsychic premise upon which psychological justice theories have been argued. Ontological opportunities thus remain curtailed by standards of positivist and dualist psychology that (1) extract the person or their cognition from their environment, (2) reduce dynamic social action to individual responsibility, and (3) see such action in quantifiable, linear, and/or causal terms.

Advocacy requires a foothold from which to enable action. But in the case of psychology and, in the present case, psychology in education, what kind of ontological opportunities are we advocating for? Recall, I began this chapter highlighting two pivotal points: (1) education should be about the pursuit of justice, and if accepted as an ontological opportunity, then (2) education can invite the pursuit of a particular kind of justice - psychosocial justice. I reckon the theory we develop and the practices we engage as psychologists (e.g. assessment, ther-apy, etc.) are inextricably linked to issues of justice (i.e. fairness and equity), not only for the way they are practiced, but also for the way in which they are invoked. Any action is always-both a response to the immediate context in which we find ourselves and a propagation or negation of emergent agencies or practices - or to the very norms that have been presumed to exist out there, seemingly beyond the psychology of the individual. In effect, the pursuit of psychosocial justice is simultaneously distributive and procedural because of the ontological opportunities enabled. As psychologists, we actively help create or sustain forms of life when we enact our professional responsibilities. Although often not explicitly recognised, this asks us to be critical of our values, able to acknowledge and understand how these might work within a 'moral science' of human action (Shotter, 1975).

I have engaged in this chapter a series of positions, largely informed by social cognition, to highlight how dualist notions of human being have been portrayed in psychological theories involving justice. These collectively support:

- Separation of the person from their world
- Treatment of the individual as the principal unit of analysis
- Ontological assumptions about the nature of people and agency
- Societal norms uncomplicatedly engaged
- Use of a range of discourse employing common psychological metaphors

The antithesis to approaches of a dualist kind cannot simply remove any understanding of personhood from social action (for one must then ask, 'Would that still be psychology?').

A non-dualist account of personhood is possible but needs to be able to find workable space between the psychological and the social. Whilst I agree with Prilleltensky's sentiment, I struggle to accept the terms of engagement as used, that is, to disentangle motivation from context or explicitly split what is considered subjective from what is considered objective. I believe we require an orientation that resists having to universally explain what psychology is, which instead implores us to listen to how lives are lived, and mental health sustained. Such reorientation shifts our work as educational psychologists in support of psychosocial justice.

Enabling psychosocial justice

Melbourne, the city I have called home for more than a decade, will forever hold an inauspicious international title. Here we experienced the longest cumulative lockdown of any city during the Covid-19 pandemic (Macreadie, 2022). I spent a lot of time walking the streets of my suburb during that period as we were regularly mandated to stay within a 5-kilometre radius of our homes. On those walks I listened to a number of podcasts, and a scholar who appeared across several was philosopher and ecological activist Timothy Morton (2016, 2018). On those podcasts, Morton would repeat this phrase: 'The how is the what.' What Morton was inviting listeners to, I believe, was a process-oriented approach to understanding life. In reference and response to the ecological crises affecting our modern world, Morton suggests: 'It's not exactly what you believe but how you believe that could be causing trouble' (2018, p. 76). What kind of trouble? you may ask. They continue: 'Being mentally healthy might mean knowing that what you are thinking and how you are thinking are intertwined' (p. 76). Having spent some time pondering Morton's invitation, I subsequently developed an idea I call ecologics (Corcoran, 2023a).

Ecologics are not just about orienting to the world but about tools for sustaining ways of knowing/being or doing onto-epistemological work. For educational psychologists, ecologics could be considered a way of thinking about and engaging with lives being lived. Foremost, in the context of this discussion, ecologics provide an alternative to constructivist orientations which centre the individual in social practice. The model most social researchers would be familiar with here is Bronfenbrenner's (1977) ecological systems theory. The classic configuration presents an individual embedded within a series of concentric circles representing environmental systems (e.g. microsystem, mesosystem, exosystem, macrosystem, and chronosystem). For what it is, Bronfenbrenner's theory was an advance on behaviourist and objectivist psychological models of human development. However, the theory today needs to be recognised for its anthropocentric orientation and grounding in scientism. In the remainder of this section, I briefly outline five prospective conditions necessary for engaging ecologics, discussing these in relation to school-based mental health work. The discussion reaches back to earlier questions concerning the onto-epistemological opportunities and psychosocial justice offered by preferred theory~practice.

Explicating orientation

Mental health has, for the past century or so, been predominantly informed by medical knowledge and, when, for example, diagnosed as defective biological pathology (e.g. neurochemical imbalance), is usually treated via pharmacological interventions and/or psychological therapy.

Of course, this orientation to mental health is founded on distinctions adjudged between health and ill health. To be considered healthy is to be considered able, that is, able to act according to prevailing moral, social, and cultural norms. If disabled, the person may not perform in ways expected by others in their immediate environment. This comparison, particularly when defects are essentialised as possessive qualities of the individual, can invoke the presence of ableism. Discrimination that accompanies ableism is often intersectional, meaning, that multiple biases can be evident at one time. For example, a student presenting with mental health concerns may also identify as indigenous and live with racism and/or also identify as gay and subsequently experience homophobia. In resisting ableism, educational psychologists support psychosocial justice. They do so by aligning their practice with theory recognising no separation in between. To paraphrase the American philosopher Richard Rorty (1999), theory is always already practice. Do practitioners purposively recognise the theory that speaks to their practice? And conversely, can practitioners examine their work and name the theories underwriting such action? If so, they are well on the way to explicating their orientation.

Affirming relationality

Use of the term *relationality*, in preference to *relationship*, should be noted. As Tynan (2021, p. 607) recognises, 'relationality actually decentres the human and focuses on the relationships between entities [and] processes of connection'. This concept is central to the idea of psychosocial justice because our attention is continuously engaged with living processes, their co-constitutive conditions, and how these potentially affect those involved. Let us consider an example. What if we understood mental wellness or ill health not as the possession of a dys/functional brain situated within an individual body but as a way of being responsive to prevailing conditions belonging to distinguishable events? Test-taking or exams remain a common practice within education, supposedly determining an individual's learning from a unit of study. I, for one, was never a fan, either as a student or as a tertiary educator. The value of rote conditioning has always seemed a questionable means to learning's ends. Practices surrounding traditional examinations invite questions pertaining to psychosocial justice. For instance, anxiety's presence in exams is uninvited and yet commonly invades educational practice. It is more likely than not that a student reporting the presence of anxiety would receive some form of adjustment or change to the exam arrangements to accommodate engagement. Inclusive assessment practice has been recognised as an area desperately in need of innovative theorisation (Tai et al., 2021). Why stop there? Surely, all aspects of education would benefit from affirming the relationality of practice.

Accepting not knowing

The attentive reader may have noticed the way in which anxiety was just discussed. Rather than fixing a disordered condition to the being of the individual, anxiety can be engaged as an affective agent contributing to an emergent relationality. Some may recognise this orientation from narrative therapy (White & Epston, 1990). A regularly used method from this approach is what is called externalising conversations. While acknowledging the less-than-preferred dichotomisation of an internal psychological space contrasted with the external material world, the move to separate the person from the problem (another narrative therapy idiom) is inspiring as much as it is aspirational. What is crucial here is to understand that how we make sense of the circumstance is potentially what matters most. Not knowing how a person might respond to an externalising conversation, for example, is critical and supports the pursuit of psychosocial justice. For some, problems existing in their lives have long been attached or affixed to who they are known to be. Adam had all but accepted he was 'bad'. In orienting to not knowing, educational psychologists create opportunity to resist their own and others' pre-formed conclusions. Blackman (2021, p. 122) explains:

> The focus on process is on composing rather than composed, pre-formed entities. The focus on composing looks at how bodies become assembled in particular ways through their coupling or conjoining with particular objects, practices, techniques and artifacts such that they are always in-making or in-formation rather than being ready-made.

Respecting unfinalisability

Over the ten years I practiced as a psychologist, other professionals (e.g. teachers, principals, etc.) and those close to the person I was engaging with (e.g. parents, carers, etc.), were keen – at times desperate – to be provided with answers. Why did Adam behave the way he did in school? As we consider the importance of process in relation to matters to do with justice, it is important that educational psychologists challenge invitations to finalisation. This is often not a simple achievement when the expert has been retained to pronounce an opinion. At times like these, we need to be able to slow down our process to acknowledge the complexities involved in relationalities. As Stengers (2018, pp. 81–82) recognised, '[s]lowing down means becoming capable of learning again, becoming acquainted with things again, reweaving the bounds of interdependency. It means thinking and imagining, and in the process creating relationships with others that are not those of capture'. In so far as understanding mental health in schools, it is impossible to ever have the last word regarding such matters. Traditionally, the relationships educational psychologists are invited to, such as performing quantified assessments, are largely intended to capture static being. Touching back to Giroux's quote from the introduction of this chapter, it is imperative that educational psychologists recognise the political conditions controlling their work. Too often in contemporary educational practice, teachers and students in classrooms are dependent on psychometric assessment to facilitate financial support. It is incumbent on us as practitioners, if committed to the pursuit of psychosocial justice, to encourage those seeking answers to live with unfinalisability as key to the prospect of lifelong learning.

Working transparadigmatically

This prospect possibly presents the most significant challenge for practitioners regarding their adoption of ecologics. Educational psychologists, depending on where they received their training, will have been exposed to particular epistemologies (Corcoran & Vassallo, 2023). Especially for our US-based colleagues, practice deviating from the scientist-practitioner model of delivery is extremely uncommon. Reports suggest that only 1.75% of US accredited school psychology programs require qualitative research coursework (Powell et al., 2008), and 13% of school psychology doctoral involve qualitative training (Rubin et al.,

2018). But interest here goes beyond a simple quantitative/qualitative split for qualitatively labelled research, and oriented practice can still maintain many similar properties to quantitative applications (e.g. alignment with realism). Working transparadigmatically means being open to inquiry, which need not exclusively adhere to practices or research criteria associated with positivism and/or Global North-oriented scientism. Neither a transparadigmatic orientation nor a need to try and forcibly synthesise varieties of knowledge. Engaging either tactic only perpetuates practice tied to dominant traditions like the inquirer-as-spectator capturing knowledge (see Stengers earlier) to abstract and represent living agents as static objects. There are alternatives. Indigenous studies scholarship asks:

> The question before us is not just how the object of our inquiries are understood differently in our inquiries, but also how are we ourselves becoming different through inquiry and how our relationships with the other agents in our inquiries are transformed.
>
> (Rosiek et al., 2020, p. 336)

Is it possible that the kinds of transformations educational psychologists desire when attending to mental health-related matters in schools fail to materialise because we have neglected an ethic of reciprocity inherent in relational engagements (Corcoran, 2017)?

Conclusion

The purpose of this chapter has been to open a door to a process-oriented account of relational practice by disrupting dualist notions of social justice and motioning toward the possibilities of psychosocial justice. Psychologists can pursue psychosocial justice in direct and fundamental ways by acknowledging our discipline's ethical, moral, and political anchoring; acknowledging the constitutive nature of our discursive and material practices; and taking responsibility for the kinds of onto-epistemological opportunities enabled by our engagements with people. Because this kind of work has the potential to simultaneously engage across emerging events, it aims to understand differing perspectives - human and non-human, discursive and material - in terms of how these contribute to constituting relational action. Our profession is uniquely placed to lead responses to mental health promotion in school communities. Transformations here will require more than what has come before. How that gets realised, again and again, with each next living moment, is a matter we are all responsible for.

Summary box

Psychosocial justice recognises the relational conditions which entwine wellbeing and ill health. Educational professionals can address matters of psychosocial justice by:

1. Naming the ideas, concepts, and theories that orient their ways of working
2. Accepting that life matters are connected and co-constituted
3. Responding to others as the experts in their lives
4. Keeping open opportunities to learn by resisting conclusions
5. Valuing knowledge derived from diverse sources

Acknowledgements

I live and work on unceded Wurundjeri Country. I acknowledge the traditional custodians of the land on which this writing was conducted: the Wurundjeri people of the Kulin nations, paying respect to their elders before and after now.

References

Adams, J. S. (1965). Inequality in social exchange. In L. Berkowitz (Ed.), *Advances in experimental social psychology* (Vol. 2, pp. 267–299). Academic Press.

Barad, K. (2007). *Meeting the universe halfway: Quantum physics and the entanglement of matter and meaning*. Duke University Press.

Blackman, L. (2021). *The body: The key concepts* (2nd ed.). Routledge.

Boeckmann, R. J., & Tyler, T. R. (1997). Common sense justice and inclusion within the moral community: When do people receive procedural protections from others? *Psychology, Public Policy and Law, 3*(2–3), 362–380.

Bronfenbrenner, U. (1977). Toward an experimental ecology of human development. *American Psychologist, 32*(7), 513–531.

Corcoran, T. (2007). Counselling in a discursive world. *International Journal for the Advancement of Counselling, 29*(2), 111–122.

Corcoran, T. (2016). What results from psychological questionnaires? In P. Towl & S. Hemphill (Eds.), *Locked out: Understanding and tackling school exclusion in Australia and Aotearoa New Zealand* (pp. 71–88). NZCER Press.

Corcoran, T. (2017). *Are* the kids alright? Relating to representations of youth. *International Journal of Adolescence and Youth, 22*(2), 151–164. http://dx.doi.org/10.1080/02673843.2014.881296

Corcoran, T. (2022, May 18). Critical educational psychology. In *Oxford research encyclopedia of education*. https://doi.org/10.1093/acrefore/9780190264093.013.1742

Corcoran, T. (2023a). From dialogics to ecologics: When the how is the what. *International Journal of Qualitative Studies in Education*. Advance online publication. https://doi.org/10.1080/09518398.2023.2233941

Corcoran, T. (2023b). Attitudes toward inclusion. In R. J. Tierney, F. Rizvi, & K. Erkican (Eds.), *International encyclopedia of education* (Vol. 9, 4th ed., pp. 328–333). Elsevier. https://doi.org/10.1016/B978-0-12-818630-5.12067-6

Corcoran, T., & Billington, T. (2015). Being well: Educated. In T. Dragonas, K. Gergen, S. McNamee, & E. Tseliou (Eds.), *Education as social construction: Contributions to research, theory and practice* (pp. 30–48). WorldShare Books. www.taosinstitute.net/education-as-social-construction

Corcoran, T., & Vassallo, S. (2021). Psychosocial justice: Always more-than to consider. *Educational & Child Psychology, 38*(2), 8–18.

Corcoran, T., & Vassallo, S. (2023). Critical psychology and education: Opportunities outside silos. *School Psychology International*. Advance online publication. https://doi.org/10.1177/01430343231187064

Corcoran, T., White, J., Te Riele, K., Baker, A., & Moylan, P. (2019). Psychosocial justice for students in custody. *Journal of Psychosocial Studies, 12*(1–2), 41–56.

Danziger, K. (1997). *Naming the mind: How psychology found its language*. Sage.

Gergen, K. J., & McNamee, S. (1999). *Relational responsibility: Resources for sustainable dialogue*. Sage.

Giroux, H. (2011). *On critical pedagogy*. Continuum.

Harre, R. (1998). *The singular self: An introduction to the psychology of personhood*. Sage.

Jackson, A. Y., & Mazzei, L. A. (2023). *Thinking with theory in qualitative research* (2nd ed.). Routledge.

Kelly, G. A. (1955). *The psychology of personal constructs* (2 Vols.). Norton.

Macreadie, I. (2022). Reflections from Melbourne, the world's most locked down city, through the COVID pandemic and beyond. *Microbiology Australia, 43*(1), 3–4.

Morton, T. (2016). *Dark ecology: For a logic of future coexistence*. Columbia University Press.

Morton, T. (2018). *Being ecological*. Penguin.

Piaget, J. (1953). *The origin of intelligence in the child*. Routledge.

Powell, H., Mihalas, S., Onwuegbuzie, A. J., Suldo, S., & Daley, C. E. (2008). Mixed methods research in school psychology: A mixed methods investigation of trends in the literature. *Psychology in the Schools, 45*(4), 291–309.

Prilleltensky. (2012). Wellness as fairness. *American Journal of Community Psychology, 49*, 1–21.Queensland Government. (1989). *Education (General Provisions) Act* (Reprint No. 4). Queensland Government Printer.

Reis, H. T. (1987). The nature of the justice motive: Some thoughts on operation, internalisation, and justification. In J. C. Masters & W. P. Smith (Eds.), *Social comparison, social justice, and relative deprivation: Theoretical, empirical, and policy perspectives* (pp. 131–150). L. Erlbaum.

Rorty, R. (1999). *Philosophy and social hope*. Penguin.

Rosiek, J. L., Snyder, J., & Pratt, S. L. (2020). The new materialisms and indigenous theories of non-human agency: Making the case for respectful anti-colonial engagement. *Qualitative Inquiry, 26*(3-4), 331–346.

Rubin, J. D., Bell, S., & McClelland, S. I. (2018). Graduate education in qualitative methods in U.S. psychology: Current trends and recommendations for the future. *Qualitative Research in Psychology, 15*(1), 29–50.

Shotter, J. (1975). *Images of man in psychological research*. Menthuen.

Shotter, J. (2016). *Speaking, actually: Towards a new 'fluid' common-sense understanding of relational becomings*. Everything is Connected Press.

Stengers, I. (2018). *Another science is possible: A manifesto for slow science* (S. Muecke, Trans.). Polity.

Tai, J., Ajjawi, R., & Umarova, A. (2021): How do students experience inclusive assessment? A critical review of contemporary literature, *International Journal of Inclusive Education*. Advance online publication. https://doi.org/10.1080/13603116.2021.2011441

Taylor, D. M., & Moghaddam, F. M. (1987). *Theories of intergroup relations*. Praeger.

Thibaut, J., & Walker, L. (1975). *Procedural justice: A psychological analysis*. Erlbaum.

Tynan, L. (2021). What is relationality? Indigenous knowledges, practices and responsibilities with kin. *Cultural Geographies, 28*(4), 597–610.

Vidmar, N., & Miller, D. T. (1980). Social psychological processes underlying attitudes toward legal punishment. *Law & Society Review, 14*(3), 565–602.

White, M., & Epston, D. (1990). *Narrative means to therapeutic ends*. Norton.

Williams, A., Billington, T., Goodley, D., & Corcoran, T. (Eds.). (2017). *Critical educational psychology*. Wiley Blackwell.

4 An inquiry into the heart of separation, selfhood, connection, and love

The implications of non-duality to relational practice

Sahaja Timothy Davis

Introduction

I'm sitting at the back of the class, notebook in hand, whilst the year 4 teacher is helping children express and manage their feelings using a PowerPoint presentation written by a mental health provider. I was observing one boy in particular as he chewed the whole of his pencil into small splinters, his face half-hidden by a black hoodie. School staff said they were really struggling with Jose, and it was clear he was really struggling too. From this privileged vantage point of an observer, a question took hold of me: might it be possible that the very basis of this situation, for all its good intention, is somehow contributing to Jose's difficulties?

What I outline here is a play of ideas, a series of thought experiments that challenge the very notions that form what is most dear to us and what we think of as real. In this chapter, I will attempt to direct our attention to a radically different way of thinking about the relational, experiencing relational, and acting rationally. The shift in perspective that I am referring to is not simply a private matter or an indulgent intellectual game. It is a shift in understanding that, if grasped by education and mental health professionals, will unquestionably have a real-world impact on the lives of children and young people.

The reading of this chapter takes us through a journey where we look into our cultural understanding of who we are, explore what we understand as things and what lies at the heart of the understanding of who we are. This is no mean feat for a reader (or writer, for that matter); at times it might feel confusing or baffling. Whilst the matters at hand, such as Jose's plight, are of a deeply serious nature, in engaging with these ideas, what is required of the reader is an openness and curiosity about their experience, but also lightness of touch, a playfulness, and an ability to literally not take themselves too seriously.

For me, Jose was the beginning of a journey that I never could have imagined would arrive here. The more I witnessed, read, and reflected on Jose's predicament, the more I became convinced that the wider mental health issues schools are facing are ontological rather than methodological. I came to believe there is a fault line in how we were understanding and responding to Jose and children in his situation. It would appear that the solutions we were deploying came from the same position as the problem, thus reinforcing that position and, in all likelihood, compounding the issue. For this reason, a solution was required that is derived from a different order of thinking.

The PowerPoint lesson that the teacher, Mr Allen, was using focused on individual children working to improve and develop themselves so they can live a better life. In this sense, to me,

DOI: 10.4324/9781003451907-4

the lesson overlooked how Jose's intentions were only a small fragment in the vast web of interrelated conditions in which his emotions and actions were arising.

Support services and schools, in a climate of what feels like ever-tightening resources, are attempting to respond to a deepening and widening issue they are seeing amongst children and young people (O'Reilly et al., 2018). Jose's lesson was a part of the schools' best efforts at helping him and his peers, as was his behaviour management program, his sticker chart, and his diagnosis of conduct disorder. Jose was clearly feeling overwhelmed by his experience, as were those who were trying to support him.

What if the antidote to this sense of overwhelm lies deeper than employing another particular method or approach but rests instead within the very heart of how we conceive of the problem? After 7 1/2 million years, Douglas Adams's supercomputer 'Deep Thought' was able to arrive at the ultimate answer: 42. The difficulty then arose that humanity forgot what the question was.

Our understanding of ourselves as an individual, distinct, separate, and at times in relation to others, is culturally fabricated, and this understanding is central in creating a point in our history understood by many as in crises (Siegel, 2022).

I hope to evoke a perspective in which everything that appears to exist inside us and around us is understood as entangled, co-existing, and in process. There are a number of terms that are used to refer to this position: *non-duality* (Blackstone, 2006), *unselfing* (Olsson, 2018), *intraconnection* (Siegel & Drulis, 2023), *interbeing* (Niforato, 2016), *fundamental awareness* (Theise & Kafatos, 2016), *Advaita Vedanta* (Blackstone, 2006), and *Rigpa* (Josipovic & Miskovic, 2020), to name a few. From this position, acting with care and love to others and the planet is not an act of personal virtue but more an uncontrived response to the self-evident condition of things.

Within our professional roles in schools, supporting the mental health of children and young people, this position can offer a refreshing alternative perspective. It situates mental health or ill health not as a thing residing in an individual but as an entangled process that lives through different bodies and systems. With this alternative understanding, our responses to children and their difficulties become more sensitive, attuned, and effective. In Kenneth Gergen's (2009) seminal work 'Relational Being', he posited that the relational precedes who we are and our actions, rather than relationships being something we do. What might at first seem like a linguistic sleight of hand is in fact a profound and momentous shift in perspective and has enormous implications for how we respond to children's mental health.

The nature of this subject matter is inherently challenging; it potentially reveals and takes us beyond our cultural horizons, going beyond what might feel permissible (Akomolafe & Ladha, 2017). McCarroll (2022) identifies intrinsic difficulties in discussing this topic: 'language inherently relies on the ground of perceiver (the reader) and perceived (that which is read), and at its core non- dualism negates assumptions of separation between the two' (p. 6). In order to meet this challenge, I have taken a number of roads up the mountain.

Culture

There is an emerging consensus among academics and professionals across the range of disciplines that we are currently living in an epoch defined by a global mental health and ecological crises (Tiwari, 2023). Akomolafe and Ladha (2017) suggest that this is a time to ask fundamental questions regarding what it means to be human, a point of existential and epistemological crises.

Daniel Siegel (2022) goes further and proposes that at the root of the crises lies our constructed view of self and other (solo-self). He likens our attachment solo-self in the Global North to cancer cells. Cells that 'go rogue' and act without regard to the whole-body system.

The current epoch principally in the Global North is a period of neoliberalism typified by free will, autonomy, and choice (Boyle et al., 2023). Our consciousness, shaped by market forces, has led to a deeply held understanding of ourselves as existing in the body, separate from each other and the earth, in a battle to achieve the goal of ontological security (Struhl, 2020b). A goal that, for the vast majority of us, is unobtainable in this lifetime and ultimately unobtainable for all. This drive for individual freedom and security is highly divisive, resulting in an appetite for consumption, competition, and conflict. This can be seen within our own individual psychology, in our social networks, in the systems and education institutions in which we work, and in the wider political forces that shape our lives.

Our 'culturally treasured notions of identity, autonomy, and independence', according to Sheldrake (2021), lie at the heart of our understanding of ourselves. There is a me that lies at the centre of this universe; beyond this lie the boundaries of my skin, my group, my nation, my species, outside of which the 'other' exists. It is a significant challenge to entertain the possibility of something beyond our horizon, to see this as simply a narrative situated in a particular time and place, as opposed to a self-evident truth. However, if we are to conceive of an alternative narrative, this is what is required.

Whilst neoliberalism continues to extend its areas of influence across the globe, there are areas of resistance from traditions who offer alternative ways of conceiving what appears inside us and outside of us. Daniel Siegel (2022) refers to specific indigenous communities of North and South America, Polynesia, New Zealand, Australia, and Southern Africa, to whom interconnection is the primary belief, as opposed to the sanctity of the individual.

Workineh Kelbessa (2015), professor of philosophy at Addis Ababa University, identified many African Indigenous cultures who have the recognition of interconnectedness and interdependence at their heart. The words *ubuntu* (explored further in Mary Chilokoa's chapter), *botho*, and *huhnu* in African languages all refer to a condition of being and state of becoming or emergence which involves existing within the complex wholeness, and that identity is not understood to be a sense of individuality but of 'living through other' (Kelbessa, 2015, p. 392).

It appears to be self-evident or common-sense to know that we and things exist, and this existence is defined by certain characteristics or qualities that belong to that person or thing. However, from a broader perspective, we can see this is only true within our cultural bubble, outside of which things may appear, feel, and be experienced very differently. How we are responding to Jose is shaped by a culture that sees understanding as knowledge creation, and knowledge creation as a means to control and exert power. Jose can be understood and therefore known through his diagnosis, and we can control Jose through the application of evidence-based interventions.

No-thingness

The ability to predict, control, and manipulate stuff is essential for our survival. In service of this has been the human ability to provide a conceptual map of experience comprising of 'things' acting on each other, such as an apple hitting the ground. The error is to mistake this conceptual map, which is a representation of reality, for reality itself, as if mistaking the images on Google Maps for the dynamic, complex world unfolding beyond the windscreen.

Essentialism regards the patterns that exist in and around us as things in themselves (Köhne, 2020). Whereas non-essentialist arguments suggest that concepts are a practise of convenience, words and maps can evolve, be contested, and bring us closer or further away from understanding. This has long been the challenge to dominant mental health discourses. These critiques contest the veracity that disorders are actual things, and that diagnosis is the verification of an essential truth as to whether a person does or does not 'have' a particular disorder.

Non-duality invites us to go further and examine our experience of all 'things' or events, such as a feeling of annoyance, a cloud, a nation, a table, even conduct disorder. When we relate to our conceptual map as a reality, it locks us into a reduced and rigid navigation of life. When we are able to see through our veil of conceptualisation, we are free to experience the 'reality of continuously intermingling, flowing lines or strands of unfolding, agential activity, in which nothing (no thing) exists in separation from anything else' (Shotter, 2014, p. 306).

Concepts can be seen as a description of a relationship as opposed to pointing to the qualities inherent in the things in themselves. Gergen talks about language as a product of coordination. Our words reference what this means to us as opposed to the essence of the thing. For example, a chair describes its function for us as something we sit on, and Jose's 'disorder' as something that we want to change in him. There are issues of power and language here that are well worth considering; however, they fall beyond the scope of this chapter.

One of the difficulties with holding too tightly to the map is that it represents a static view of the world containing immutable truths. Such as 'I am a man', 'I am British', 'I am dyslexic'. These miss the fluid, ever-changing nature that lies at the heart of existence. Brown et al. (2020) suggest that '[t]hese binary human discourses extend their reach into all aspects of educational practice, forming limited and limiting ideas and stories of human versus nature, male versus female, black versus white, and mind versus body' (p. 229). This brings to mind some of the questions school staff were asking me about Jose: Can he help it? Does he have autism, or is it trauma? Does he have learning difficulties?

To acknowledge that what we experience in and around us is a dynamic flux, and the abstraction we refer to with our words and concepts as a convent representation of the temporary patterns that appear to take place, changes how we behave and relate to everything. It changes how we respond to a feeling that might arise in us, the white formations in the sky, a giant emergence from the forest floor, or the structure that our book or laptop is resting on. Importantly, it also changes our relationship to a diagnosis of conduct disorder and to a child who is lashing out at his or her teachers and, ultimately, the questions we ask about Jose.

No-self

Buddhist scholars suggest that the critique of essentialism can be most powerfully applied to that which we hold most dear to ourselves. The political and social writer Antonio Gramsci (1971) encouraged us to turn our critical gaze even towards what might appear to us as common-sense. I would argue that at the heart of our common-sense notions is what appears to be a someone, a self, the homunculus, reading these words, sitting in our body, observing, making decisions, controlling our thoughts and actions.

This notion of the self is the core premise for most mental health inventions with young people and our understanding of our experience of ourselves. It is the premise that sits underneath the year 4 lesson on managing emotions, Jose's sticker chart, and in his diagnosis. The self here is understood as a fixed, independent, unitary entity that has some kind of overview and executive control over thoughts, feelings, and actions (Struhl, 2020a). The novelist and philosopher Iris Murdoch (1970) suggests that we cling to our sense of self to feed our desire to be significant and make existence bearable.

It is more than a little unsettling to consider that the self's existence is generally thought of by both social and neuropsychologists alike as having no substantial material existence and might, in many respects, contribute to mental ill health (Siegel, 2022).

Famously, in the 1980s, the neuropsychologist Benjamin Libet (2009) asked participants to choose a moment to move their finger whilst he measured their associated brain activity. What surprised Libet and his colleagues most was that the intention to move the finger followed, not preceded, the action. In fact, the intention occurred half a second after moving their finger. Neuroscientists in this field argue that the awareness of making a decision is but an afterthought and does not affect, let alone drive, the decision (Smith, 2011).

An intriguing question to ask ourselves is, Where does this me exist or reside? In this sense, there is often thought to be a core or essence that inhabits the body or is the body, what some religions might refer to as the soul.

When we look in the mirror as years go by, we see that this body changes, sometimes quite drastically, perhaps indicating that we are not the body. It might, however, appear that there is a 'someone' looking in the mirror and they are the same from one day to the next, year after year.

What or who is this person that appears to be the witness? When asked to locate this observer, it is common for people to point to their heads, their mind. When we are asked to identify the distinctive qualities of the witness or pinpoint the witness as qualia, we find ourselves only having access to the contents in our field of awareness, but not the awareness itself, that is, thoughts, feelings, and sensations. We may rarefy the observer into a thing that is witnessed; however, this can only lead to an infinite regression in which the witness can never be located. Might it be there is no homunculus sitting in our mind, located in the brain, with an overview of experience, that there is no 'thinker behind the thoughts' (Struhl, 2020b, p. 100)?

It is also interesting that the existence of a self might even have no foundation in our phenomenological experience. Whilst the idea or concept of self is readily applied to our experience of our thoughts or decisions (perhaps as an afterthought), with some concerted introspection, we can become aware that, in any moment, there is not a coherent thing called me but merely a stream of thoughts and feelings that appear to arise without volition. Blackman suggests that what we think of as the self is nothing more than 'momentary flashes of experience: disparate, fragmented thoughts, emotions, and sensations' (Blackstone, 2006, p. 49).

Overidentification with what Siegel (2022) refers to as the solo-self creates a sense of aloneness, separation, and individuals competing for resources. It also creates an illusion that at the core of Jose biting his teacher lies a decision-maker, a wilful actor that can be taught to manage his feelings better, whereas surrounding the moment Jose bites his teacher are interrelated conditions. The skin around Jose's body does not represent a fixed boundary of causal conditions. In this sense, these boundaries are permeable or even illusionary. His thoughts are borrowed from those around him, his sensations are the result of biological processes beyond his control, and his actions are responses to conditions within the classroom and further afield. By reducing Jose into a distinct child who has conduct disorder, we are confining him to a view that is overly simplistic and narrow. It confines the problem to exist within what is perceived as Jose's personhood. This view is dangerously deterministic and offers little hope for authentic, substantial change. It also reflects the sense of overwhelm that Jose's teachers feel when so much time and effort are put into interventions that appear to have little or no impact on Jose's experience in the classroom.

What is required is a response to Jose's experience that is attuned to all the conditions that surround his feelings and actions. That the problem is not located within Jose and the action that he performs is not considered 'his' action or belonging to him. Instead, the act of biting a teacher or chewing a pencil to bits belongs to all the conditions from which it emerged.

Impermanence

We have explored our understanding of ourselves and the world as culturally conditioned and given a critique of the essential nature of 'things', which was then applied to our own sense of self. The next path I wish to take up the mountain is to explore the notion that everything is in process and entangled with each other. There is some risk here of repetition; invariably, these paths cross and overlap. After all, there is only one mountain being explored here. However, it is sometimes useful to look at the same phenomenon from slightly different perspectives.

According to Buddhism, one of the marks of existence is that everything is impermanent, in process. Whilst this might seem obvious, it is noteworthy that Buddhists place such great emphasis on this observation, it is seen by Buddhist practitioners as a lifetime's work to realise.

The conceptual map we referred to earlier in order to be made up of 'things' requires them to have arrived at a state of completion. One of the significant differences between our concepts and the processes that they refer to is that our concepts, like maths, offer us a fixed entity that does not change.

When we look into our internal experience, it is easy to see that everything is fluid and in a state of flux. What we might conceptualise as being annoyed is, in fact, a dynamic movement of certain thoughts and feelings that arise and pass way from one moment to the next. The same could be said of everything around us. Through our conceptualisations, we create fixed entities; this obscures that everything is in a state of flux. The chair we are sitting on and the building we are sitting in are in process. What appear to be inanimate objects are breathing, literally filled with life. The paint is gradually lifting off its surface; the glue holding the legs in place is slowly deteriorating; mould and fungi are infiltrating the brickwork. Without the constant efforts of people to resist, hold off, and repair this decay, the chair and the building will eventually crumble back into the soil. Admittedly, hopefully, the tangible result of this decay is some way off yet.

Despite ourselves, we are very attached to our conceptual formations. Occasionally, we can be unexpectedly arrested in our tracks by a tree, its unique formation, the ridges on the bark twisting one way and then another, as if it were expressing some unique character; however, for most of us, most of the time, it is simply a tree. In seeing this event as simply a tree, we miss the uniqueness of its formation, the detail and atmosphere that it appears to be emanating. The concept of the tree is a much-reduced version of what we might potentially see before us. The same might be said of Jose, who is defined by certain key attributes: he has conduct disorder, he is a difficult child, he has SEBD (social, emotional, and behavioural difficulties). These narrow attributes reduce Jose and narrow our vision of him.

The willingness and ability to distinguish between our conceptual formations and the fluid alive experience are not always as simple as lifting our gaze. When I earlier referred to Google Maps characterising the conceptual formations, this is more akin to an augmented reality than a phone attached to the dashboard. There is work to be done to distinguish the map from the experience. This is not simply a theory that we can apply to certain things in particular circumstances; as will be discussed later, this is a lived experience and therefore requires what might be seen as practice.

Steven Hayes (2019), the founder of acceptance and commitment therapy (ACT), referred to our tenacious attachment to language as 'cognitive fusion'. Non-duality invites us to disentangle ourselves from Google Maps to 'cognitively defuse' and acknowledge the vast complexity that is in front of us.

For Jose, non-duality is asking us to lift our gaze from diagnostic manuals, labels, simplified models, and theories to Jose, a living person in the process of becoming and never arriving. He is a complex alive, unique person who, at any given moment, is acting and responding within a live complex open system.

Dependent arising

From a non-dual perspective, it is not only important to recognise that we are fluid processes; it is also that these processes cannot meaningfully be seen as separate from the conditions they exist within. Traditionally, this is termed *dependent arising* or *dependent origination* (Struhl, 2020b) and is explored in Mary Chilokoa's chapter.

For a psychologist to take Jose out of one set of conditions (the classroom) and receive him in their clinic, to then make an assessment of him is to assume that Jose can be viewed independently. Independently from the psychologist and independently from their clinic. However, we know that who Jose is for that hour is a result not just of Jose but of who the psychologist is, how the psychologist is feeling that day, whether Jose has had breakfast that morning, whether at that time the environment feels safe or threatening. In fact, there is a mind-boggling array of conditions that will result in the psychologist meeting a particular Jose. To recognise this is to acknowledge that no one thing can be separated from the conditions within which it arises; there can only be different conditions, not a different Jose.

Jose, like many other pupils I have worked with, has spent some time in a resourced provision with fewer pupils, more teachers, and less demands on formal education. Jose spent 12 weeks in this provision, and in that time, staff described him as being a lively, funny, warm, and affectionate boy who, on the whole, cooperated with the agenda of the staff. It was felt that after his 12 weeks, things had changed enough for him to be re-integrated back to his mainstream class. However, on his return, Jose began to experience significant difficulties.

At his second re-integration meeting, there appeared to be some frustration on why the changes they had seen in Jose had not sustained themselves. What was not understood at that time was that Jose was not one thing. What they were witnessing in these different environments were emotions and behaviours that arose dependent on the conditions that surrounded them.

Entanglement

The sense that one thing cannot be separated from that which surrounds it is often termed *entanglement* (Barad, 2007). It communicates that the boundaries we put around things, processes, and events are imposed by us and cannot be seen in the things themselves.

What lies at the heart of much of psychological suffering and human exploitation is the belief that we are separate from others and the environment. However, this could not be further from the truth. The bubble we might find ourselves in when surrounded by other people or the alienation we might experience from our environment is a self-imposed illusionary barrier that we actively build moment by moment.

Greif (2017) suggests that cognition is not something that resides in the individual but extends beyond our somatic boundaries into our environment. From a non-dual perspective, learning is not something that an individual does but is a cooperative activity (Gergen, 2020). It is not the teacher who imparts knowledge to the students but the community of learners who partake in a shared endeavour in which new understanding and insights emerge. Every word I type here is not in isolation but very much with you in mind. My imagined reader made up of the personalities I have curated.

The divisiveness of separation bids us against each other, where children compete for better grades from their neighbours, whereas entanglement draws us together through recognising that we are intimately connected to one another.

Jose has missed a lot of school. The approaches to learning in school in numerous ways compel him to compare himself with his peers. As a separate person, he feels diminished, and even a sense of shame. Feelings that, at times, are unbearable for him, that provoke behaviour which attempts to rescue himself from these feelings.

Jose's sense of isolation is evident. He tells me that teachers do not like him and that they are always picking on him; he says he hates school and does not see the point. Mr Allen describes himself often battling with Jose when trying to correct his behaviour. These all point to the sense of alienation that is Jose's experience in school. It is not a place where he experiences a sense of belonging. The lack of ease that he feels is a response to his evaluation that the environment is not safe, that he needs protection. All of which hardens the boundary between himself, others, and his environment. It is not only Jose who is hardening his imagined boundary. For Mr Allen, Jose is a threat, not only a physical threat, but also a threat to his sense of ease in the classroom. He feels that sense of comparison with his peers when the head teacher is called to intervene, again. With all this anxiety in the room, it is no wonder that the dynamic becomes a battle. 'No matter how much we try to escape it, we are part of a cacophonous parliament of things' (Akomolafe & Ladha, 2017).

The physicist Karen Barad's (2007) term 'intra-action' and the psychologist Siegel's (2022) 'intra-connection' suggest that all actions exist within relationships. The use of *intra*, from the Latin 'inside', implies that these relationships are not to be conceived of as one thing acting on another; it indicates something far more intimate, that we are intricately entangled with others and our environment.

The implications of non-duality for Jose are that attention needs to be paid, not so much to Jose himself, but to the dynamic that exits within these relationships. It is not that the relationships in the school setting should be strengthened; as we have seen, we cannot escape our entanglement with each other. For Jose in school, these relationships are predominantly defined by fear, opposition, threat, and humiliation. It is a subtle but significant shift to become less curious about who Jose is and why he is acting the way he does and towards placing our careful attention to particular nodes within the entangled web that surround Jose, the encounters with teachers, pupils, and the school environment. These include requests, demands, praise, hiding, biting, shouting, being judged, and judging. According to Akomolafe and Ladha (2017), 'reconfiguring of our familiar understandings of causality, locality, agency, intentionality, individuality, choice, and subjectivity will constitute a potent ethical intra-vention' (p. 822).

Love

I still carry with me an incident in my first year of educational psychology practice at a review meeting of Pete in an inner-city high school. I met with the young person half an hour before the meeting. Around the table were the head of year, police liaison officer, class teacher, and a number of other professionals. We were going around the table, offering our insights into the young person's situation. As it came closer to my contribution, I began to panic; I had nothing worthwhile to say. Thoughts were racing through my mind: 'I am a useless psychologist', 'They are going to know this', 'What on earth is psychology, anyway', 'I have to prove myself'. When it was finally my turn to speak, I said something about the stages of change that I remembered from a seminar on motivational interviewing. To my shame, what struck me afterwards was, in that moment, how little regard I had for Pete. I was full of anxiety, felt threatened, and was compelled to protect my sense of self, my professional standing. As opposed to being attuned to the young person, motivated by concern and care for him, my attention was largely focused on me.

Steven Hayes (2019) would regard this as a typical example of cognitive fusion driven by experiential avoidance. In hindsight, I can see how the unselfing process would have significantly helped the situation. By acknowledging my feelings as transient and the selfing processes as insubstantial, I can see how my attention could have been released from the eddy it had created and brought my awareness back to what mattered, this young person. The American philosopher Karen Barad and novelist Iris Murdock both saw unselfing as a moral imperative.

The artist and non-duality commentator Rupert Spira describes the subjective experience of non-duality when in contact with the inanimate as beauty and when in contact with other people as love. Interestingly, the educationalists Maija Lanas and Michalinos Zembylas (2015) have contested the notion of love as a 'feminized, soft topic' (p. 32), suggesting that it is a powerful transformative tool.

Whilst more detached terms such as 'connection', 'the relational', 'relatedness', or 'attunement' may feel safer, love might be said to be closest to what Jose and all children in his situation need most. Love is not a theory, skill, or tool; love suggests something fully felt. This book typifies a growing interest by professionals working with children and young people in theories surrounding attachment and trauma, demonstrating an understanding in the need to address the relational field of the child. However, more crucially, these theories point to the need for love. Lana and Zembylas (2015) suggest that 'the transformational power of love arises precisely from the fact that it breaks the I' (p. 37).

Cross-disciplinary

As an educational psychologist with a particular interest in children's mental health who came across non-duality as a way of responding to a problem in my field, I find myself in interesting company. Within the academic literature, there is a growing interest in non-duality across different disciplines, often as a way of reconciling new findings in their field.

The flourishing of thoughts and ideas emerging from non-duality across different disciplines implies that there is something fundamental to existence that is being approached here, and if this is the case, it would naturally be applicable in all areas of our lives. As such, it inevitably pertains to children's mental health and, specifically, children like Jose.

Koning and Van Willigenburg, in their paper published in *Physics Essays* in 2020, put forward the proposition that *non-duality* is central to a coherent understanding of the universe in which 'everything is connected and depends on everything else' (p. 299). The microbiologists Bapteste and Huneman (2018) point to the limitations in seeing organisms as entities in themselves and suggest that, for microbiology to progress, a theoretical shift is required towards seeing life in dynamic, complex networks of interaction. Also, the immunologist Alfred Tauber described the notion of the self as an impediment to furthering immunology, referring to the self as simply a metaphor.

The term 'unselfing' was coined by the novelist and philosopher Iris Murdoch (1970), in which she speaks of the transformative power of undoing our sense of self to allow a greater attunement to the surrounding world. Art and poetry across the world have been replete with references to what might be described as non-duality and, for many, like myself, is a constant source of inspiration. From the 14th-century Islamic poet and mystic Mahmud Shabistari (Jamal, 2009) to the modern American poetry of Mary Oliver (2014).

Implications for practice

The implications of non-duality for how we understand and respond to children and young people are significant. The ecologist and transpersonal psychologist John Davis (2011) stressed that it was important for non-duality to be seen 'not as an end to action but the beginning of a new source of action' (p. 144).

For almost all of us working in education and mental health, our primary lever of change for any child or young person are the interactions we have with and around them. A key area of exploration by academics is the potential of non-duality in cultivating flexible, sensitive, attuned response to who we encounter (Blackstone, 2006).

The non-dual perspective offers a concrete means by which interactions can be experienced as one typified by love. By cultivating a non-dual perspective, we extract ourselves from the barriers of separation that remove ourselves from the child. This is not a behaviour or skill that can be learnt but an embodied authentic response to how we are experiencing the situation. I would suggest that the authenticity of our response can be felt by the other, especially by children. Jose, like many other children who have had similar experiences, has developed a highly sensitive antennae for interactions that feel unsafe. Those of us who are used to working with children who are sensitised in this way will know how important authenticity is.

Many of the psychological theories and models that are founded on relationships and attunement can easily be adopted in a performative manner, learning scripts or steps of interaction. For many children like Jose who, whilst having a high need for connection, also have a high need for safety, such interactions can, at times, have little impact. I would suggest that these interactions can, on occasion, feel synthetic or insincere for the receiver and therefore potentially unsafe. The phenomenologist and existentialist Jeff Malpas (2015) suggested that self-release directs us to a more encompassing authenticity. My personal experience is that this authenticity is felt by parents, teachers, children, and young people, resulting in more open, trusting communication. I would also concur with Lana and Zembylas (2015) that love in and of itself is transformative in these interactions.

Another aspect of non-dualities' encounter with children's mental health which has been discussed is a shift in where the problem is understood to be located. From a non-dual perspective, mental suffering and what is regarded as problematic behaviour are not something that can be seen as residing in or arising out of the person. Neither can it be isolated from the conditions in which it arises. Non-duality encourages us to look at the whole complex, interrelated systems surrounding the young person from the school system, friendship groups to diet and physical activity – it even includes the agendas and emotions of those that define the problem. By witnessing things as dynamic and interrelated, we are invited to take what Zen practitioners refer to as the backward step. We disentangle ourselves from a narrow field of vision of labels, simplistic causes, and apportioning blame to seeing any action or emotion as arising from a wider field of conditions, like a wave that rises and falls in the sea. Practically, this encourages us to pay attention to what flowed through and around a particular event. When Jose bit his teacher, what feelings were flowing through Jose, what led to Jose's compulsion arising from the ground of his feelings, and what were the distal events that led to these feelings and compulsions?

Having explored what non-duality is and what it has to offer professionals working with children and young people who are experiencing difficulty, I would finally like to make the distinction between a cognitive comprehension of non-duality and an awareness of what non-duality is pointing towards. Unlike discursive psychology, non-duality encourages an embodied, felt apprehension of its position. As I mentioned at the start of the chapter, there are certain insurmountable barriers to writing and reading about this area in that non-duality is not something that can be grasped by the conceptual mind; it is this very mind that is seen to obscure the fluid, complex phenomena that pervades our experience.

Many psychologists have developed systems of practice that facilitate a felt sense of this perspective. Mindfulness, as it has been translated in the Global North, tends to focus on one aspect of what is practised by most Buddhist practitioners. Mindfulness in the Global North tends to focus on what is termed as *sati* or *concentration*, which generally is understood as merely a precursor to vipassana. *Vipassana*, translated as 'to see things as they really are', is to direct one's focused mind towards simply looking at what arises in our experience. When this is done simply, without expectation or a theory, what is understood to be revealed is a direct witnessing of non-duality. Once this has been witnessed, what is thought to occur is an ontological shift which immutably changes our perception of things. Whilst the conceptual mind is still effectively functioning, it is seen in the context of a more expansive awareness of things.

To this end, Steven Hayes (2019), through acceptance and commitment therapy, has created a range of innovative exercises which he terms 'self as context'; these exercises have been expanded on and added to by psychologists since its inception in the 1980s. More recently, Dan Siegel (2022) has developed what he refers to as 'the wheel of awareness', in which he asks participants to shift their attention from their objects of awareness, such as external entities, thoughts, feelings, light (the rim of the wheel), to that which is aware, the hub of the wheel.

Concluding remarks

It is my belief that, engaging with these kinds of practices as education and mental health professionals, we are able to offer children and young people meaningful relationships that nourish their sense of connection and safety. It is my experience that an embodied non-dual understanding encourages professionals to look beyond the individual child and develop the conditions that lead to the wellbeing of everyone within their relational field.

Summary box

This chapter has attempted to evoke a way of relating to ourselves and others, described as non-duality. It is hoped that this has sparked a curiosity and interest in who we are and the possibilities available to us in experiencing and responding to others.

For those interested in exploring or deepening an understanding of non-duality, the internet is replete with resources, materials, seminars, and literature around this subject.

Under the umbrella of acceptance and commitment therapy, Steven Hayes and his colleagues (Hayes et al., 2011) offer a range of practical literature and resources for working with children and parents. Approaches relating to 'self as context' correspondence closely with non-duality.

Recently, Dan Siegel (2022) has developed a discipline which he has termed as 'interpersonal neurobiology', which offers both a rationale for a non-dual perspective and practical exercises to help us become more aligned with this positioning.

The implications for education settings are very well articulated by Kenneth Gergen and his colleagues. Much of their work can be found in the Taos Institute.

Finally, a personal hero of mine is Bayo Akomolafe, who is described as a philosopher, writer, activist, and psychologist. His work might be understood as a call to decolonising psychology to open up alternative ways of being.

References

Akomolafe, B., & Ladha, A. (2017). Perverse particles, entangled monsters and psychedelic pilgrimages: Emergence as an onto-epistemology of not-knowing. *Ephemera: Theory & Politics in Organization, 17*(4).

Bapteste, E., & Huneman, P. (2018). Towards a dynamic interaction network of life to unify and expand the evolutionary theory. *BMC biology, 16*, 1-16.

Barad, K. (2007). *Meeting the universe halfway: Quantum physics and the entanglement of matter and meaning*. Duke University Press.

Blackstone, J. (2006). Intersubjectivity and nonduality in the psychotherapeutic relationship. *Journal of Transpersonal Psychology, 38*(1).

Boyle, M., Hickson, J., & Ujhelyi Gomez, K. (2023). Me, myself, and I? The neoliberal citizen. In *COVID-19 and the case against neoliberalism: The United Kingdom's political pandemic* (pp. 139-154). Springer International Publishing.

Brown, S. L., Siegel, L., & Blom, S. M. (2020). Entanglements of matter and meaning: The importance of the philosophy of Karen Barad for environmental education. *Australian Journal of Environmental Education, 36*(3), 219-233.

Davis, J. V. (2011). Ecopsychology, transpersonal psychology, and nonduality. *International Journal of Transpersonal Studies, 30*(1-2), 137-147.

De Koning, W. L., & Van Willigenburg, L. G. (2020). The essence of everything. *Physics Essays, 33*(3), 299-301.

Gergen, K. J. (2009). *Relational being: Beyond self and community*. Oxford University Press.

Gergen, K. J., & Gill, S. R. (2020). *Beyond the tyranny of testing: Relational evaluation in education*. Oxford University Press.

Gramsci, A. (1971). *Selections from the prison notebooks of Antonio Gramsci*. International Publishers. (Original work published 1891-1937)

Greif, H. (2017). What is the extension of the extended mind? *Synthese, 194*(11), 4311-4336.

Hayes, S. (2019). *A liberated mind: The essential guide to ACT*. Random House.

Hayes, S. C., Strosahl, K. D., & Wilson, K. G. (2011). *Acceptance and commitment therapy: The process and practice of mindful change*. Guilford Press.

Jamal, M. (Ed.). (2009). *Islamic mystical poetry: Sufi verse from the early mystics to Rumi*. Penguin UK.

Josipovic, Z., & Miskovic, V. (2020). Nondual awareness and minimal phenomenal experience. *Frontiers in Psychology, 2087*.

Kelbessa, W. (2015). African environmental ethics, indigenous knowledge, and environmental challenges. *Environmental Ethics, 37*(4), 387-410.

Köhne, A. C. (2020). The relationalist turn in understanding mental disorders: From essentialism to embracing dynamic and complex relations. *Philosophy, Psychiatry, & Psychology, 27*(2), 119-140.

Lanas, M., & Zembylas, M. (2015). Towards a transformational political concept of love in critical education. *Studies in Philosophy and Education, 34*, 31-44.

Libet, B. (2009). *Mind time: The temporal factor in consciousness*. Harvard University Press.

Malpas, J. (2015). From extremity to releasement: Place, authenticity, and the self. In H. Pedersen & M. Altman (Eds.), *Horizons of authenticity in phenomenology, existentialism, and moral psychology. Contributions to phenomenology* (Vol. 74). Springer.

McCarroll, V. (2022). Mysticizing medicine: Incorporating nondualism into the training of psychedelic guides. *Interdisciplinary Science Reviews, 48*, 752-767.

Murdoch, I. (1970). *The sovereignty of good*. Routledge.

Niforatos, J. D. (2016). The decent care movement: Subsidiarity, pragmatic solidarity, and cross-cultural resonance. *Journal of Religion and Health, 55*, 206-216.

Oliver, M. (2014). *Dream work*. Open Road+Grove/Atlantic.

Olsson, A. L. (2018). A moment of letting go: Iris Murdoch and the morally transformative process of unselfing. *Journal of Philosophy of Education, 52*(1), 163-177.

O'Reilly, M., Svirydzenka, N., Adams, S., & Dogra, N. (2018). Review of mental health promotion interventions in schools. *Social Psychiatry and Psychiatric Epidemiology, 53*, 647-662.

Sheldrake, M. (2021). *Entangled life: How fungi make our worlds, change our minds & shape our futures*. Random House Trade Paperbacks.

Shotter, J. (2014). Agential realism, social constructionism, and our living relations to our surroundings: Sensing similarities rather than seeing patterns. *Theory & Psychology, 24*(3), 305-325.

Siegel, D. J. (2022). *IntraConnected: MWe (Me+ We) as the integration of self, identity, and belonging (Norton series on interpersonal neurobiology)*. WW Norton & Company.

Siegel, D. J., & Drulis, C. (2023). An interpersonal neurobiology perspective on the mind and mental health: Personal, public, and planetary wellbeing. *Annals of General Psychiatry, 22*(1), 5.

Smith, K. (2011). Neuroscience vs philosophy: Taking aim at free will. *Nature, 477*(7362), 23-25.

Struhl, K. J. (2020a). What kind of an illusion is the illusion of self. *Comparative Philosophy, 11*(2), 8.

Struhl, K. J. (2020b). Ecosocialism: A Buddhist-Marxist approach. *Radical Philosophy Review, 23*(1), 89-115.

Theise, N. D., & Kafatos, M. C. (2016). Fundamental awareness: A framework for integrating science, philosophy and metaphysics. *Communicative & Integrative Biology, 9*(3), e1155010.

Tiwari, M. (2023). Young people can help to ease the global mental health crisis. *Nature Human Behaviour, 7*, 831-832.

5 'I am because we are'

African and Buddhist perspectives on 'relationship' and human flourishing

Mary Chilokoa

Introduction

This chapter seeks to engage in a bit of cultural 're-appropriation' on matters relating to human development and 'flourishing'. It seeks to offer some alternative sources of wisdom, counter and complementary narratives to perspectives (primarily based on White Western paradigms) which have existed as dominant discourses within contemporary psychological theory and practice.

In highlighting particular cultural and spiritual perspectives, this chapter seeks to engage in a process of 're-balancing' which celebrates and, in so doing, privileges different ways of seeing and being in the world. These 'different ways', while not traditionally considered within the 'mainstream', can nonetheless be seen as having value: with regard to supporting human wellbeing and in understanding the significance of how our relationships with one another are expressed.

It is certainly true that what is considered worthy of general consumption, of study, and of discussion is subject to change over time. In this regard, aspects of African culture, such as its music and food, for the longest time ignored or demeaned within the context of the White Western gaze, are now lauded in certain quarters of British youth and popular culture. Despite a largely unacknowledged history of African music in Britain dating back to the 1920s, for example, we now see 'Afro-beats' artists commanding mass followings, made up as much from White British teenagers as African ones. Similarly, 'jollof rice', a traditional staple of West African households, is now a mainstay of many a 'hipster' street food market in cities all across the UK. We have come a long way – and as a child growing up in the UK of the 1970s and 1980s, where to be African was definitely not something to shout about, I know this as part of my lived experience.

Within the academic sphere, however, while the burgeoning discipline of African psychology (Nwoye, 2015) is gaining credence and developing its own distinctive voice, there is still some way to go. By the same token, the acceptance within mainstream academia of matters pertaining to 'spirituality' is certainly far from unequivocal. While there is evidence that the exploration of spiritual ideas within contemporary mainstream psychological discourses is becoming more widespread (Kwee et al., 2006; Gersch et al., 2008; Ruddock & Cameron, 2010) and the appropriate inclusion of religious or spiritual considerations within academia can be regarded as having merit (Gergen, 2009), there is still perhaps a degree of uncertainty about the place of spiritual matters within secular, mainstream domains.

This chapter will seek to put forward an argument for the legitimate consideration of these cultural and spiritual perspectives in relation to practice and approaches which can be meaningful in our work with young people.

DOI: 10.4324/9781003451907-5

Philosophy, Buddhism, and the meanings in life

Philosophy has been concerned with the nature of human experience and what connects human experience as it is lived to the real world. Dictionary definitions of *philosophy* as the study of 'the fundamental nature of knowledge, reality, and existence' and a theory or attitude 'that acts as a guiding principle for behaviour' (*Oxford Dictionaries* Online) emphasise its function as something which not only informs the sense of what we 'know' about the world but also shapes the way we live in it.

Western philosophy has grappled with questions concerning the human search for knowledge and meaning – those questions, as Nagel (1979) put it, relating to 'mortal life: how to understand it and how to live it' (Nagel, 1979, p. ix). These are perennial concerns and are played out in a myriad of ways, across different cultures and contexts. Today, it could be argued that these same questions are now being explored by forms of neuroscience as they attempt to map conscious experiences (such as feelings and emotion) onto the workings of the brain and towards an understanding of a distinct concept of 'mind'. As Damasio ponders:

> Are mind and body two different things, or just one? If they are not the same, are mind and body made from two different substances or just one? . . . These are some of the main issues involved in the so-called mind-body problem, a problem whose solution is central to the understanding of who we are.
>
> (Damasio, 2003, p. 183)

Such questions exploring fundamental aspects of life resonate with those within some Eastern philosophies. Buddhism is one such philosophy, originating in India in the 4th or 5th century BCE, with the Prince Siddhartha Gautama (later to become known as Shakyamuni Buddha) and his search to understand the nature and causes of human suffering and how it could be overcome. The Sanskrit word *Buddha* means 'one who is awakened [to the truth]' and reflects an idea that, through the process of 'enlightenment', living beings can see the world as it truly is. In Buddhism, this relates to recognising the qualities of courage, compassion, and wisdom as inherent within the lives of all living beings, rendering them worthy of respect and dignity. Although innate in all people, these qualities may remain latent for any number of reasons, including life experiences. The primary purpose of Buddhist practice is the 'awakening to' and unlocking of this innate positive potential and capacity and, in so doing, to create value in one's own life and in that of others.

The concept of 'ubuntu'

Ubuntu is an indigenous African philosophy and way of life and part of a long oral tradition. As expressed through the southern African 'Nguni' proverb that 'umuntu ngumuntu ngabantu', often translated as 'a person is a person through other persons' (e.g. Nwoye, 2017), ubuntu dates back to before the colonisation of Africa. Popularly traced to the Bantu peoples of southern Africa (Bolden, 2014), the concept is considered by some to have origins dating right back to Ancient Africa (Ramose, 2002). Ubuntu can be understood as a social philosophy: based on principles of care and community, harmony and hospitality, respect and responsiveness, it expresses the fundamental interconnectedness of human existence

(Bolden, 2014) and has been used for many centuries to shape, guide, and maintain positive human interactions, relationships, and wellbeing among African communities (Ramose, 2002). The proverb has equivalent versions in other African dialects, but for the purposes of this chapter, we shall stick with the Zulu/Khosa translation, as it has received some popularisation in recent years, not least in the writing of the late Desmund Tutu, who described it as 'the essence of being human', where 'we need other human beings in order to be human' (Tutu, 2004, p. 25).

Ubuntu philosophy is grounded in humanistic values and principles of solidarity, cooperation, and compassion (Ngubane & Makua, 2021). It is an expression of deeply held African values which emphasise reciprocity within relationships, where one's personhood is rooted in one's interconnectedness with others and one's own good is found in the communal good. Whilst the origins of ubuntu can be seen as distinctly African, parallels have been drawn with similar concepts in other societies, including the Chinese philosophy of *jen*, the Filipino philosophy of *loob*, and the Russian concept of *obschina* (Bolden, 2014).

Ubuntu can also be paraphrased as 'I am who I am because of who we all are', highlighting values linked to the importance of family, community, and respect and humility, particularly in terms of our relationship with the land and with nature. Thus, ubuntu offers a holistic perspective on 'relationality' as a core aspect and function of existence: of 'being' and 'doing' in the world.

The relational Buddha (and the lotus flower)

As Buddhism travelled eastwards along the 'silk road', various schools and traditions developed along the way, some focusing on particular sutras (oral teachings) expounded by Shakyamuni. Nichiren Buddhism is one such tradition and will form the main focus for the 'Buddhism' described within this chapter. Originating in Japan, and following the teachings of the 13th-century monk Nichiren Daishonin, Nichiren Buddhism takes as its primary text the *Lotus Sutra*, the final sutra of Shakyamuni, which emphasised the equality of all living beings to attain Buddhahood (a state of life where courage, compassion, and wisdom can be freely expressed), which was unusual for the time and context. The central message of the *Lotus Sutra*, with the metaphor of the lotus flower blooming in a muddy pond, is that this is possible for everyone, in the midst of life's challenges and hardships. The belief is that the hardships themselves can constitute the essential ingredients for this 'flourishing', and this process plays out as individuals awaken to their potential in the present moment and from moment to moment.

In terms of an understanding of life and how it is experienced, the idea of a separateness between mind and body, as first described by Descartes (1596-1650), contrasts with the 'non-duality' expressed within Buddhist philosophy. Buddhism resists engaging with dualistic understandings of phenomena, holding that the mind and body, for example, co-exist on an interdependent basis. This understanding is extended to life and its environment, and this 'relationality' is beautifully expressed within the fundamental Buddhist concept of interconnectedness, known as 'dependent origination':

> In Buddhist terms, the great universe and the self - the great macrocosm and the microcosm - are one. . . . Since the self and all phenomena are one, all things are interrelated. All things weave a single whole in which individuals live in relation to all others. In other

words, all beings and phenomena exist or occur because of their relationship with other beings and phenomena, and nothing in either the human or the non-human world exists in isolation. All things are mutually related to and interdependent with all other things.

(Ikeda, 2006, p. 248)

Thus, all phenomena are seen as arising from mutually interdependent relationships in response to various causes and conditions: all life as primarily relational (Gergen, 2009), conditions within it intrinsically related and influencing one another. The term 'esho funi' in Nichiren Buddhism expands on this concept further. Translated from the Japanese as the 'one-ness of self and environment', it also has the meaning 'two but not two' and proposes the idea that we, as individuals, are not only not separate from our environment but also exert a profound (metaphysical) influence on it. It requires the holding together in mind of two seemingly distinct concepts, of 'self' and 'environment', as one – and again contrasts with 'binary' modes of constructing the world often associated with Western ways of thinking.

Buddhism exists as a supremely optimistic philosophy which emphasises the dynamic potential within life and our living of it. It offers a uniquely relational perspective on the function and meaning of life and how we perceive what is possible within and through human relationships.

'A person through other persons': 'Ubuntu' as African humanism

Ubuntu can be seen as existing as part of an 'African worldview' (Nwoye, 2017) which is expressed through various aspects of its culture. 'Culture' may broadly be understood here as including thoughts, beliefs, and norms for interaction and communication, all of which may influence cognitions, behaviours, and perceptions (Ingraham, 2000), and when attempting to define the values and beliefs of any cultural group, it is of course important to recognise that all cultural groups have diversity within them. Particularly given the vast number of countries and territories within the African continent, it would be unreasonable to think of its people as one homogenous group; it is also known that 'ubuntu' itself has multiple localised meanings and diverse forms in different communities throughout Africa (Muwanga-Zake, 2009). Nonetheless, the concept can be seen as having commonality throughout Africa, albeit in slightly varying forms.

In rhythm with those described earlier, significant core values of ubuntu have been identified as those pertaining to survival, solidarity, compassion, and dignity. Through ubuntu, the African person sees the benefit of engaging in reciprocity and mutuality, particularly in times of need. These values support a sense of identity and belonging, where each person knows themselves as a member of a people and, through stories, myths, and other cultural practices, to have rootedness in their community Nwoye, 2017).

Through a sense of ubuntu, the individual is able to perceive their existence as relative to that of the group, and there is an awareness of individual responsibility to something greater than oneself – the collective – to which each person contributes. It is important to note that individuality is not negated but simply seen as secondary to the wellbeing of the community. As Nwoye (2017) points out, the ubuntu orientation to living, therefore, contrasts greatly with the 'individualistic' notion of identity proposed in the West, which emphasises the idea of humans as self-contained units in control of their own destinies (Nwoye, 2017).

As such, ubuntu can be seen as a humanistic philosophy which exists in opposition to the often-adversarial discourses which prevail in societies based on competition rather than on community – narratives which reflect attitudes that 'my freedom depends on your lack of freedom', for example. In resisting these values, ubuntu moves towards a sense of mutuality, where freedoms can, in fact, co-exist.

While the concept of ubuntu may have originated within rural African communities, it still has traction and relevance in urbanised and Westernised communities across the African diaspora. In my own experience, growing up in the East End of London, I was very aware of aspects of my everyday life which served to relocate me to my African heritage. Just as within rural communities it is common to have more than just one 'mother' figure, with other women taking on that role as needed, I have memories of an extended network of family friends who were an integral part of my childhood growing up. They were respectfully referred to as 'auntie' or 'uncle', regardless of any blood connection, the connection through culture, community, tradition, and history being enough. This is the proverb 'It takes a village to raise a child' in action and is an example of what can happen within 'collectivist' cultures, where responsibility for the upbringing and wellbeing of children within the community is taken as a shared responsibility.

My sense of African culture is that one person's situation is very much connected to that of the group – socially and also economically. I know that my own parents, as new immigrants to the UK, were dependent upon the patronage of fellow Nigerians in finding work and a place to live. There is something of a running 'in-joke' about immigrant parents from certain communities being obsessed with their offspring taking up jobs in safe and prestigious professions, such as medicine and law; while there may well be a strong competitive element being played out, what is also clear is that the job of one within the community can have significant implications for others within that community. These relate ultimately to the quality of life that is possible for a whole community, where benefits and resources can be shared. Such factors have particular significance for racialised communities, for whom the impacts of racism and discrimination, connecting with wealth and health disparities, are now increasingly acknowledged. The spirit of ubuntu enables and facilitates this sharing of resources, where not only the wellbeing but also the survival of a community may be at stake.

Nwoye (2017) proposes an 'Africentric' theory of human motivation and personhood as a lens through which to explore ubuntu and seeks to use this paradigm 'to demonstrate that, in Africa as in other parts of the world, mature human beings are not born but made' (Nwoye, 2017, p. 42). In this respect, African 'personhood' is seen as socioculturally derived and influenced by a range of forces, both ancient and contemporary (Nwoye, 2017). In common with Buddhist thinking, 'Africentric' perspectives, unlike 'Eurocentric' ones, see reality in holistic (both-and) rather than dualistic (either-or) terms (Nwoye, 2017). In particular, they recognise not only the physical but also the spiritual dimensions in being a person and, specifically, an African person and exist as an 'alternative to the currently pervasive Eurocentric hegemony in the personality field that gives little room for the accommodation of other accounts of how human subjectivities are crafted' (Nwoye, 2017, p. 3).

This 'African worldview' encompasses internalised basic moral virtues, such as respect for elders, traditions around birth and death, and norms for social interaction. I remember my mother telling me of how she was regularly misunderstood when responding with a 'sorry' when a colleague at work, for example, might inadvertently have hurt themselves.

The confused colleague would not have known that in Nigerian culture, there is a specific meaning for this type of 'sorry'. This 'sorry' (*'ndoh'* in my own native dialect) is not given as an apology or admission of culpability; rather, it constitutes an expression of empathy in the face of the other person's hurt (which could be physical or emotional). In this way, a sense of ubuntu can be manifested within even 'micro' aspects of everyday human interaction.

While Nwoye (2017) champions ubuntu as a resistance to the hegemony of Western models, Hanks (2008), also referencing ubuntu, calls for a re-visioning of some of the traditional parameters of Western humanism:

> We must build a modern, (and more importantly, humane and just) psychology from within the traditions of humanism that can be expanded and adapted to serve our increasingly global, increasingly complex community. It is time for a humanistic reformation that goes beyond a call for the opportunity to develop *individual* potentialities and *self*-actualization. It is time for a unifying psychology that recognizes *cultural* and societal *potentialities* and offers the opportunity for *universal* actualization.
>
> (Hanks, 2008, p. 118)

This statement would seem to be suggestive of a need to open up to new possibilities for understanding our human motivations, which include perspectives which are more inclusive and culturally sensitive and relevant for what is needed today in our quests for fulfilment and wellbeing.

Buddhist humanism: 'Flourishing in a muddy pond'

The fundamental objective of life for Buddhists is to become happy and fulfilled. For Nichiren Buddhists, this is conceptualised as 'happiness for self and other', whereby one's own happiness cannot be separated from the happiness of those in one's environment. For Nichiren Buddhists, therefore, the concept of 'flourishing' is specifically a relational one. For example, as we seek to understand the vastness of our own potential, we must also understand and acknowledge the equal potential of others, and to see both as intrinsically linked. Similarly, just as the Buddhist proverb 'When one carries a lantern for another, one's own way is illuminated' suggests, as we take steps to support others' development, our own aims and needs are also supported. This has clear parallels with ubuntu values of interconnection and solidarity, where one's own wellbeing is intrinsically linked to the wellbeing of the group, and vice versa.

Within Buddhism, the focus is very much on happiness as residing within our own lives, as a process of 'becoming' and 'realisation', rather than an end point. Further, a distinction is made between 'relative' happiness and 'absolute' happiness (Ikeda, 2006), where the former refers to short-term pleasure or satisfaction in response to immediate, external needs being met, as opposed to a more enduring state of wellbeing which exists regardless of circumstances and 'happenings' within our lives; this speaks to the significance of how we are able to respond to difficulties, rather than the absence of difficulties themselves. Thus, in a Buddhist sense, the problem is not the 'problem'; it is the internal resources available to us with which to engage with the problem, which is key. And by engaging with one's 'Buddhahood' (e.g. with courage, compassion, and wisdom), which then also engenders a sense of hope in our lives, the problem or difficulty can be perceived differently, challenged, and ultimately transformed. Problems are thus conceptualised as 'events' which provide the opportunity for personal growth through engaging with the struggle of the problem. The 'muddy pond' which facilitates the blooming of the lotus flower.

Within Nichiren Buddhism, the character symbols for 'heart' and 'mind' are the same. The belief is that an inner change, a process of inner transformation of heart and mind through faith in the unlimited potential of one's life (self), has the capacity to transform any external situation (our environment) for the better. This is the Buddhist concept of 'human revolution', which takes place as we struggle against life's hardships and challenges and is a process which enacts a dynamic interplay:

> When we change, the world changes. The key to all change is in our own inner transformation – a change in our hearts and minds. . . . When we realise this truth, we can bring forth that power anywhere, anytime, and in any situation.
>
> (Ikeda, 2007, p. 51)

There is, therefore, an understanding that this process of struggle and transformation can yield benefits perhaps initially unforeseen, a capacity also acknowledged by non-Buddhist theorists:

> It is in the course of the quest and only through encountering and coping with the various particular harms, dangers, temptations and distractions which provide any quest with its episodes and incidents, that the goal of the quest is finally to be understood. A quest is always an education both to the character of that which is sought and in self-knowledge.
>
> (MacIntyre, 2000, p. 219)

Nichiren Buddhism positions itself as a philosophy for navigating these struggles of everyday life, the facing of which has the effect of bringing forth inner resources – with 'happiness' located within this very struggle. This principle has parallels with those Western humanistic approaches which emphasise personal growth and fulfilment as a basic human drive, and the notion that, in different ways, humans continuously seek to grow psychologically. This has been captured by the term 'self-actualisation' (Maslow, 1943; Rogers, 1943). Maslow (1954) described the idea that as one becomes more self-actualised and self-transcendent, one develops greater wisdom for use in a wide variety of situations. Alderfer's (1972) hierarchical conceptualisation of motivational needs stressed the notion that individuals are intrinsically connected to each other, and that the need for connectedness is a central human motivation. These ideas offer hopeful and optimistic conceptualisations of human beings as having great potential for engaging with the environment and with each other in endeavouring to solve the problems which arise in those environments. In a similar way, Nichiren Buddhism proposes that in revealing our potential through the qualities of 'Buddhahood', we can manifest those qualities in actions which 'create value' within our relationships and within the environment. As Ikeda (2004) asserts:

> A great human revolution in just a single individual will help achieve a change in the destiny of a nation and, further, will enable a change in the destiny of all humankind.
>
> (Ikeda, 2004, quoted in Ikeda, 2007, p. 306)

Thus, there is a profound connection between the 'flourishing' of an individual and the potential for corresponding positive effects, or 'flourishing', in the people and situations around the individual.

The Ancient Greek concept of 'eudaimonia' (sometimes translated as 'happiness' but thought to translate best as 'wellbeing' or 'flourishing') expresses the idea that we become better persons through practice. It was felt that someone who is flourishing is living the 'good' or 'virtuous' life, and according to Aristotle, all people seek to flourish, and these aspirations for 'good' lead to 'good' habits.

In secular life, 'happiness' is certainly something of a slippery concept, not least because of its subjective nature. Whether we construct 'happiness' and 'wellbeing' as the same thing is a question in itself and may depend upon how we are orientated towards these concepts through our social and cultural influences. In recent years, the concepts of 'happiness' and 'wellbeing' have become the focus of much study and research (e.g. Seligman, 2002; Haidt, 2006), yet at the same time, we are confronted by statistics which tell us how poorly we are scoring on indexes measuring the happiness and wellbeing of our young people (Prince's Trust, 2003). These consistently poor ratings have become social and, rightly, political issues and reflect deep-rooted problems which are proving far from easy to put right – despite the investment in short-term therapies through various government initiatives. It seems clear that more nuanced and human-focused approaches to supporting mental health and wellbeing are needed at this time.

For us as professionals, perhaps one of the most important questions is how we may facilitate and encourage those processes which can enable 'flourishing' in the context of our institutions and educational systems: how, through our conscious actions and efforts, we create value in our social, cultural, and educational environments.

The call for 'humanising' work with children

To put relationships at the centre of professional practice is to engage in 'humanising' work with people: work which emphasises and embodies empathy, connection, and empowerment. The importance of this 'humanising' work is captured very well within the African proverb which gently, but ominously, warns that 'a child who is not embraced by the village will burn it down to feel its warmth'.

And if we are to engage in humanising and transformational practice, with relationships at their core, perhaps we must start with the way that we perceive children and how we position them within our familial and societal structures.

In the UK, parents are now much more involved in their children's lives than in previous generations, as they seek to parent in the 'best' way, and to protect children from perceived harms (Ellyatt, 2011). This contrasts with how children within traditional African communities may be positioned: perhaps operating with much more independence, absorbing aspects of education and culture through observation, 'at the elbow' of elders, whose primary role might be seen, as expressed within 'ubuntu', as supporting the child to become a contributing part of the community.

In terms of professional practice, and in reference to the questions Billington (2006) has encouraged us to reflect on, in how we write and speak of, and how we speak with and listen to, young people (Billington, 2006), it is clear also that how and what we think about and how we position young people influence our engagement with them. Alongside our own personal biases, these perceptions will necessarily reflect the dominant discourses in our cultural and professional landscapes which construct and position children in particular ways (Gergen, 1999; Burman, 2008). In professional contexts, especially where adults hold positions of power and influence that children do not hold, we need to be particularly mindful of the actions and decisions that we take in relation to young people, and what those actions and decisions are based on. Often, these narratives and constructions may be subtle and implicit, at other times more explicitly known to us. It becomes important to take time and space to reflect on exactly how and why we do what we do: 'how we perform our work, the ideas and theories that we employ, the ideas upon which we base our advice and interventions; the evidence base for our theories or chosen intervention' (Billington, 2006, p. 7). Certainly, without this mindfulness, there may be a danger that we become adults whose actions serve to dominate, or patronise, or worse still, close off possibilities of 'being' (Billington, 2006; Mercieca, 2011) for the children in our care. As Billington (2006) reminds us, 'professional theory-choice' has an impact on children's lives and can lead to particular forms of language being used with regard to children, and in particular representations of them prevailing as 'truth' (Billington, 2006).

For children from particular communities, this is especially relevant. Cases which have recently come to general attention in the media involving 'adultification', for example, speak to the danger of this mis-representation. The term refers to the perception of Black children as less innocent and more adult-like than White children of the same age, with far-reaching implications for how they are responded to, and for their overall outcomes within, our educational and judicial systems (Epstein et al., 2022). In Epstein et al.'s study, Black girls were perceived as needing less nurturing, protection, and support, with these perceptions seen as leading to more punitive treatments:

> Ultimately, adultification is a form of dehumanization, robbing Black children of the very essence of what makes childhood distinct from all other developmental periods: innocence. Adultification contributes to a false narrative that Black youths' transgressions are intentional and malicious, instead of the result of immature decision-making.
>
> (Epstein et al., 2022)

Our actions and interactions with children are always of significance. They constitute a relationship of connections which are ultimately influenced and reinforced by what each has experienced and by the various and shifting constructions of the world in which we exist as adults and children. As with ubuntu principles, it becomes important to understand people as interconnected social and cultural beings and, as taught within Buddhism, as respect-worthy, dynamic protagonists within their social contexts. This chimes also with social constructionist ideas that we construct the world in the context of our relationship with others (Gergen, 1999).

It is important, then, that our models for professional practice with children are informed by holistic and humanistic perspectives, as a counter to overly rational and mechanistic methods which fail to engage with children and young people as 'whole' beings who are part of a sociocultural and community ecosystem. Educational systems such as those in the West which are often in the business of compartmentalising different aspects of children's capacities go contrary to this sense of the 'whole' person, and, for example, cultural and spiritual aspects are often overlooked in the assessing and supporting of children's human needs.

This attention to their 'whole' selves is important for all children, but even more so for children from particular groups. Nwoye (2017) has highlighted the 'problem' of educational systems in Africa, meant for Africans, but often based on non-African pedagogy. A related problem exists for many children of African and Caribbean descent across the diaspora, those directly or indirectly impacted by colonialism and imperialist value systems which often served to denigrate and diminish. Equally, the enactment of the transatlantic slave trade involved not only the separation of a people from their homelands but also a separation from their culture and ancestry. The implications for those descendant communities have continued to be seen and felt across family systems and in the ways that intergenerational trauma is being played out across our social landscapes today. The education system in many Western countries, including the UK, continues to disadvantage children who are racialised as 'other than White', something which is consistently borne out by data which highlights discrimination and inequality within the system (see, for example, Long et al., 2023, for a recent summary of research in this area). People of African heritage (along with other marginalised groups) may also suffer an additional harmful injustice when systems problematise and penalise them through the use of methods and tools (often with dubious 'eugenics' histories) which do not acknowledge significant aspects of their culture; this has the effect of failing to recognise them as 'whole' beings, and of effectively separating them from their rights to 'flourish'. The narrative around a young person may become skewed and problematised simply because they or their behaviours are viewed from particular perspectives which are informed by Western constructs and which can render them as 'other'.

'Cultural competence' describes 'the awareness, knowledge and skills that enable a person to interact effectively in a culturally diverse environment' (Harkins, 2010, p. 2). Although contentious in some quarters, developing cultural competence has the aim of supporting professionals to reflect upon the impact of culture on the way individuals and groups experience the world – this in order, ultimately, to work together as a wider community to reduce the institutional barriers and structural inequities that disproportionately affect the educational experiences of marginalised populations. This can be an important part of developing systems which can respond sensitively and appropriately to the children it hopes to support, systems which acknowledge and recognise the splitting and disconnection that exist and which have been produced within family and social systems (for example, as a legacy of slavery and colonialism) and which can take on the role of the 'village' to nurture, support, and embrace every child. These are systems which can become more humane through their 'humanising' social action.

It takes a village: Buddhist philosophy and ubuntu pedagogy informing relational and transformative action in practice

This chapter has proposed new ways of looking at and conceptualising our work with children and young people, which truly honours a spirit of relational practice. It has explored how we might engage in practice which is able to venture into new domains, towards that which emphasises the interconnectedness of things and the potential in every situation. The specific use of a spiritual dimension alongside other perspectives, in work with people, has been explored by others: Myers (1993) has suggested an 'optimal psychology' based on a holistic conceptual system utilising Eastern philosophies and African folk beliefs, and the intersection between spirituality and the aims of social justice are specifically emphasised within the framework proposed by Pigza and Welch (2010). They termed this 'spiritually engaged pedagogy', and it is described as a framework which draws on a broad conceptualisation of spirituality as involving development of the 'authentic self' and constructions of meaning and knowledge, emphasising relationship and interconnectedness (English, 2000; Tisdell, 2003).

Buddhism emphasises the interconnectivity within all life and the potential in each life moment. It also resists dualistic thinking around 'right and wrong', 'good and bad', and so encourages a worldview where difficulties are seen as part of life, where everything has the capacity for positive change. The concept of 'karma', now well embedded within the zeitgeist, can sometimes be taken negatively but simply refers to the accumulation of causes, good and bad, that we make (over lifetimes) and their effects. The Sanskrit word *karma* originally meant 'action', and in Buddhism, this means that every thought, word, and deed imprint a latent influence in one's life. This influence, or karma, has a dynamic element and becomes manifest when activated by an external stimulus, which then produces a corresponding effect. According to this concept, our actions in the past have shaped our present, and equally, our actions in the present, in turn, determine our future. Within Buddhism, this can be seen as a profoundly optimistic principle because it emphasises the agency we all have to make positive causes in this moment.

Ubuntu stresses that there is no separateness between our own and others' needs and motivations. Within our diverse, multicultural environments, ubuntu pedagogy can be seen as having the potential not only for connecting and reconnecting students with important indigenous values and cultures but also for enabling within the wider group the cultivation of social values of solidarity, co-existence, respect, and cooperation among all students: ubuntu pedagogy as a transformative and decolonial approach that promotes inclusion and social justice (Ngubane & Makua, 2021, p. 1). In practical terms, this might involve cultivating an educational culture which focuses on 'interdependence' and peer support rather than just 'independence' and the working towards individual goals, one which privileges methods for approaching problems which are holistic rather than binary and dualistic and modes of engagement which are inclusive and culturally competent in nature.

For us as educational professionals, often working within imperfect systems, holding to the concept of 'relationality' may be part of seeing that everything becomes an opportunity to create value, even (or particularly) if through having to challenge personal feelings of doubt, overwhelm, or insecurity in the face of difficult work environments. It involves seeing the potential in each moment and having faith in the causes we are making, even if the positive 'effects' may not be immediately apparent. In our work with schools, children, and families, we are often involved in situations where we are trying to make a positive difference, where it may not always be clear exactly what that difference is. It then becomes important to trust – in the significance of each action that is carried out with sincerity, with the wellbeing of that child or situation at the centre of our actions. In this way, we honour our professional values and elevate our professional lives.

We, as professionals within the education system, also need to take responsibility for being the 'village' around the child. In this very respect, this famous quote from the work of Buddhist philosopher Thich Nhat Hanh seems very relevant:

> When you plant lettuce, if it does not grow well, you don't blame the lettuce. You look for reasons it is not doing well. It may need fertilizer, or more water, or less sun. You never blame the lettuce.
>
> (Hanh, 1995, p. 78)

We need to know that when we enact practices which do not honour, respect, and nurture all aspects of a child's being, this will inevitably lead to damaging consequences for all of us within the system. We, the adults, need to be, or contribute, the 'nutrients' for the soil that encompasses a child's life so that the child's potential can be revealed and they are able to flourish. And we must trust that the causes we make and the actions we take, in the spirit of 'I am because we all are', will definitely manifest positive and transformational effects for all of us.

Summary box

- This chapter has sought to highlight key aspects of particular African and Buddhist philosophy and how they might usefully be applied to support relational practice.
- This has involved highlighting core values of Buddhism as acknowledging and respecting the dignity and value of every individual and the potential within each moment, and of ubuntu, as embodying a spirit of solidarity and collectivism, and the sense that the greatest good that we create is in relation to others.
- It has privileged non-dualistic thinking which acknowledges the interconnectedness between all things, emphasising the relationality and possibilities within all phenomena and circumstances.
- Finally, these key themes gravitate towards an idea that one important way to create and contribute towards a hopeful, respectful, and equal society (which enables the flourishing and wellbeing of all) is through education systems which are informed by humanistic values and which embody culturally inclusive and relational practice.

***

This chapter has been both rewarding and very difficult to write. The 'reward' has come from the fact that my identity as a practising Buddhist and as a person of African descent is such a big part of my life that to share and explore these aspects in relation to the professional life that I lead has been a profound and liberating experience. It has been 'difficult' for the very same reasons. I have felt a weight of responsibility in trying to give an accurate account of theories and philosophies which represent so much to me, and to be able to share them in an unbiased, accessible way for fellow practitioners: it has felt very important to 'get it right'.

What I have learned through the process of writing this chapter is that to 'walk the talk', for me, means really embracing the idea that 'difficult' things are often important in what they have to teach us, and that doing important things is often difficult. And to trust the process nonetheless.

References

Alderfer, C. P. (1972). *Existence, relatedness and growth*. Free Press.

Billington, T. (2006). *Working with children: Assessment, representation and intervention*. Sage.

Bolden, R. (2014). Ubuntu. *Encyclopedia of Action Research, 21*, 800-802.

Burman, E. (2008). *Deconstructing developmental psychology* (2nd ed.). Routledge.

Damasio, A. R. (2003). *Looking for Spinoza: Joy, sorrow and the feeling* brain. Harcourt.

Ellyatt, W. E. N. D. Y. (2011). Democratization of learning in R. *Too Much, Too Soon: Early Learning and the Erosion of Childhood, 1*, 160-180.

English, L. M. (2000). Spiritual dimensions of informal learning. In L. M. English & M. A. Gillen (Eds.), *Addressing the spiritual dimensions of adult learning: What educators can do* (pp. 29-38). Jossey-Bass. Cited in: Pigza, J. M., & Welch, M. J. (2010). Spiritually engaged pedagogy: The possibilities of spiritual development through social justice education. *Spirituality in Higher Education Newsletter, 5*(4), 1-12.

Epstein, R., Blake, J. J., & Gonzalez, T. (2022). *Girlhood interrupted: The erasure of Black girls' childhood*. The-Georgetown.

Gergen, K. J. (1999). *An invitation to social construction*. Sage.

Gergen, K. J. (2009). *Relational being: Beyond self and community*. Oxford University Press.

Gersch, I., Dowling, F., Panagiotaki, G., & Potton, A. (2008). Listening to children's views of spiritual and metaphysical concepts: A new dimension to educational psychology practice? *Educational Psychology in Practice, 24*(3), 225-236.

Haidt, J. (2006). *The happiness hypothesis: Finding modern truth in ancient wisdom*. Basic Books.

Hanh, T. N. (1995). *Peace is every step: The path of mindfulness in everyday life*. Random House.

Hanks, T. L. (2008). The Ubuntu paradigm: Psychology's next force? *Journal of Humanistic Psychology, 48*(1), 116-135.

Harkins, M. J. (2010). Teachers' perceptions of their cultural competencies: An investigation into the relationships among teacher characteristics and cultural competence. *Journal of Multiculturalism in Education, 6*, 1-30.

Ikeda, D. (2004). *Unlocking the mysteries of birth & death: . . . And everything in between, a Buddhist view life*. Middleway Press.

Ikeda, D. (2006). *Buddhism day by day: Wisdom for modern life*. Middleway Press.

Ikeda, D. (2007). *Lectures on "On attaining Buddhahood in this lifetime."* Soka Gakkai Malaysia (SGM).

Ingraham, C. L. (2000). Consultation through a multicultural lens: Multicultural and cross-cultural consultation in schools. *School Psychology Review, 29*(3), 320-343.

Kwee, M. G. T., Gergen, K. J., & Koshikawa, F. (Eds.). (2006). *Horizons in Buddhist psychology*. Taos Institute Publications.

Long, D. A., McCoach, D. B., Siegle, D., Callahan, C. M., & Gubbins, E. J. (2023). Inequality at the starting line: Underrepresentation in gifted identification and disparities in early achievement. *AERA Open, 9*, 23328584231171535.

MacIntyre, A. (2000). *After virtue: A study in moral theory* (2nd ed.). Gerald Duckworth and Co Ltd.

Maslow, A. H. (1943). A theory of human motivation. *Psychological Review, 50*, 370-396.

Maslow, A. H. (1954). *Motivation and personality*. Harper.

Mercieca, D. (2011). *Beyond conventional boundaries: Uncertainty in research and practice with children*. Sense Publishers.

Muwanga-Zake, J. W. (2009). Building bridges across knowledge systems: Ubuntu and participative research paradigms in Bantu communities. *Discourse: Studies in the Cultural Politics of Education, 30*(4), 413-426.

Myers, L. J. (1993). *Understanding an Afrocentric world view: Introduction to an optimal psychology*. Kendall/Hunt Publishing Company.

Nagel, T. (1979). *Mortal questions*. Cambridge University Press.

Ngubane, N., & Makua, M. (2021). Ubuntu pedagogy – Transforming educational practices in South Africa through an African philosophy: From theory to practice. *Inkanyiso: Journal of Humanities and Social Sciences, 13*(1), 1–12.

Nwoye, A. (2015). What is African psychology the psychology of? *Theory & Psychology, 25*(1), 96–116.

Nwoye, A. (2017). An Africentric theory of human personhood. *Psychology in Society, 54*, 42–66.

Pigza, J. M., & Welch, M. J. (2010). Spiritually engaged pedagogy: The possibilities of spiritual development through social justice education. *Spirituality in Higher Education Newsletter, 5*(4), 1–12.

Prince's Trust. (2023). *The Prince's Trust NatWest Youth Index 2023*. www.princes-trust.org.uk/about-us/news-views/princestrustnatwestyouthindex2023

Ramose, M. B. (2002). The philosophy of Ubuntu and Ubuntu as a philosophy. In P. H. Coetzee & A. P. J. Roux (Eds.), *Philosophy from Africa: A text with readings*. Oxford University Press.

Rogers, C. R. (1943). Therapy in guidance clinics. *The Journal of Abnormal and Social Psychology, 38*(2), 284.

Ruddock, B., & Cameron, R. J. (2010). Spirituality in children and young people: A suitable topic for educational and child psychologists? *Educational Psychology in Practice, 26*(1), 25–34.

Seligman, M. E. (2002). *Authentic happiness: Using the new positive psychology to realize your potential for lasting fulfillment*. Simon and Schuster.

Tisdell, E. J. (2003). *Exploring spirituality and culture in adult and higher education*. Jossey-Bass. Cited in: Pigza, J. M., & Welch, M. J. (2010). Spiritually engaged pedagogy: The possibilities of spiritual development through social justice education. *Spirituality in Higher Education Newsletter, 5*(4), 1–12.

Tutu, D. M. (2004). *God has a dream: A vision of hope for our time*. Rider.

6 Personal selves, professional lives

Engaging the 'self' in work with families and young people

Mary Chilokoa and Emily Jackson

Introduction

A key endeavour for many educational practitioners is the search for, and exploration of, ways of enacting meaningful practice. This might be characterised as work which feels consistent with personal and professional values and which connects us in productive ways to the families and young people that we are engaged with in our professional lives.

In this chapter we are writing as individual authors to co-author a collaborative piece. As we are writing about personal experiences, we have chosen to write in the first person, and there are certain sections where we have indicated individual accounts, through highlighting in italics. The focus of this chapter has been the exploration and development of ideas for practice. For one of us (Mary), these ideas had their genesis during the often-uncomfortable process of revealing vulnerability as part of doctoral research some years back, and for the other (Emily) emerged as a strong theme after returning to work following maternity leave. These ideas place the relationship with self, and with others and self, at the centre of our professional endeavours.

Our hope for this chapter is that it will, in some way, speak to you, the reader, either through ideas which may resonate with your own thinking or through ideas which may provoke reflection, questions, or even discomfort. While reflecting together, we have been reminded of the resonance between personal experiences and the universality of our most personal feelings, as Rogers (2004) has beautifully described it:

> I have almost invariably found that the very feeling which has seemed to me most private, most personal and hence most incomprehensible by others, has turned out to be an expression for which there is resonance in many other people. It has led me to believe that what is most personal and unique in each one of us is probably the very element which would, if it were shared or expressed, speak most deeply to others.
>
> (Rogers, 2004, p. 26)

In this chapter, we will start by considering the interconnectedness of all phenomena, reflecting on why this idea feels particularly salient to us as practitioners. We consider what it means to connect with our 'whole selves' within our work and the impact of the social, cultural, and political contexts which we work within. We reflect on our personal experiences of vulnerability and loss, and on our professional context of working within an educational

DOI: 10.4324/9781003451907-6

psychology team, before concluding with the consideration of what some of these ideas might mean for relational practice.

As a way of engaging you further with the ideas at the heart of the chapter, and to bring them to the forefront of your own thoughts and experiences, we would like to invite you to answer a series of questions which we pose as offerings at the end of each section.

Question for the reader: What has resonated for you in choosing to read this chapter? What are your hopes for reading this chapter?

Our starting point: The 'personal'

Whilst writing this piece, we have reflected on why the ideas within this chapter feel particularly salient and important to us as practitioners and as human beings.

Emily's reflection:

Over the last five years, there has been an ongoing experience of trying to find places of balance from the tension of trying to fulfil various different roles which have involved negotiating demands between my personal and professional selves. Of most importance has been the experience of becoming a mum and trying to be the mum I want to be, whilst also being in the role of daughter to ageing parents and accompanying them in the process of dying, whilst experiencing other losses and continuing to be an educational psychologist (EP) throughout the COVID-19 pandemic and at a time when services within local authorities have been particularly stretched. I have been acutely aware of the interface between the public and professional and the private and personal, and at times, this has felt uncomfortable. I have reflected on some of the narratives around being 'good enough' and how inadequate this can feel when there is a personal experience of an emotional need to give as much presence as I can to those I love the most. I have searched for ideas which feel affirming and have particularly connected with accounts of personal experience and with some narrative ideas which I have been introduced to through the Institute of Narrative Therapy. I have also tried to reflect on how these experiences, while difficult, may provide 'relational resources' of greater empathy, understanding, and compassion which I hope can aid my work and development of being a psychologist.

Mary's reflection:

My personal history and lived experience as a child of Nigerian immigrants, growing up in a working-class area of inner-city London, have inevitably shaped my approach to many things, including the professional practice I enact today. For myself at that time, navigating an often-opaque and confusing - sometimes even hostile - education system meant it was difficult to feel 'good enough'. The system seemed to consist of winners and losers, and for young people like me, trying to survive amidst personal and social challenges (and without the 'cultural capital' of family privilege or the sense of entitlement that some seemed to have), I learned that educational success, and the social acceptance that came with it, was certainly not a 'given'. I have reflected on these experiences as foundational stones for my later identification with some of the marginalised

---

children and families I later came to work with. Just as I had once felt lost, invisible, and voiceless, by virtue of my class, my 'race', and my culture, I can identify with those lost, or rendered voiceless, 'hidden in plain sight' within an imperfect system. I know that these experiences have been important: they have led me to hold close a set of values and beliefs about the world which have subsequently informed the lens through which I view the scope and possibilities of my professional work. Some of these beliefs and understandings have invariably been further developed through encounters within my social, professional, and later, academic life, the old and new weaving together to form a 'technicolour dreamcoat' of perspectives and possibilities for practice.

As Jon Kabat-Zinn (1994) reminds us, 'wherever you go, there you are', and his book title seems to emphasise an idea that it is impossible to leave your 'self' behind, even if you wanted to. In our professional lives, too, we cannot help but embody and carry around with us a collection of characteristics and history which might broadly make up an 'identity', all of which invariably contribute to how we engage with the world.

We think it is important to work with the notion that identity is multi-layered, and that there may be parts of our identity which most resonate, or which feel most relevant to us, in working and connecting with particular young people and their families. Engaging with tools for practice such as the 'social graces' model (Burnham, 2012; Roper-Hall, 2008), a process to support awareness of, and sensitivity to, issues of social difference and intersectionality, can help us bring some of these considerations to the fore of our consciousness: to acknowledge that all of 'ourselves' are part of, not separate to, the ecosystem of our relationships with others. We can appreciate also that these parts of our identity exert a subtle but nonetheless significant influence on who we are within our professional roles – whether we are consciously aware of it or not. We can acknowledge that each aspect of our 'selfhoods' (whether relating to gender, race, religion, age, and so on, as expressed in the social graces model) is contributing to 'the construction of social realities, as well as part of and making a person's experience, shaping their identity . . . and influencing their positioning' within social relationships (Burnham, 2012, p. 142). It is helpful also to have an awareness of those aspects of ourselves which are both 'voiced' and 'unvoiced' (Burnham, 2012) within our professional relationships, those aspects both visible and less visible to others, and those aspects of which we ourselves may be less aware. These latter aspects may constitute 'blind spots', as described within the Johari Window concept (Luft & Ingham, 1961), which explores our awareness of what we know and understand, and what others know or otherwise, about ourselves. Part of our hope for this chapter is that exploring these considerations can support a more conscious awareness of these aspects of our relationships with 'self' and with 'other'.

Question for the reader: Within the context of social graces (gender, geography, race, religion, age, ability, appearance, class, culture, ethnicity, education, employment, sexuality, sexual orientation, and spiritualty), which aspects of your identity feel the most relevant, useful, and/or significant in the context of your personal selves and professional selves?

Interconnectedness of self and environment

The Buddhist concept of 'dependent origination' relates to the interconnectedness of all phenomena: mind and body, self and environment, microcosm and macrocosm, as also discussed in Sahaja Timothy Davis's chapter. It relates also to the idea that our inner world exerts an influence on our environment and those around us, just as we are influenced by all elements within our environment. This concept, if applied to professional practice, would suggest that there exists a profound connectedness between people, regardless of role or status within a relationship. On a psychic and emotional level, therefore, we both affect and are affected by relationships and events in our environment, whether we are cognisant of this or not.

At a time in history which has seen seismic societal shifts and reverberations with regard to 'race' and sexual politics, and to health and wealth inequality, new understandings around the things we see as most important have emerged and been brought to the surface for many of us. Whether through grief, anger, or the reconceptualising of things we may previously have accepted or simply taken for granted, individually and societally, we cannot fail to have been changed in some way. We feel that seeing these transitions as opportunities for new ways of moving forward as a society of people, and for re-visioning the ways we relate to each other as human beings, offers hope which is sorely needed. Similarly, within the professional domain, there is an opportunity to reflect, reconsider, and recalibrate the ways in which we relate to the people we are working with, and to acknowledge the influence that the wider social and political context may be having on our professional practices.

> *Question for the reader: Can you think of moments in your work which have reminded you of the profound connectedness between people, regardless of role or status within a relationship?*

Enabling the 'whole' self in our work

Bell hooks (1994), writing from an anti-colonialist, critical, feminist, and multicultural perspective, conceptualised the educational space as a space for empowerment. She saw possibilities for teaching as a catalyst for shared and equal engagement, and for students becoming active participants in their learning: 'There must be an ongoing recognition that everyone influences the classroom dynamic, that everyone contributes' (hooks, 1994, p. 8). Centring her gaze on classroom practice in particular, hooks explored an idea of what it would mean for the educational professional to enact their role differently – not just through the traditional, institutionally sanctioned construct of 'teacher', for example, but as a 'whole' being, with mind, body, and soul integrated, rather than as compartmentalised entities. For hooks, the 'practice' – of professionals working with people in the realm of support and education – should be directed towards him or herself first. This involves turning the gaze inwards and striving towards a sense of personal and professional integrity. This mode of professional practice, what hooks terms 'engaged pedagogy', also involves being willing to make oneself vulnerable and not to expect any student (or any other) to take any risk within the professional relationship that we, as practitioners, would not be prepared to take ourselves:

> When education is the practice of freedom, students are not the only ones who are asked to share, to confess. Engaged pedagogy does not seek simply to empower students. Any classroom that employs a holistic model of learning will also be a place where teachers grow and are empowered by the process. That empowerment cannot happen if we refuse to be vulnerable while encouraging students to take risks.
>
> (hooks, 1994, p. 21)

Citing Paolo Freire (1998), hooks states that 'education can only be liberatory when everyone claims knowledge as a field in which we all labour' (hooks, 1994, p. 14).

These principles, for enabling participatory spaces for the sharing of knowledge and experience, can equally apply to any endeavour involving work with young people and their families. Here, the intention of the practitioner is central: to be open to our own subjectivities, and to appreciate the impacts of our histories and past experiences in our work. We acknowledge the part of these histories in creating new experiences and narratives alongside the young people as our lives and stories intersect. We can view ourselves as non-unitary entities, with multiple and contradictory subjectivities (Hollway, 1994) which reflect, and, to some extent, are a response to, the complexities that we face as human beings in the world. Embracing this complexity and seeing it as part and parcel of who we are (Mercieca, 2011) can be a key part in any move towards more 'authentic' practice.

Hooks also makes links with Freire's emphasis on 'praxis' – action and reflection upon the world in order to change it – and views this 'engagement' as a path which requires some emotional labour on the part of the practitioner, because '[teachers] must be actively committed to a process of self-actualization that promotes their own wellbeing if they are to teach in a manner that empowers students' (hooks, 1994, p. 21).

As former teachers who have experienced and been part of the traditional playing out of power dynamics within the classroom, we are struck by what is proposed as the true, meaningful function of relationships within the learning space, which is described as:

> [W]hen there are two learners who occupy somewhat different spaces in an ongoing dialogue . . . both participants bring knowledge to the relationship, and one of the objects of the pedagogic process is to explore what each knows and what they can teach each other. A second object is to foster reflection on the self as actor in the world in consequence of knowing.
>
> (Aronowitz, 1998, (Introduction) in Freire, 1998, p. 8)

'Know Thyself' is famously inscribed on a wall at the ancient Temple of Apollo at Delphi, and Socrates is recorded as saying that to know oneself is the beginning of wisdom. In line with these aspirational and transformational ideas about education, we contend that to create value in our work, we need to be alert to and aware of our own constructions, prejudices, beliefs, and judgements, particularly those emanating from our own personal landscapes. With this awareness in place, utilising the 'self' can become an important part of 'relational' practice and might, for example, include the sensitive use of self-disclosure to support trust, transparency, and genuineness within professional relationships. In order to do this safely and well, we must be mindful of when and in which situations this opening up of ourselves, in ways which might otherwise feel exposing, might be most (and least) appropriate. It becomes important, then, to have a clear sense of who and for what purpose this 'opening up' is serving, and what value it is creating as part of the dialogue or interaction. This requires a level of reflection and reflexivity in practice which necessarily requires an opening up of 'self' to 'self'.

Question for the reader: Can you think of a time when it has felt appropriate to be open about yourself and to share your vulnerability during an interaction within your professional relationships?

'Being' in 'professional' practice: Personal experiences of vulnerability, grief, and sharing

---

Emily's reflection:
As the contexts we work within are constantly changing, so within ourselves there are ongoing processes of transition and flux. It has been my experience that at times of personal challenge, I have felt more vulnerable as a practitioner, and my own emotions have felt closer to the surface, so that I have quickly felt very moved or touched by the experiences of those I have worked with. Examples relate to moments when I have felt moved by great sadness or despair in hearing about a situation for a child or family, or at other times great happiness and joy. At these times I have also noticed that I can more quickly feel an experience of emotional overwhelm, as if some of the emotional filters which are used to relate to the world have been removed.

We have each experienced the death of both parents over the last five years. This has led us to consider some of the implications of significant loss at a more personal level. While being mindful of the importance of accepting that these experiences are deeply individual, it has led us to think about the enormity of some of the losses which the children and families we work with experience. There are some experiences which change us beyond measure; there is the self before and the self after, and there is no going back to the person who existed before. Perhaps accepting this gives some respect to the enormity of the change, an acknowledgement of the level of love and the scarring which is left. As Adichie (2022, p. 13) writes after experiencing the death of her father: 'I have mourned in the past, but only now do I touch grief's core. How do people walk around functioning in the world after losing a beloved father?' (Adichie, 2022, p. 13). We are reminded of the Japanese art of 'kintsugi', meaning 'golden joinery', also called 'kintsukuroi', meaning 'golden repair'. Broken pottery is mended by using lacquer combined with platinum, gold, or silver so the breakage and repair is embraced as part of the experience of an object rather than something to cover up and hide. These cracks are viewed as important events in the life and history of an object and have also been viewed metaphorically as a way to view the broken, damaged, and difficult parts of our lives (Kuma, 2018).

Experiences of loss and grief are reminders of the human frailty within all our lives. We are not set apart from these experiences because we have undergone some form of professional training or because we are used to being on the 'helper' side of therapeutic encounters. Loss and grief are great equalisers; we are all in it together. It has been our experience that grief can feel extremely isolating and a reminder of the limitations of being able to enter the subjective experience of another. Words and language can seem very inadequate: 'Grief is a cruel kind of education. . . . You learn how much grief is about language, the failure of language and the grasping for language' (Adichie, 2022, p. 5). In reflecting on how our personal experiences can influence our work, we have wondered if these experiences of loss, pain, and grief can become 'relational resources', if they can deepen our personal skills and abilities in enabling us to relate, attune, understand, and imagine more about the worlds of those we are working with.

> **Mary's reflection:**
> *My experience of doctoral research was pivotal in my development of a new way of seeing myself as a 'professional'. What emerged through this process of study was the realisation that my professional experience and identity were not separate from my personal identity, that each was feeding into the other in a way which could be used positively. In the same way, Field (1936, p. 14) allowed herself to be part of the data of her research; acknowledging that 'the personal is everywhere', she uncovered a method for 'finding and setting up a standard of values that is truly one's own and not a borrowed mass-produced ideal'. Here, Field centres on the importance of being able to act in ways which feel coherent within a set of personal values.*

Through acknowledging and reflecting on the interface between our personal and professional selves and the possibilities for practice which this throws up, what comes to the fore is a sense of the importance of the values and principles which ground us: values connected strongly to social equity and the need to address power imbalance, values around the need to resist the structures which serve to reinforce disadvantage, and values relating to authenticity, openness, collaboration, and compassionate action. Other significant values relate to a belief in the potential of each situation and of each individual within that situation. These values and beliefs have all been borne and formed from our experiences, and once open to them, as Field (1936) found, we have found that we are able to acknowledge the ways that they consciously and unconsciously inform our professional approaches and actions.

> **Mary's reflection:**
> *This openness to the validity of my own experiences led to a new trust in my own practice and a developing confidence that came from feeling somehow less constrained by prevailing notions of what constituted 'good' professional practice: 'not sticking to a rigid system as a substitute for using my mind' (Bion, 1970, cited in Mercieca, 2011,*

> p. 60). This led to a further willingness to explore and call upon the other, often hidden, textures and dimensions of my personal self which I had not previously acknowledged as having value. I recall an incident where my response to a highly distressed parent overwhelmed by the situation she and her son found themselves in was to offer comfort through a hug. This was a simple gesture, which might seem to fall outside the remit of the 'professional' relationship but nevertheless felt right in the circumstances, as we sat together in the parents' living room. Similarly, there are times when my own minor challenges (dealing with teenage children seemingly 'surgically attached' to games consoles, phones, or other electronic devices) have seemed very appropriate to share, in the spirit of acknowledging and normalising some of the struggles of parenting.

These moments become a sharing of humanity, as well as a contribution towards the problem-sharing and solution-generating that is part of many EP consultations. Rather than existing as the hidden sub-text within the stories we are part of creating in our practice (in our accounts and our reports about young people and their families), these dimensions of ourselves can be allowed to become, unselfconsciously, living, breathing, value-creating parts of the stories themselves. This can become a conscious choice within practice, enabling a sense of 'the personal self as participating with the professional self' (Mercieca, 2011, p. 114).

> Question for the reader: We would like to ask you to reflect on your own experiences of personal significance and how these may have transformed you . . . perhaps beyond measure?

'Being' in 'professional' practice: Engaging with the personal, social, cultural, and political

Educational psychologists are focused on applying psychology to educational and developmental difficulties. This privilege allows us great access to people and to interface with a range of social, cultural, and familial contexts. Moreover, this privilege is granted to a wide range of practitioners within education, health, and social care who have the opportunity to connect with people and to gain a window into their lives. In taking these roles seriously, it could reasonably be considered that, as practitioners, we have a responsibility to engage in practice which acknowledges the social, cultural, historical, and political factors which may affect the lives and experience of particular individuals or groups but which invariably exert an influence on us all. In this sense, as previously mentioned, we can also hold an awareness that our professional practice does not exist in a vacuum but is part of an ecosystem of narratives, beliefs, and behaviours within a social context, both individual and institutional. At its most basic level, we are human beings working with and alongside other human beings in a socio-cultural-political landscape which constitutes our collective environment at a particular point in history.

In terms of this socio-cultural-political landscape, at the present time, it could be argued that we are living in an increasingly mechanistic, adversarial, and competitive time. Political and other leaders can often model a way of being which eschews vulnerability and human 'not knowing' (Anderson, 2005) in favour of a facade of infallible competence. This has implications for the ways in which particular versions of 'being' are sanctioned and reinforced as desirable and 'appropriate' in how we relate to one another. Accepted codes of 'being' evolve within different professional spheres, and to some extent, these can act as barriers which create distance from those we work with. This might relate to the language and terminology which is used, how information is communicated, and even the assumed dress codes associated with 'being professional': the way in which power is worn lightly or heavily. In educational settings, where the 'core business' is surely to support the flourishing of individuals, often in the midst of many challenges, it feels clear that a strong relational focus to practice should be encouraged. As such, this might be framed as a highly personal, but also ethical and political, endeavour, shaped and informed by humanistic values and ideology which place the person at the centre.

We have reflected on moments in our practice when we have been aware of our own identification with aspects of the lives of the children and families with whom we work. On some occasions, this has been a conscious process when we are cognisant of how we are linking our own stories with the stories of the people we are working with as a way of engendering empathy and understanding. This process of connecting with our personal lives can be seen to enable us to be more aware of our own emotions and responses. Moreover, when we go through the process of placing ourselves in someone else's shoes, we see the people we work with as 'people' rather than 'cases' or numbers on spreadsheets to be allocated (Mercieca, 2011). Sometimes we have reflected on and briefly referred to experiences in our own lives, a conscious sharing to support the people we are working with to feel less alone and more contained (whilst mindful of the inherent power imbalances and boundaries which are needed to enable effective therapeutic working). On other occasions, it has been less conscious, a process of triggering which may occur outside conscious awareness, but which has left us with emotions which have stayed with us after our period of involvement was over. We have reflected on how, as practitioners working in education, we have a particular vulnerability as we are coming from a position of wanting to help. As Mercieca (2011) describes:

> When a professional decides to work with children with the intention of doing something to make changes for the better, there has to be that person's self in the professional self. This means that the professional has a stake in what they are investing so much energy into.
>
> (Mercieca, 2011, p. 77)

This intention, desire, and the need to be useful mean that already we have a personal investment in our work, and this engenders a level of risk. There is a risk to investing too much of ourselves personally. We may then find it hard to separate from our work and to hold boundaries between our personal and working life, and ultimately, we can feel overwhelmed by the difficulty of being able to help when working within systems which are often bureaucratic and overloaded. There is also a risk of not investing, of keeping ourselves too far removed. If we are not able to see ourselves in the feelings and struggles of those we are working with, and if we fail to show that we care, then it is likely that people will also experience this lack of caring, of being valued, and of mattering. If there is risk either way, then it seems that the optimal position is one of balance, and this is a dynamic process, as our positioning will also be affected by our own resources and personal capacities, which are constantly in flux.

Attending to the level of our own resources and capacity can be seen as an act of caring for ourselves, which ultimately benefits those we work with, as it affords us the ability to be fully present and focused on the purpose of our work. As Reynolds writes, 'we have an ethical responsibility to engage with enough self-care to be able to be fully present with clients, keep their suffering at the centre, and bring hope to the work' (Mercieca, 2011, p. 29).

Emily's reflection:

I had a particular encounter working with a family who had experienced a great deal of loss. After working with them for some months, I attended a further multi-agency consultation and was aware during the consultation that I was shifting position to a viewpoint which did not feel comfortable, espousing views which I felt might need to be articulated, but afterwards, I questioned whether these views were really mine or views which I felt I 'should' be putting forward. Years later, when I thought about the family, I had an uneasy, uncomfortable feeling. After experiencing personal losses myself, I felt even more uncomfortable about how the situation had developed, a feeling that perhaps, as professionals, and within the systems we are part of, we can create distance between ourselves and others. However, this distance can remove us from grasping the enormity of the losses which some children experience as opposed to really connecting in a personal and deeply human sense. Through reflecting on how closely we are relating or distancing ourselves from those we work with, we can be mindful of the position we are taking and the extent it engenders possibilities for relating and compassionate understanding.

Question for the reader: Thinking about the professional experiences which have moved you, what emotions have stayed with you, and which values have they connected with?

'Being' and 'doing' in our professional work

Within the educational psychology (EP) service where we are based, there have been a series of working groups looking at the values which underpin professional practice. Following the COVID-19 pandemic, we were also involved in a group which was established to explore 'authenticity' and what it means to be an 'authentic practitioner'. In the context of the pandemic, an experience which touched the lives of everyone, it felt important to reflect and acknowledge the impact of these experiences on a personal, as well as professional, level. Questions around authenticity, what this means and how this is embodied, are ongoing and fluid within us and also within our service.

Mary's reflection:

I have been part of establishing group peer supervision within our EP service, and this has been very personally significant in supporting (my confidence in) the way I am able to perform my professional 'self'. The sessions take place on a fortnightly basis and are 'opt-in', with the respectful expectation that colleagues commit to most sessions within any one term so that continuity and emotional safety within the group can be preserved. For me, these group supervision sessions have been something of a lifeline: they have provided space for supportive and insightful reflection on all aspects of our (often challenging) work; they have enabled me to develop my practice and skills in an environment of care, respect, and non-judgement; and they have supported my emotional wellbeing. Most recently, during the COVID-19 pandemic, group peer supervision was a space to express the loss, confusion, and uncertainty many of us were feeling. For me, this space has represented something fairly unique within my everyday professional life, where it often feels as if EPs are looked to as having 'all the answers', and there are often expectations around definitive judgements. I have been grateful to colleagues within the peer supervision group for providing me with a space for reflection on the internal and external influences on my work and practice: where vulnerability has been shared between us, and where we have encouraged each other to live out our professional selves as 'whole beings' rather than compartmentalised ones, as hooks (1994) suggests. We have settled into using a model based on reflecting teams (Andersen, 1987), and we have supported each other using some essential ingredients, including attention, trust, safety, and containment (Scaife, 2014). Using ideas informed by narrative therapy, we have made space to challenge taken-for-granted ideas and utilised an 'outsider-witness' (White, 2000) perspective to explore and retell our realities.

Among other things, peer supervision can be important for enabling us to feel that we are not alone, as some professional experiences can feel deeply isolating: if no one else is speaking about them, it may feel as if they do not really exist. We have noticed, within the systems in which we work, that experiences can often be internalised so that some individuals may feel that they are not doing/being 'good enough'. We have also noticed that if that experience is shared and talked about together, then it becomes a collective experience. When we acknowledge and understand experiences as being collective, then this often shifts thinking about change to a systemic rather than an individual level. For example, if the systems are creating a level of work which many are finding unmanageable, then this is surely a failing of the system rather than of the individual, and individuals working together can harness the power to change or influence the system. This experience of honest sharing of practice has now become an imperative for us, which allows us to regularly practice letting go of misguided expectations (including around having to have 'all the answers') and enables us to know that we are not alone in our confusions or uncertainties around aspects of work. Moreover, this sharing enables us to become aware of the interface between our personal and professional selves; we can reflect on pieces of work which have connected more deeply with us on an emotional level, and being part of a group enables us to experience being emotionally held and supported by one another. We think this is an example of one important way in which everyday, professional working contexts have the opportunity to become participatory and even emancipatory spaces, which can facilitate the professional 'flourishing' of individuals, in order that 'good' work (of value and meaning) can be done.

> **Emily's reflection:**
> I have been inspired by training from Vikki Reynolds (2011b), who has spoken about the practice of creating a solidarity team. This can include membership from people who are alive, but also people who you may never have met, or no longer have physical contact with, and may include mentors and guides who are no longer alive. This invites the possibility of holding an invisible support team in mind who can powerfully contribute to our work without being physically present. The internalising of important figures creates a way of refuting the isolation and individualisation which therapists can experience; as Reynolds reflects, 'the greatest resource available to us in the relational work that we are doing is ourselves and each other' (Reynolds, 2011a, p. 33).

We have also connected with other ideas and practices within narrative therapy which explore identity through practices of re-authoring in line with the values and aspirations which are personally salient. Through the experience of using practices such as the 'tree of life' (Ncube, 2006), we have been able to relate to our own histories, stories, and values and how these connect with what is meaningful within our professional work. By engaging in asking ourselves the questions which we would also ask of those we work with, we are reminded of how it feels to be vulnerable. Moreover, our experience has been that when we have space to connect with our own stories and histories and the opportunity to explore what we give value to, this can be deeply energising and sustaining for our professional work.

> Question for the reader: What are the practices in your work which engender support and solidarity?

Conclusion

Throughout this chapter, we have questioned how free we are to express our inner 'selves' and emotions, to feel moved and to show that we are moved, and the extent to which this is accepted or valued within professional practice. It has been suggested that when professionals endeavour to be more authentic, to be honest about the ways in which professional practice may be distancing, and about some of the power imbalances inherent in our work, we can move closer to methods of relating which are based more around what it means to be human. This entails an openness, but also an acceptance, that as part of this process of connecting, we will also be changed through the professional experiences. The ability to be moved and affected by the work we do is a valuable part of how we relate and of the reciprocal nature of relationships. As Rosa (2019) proposes through his theory of resonance, 'educational processes, on the other hand, if they are to be successful, require *encounter*, genuine sympathy and concern, and the ability to both touch and be touched' (Rosa, 2019, p. 11).

This openness also involves an honesty in being able to really listen to ourselves and connect with the vivid texture of our own internal feelings and experiences. In the same way that we consider the importance of giving space and presence when listening to others, the same conditions for listening are needed for listening to ourselves. Times of challenge present us with opportunities to try to practice some of the values of authenticity, to be honest with ourselves about the impact of the personal difficulties which we experience, and how this continues to shape us as practitioners. Within our professional spheres in education, it is important to reflect on the space which is given for deeply reflecting on the inter-relationships between our personal and professional worlds. We suggest that our emotions can be an additional resource for how we relate to others, and that by connecting with our inner worlds, this has a positive impact on how we relate professionally. As Mercieca (2011) writes: '[I]n the area of educational psychology and other caring professions, I argue that when a practitioner takes their emotions into consideration, this is a better indication of their professionalism than otherwise' (Mercieca, 2011, p. 75).

What has been proposed is a form of 'engaged' practice, where we seek to meet human needs in a human way, perform practice which is grounded in a 'relational shift' from a 'mechanistic' way of understanding the world, to acknowledging, celebrating, and fully utilising the relational in our work (Spretnak, 2011). We hope that this form of practice can embolden and empower practitioners towards a more honest, authentic, and integral way of relating with others and with ourselves as we carry out our valuable and meaningful work with people.

Question for the reader: We would like to ask you to reflect on the thoughts, images, and ideas which are staying with you as you reach the end of this chapter.

Summary box

- This chapter has encouraged practitioners to consider the relationship between our personal and professional lives and consider the value which our personal experiences can offer our professional work.
- It has sought to emphasise the value of connecting with human beings as human beings. We have endeavoured to challenge some of the ideas and narratives around what it means to be 'professional' and to explore how our professional experiences are shaped by the social, cultural, and political contexts which we work within.
- For colleagues who are interested in exploring some of the ideas mentioned in this chapter, we would encourage you to consider the following given references, particularly the ideas regarding the use of reflective group peer supervision (e.g. Scaife, 2014) and solidarity teams (Reynolds, 2011b).
- If you are interested in the ideas we have proposed within this chapter and would like more information, please do contact us at Leeds Educational Psychology Service.

References

Adichie, C. N. (2022). *Notes on grief*. 4th Estate.

Andersen, T. (1987). The reflecting team: Dialogue and meta-dialogue in clinical work. *Family Process*, *26*(4), 415–428.

Anderson, H. (2005). Myths about 'not-knowing'. *Family Process*, *44*(4), 497–504.

Aronowitz, S. (1998). Introduction. In P. Freire (Ed.), *Pedagogy of freedom*. Rowman & Littlefield Publishers.

Bion, W. R. (1970). *Attention and interpretation – A scientific approach to insight in psychoanalysis and groups*. Tavistock [cited in Mercieca, D. (2011). *Beyond conventional boundaries – uncertainty in research and practice with children*. Sense Publishers].

Burnham, J. (2012). Developments in social GRRRAAACCEEESSS: Visible – invisible and voiced – unvoiced 1. In *Culture and reflexivity in systemic psychotherapy* (pp. 139–160). Routledge.

Field, J. (Marion Milner) (1936). *A life of one's own* (2nd ed.). Chatto and Widus [Reprinted New York].

Freire, P. (1998). *Pedagogy of freedom: Ethics, democracy and civic courage* (pp. 1–19). Rowman and Littlefield Publishers.

Hollway, W. (1994). *Subjectivity and method in psychology*. Sage [Cited in: Mercieca, D. (2011). *Beyond conventional boundaries*.]

hooks, b. (1994). *Teaching to transgress: Education as the practice of freedom*. Routledge.

Kabat-Zinn, J. (1994). *Wherever you go, there you are*. Piatkus.

Kumai, C. (2018). *Kintsugi wellness: The Japanese art of nourishing mind, body and spirit*. HarperCollins.

Luft, J., & Ingham, H. (1961). The johari window. *Human Relations Training News*, *5*(1), 6–7.

Mercieca, D. (2011). *Beyond conventional boundaries – uncertainty in research and practice with children*. Sense Publishers.

Ncube, N. (2006). The tree of life project: Using narrative ideas in work with vulnerable children in Southern Africa. *International Journal of Narrative Therapy and Community Work*, *1*, 3–16.

Reynolds, V. (2011a). Resisting burnout with justice-doing. *The International Journal of Narrative Therapy and Community Work*, 27–45.

Reynolds, V. (2011b). Supervision of solidarity practices: Solidarity teams and people-ing-the-room. *Context*, *116*, 4–6.

Rogers, C. (2004). *On becoming a person – A therapist's view of psychotherapy*. Constable.

Roper-Hall, A. (2008). Systemic interventions and older people. In *Handbook of the clinical psychology of ageing* (pp. 489–504). Wiley.

Rosa, H. (2019). *Resonance – a sociology of our relationship to the world*. Polity Press.

Scaife, J. (2014). *Supervising the reflective practitioner: An essential guide to theory and practice*. Routledge.

Spretnak, C. (2011). *Relational reality*. Cavite State University, Green Horizon Books.

White, M. K. (2000). Reflecting teamwork as definitional ceremony revisited. In M. White (Ed.), *Reflections on narrative practice: Essays and interviews*. Dulwich Centre Publications.

7 'There's TRUST there at the heart of it'

Co-creating inclusive cultures in a relational way through the four cornerstones approach

Claire-Marie Whiting and Scott Johnson

Introduction

If co-production is working together as equal partners from the start, then it inevitably means considering power and privilege within the relationships involved. We wanted to co-create the chapter together with the young people, parent/carers, and schools/settings for whom it is written, adopting an ethical approach to working together by privileging their voices. Feeling part of a growing community oriented around the cornerstones and making relational practice a core element, we facilitated and participated in conversations with these groups to explore what it is about the process that we all connect with at a human level, and what it is through the chapter we need to communicate. We could not have written it any other way.

Acknowledgements

The chapter was co-created with young people, parent carer, and practitioner representatives of the Genuine Partnerships team, in which members of Guiding Voices, Rotherham Parent Carers Forum, and Rotherham Educational Psychology Service participate as equal partners.

The chapter has evolved into two sections:

Part 1: The four cornerstones' story
Part 2: Relational practice at the heart of the cornerstones approach:
- Experience and embodiment
- Reflection and relational reflexivity
- Relationships, community, and connection
- Positivity and celebration
- Empowerment
- Culture, ethos, and mindset

Part 1: The four cornerstones' story

'What does it feel like?'

It was 2009, and we were a group of Rotherham practitioners who had become involved in a pilot for the Inclusion Development Programme (IDP). This was a web-based resource published

DOI: 10.4324/9781003451907-7

by the then Department for Children, Schools, and Families. The programme was designed to improve 'quality first teaching' in mainstream schools, which is a term used to describe children and young people experiencing special educational needs being better included in their class-rooms through good-quality differentiation (Department for Children, Schools and Families, 2008). We had been tasked with evaluating the pilot and discussed what it was that we wanted to know. It was suggested by a trainee EP who was using a narrative approach to complete her thesis that adopting this methodology might also help us explore the questions to which we kept returning: What does it *feel like* if you are a child or young person with an additional need at one of our schools? What does it *feel like* if you are their parent or carer?

These questions were intentionally open. We decided that creating the physical and meta-phorical space for children, young people, and parent/carers to tell their stories in relation to these questions would enable us to have a richer insight into the landscape of inclusion within our schools from the perspective of those for whom this matters the most. We antici-pated that in sharing their narratives, the participants would have the opportunity to organ-ise and give meaning to their lived experience of school (White & Epston, 1990) in ways that may not so far have occurred. Drawing upon principles from systemic practice, we wanted to support the voicing of the 'not yet said' (Anderson & Goolishan, 1988).

The IDP pilot schools welcomed us into their settings to carry out this research, and we were grateful for their openness to learning from their children and parent/carers. We opted to facilitate separate focus groups for children/young people and parent/carers. In narrative practice, when people meet together to hear, respond to, and acknowledge the preferred accounts of people's lives, it can be referred to as 'outsider witness practice' (Walther & Fox, 2012). We had a sense that it was important for the stories shared to be heard in a support-ive, relational space that might foster human connection. Offering an immediate network of mutual understanding was an ethical option.

Despite understanding that we might witness some painful narratives, we were unpre-pared for the intense emotional experience of hearing the stories; we were glad for the emo-tional containment made available within the focus groups.

'The worry I have' – the relational things that can make a big difference

We heard from many of the children/young people that they frequently felt inferior to their classmates, and that they did not think their needs were always fully understood. Their sad-ness, and at times distress, was impacting significantly upon the emotional wellbeing of their parent/carers. Parent/carers talked about their frustration within systems that seemed to prevent them from advocating for their children, which made them feel impotent and affected their confidence and added to their worry about their child's future.

We also heard that small things could make a big difference to these experiences. These small things were relational. They stemmed from the quality of the relationships made pos-sible within the school environment.

Hearts and minds met

Brian Lamb published his report following an inquiry focusing on improving parental confi-dence in special educational need systems (Department for Children, Schools and Families,

2009). A conference for special educational needs coordinators (SENCos) was held in Rotherham, to which the newly formed Parent Carer Forum (PCF) was invited to give a keynote speech. We had also been asked to facilitate a workshop; we were keen to seek feedback from SENCos in response to the narratives we had gathered.

The PCF speech was powerful, conveying more parent/carer stories resonating with the narratives we had gathered. The presenters encouraged us to build a colourful bridge of Post-it notes identifying how barriers to parent/carers and practitioners working together might be overcome. The bridge was abundant with examples of human connection. Realising that our stories were converging, we began to work in partnership with the PCF to co-create a more hopeful chapter from our sea of mutually painful stories. One of the team suggested generating a charter for schools.

The Rotherham Charter for parent and child voice

The Charter was developed following a successful Brian Lamb innovative project bid to increase parental confidence in SEN systems within our area. Because the sharing of stories and fostering relationships had been such a fundamental element within our work so far, we agreed to model this approach as a team of parents/carers and practitioners working together. We invited SENCos and head teachers who had shown interest to join us, together with more parent/carers and a wide range of local authority practitioners. We began by sharing some of the original narratives and asked what it was that would have made a positive difference to these experiences. There were big blank sheets of paper, and the passionate discussions and scribbles that followed were exciting to witness, generating more relational layers as the collaborative nature of the session established stronger relationships. There was purposeful commitment to privileging quieter voices in the room. Although we may not have described it thus at that time, in hindsight, we realised that we had been starting to co-produce *and* engage in community psychology:

> [S]elf-aware social change, with an emphasis on value based, participatory work and the forging of alliances . . . It is community psychology because it emphasises a level of analysis and intervention other than the individual and their immediate interpersonal context. It is community psychology because it is nevertheless concerned with how people feel, think, experience and act as they work together, resisting oppression and struggling to create a better world.
>
> Burton et al. (2007, p. 219)

Some keywords were mentioned repeatedly, but it took three such meetings to agree that **trust** was a fundamental aspect of the change we needed to nurture through the Charter we were co-creating. By focusing on trust and what this means within relationships and systems, four Charter principles emerged that were fundamentally about cultivating relationships:

Welcome and care
Value and include
Communicate
Partnership

More than a Charter on a wall

We continued working together, but the notion of a charter was challenged: What difference would having these words on a wall make if they do not change experience? We decided to consider what each of the principles means in practice: for example, what would the experience of 'welcome and care' in a school mean for children/young people in school, and for their parent/carers? What happens that makes them feel valued and included? What does good communication involve? What *is* equal partnership? What would be happening within a school or setting to make each of the principles genuine and meaningful?

We had established a way of working together that was open to different perspectives and began to generate indicators and examples that would help schools/settings understand how best to implement the Charter's principles. Over time, a self-evaluation tool was co-created. Again adopting systemic ideas, it was suggested that if this is a partnership approach, it should feel positive, removing the need for blame (see Partridge & McCarry, 2009). We wanted good relational practice to be celebrated, shared, and modelled. A toolkit was generated, illustrating the Charter in action within Rotherham schools and settings. The school leaders involved felt that staff may need more support to confidently work in this way, so training and an appreciative inquiry approach (see Whitney & Trosten-Bloom, 2003) evolved to help schools notice, embed, and build on great relational practice. This culminated in an accreditation process going beyond SEN to involving the whole school community. We wanted the Charter principles to live within everybody's experience, and to have integrity.

Being the change

A significant element to this work was how we interacted as a team. We were committed to modelling the principles within our own relationships but quickly realised that this came with challenges. We wanted to have open, honest conversations, and we talked about equal partnership, but not blithely. We interrogated the ideas and why they might feel difficult, realising that self-reflection was needed. Over time, we came to admit to our prejudices and relative positions of privilege and power, becoming more conscious of unconscious biases. This was hard and could feel exposing and raw but also enabled greater emotional connectivity and empathy. We tackled language that might divide us, such as the word *professional*, whilst being respectful of individual and collective skills and expertise. We found that being solution-focused, strength-based, and appreciative created a supportive space through which some of these difficult conversations could be contained. We also came to learn that we were asking the organisations with which we were engaged to work through the same process, and this takes time.

Reforms and inspections

Section 19 of the Children and Families Act 2014, also reflected in Chapter 1 of the 2015 SEND Code of Practice, makes clear that children and young people with special educational needs and disabilities (SEND), and their families, must be supported to be involved in decisions that are made concerning their lives (DfE, 2015). This emphasis is now often termed *co-production*. When the reforms were launched, Brian Lamb was invited to Rotherham as a keynote speaker at an event called *In It Together*, which brought together young people, parent/carers, schools/settings, and services across education, health, and social care. He affirmed the work of the team and how the collaborative approach being promoted through the Charter principles had informed the new legislation. We had frequently found ourselves in the position of needing to justify our work, so this was a welcome and exciting boost to our confidence. There was also a realisation that the relational, partnership-based way of working we were advocating needed to extend beyond schools to encompass children/young people 0–25 and the services they encountered across education, health, and care. In 2015, we re-named the team Genuine Partnerships to better reflect the essence of our approach and, at the same time, enable broader application.

The four cornerstones

Two years later, Ofsted and the Care Quality Commission (CQC) launched local-area SEND inspections. It was becoming apparent that the co-production made explicit in the new code of practice was difficult for local areas to achieve. Genuine Partnerships was invited to a meeting in London facilitated by national charity Contact, also attended by key national SEND partners. We presented the story of the Charter model, how we work together as a team, and the relational basis for the principles. It was agreed at that first meeting that the principles were a strong foundation for co-production and inclusive practice. They were re-named the *four cornerstones*.

Since then, Genuine Partnerships has continued promoting and supporting the development of the *four cornerstones approach* locally, and nationally, and the team has extended to include Rotherham young people's group *Guiding Voices*. There has been a strategic impact within local area systems and policies, making the approach a key consideration in new initiatives. Fundamentally, the model is asking schools, settings, and services to involve children and young people and their families in working together with practitioners to reflect upon and evaluate practice, embed changes that build trusting relationships, and enhance wellbeing.

The psychology

By considering what the cornerstones mean in practice, the Genuine Partnerships team attempts to make some of the psychology underpinning the approach more explicit. Key psychological ideas include:

Collaborative systemic thinking: for example, the importance of narrative practice, not blaming, curiosity, not knowing, privileging marginalised voices, and perspective-taking.

Psychodynamic thinking: acknowledging and validating the emotional context of relationships, considering attachment theory, trust within relationships, and empathy.

Appreciative inquiry as a collaborative, strengths-based approach to achieving organisational and systemic change and positive psychology more generally.

The importance of reflectivity and reflexivity to increase awareness of one's own social constructs, prejudices, and unconscious biases.

Critical social psychology: considering and addressing power differentials to introduce agency and empowerment.

Critical community psychology.

Part 2: Relational practice at the heart of the cornerstones approach

Embodiment (modelling) the cornerstones and the power of this experience

- 'Modelling it . . . it's not just something that you say you do, a tickbox. It's something that you have to constantly work at. It's not an overnight fix. It's a culture change. It's systemic. And so it takes time.' (parent/carer)
- 'You take one foot over the threshold, and you know, you know instantly. It's that warm welcome. It's the smiles. Its people are friendly. Literally, as soon as you've signed in, you know, you know . . . if it embodies the principles or not. . . . It's that "welcome and care". . . . It's the tone, isn't it, it's being friendly and relatable?' (practitioner)
- 'The cornerstones model asks schools, settings, and services to collaborate with the whole community to explore experience using the four principles. This inevitably means considering the quality of the human relationships. Because trust is at the heart of the cornerstones, we try within Genuine Partnerships to model the principles in our own relationships with each other, and with anybody we encounter. Responding in this way, ultimately, becomes a way of being.' (practitioner)
- '[Y]ou can definitely see different people and what their ethos is and practitioners . . . that work in this way, whether they realise they're working in this way or whether they don't. But I think it, yeah, it's just about modelling it amongst each other . . . and forgiving each other when we get it wrong.' (parent/carer)

Humans are social beings, and it is possible to refer to traditional psychology, for example, Bandura's social learning theory, to evidence that we copy the behaviour and emotions of others (Bandura, 1977a). When people smile, we smile. When people panic, we panic. We can learn how to respond differently when our experience of relationships offers an alternative way of responding:

> '[I]t is something that has to be embodied by individuals. You know, it's not just something that you read and go away and reflect on. . . . You have to embody it.' (practitioner)

However, modelling the four cornerstones goes beyond social learning theory to consider the social construction of knowledge from a critical stance, acknowledging that language can convey powerful meanings and serve some interests rather than others: 'Social constructionism regards as the proper focus of enquiry the social practices engaged in by people, and their interactions with each other' (Burr, 2003, p. 9). This position also allows for the possibility of a reconstruction of language and transformation of discourse that deliberately privilege those who might be marginalised. There is a focus on process and language as something people do together, which is engrained within the way the four cornerstones impact on relationships and culture within organisations. This can be why it is sometimes difficult to convey the strength of the model purely in words. It has greater authenticity when it is experienced, moving beyond tokenism and a tickbox exercise to a living experience and relational way of being:

> 'As a human being. You need to experience it for a while to see what it all means. You need to go in a charter school to get really that sense of what that means.' (practitioner)

'When you hear, you know, our Charter Champions talk and some of the head teachers, like [X] . . . full of compassion when she's talking about experiences of families.' (practitioner)

'It's more the modelling, more exposure, more being part of it . . . you know? And then eventually you do get it when you've been part of the process more and part of the team more.' (parent/carer)

'I do apply it now to the shopkeeper, you know, or somebody I bump into in the street who's banged into me or not smiled at me, and I might just think, 'They might not be having a good day, actually.' I apply it everywhere. Yeah, definitely.' (parent/carer)

'Because I'd read it and I was like, "Oh, that sounds really interesting." But thinking, "What is it?" I didn't, you know, until I'm like, until I started doing it. You genuinely don't, you can't grasp it, that passion and true working way . . . because I'd witnessed it and been part of it. . . . It gave us the confidence.' (parent/carer)

'It's a way of being. . . . It's not just something that you're leaving in the classroom.' (practitioner)

Modelling the cornerstones, therefore, is a relational embodiment through which trust can eventually be forged and positive changes experienced over time, encompassing ideas described within systemic practice: 'It is in our physical biological bodies that we feel an act in relation to ourselves and others' Bownas and Fredman (2017, p. 5). This can be impactful even when there might initially be significant tensions:

'[T]hen they wanted to work with us, and the learning mentor who deals with most of the SEND children at that school . . . they seem to have a very different approach . . . working with families much more and believing families much more. And I bumped into the learning mentor in *Home Bargains*, of all places. And she said that how we've been as a family and kept them relationships open, it impacted on how she worked with other families now and how she believes other families [when she did not believe us before].' (parent/carer)

For young people, it is when practitioners realise that they need to be proactive and do what it takes to earn the trust of young people, sometimes being prepared to make adjustments to usual ways of working to ensure that they feel included as partners:

'Well, I think for "value and include" I think like having all the different people like come to the meetings and involve us in projects. I think that helps like me to feel included.' (young person)

By working in this way, enabling different perspectives and focusing on empowerment, when things do go wrong, forgiveness at a human level, rather than blame, defence, and animosity, is made possible.

Reflection and relational reflexivity

'I think for me it's mindfulness. So when I first started this volunteering, you were saying about "welcome and include". And I'd think of an example that you know, and one of them that I'll always go back to . . . the receptionist getting B into school. That was the only way to get her into school, if that receptionist was there, and so that's just like a minute part of the day. And it was just a smiley woman. So that's mindfulness. But it's coming back to the small, tiny things that make a huge impact, a huge difference.' (parent/carer)

When we listened to team members reflecting on their experience of being involved in Genuine Partnerships, reflection and relational reflexivity in the application of the cornerstones began to emerge as a subtle but powerful narrative (Burnham, 2005).

As indicated, ideas drawn from systemic practice have influence within the four cornerstones model, illustrative of the potentially therapeutic nature of the relational ideas being nurtured. When schools, settings, and service contexts are recognised for their 'welcome and care', it is understood that they are providing open and, at the same time, safe spaces in which people are encouraged to tell their stories, whether this is a parent/carer having a conversation with the learning mentor at the gate about an incident at home, a child in a school council meeting feeling able to tell the head teacher about their idea for new playground equipment, or a teacher sending an email to the chair of governors saying that they are not coping. There is trust that these stories will be heard empathetically, and the person entrusted with the story is also a participant in the unfolding narrative, collaborating and connecting, demonstrating a curious, 'not knowing' position (Anderson, 1997), even if the story might be challenging to absorb:

'I try to go to places with sort of a fresh mind and just, "OK, what, what am I going to learn from this situation? What will people share with me? What will I learn?" Rather than already go in there with preconceptions as to what I think might be happening.' (practitioner)

At the same time as hearing the story, the listener will be engaged in a dialogical conversation with themselves, actively preparing and forming their response. Anderson (1992) states: 'When I talk with others, I partly talk with the others, partly with myself.'

As in the other relational Rotherham model described in this book, REFLECT, we were reminded of the questions for research and practice Billington (2006) asks us to consider when we think about children, which he gave us permission to adapt more widely to people:

How do we speak with children [people]?
How do we speak of children [people] (to others)?
How do we write of children [people]?
How do we listen to children [people]?
How do we listen to ourselves [when working with children [people]?
Billington (2006, p. 8)

Burnham (2005) affirms that self-reflexivity involves paying attention to how we act in relation to others, considering the social constructs and unconscious biases that we might be taking into a situation related to our power and privilege, considering our responses and the questions we may wish to ask.

> '[I]t's really reflective process, I think. . . . You have to go away and reflect on something and think, "Oh yeah, yeah", and I might need to change because I didn't think about it that way, but what we're trying to do is to support staff in schools and in services to think in that way as well.' (practitioner)

Schön (1983) distinguishes between reflecting *on* action (in hindsight) and reflecting *in* action (in the moment). This means attempting to be mindful of ourselves and what it is that we are bringing to a situation and making adjustments accordingly even as we engage in these interactions:

> 'How you really need to think about other people you're encountering as a practitioner, how you might need to change the way you think about things.' (practitioner)

Being relationally reflexive goes beyond this to engage others in the internal process in which we are involved, asking questions about the questions we next need to ask and collaborating about the best way to respond. In this way, 'expertise may be thought of as being co-created' (Burnham, 2005, p. 16).

Having the four cornerstones can bring resolve and confidence when trying to work relationally. Encouraging everybody to genuinely consider the cornerstones within interactions, aiming to create environments within which they are cultivated, supports reflection about what the principles mean in practice and hopefully enriches lives with an abundance of sparkling relational moments:

> 'I think having the cornerstones as a thing, as something that you can look at, it just helps you to have the confidence in. You can keep relating back to it and keep thinking in the back of your head.' (parent/carer)
>
> 'And so then we drilled down and thought, "What does 'welcome and care' mean?" And that's when . . . that reflection happens. But what do those things mean? So I've been amazed, and I know I'm speaking as a practitioner, but I've been amazed by what schools do when they start to think about it, when they really start to think about it.' (practitioner)
>
> 'And it's a framework, isn't it, for thinking? I think the repetition part is essential. . . . You can be going, "What do I need to do to make this person feel welcome? What do I need to do to make this person recognise that we care about them?"' (practitioner)

When being relationally reflexive, this can generate, and has generated, some challenging conversations that have involved considerable soul-searching for team members, as well as rich learning and personal and collaborative growth:

> 'We were learning how to communicate with each other, and it felt threatening. . . . I think that some of those difficult, challenging conversations that we've had . . . I'm not sure we would have really . . . challenged ourselves . . . without those conversations.' (practitioner)

Being sensitive and thoughtful about how best to communicate and the language to adopt within interactions is an aspect of reflecting *in:*

> '[I]t's sometimes just having that honesty to say it in a clear, well-delivered way rather than in a flippant comment. . . . [I]t's just being conscious of that communication, that language.' (parent/carer)

The depth of reflection involved in authentically applying the cornerstones transforms them from a useful model to a way of working. a way of life:

> 'Those of us who are involved in that team take that out of the team and into every other interaction that we do. Yeah.' (practitioner)

Relationships, community, and connection

Central to the cornerstones model are relationships and the trust that working together will facilitate the best experiences and outcomes for young people. The impact of this approach to practice is the fostering of a sense of belonging, understood to be a fundamental human motivation (Maslow, 2013).

Feeling connected and holding a sense of belonging are recognised to have a significant impact for children/young people, particularly for those with special educational needs (Hebron, 2017). It is recognised that fostering a sense of belonging for SEND young people enables the potential for social inclusion and understanding where there may otherwise be an absence of connectedness (Cullinane, 2020). Acceptance and belonging are therefore necessary for the inclusion of children/young people with SEND (Rose & Shevlin, 2017).

Young people, families, and practitioners immersed in the cornerstones approach note how the model has enabled the development of relationships that have supported their community and connection:

> 'Yeah. I think that makes it different. It's about building that relationship in the setting.' (practitioner)

The starting point is often related to reaching out to others and considering the ways in which to connect and communicate with parent/carers, wider family, and young people. Champions of the model report it being 'the simple things' that make a difference. Practitioners often speak of considering ways in which to personalise their approaches when communicating with families:

> 'I think that most of us have somebody on the gate in the morning, whether that's a member senior leadership team or a kind of family liaison worker.' (practitioner)
>
> '[Y]ou know, giving those personal invites, and I've sent emails before, personal emails rather than just the banket email and . . . [y]eah, and building those relationships, like we said earlier, out on the gate, and I'm out on the gate every morning.' (practitioner)

Establishing a felt experience of care is recognised to be fundamental in helping individuals be included, building connection. Empathy, understood as 'other-oriented' (Noddings, 2012), is commonly reported to be engendered through considerations of the cornerstones and is expressed through the ways in which individuals interact:

> 'And children, they sense everything. And if they don't sense that you care for them or you value them, you've not got a good relationship, and so you've lost them basically.' (practitioner)

Experiencing relational practice is expressed in the experiences of children/young people when interacting with practitioners, particularly when they feel heard and are not positioned to explain difficulties repeatedly. One young person recounted the moment of a difficult experience when they feared they would need to explain something to multiple adults, reliving the moment over and over, and how this can be overcome when there are good communication systems:

> 'Then, like if, like you flag or you tell somebody something, then . . . [i]t's like I think it's on a system somewhere, but somehow the next morning, or like your staff for that day and your tutors already know. So you don't have to explain the same story 50 times because everyone . . . like, they communicate.' (young person)

An important part of supporting the work completed in settings through a cornerstones model relates to how to build connections between stakeholders. Practitioners talked about the work they do to facilitate families feeling invited into their settings and ways to 'get them through the doors'. The model supports the potential for considering creative ways to enable families to feel welcomed:

> 'It's . . . family support from their liaison. We have a member of SLT as well. So we, you know, we're out there morning and, you know, and . . . chatting and building those relationships. So they feel that they can come through that door at any time.' (practitioner)
>
> 'We've also got quite a few events, weekly events that we run for parents and staff and children altogether. So we have a family boot camp . . . which a couple of our TAs run, which is for children and parents and grandparents and stuff all to go and do a bit of a fitness class. And we've had a staff and parent netball team.' (practitioner)

Parent/carer involvement within schools and with practitioners is closely associated with a sense of trust in a setting (Santiago et al., 2016). The importance of the model's potential for building trust is highlighted by individuals working within the cornerstones framework, with one parent/carer saying, '[B]ut actually it's about trusting it and working with school as well' (parent/carer). Practitioners indicated the cornerstones helped them consider

> 'ideas for how to collaborate with everyone and fill them trusting relationships so you know, you can always help them throughout their journey in school, not just, you know, one-off meetings and stuff like that.' (practitioner)

The framework offers practitioners a reflective guide through which it is possible to establish trust, enabling closer relationships to be developed that facilitate a sense of community. Connection and disconnection are closely associated with wellbeing (Klussman et al., 2020), and the cornerstones model supports the establishment of genuine relationships and connection.

Practitioners report using creative ways to support building relationships with families. The cornerstones help settings and organisations consider different ideas through the four foundations of the model. Examples range from community meeting spaces, in-school 'escape room' experiences, to virtual accessibility for parent/carers. These different approaches are broad in nature but are fundamentally grounded in the principles of the cornerstones approach. They seek to increase the openness of the settings in different ways in order that parent/carers and children/young people feel invited to participate actively as partners in their school community.

Positivity and celebration

'Being the beautiful you is always a treasure to behold, that sparkling rare diamond of the world.' (young person)

The cornerstones model seeks to enable stakeholders and the different communities in and around settings to flourish. The approach leans into positive psychology (Gable, 2005) and is purposefully implemented in a non-judgemental way that seeks to identify good practice:

'Because we know that it can really destroy somebody when all you receive is critical feedback . . . what we're trying to do is empower.' (practitioner)

When engaging with the cornerstones, settings/services embark on a journey to consider practice that is working well and ways that they can extend their approach based on the narratives of their stakeholders. The appreciative inquiry approach seeks to recognise and support best practice in relation to each cornerstone. This establishes a generative process that, in essence, is collaborative and creative (Cooperrider & Srivastva, 1987).

'Like that we said that its, you know, identifying what you are doing for these children, these families, and your staff.' (practitioner)

Challenges are faced within settings to support the development of children and young people. The model centralises collaboration in overcoming difficulties, celebrating practice that embodies the cornerstones, bringing them to life for children/young people, parents/carers, and practitioners together. The theoretical foundations recognise the ways some psychological approaches may predominantly focus their attention on negative bias, exploring deficit, diagnosis, and pathologies (Sheldon & King, 2001). The cornerstones involve a stance that extends beyond blame towards collaborative, solution-focused ways of working:

'It's about celebrating each other's strengths.' (practitioner)

The approach forms the basis for settings and services to be able to develop their relational practice. The Genuine Partnerships team works together with staff to reflect on where they are in their development of co-production and how they can begin engaging in conversations with young people and families to consider what they feel is working well.

Through narrative focus groups with children/young people and parent/carers, the team explores experiences around each cornerstone in greater depth. The aim is to seek out positive aspects of practice as well as opportunities for development in order to strengthen working towards authentically embodying the cornerstones' ethos. This forms the basis of the journey to 'Charter Gold', which is an award to recognise where good relational practice has been generated, developed, and established in true co-production. Celebration and the expressed aim to highlight positive practice that underpins the model have been a great motivator for engagement and inclusion:

> '[Y]ou will remember that when we had our first Gold Event, we literally got them [parents/carers] queuing down the street.' (practitioner)

Celebration events are developed with settings and services to bring communities together to recognise the positive impact of embedding of co-production with, and between, young people, families, and practitioners. This helps all stakeholders feel a sense of pride in working together through the cornerstones:

> 'Using and thinking things like the Charter Gold celebration when we're really showcasing our schools and the challenges.' (practitioner)

Recognition of the positive impact of the inclusion of the cornerstones as a way of enhancing partnership working and school culture has also been praised by external bodies such as Ofsted:

> 'Ofsted have given positive feedback about it as a model.' (practitioner)

Empowerment

The marginalisation of young people with special educational needs is well documented and is recognised to lead to poorer outcomes (Messiou, 2012; Mowat, 2015; Rose & Shevlin, 2004). The concept of partnership embedded within the cornerstones approach is purposefully designed to address power dynamics within organisations and settings. The aim of the approach is to increase partnership through the more equal distribution of power amongst those involved, and to generate agency for those who may otherwise feel their voice is oppressed.

Agency, understood as '[a] group-based, participatory, developmental process through which marginalized or oppressed individuals and groups gain greater control over their lives and environment, acquire valued resources and basic rights, and achieve important life goals and reduced societal marginalization' (Maton, 2008, p. 5), is reflected in the fabric of the cornerstones, with *partnership* being synonymous with the participatory nature of agency.

The emergence of partnership in practice encourages group ownership and responsibility. Voices are enabled, as listening is essential to how individuals feel valued and included. Hearing what others wish to express is a fundamental part of communication that supports engagement and empowerment. For leaders, who might feel under pressure to exert authority, the model invites a 'decentred but influential' position (White, 2007).

Parent/carers speak positively of seeing themselves as empowered within their child/young person's setting. The model supports them in feeling able to approach issues in different ways and leads to increases in their sense of wellbeing:

> 'But I think for me, as well, it's about how much it empowers parents to work in a different way that I can completely say that, sometimes, when I'm asking for things for my

child, it would come in from a point, a naivety sometimes . . . and actually being able to have that open, honest conversations and saying, actually, if you look at it this way or that way or from a different perspective, what a difference that can make.' (parent/carer)

'I know that, since being part of the team and feeling empowered and working in this way, my mental health clinically improved, because [I'm] just naturally thinking about what's working well rather than looking at what could go wrong constantly.' (parent/carer)

'[It] makes it lovely being in that environment, and so it empowers them and engages them, and it gives a confidence.' (parent/carer)

Partnership within the cornerstones encourages reflection and joint thinking on how to ensure stakeholders establish practices that facilitate choice and decision-making. Practitioners report different ways they have supported young people and families to guide the direction of practice based on understanding and attempting to meet their different needs:

'And we've also had community cafÈs, where we've had a specific focus as well. So we . . . you know, we'd have a suggestion box for . . . the topics they want to discuss. It might be, it might be budgeting, it might be the transition.' (practitioner)

Engaging in the cornerstones approach requires consideration of how to ensure individuals feel valued and included. Fundamental to this aspect of the framework is enabling them to recognise they are heard and their voices make a difference. Young people with special educational needs have reported feeling that practitioners can engage with them in tokenistic ways that leave them believing their voices are collected but have no influence. Ensuring individuals feel valued and included means considering ways to avoid tokenism. The following extract from a conversation between a young person and practitioner demonstrates that a simple process of returning to young people who have shared their views, and explaining the difference this has made, supports their sense of empowerment:

Young person:	'I think it's cool when [XXXX] comes and asks us about that. . . . It's like a panel or a board where they decide . . . [l]ike how to help young people?'
Practitioner:	'Yeah, the inclusion panel stuff.'
Young person:	'Yeah, I think that's it, yeah. . . . Yeah, I think it's really good that she, like, makes the time to come back and, like, update us all. What she's been up to and things because. I think it helps, like . . . you can tell she's actually listening.'

Practitioners also recognise the importance of highlighting clearly where voice has had a meaningful impact and influence on practice:

So thinking about people with really difficult needs and what can we do to make the model accessible, to make it feel like it's a choice for them to be part of something that has no compulsion, it's thinking about them, it's hearing them, it's valuing what they have to say, and it's demonstrating that things happened as a result of what they say. I think it has a massive impact on "voice and influence". That has huge implications for the wellbeing of those young people and their sense of what they can do, which I think is often absent for some reason for young people with special educational needs who feel very stuck and very limited and trapped. And other people hold the same kind of sense of them. And actually working with that group of young people, you can demonstrate, actually, how much they can do. And yes, with that support, they can achieve great things and feel, just feel good about themselves.' (practitioner)

Culture, ethos, and mindset: Whole system change

'Because we're looking at whole school or whole school and setting, organisational change . . . and that's what's really important.' (practitioner)

Parent/carers, practitioners, and young people engaging in a cornerstones-based approach often desire changes in a setting/service culture, ethos, and mindset to happen quickly, but it is acknowledged that embedding change within organisational culture takes time:

'Modelling it, I think really need to emphasise on the modelling. It's not just something that you say you do, a tickbox; it's something that you have to constantly work at. It's not an overnight fix. It's a culture change, its systemic. And so it takes time.' (parent/carer)
    'There's, like, lots of conversations about how you have to, like, respect each other's, like, needs and things. (young person)
    '[T]hey're still valuing it . . . as a model, as an ethos; it's something you live and breathe. You know, it's not . . . [i]t's not a gimmick, it's not something that you do and collect the badge, then, "OK, well, what should we do next? Let's find another badge."' (parent/carer)
    'Just exactly the same. It's just fundamentally what you do in a school, it's just the whole ethos of what we're about, and it . . . it's good to have the cornerstones there, but it's just there . . . that is just what you do.' (practitioner)

The cornerstones model supports organisational change by providing a relational framework through which practice can be considered. The guiding principles of 'welcome and care', 'value and include', 'communicate and partnership' encourage practitioners, parents/carers, and children/young people to reflect on policy and practice. It is only through an adaptation in mindset that systemic change can become established as the new norm (Wedell, 2008). The approach supports the development of a cornerstone-framed mindset that is instrumental in galvanising systemic change.

The sustainability of organisational change is difficult (Adelman & Taylor, 2003), particularly as the diversity and range of individuals coming together within educational institutions are potentially vast. This presents a challenge, as flexibility and individualised approaches are important. The cornerstones model does not provide hard and fast rules to guide creating change but instead acts to guide how stakeholders build relationships and work together in considering:

• How do we show 'welcome and care'?
• How do we make people feel 'valued and included'?

- How do we 'communicate' well?
- How do we make working together a true 'partnership'?

These questions seek to draw attention to practice connected with empathy, agency, accessibility, and empowerment. The operationalisation of each of the cornerstones is then context-specific, allowing for reflection and the ability to adjust approaches to meet the needs of those with whom we wish to build trusting relationships:

> 'Another parent or another practitioner and . . . if somebody does it differently, it doesn't mean it's not as good. And so schools might each do it differently, but actually, as long as the core ethos is there, does it matter, as long as people have a better experience?' (parent/carer)

As indicated earlier, central to the model is the consideration of power within relationships, recognising the imbalances that can exist within organisational structures. The influence of power on voice can lead to social dominance (Islam & Zyphur, 2005), thereby minimising some voices and amplifying others. The cornerstones help establish a sense of balance within relationships, meaning, that all voices can be heard and supported:

> 'So like how working in partnership and using the cornerstones can enable you to have stronger meetings with families and to feel equal.' (parent/carer)

Where mindsets are stuck within hierarchies of power, it can be more difficult to accept help, particularly if one partner is positioned as an expert who will provide the answer. In addressing power through the cornerstones, permission is given to hold challenges together, and for partners to jointly find solutions where answers may be illusive and initially difficult to capture.

Systemic relational change is possible through integrating the cornerstones into how stakeholders think, but it takes time to embed the approach. From our experience, once the model is adopted, practitioners find it is time well spent that, ultimately, supports everybody's wellbeing:

> 'And I just wanted to comment on how time-poor we are as . . . as school staff . . . but the cornerstones actually make that something that you've got to really pay attention to and you . . . you really need to. And self-critique what . . . what we actually do deliver for parents with regards to quality communication and . . . and not just a rushed, quick chat on a phone call. It is more than that. It's getting to know the parent. It's becoming a confidante for that parent, as well [as] for that family, so then they feedback information that they wouldn't normally do. . . . [T]hat's where it becomes a more quality role, really. When you . . . you set that time aside and you . . . you work hard to get it sorted out for them.' (practitioner)

Conclusion

The four cornerstones approach is a relationally based model that invites children/young people, parent/carers, and practitioners to work together as partners to create and celebrate positive organisational change. The model builds upon lived experience by enabling safe spaces through which the 'not yet said' can be safely voiced and acted upon. Embodying the depth of reflection, empathy, and human connection implicit within the model is radical, at once personally challenging, empowering, and generative, encompassing every dimension of experience. This was exemplified in the writing of this chapter. We believe that the cornerstones approach ultimately offers a more authentic way of working, creating a sense of community, **TRUST**, and belonging within organisational cultures that makes everybody's experience, and wellbeing, better.

Summary box

- This chapter tells the story of Rotherham's Genuine Partnerships and the evolution of the four cornerstones approach as a process that makes the quality of relationships the foundation for organisational values and culture.
- The four cornerstones are principles that create the context for genuine co-production and inclusive practice; they are 'welcome and care', 'value and include', 'communicate and (equal) partnership', and at their heart is **TRUST**.
- Co-writing and organising the chapter with young people, parent/carers, and schools/settings model the integrity of the approach.
- Psychological thinking made explicit when discussing the cornerstones include collaborative systemic thinking incorporating narrative practice, not blaming, curiosity, not knowing, privileging marginalised voices and perspective-taking; psychodynamic thinking, for example, attachment theory, what generates trust within relationships, and empathy; appreciative inquiry and positive psychology more generally; reflectivity and reflexivity, considering one's own social constructs, prejudices, and unconscious biases; critical social psychology, reflecting on, and addressing, power differentials to introduce agency and empowerment; critical community psychology.
  - Relational practice at the heart of the approach consists of:
  - Embodiment of (modelling) the cornerstones and the power of this experience
  - Reflection and relational reflexivity
  - Relationships, community, and connection
  - Positivity and celebration
  - Empowerment
  - Culture, ethos, and mindset: whole system change

Consider collaboratively:

- How do we show 'welcome and care'?
- How do we make people feel 'valued and included'?
- How can we 'communicate' well?
- How do we make working together a true 'partnership'?

See the Genuine Partnerships and Guiding Voices websites for helpful tools and materials to support the implementation of the cornerstones approach:

www.genuinepartnerships.co.uk
Guiding Voices – Rotherham SEND Local Offer

References

Adelman, H. S., & Taylor, L. (2003). On sustainability of project innovations as systemic change. *Journal of Educational and Psychological Consultation, 14*(1), 1–25.

Anderson, H. (1997). *Conversation, language and possibilities: A postmodern approach to therapy*. Basic Books.

Anderson, H., & Goolishan, H. A. (1988). Human systems as linguistic systems: Preliminary and evolving ideas about the implications for clinical theory. *Family Process, 27*, 371–393.

Anderson, T. (1992). Reflections on reflecting with families. In S. McNamee & K. J. Gergen (Eds.), *Therapy as social construction* (pp. 54–68). Sage.

Bandura, A. (1977a). *Social learning theory*. Prentice Hall.

Billington, T. (2006). *Working with children*. Sage.

Bownas, J., & Fredman, G. (Eds.). (2017). *Working with embodiment in supervision: A systemic approach*. Routledge.

Burnham, J. (2005). Relational reflexivity: A tool for socially constructing therapeutic relationships. In C. Flaskas, B. Mason, & A. Perlesz (Eds.), *The space between* (pp. 1–17). Karnac.

Burr, V. (2003). *Social constructionism: A new force in psychology*. Routledge.

Burton, M., Boyle, S., Harris, C., & Kagan, C. (2007). Community psychology in Britain. In S. Reich, M. Riemer, I. Prilleltensky, & M. Montero (Eds.), *International community psychology: History and theories* (pp. 219–237). Kluwer Academic Press.

Cooperrider, D. L., & Srivastva, S. (1987). Appreciative inquiry in organizational life. In W. A. Pasmore & R. W. Woodman (Eds.), *Research in organizational change and development* (Vol. 1, pp. 129–169). JAI Press.

Cullinane, M. (2020). An exploration of the sense of belonging of students with special educational needs. *REACH: Journal of Inclusive Education in Ireland, 33*(1), 2–12.

Department for Children, Schools and Families. (2008). *The Inclusion Development Programme. Supporting children with speech, language and communication needs: Guidance for practitioners in the Early Years Foundation Stage*. GOV.UK. https://webarchive.nationalarchives.gov.uk/ukgwa/20110202122217/https:/nationalstrategies.standards.dcsf.gov.uk/node/161358

Department for Children, Schools and Families. (2009). *Lamb inquiry: Special educational needs and parental confidence*. DCSF.

Department of Education. (2015). *Special educational needs and disability code of practice: 0–25 years*. GOV.UK. https://assets.publishing.service.gov.uk/government/uploads/system/uploads/attachment_data/file/398815/SEND_Code_of_Practice_January_2015.pdf

Gable, S. L., & Haidt, J. (2005). What (and why) is positive psychology? *Review of General Psychology, 9*(2), 103–110.

Hebron, J. S. (2017). School connectedness and the primary to secondary school transition for young people with autism spectrum conditions. *British Journal of Educational Psychology, 88*, 396–409.

Islam, G., & Zyphur, M. J. (2005). Power, voice, and hierarchy: Exploring the antecedents of speaking up in groups. *Group Dynamics: Theory, Research, and Practice, 9*(2), 93.

Klussman, K., Nichols, A. L., Langer, J., & Curtin, N. (2020). Connection and disconnection as predictors of mental health and wellbeing. *International Journal of Wellbeing, 10*(2).

Maslow, A. H. (2013). *Toward a psychology of being*. Simon and Schuster.

Maton, K. I. (2008). Empowering community settings: Agents of individual development, community betterment, and positive social change. *American Journal of Community Psychology, 41*, 4–21.

Messiou, K. (2012). Collaborating with children in exploring marginalisation: An approach to inclusive education. *International Journal of Inclusive Education, 16*(12), 1311-1322.

Mowat, J. G. (2015). Towards a new conceptualisation of marginalisation. *European Educational Research Journal, 14*(5), 454-476.

Noddings, N. (2012). The caring relation in teaching. *Oxford Review of Education, 36*, 771-781.

Partridge, K., & McCarry, N. (2009). Dissolving blame: Systemic therapy in action. *Healthcare Counselling & Psychotherapy Journal, 9*(3), 12-16.

Rose, R., & Shevlin, M. (2004). Encouraging voices: Listening to young people who have been marginalised. *Support for Learning, 19*(4), 155-161.

Rose, R., & Shevlin, M. (2017). A sense of belonging: Childrens' views of acceptance in "inclusive" mainstream schools. *International Journal of Whole Schooling, 13*(1), 65-80.

Santiago, R. T., Garbacz, S. A., Beattie, T., & Moore, C. L. (2016). Parent-teacher relationships in elementary school: An examination of parent-teacher trust. *Psychology in the Schools, 53*(10), 1003-1017.

Schön, D. A. (1983). *The reflective practitioner: How professionals think in action*. Temple Smith

Sheldon, K. M., & King, L. (2001). Why positive psychology is necessary. *American Psychologist, 56*(3), 216.Walther, S., & Fox, H. (2012). Narrative therapy and outsider witness practice: Teachers as a community of acknowledgement. *Educational and Child Psychology, 29*(2), 8-17.

Wedell, K. (2008). Inclusion: Confusion about inclusion: Patching up or system change? *British Journal of Special Education, 35*(3), 127-135.

White, M. (2007). *Maps of narrative practice*. Norton.

White, M., & Epston, D. (1990). *Narrative means to therapeutic ends*. Norton.

Whitney, D., & Trosten-Bloom, A. (2003). *The power of appreciative inquiry: A practical guide to positive change*. Berrett-Koehler.

8 A reflection on how a relational approach supported an Educational Psychology Service's work on antiracism

Pauline Clarke and Jo Marriott

Equality: Everyone's business – a tool to support the development of antiracist practice in education settings

Introduction

In 2019, a year prior to George Floyd's murder, in my role as an educational psychologist (EP) supporting a dual-heritage young man, I became interested in how we could better support young peoples' identity development, particularly when they come from marginalised backgrounds. I am of White heritage, within a mixed-race relationship, and have dual-heritage children, which has influenced my interest in educational and social equity for racially minoritised children and young people. The piece of casework I was involved with led to me having a conversation (over the photocopier!) with a colleague from the Tackling Emerging Threats to Children (TETC) team whom I had worked with previously. We knew we had aligned values and interests, and I thought she might be willing to work with us on this topic. Together, we agreed to set up a working group to focus on identity and to consider how we might, as an Education, Learning, and Inclusion (ELI) department, support schools in this area. The group consisted of individuals from a range of backgrounds, including White, Black, and mixed heritage. The group had already met twice by the time George Floyd was murdered in Minneapolis, USA, on 25 May 2020. In June 2020, we were scheduled to meet for a third time, and understandably, all we could talk about was George Floyd, his murder, and the subsequent uprisings. As we explored our feelings and reflections with each other, there was a strong sense of wanting to do something. Our TETC team colleagues shared that they had been receiving a number of requests from schools and professionals within Nottinghamshire for guidance and direction on George Floyd in particular, and antiracism more generally. The requests included questions such as, 'How do we respond when a child asks what "All Lives Matter" means and why it upsets some people?' School staff were keen to support children and wanted to do so in partnership with parents and, in line with LA guidance, with the accountability that brings. We discussed how we could best respond to these requests, and the idea for developing a resource for schools was born.

What do we mean by racism and antiracism?

Within our Nottinghamshire cross-service working group, we co-produced our shared understandings of what we mean by *racism* and *antiracism*.

DOI: 10.4324/9781003451907-8

Racism

In the antiracism resource, we adopted the following definitions of *racism*:

> In the UK, major institutions operate in ways that discriminate against Black, Asian and minority ethnic (BAME*) people including children. This includes education, health systems, employment and the criminal justice system. This is structural racism.
>
> Barnardo's (2020)

We included a range of examples to illustrate how racism can affect the lives of people, including schoolchildren:

> Fixed-term and permanent exclusions are issues which disproportionately affect Black Caribbean and Black African children, particularly boys. Black Caribbean boys are three times more likely than their white counterparts to be excluded and Mixed: White/Black Caribbean students are also more likely to be excluded than their white counterparts.
>
> (Gillborn & Demack, 2018)

The same report noted that '[t]eachers' greater sensitivity to the behaviour of Black students can lead to them being singled out for harsher treatment' (p. 2).

Antiracism

We developed this definition of *antiracism*, drawing upon the literature:

> Antiracism is acknowledging that racism does exist in our schools and settings and supporting those who do not recognise this to develop their knowledge and understanding of British history. It is important to recognise harmful stereotypes and assumptions, and to listen, reflect and respond appropriately to the lived experiences of black and brown people.

The key sources that informed our definition included:

- *We're All White Thanks*: the persisting myth about white schools (Gaine, 2005)
- *Race and Racism in English Secondary Schools* (Runnymede Trust, 2020)
- *Natives: Race and Class in the Ruins of Empire* (Akala, 2018)
- *How to Be an Antiracist* (Kendi, 2019)

Developing the resource

During the summer term 2020, when we were in pandemic lockdown, the members of the cross-service working group collaborated virtually over a number of months to think initially about what a useful resource might look like, and then develop it. The resource became known as *Equality – Everyone's Business – a tool to support the development of anti-racist practice in education settings* (Nottinghamshire County Council [NCC], 2021). We wrote some sections together, some individually, then edited in groups (all virtual!). Resources were gathered from publications' websites, discussions, and via social media. We selected materials from sources that were consistent with our working definitions of *racism* and *antiracism*, and those which were evidence-based. We quality-assured these for content and validity before adding them to the resource, to ensure they were consistent. School colleagues were generous in sharing resources they had. The TETC team were having ongoing interactions with school staff who continued to ask and seek support from them. This demonstrated the importance of a trusted relationship (Brennan et al., 2013) and emotional safety as a precursor to learning (Maslow, 1943) for people to be able to ask difficult questions, as there is a vulnerability in doing so, especially on a topic as sensitive as racism. We recognised what a challenge it is to create a space where people feel able to take risks to learn. We also realised we needed to start where the school staff were, that is, respond to their most pressing concern, whether it was how to use language appropriately or how to build their library so it was more inclusive.

As we considered how to structure the resource, we thought back to the questions school staff had wanted support with. We decided to structure the central section of the resource as a 'Q and A', so it appeared more interactive and focused specifically on questions school staff had asked and might ask.

Due to the positive, established relationships the working group had, we were able to sensitively challenge each other during this process; for example, we were able to share our views and debate whether certain resources ought to be included or not. We were able to listen to and agree together what the context should be and kept coming back together as a group to discuss and review our progress. As EPs in a service where all our project and strategic work is undertaken collaboratively, with distributed responsibility, we brought this approach to the work on the antiracism resource.

Alongside our work developing the resource, we introduced an *Equity and Inclusion* agenda item to our EPS team meetings to support each other in having conversations about antiracism. We recognised that some people felt more comfortable having difficult conversations in smaller groups, with colleagues they had closer working relationships with. Over time, we noticed that within these trusted contexts, people were more willing to ask questions or share their own personal experiences. We became aware that education staff were not merely looking for resources to use directly with school staff or children but also wanted (and needed) to further their own understanding of antiracism so that they could feel competent talking to children about it. With the openness we created within team meetings, conversations began to flow better, and more members contributed, which led to richer discussions. This subsequently meant EPs were able to make changes to their practice as they became more confident speaking to school staff and families about antiracism.

Following ongoing discussions with school staff and children, we developed our aspirations for the resource as follows, to ensure a focus on what would be most supportive:

- For all educational professionals to move into the growth zone and towards the transformational zone in the *becoming antiracist* image (see Ibrahim, 2020).
- For education professionals to be confident in challenging racism in an active and effective way as they come across it.
- For antiracist principles and practices to become a part of not only our working lives but also our personal lives.
- For all education professionals to consciously and proactively address race-based inequalities in their individual classrooms and at a whole-school level, regardless of their community demographic.
- For our children to develop their racial literacy and commit to antiracism.

Reflections as a service

As the work on the resource progressed and we began to have regular conversations with the wider EPS about antiracism, we recognised the need for our own personal and professional learning and reflection on antiracism. In fact, we viewed it as essential if we were to be in a good position to support schools/settings with the implementation of the resource. We had noticed that conversations within the service around antiracism were not always comfortable; for example, at times EPs were not confident with their use of terminology, how to refer to certain ethnic groups, or how to challenge racism when they witnessed it within professional spaces. We acknowledged that, in order for this hesitancy to shift, we needed to create a trusting space where EPs felt able to be vulnerable and ask questions. Acknowledging tensions in creating a safe space for discussions was key, and we asked ourselves, 'Safe space for whom?' That is, how could we support minoritised staff in these discussions, as well as those from the majority culture, recognising that they might have very different experiences and emotional responses?

One of the ways we tried to address this was through the creation of a new Equity and Inclusion Strategic Psychology (Project) Group (SPG) that has since focused on continuing professional development (CPD) for the EPS. The group has led on the development of an antiracism self-evaluation framework, and *equity and inclusion* as a topic is now a standing item on team, supervision, and SLT meeting agendas. EPs were invited to bring topics or questions for discussion, for example, an experience of racial stereotyping in a consultation, or something in the media that had resonated with them. In addition, our service work on a 'story for change', described in the following, was contributing to wider discussions about privilege within the service. All these changes have enabled us to have regular, open discussions about antiracism as well as other areas of equity and inclusion. Through this process, over time, we were able to create trust between us, and EPs have been more able to engage in discussions about antiracism and its implications for EP practice. Having permission to raise topics and ensuring there was protected time to explore them led to conversations we had never had before, both about our own experiences and hearing those of others. We regularly turn to the 'becoming antiracist' image (Ibrahim, 2020) to help us look forward to where we need to go next, and backwards to see how we have moved on.

Ongoing collaboration and development

As the antiracism working group continued its work on the resource, we extended the membership to include more teams within Education, Learning, and Inclusion (ELI), for example, colleagues from 'achievement and equality', 'education improvement', 'fair access', specialist teachers, and teaching assistants. Additional members were predominantly from a White background (which reflects the demographic of Nottinghamshire) and also from Black and South Asian heritage. Everyone who participated did so voluntarily. We met regularly as a whole group to share views, resources, and to edit drafts. We had wanted to co-produce with schools/settings at this stage; however, schools were under immense pressures because of the pandemic, so it was later on, when the resource was launched, that we were able to start receiving and building on feedback from school staff.

Webinars and feedback

We launched the resource to Nottinghamshire's school/settings via a series of webinars. Colleagues from all the ELI teams were invited to share the resource during their regular contacts with education settings, and EPs were able to do this as part of their termly planning (Springboard) meetings.

Once education colleagues were familiar with the resource, we began to receive feedback informally, and also formally, via a questionnaire. Hearing feedback involved email threads, face-to-face meetings, and incidental conversations. This led to a number of co-produced amendments, and we are now on version 4 of the resource. Some of the feedback was extensive and led to significant discussion and reflection over many months and, although challenging at times, resulted in deeper learning for those involved. We found that we had to use relational approaches to address the challenges of working on racism and to manage the avoidance and defensiveness that can often arise. For example, we listened with empathy as colleagues shared how difficult they found some of the conversations, and also challenged each other with the need to persist with the discussions despite our discomfort. We valued different perspectives and the lived experiences individuals brought to the conversation.

Responding to feedback on the antiracism resource

One example of responding to feedback illustrates how our relational approach supported and sustained us; a small group of us worked together to respond to an interaction with a member of school staff. We found the conversations challenging, as the feedback was extensive and wide-reaching, and we needed to plan our responses and debrief with each other after each exchange. Different interaction styles were needed over time to maintain our communication and keep a positive momentum. This felt a little like geese flying in formation, as one of us would take the lead while the others supported, until they became overwhelmed and needed to hand the baton over. This required self-awareness, knowing when we were struggling, as well as trust in each other to be able to ask for support when needed. Through this support, co-regulation, and care of each other, we were able to empathise and recognise that the person providing the feedback was bringing their previous personal and professional experiences to the conversation, which included much anger and sadness, and was wider than content of our antiracist resource.

Throughout the process, our small group persisted with the shared goal of resolving the issues and moving towards a shared understanding, which required listening, empathising, and recognising that it would take time to find a mutually agreeable solution with the person concerned. As is the case in restorative work, there was a high level of challenge alongside a high level of support (Hopkins, 2012). On reflection, we were able to sustain these interactions, valuing his perspective and bearing witness to his pain, because we were committed to the resource being as inclusive as possible to the lived experiences of those affected by racism.

Eventually, we were able to reach agreement about the content of the resource. However, the process taught us that, regardless of how relational we think we are being in our interactions, this work is incredibly challenging to navigate and often brings with it a range of human emotions and pain. We can only do our best to be respectful and empathetic and to trust in our values to guide us.

Sharing the resource more widely

The resource was later shared on a national level at the educational psychologists' 'Race' and Culture Forum event (June 2021) and has subsequently been published on our website.

Collaborating with, and hearing from, schools who have used the resource

In March 2023, we canvassed schools for further updates on their work in this area following the resource launch (almost two years on) and received comments as follows:

> *The curriculum reflects equality and diversity and challenges any stereotypical behaviours. The tool has supported the changes in school.*
>
> *Higher profile and more frequent discussions have resulted in greater awareness of the overt and covert presence of discrimination. Adults act swiftly to address inappropriate comments or actions. Some children are quicker to report concerns.*

These comments are encouraging and reflect our initial hopes when developing the resource:

> *The tool was developed to provide schools and other education settings with initial guidance around antiracism. This work is necessary for all schools/settings everywhere, regardless of their demographic and regardless of whether people consider that these issues affect them personally.*
>
> *Schools and other education settings play an important role in supporting children and young people to understand racism and to become anti-racist. They can create an inclusive environment where learners feel welcome and valued.*

Continuing this important work

Having worked on antiracism within our service, and in developing the resource, we recognise that our work in this area is not done, and we have plenty more to do. We are continuing to explore ways to support schools and settings to engage authentically with the resource, to reflect on their own practice, and to implement the ideas within it. The resource has supported EPs, colleagues, and school staff to become more aware of antiracism and provided a framework of support, but we feel that changes to practice will take time and continued engagement with this work will be needed if we are to move towards greater social justice and better outcomes for children and young people. As EPs, we are still working on our own antiracist practice and recently spent time looking at next steps for our CPD. Our SPG will move into its fourth year in September, and we are continuing to work on our self-evaluation framework and a 'story for change'.

The development of our antiracism story for change, 'The Shimmer'

How our relational approach led to fiction being adopted to create a safe metaphorical space for connecting, sharing, and listening across the chasm created by racism

The intention

The 'story for change' emerged as an idea for a therapeutic story alongside the development of the *Equality – Everyone's Business* tool. It was thought to be a vehicle by which we could bring to life the themes that were being asked about by children in our schools, such as what is meant when people say, 'All Lives Matter'. The intention was to make the discourses they were hearing meaningful for them, and to create connection and resonance, especially for children whose lived experience is not racism. It was an attempt to reduce othering within a county where many schools have predominantly White populations of children and staff. This was an attempt to engage adults and children emotionally with the resonance for them, and their personal journeys with White privilege and antiracism (as opposed to engaging on a cognitive and psychoeducational level alone). We hoped that sharing a fictional story would open up a relational space within classrooms and staffrooms and, more widely, for sharing personal journeys with each other. The hope was that this might bridge the chasm of experience created by racism through developing empathy and, through the story, provide a shared metaphorical space for asking each other about our ignorance of racism and/or our experiences of racism.

Whilst there are lots and varied stories and life histories within the *Equality – Everyone's Business* tool, the idea behind creating a fictional, fantasy-based story came with curiosity about how metaphor, fictional plots and characters, and imagination could create genuine emotion and reflection to bring about a shift and change in our constructs and narratives (Sunderland, 2001). As stories are inherently relational (often spanning generations as well as being relevant to our immediate relationships), this would occur within the shared collaborative space created by the story to promote authentic connection in discussing privilege and antiracism.

This is the definition that we created as a service for our story-writing as Nottinghamshire psychologists:

> Stories create a rich and safe metaphorical space where we are alongside children (people) in exploring constructs, emotions and experiences. This offers the opportunity for reflection to tune the child into their own resources and relationships, to clarify and challenge constructs, to provide the broader means by which the child can understand and make sense of a situation and identify ideas and a next step for them. These stories increase the understanding of the child's constructs and enable attunement. . . . Stories can also provide insights for re-authoring.

In this work, we have drawn on narrative psychology in the broadest sense of considering the psychological advantages of adopting the medium of story/narrative and the more specific principles of narrative therapy (White & Epston, 1990). We have been influenced by the idea of re-authoring (altering our previously held narratives of life) and the powerful sense of agency this produces, and how fictional stories can propel this (Freeman et al., 1997). We thought that finding ways to re-author at an individual or small systems (such as schools) level could be a bottom-up way of creating antiracist practice. When re-authoring, we tap into alternative narratives, alternative ways of viewing our world that connect with our values, the people we wish to include, our history, our present context, and our future as we see it, developed in our thinking as a narrative structure. These may challenge societally dominant narratives which are based on the politics and power of our cultural time in history, but not necessarily reflective of our lived experience (White & Epston, 1990).

This understanding of narrative reflects our group's focus on the psychology of relationships, building trust, being alongside, considering personal and shared (societal) constructs, and creating (and recognising) the narratives around us, including dominant narratives and potential alternative narratives. Hasson (2016) has brain scan evidence that attunement occurs at a neurological level, as well as at a psychological level, when sharing stories. Our experiences of creating stories, especially this antiracism story, would suggest that this definition can be just as true about creating a story together as sharing a completed one. Since 2020, the safe metaphorical and relational space created in writing, 'The Shimmer', has been fundamental to our powerful journey of antiracism.

The surprising journey

In 2020, the COVID pandemic created a space in our work that needed to be filled in a reflective and curious way. Not in a panic, although we felt this intensely, one of our responses to the situation was to produce a short series of therapeutic stories featuring the character Little Elf. By creating an illustrated set of stories about the experiences of Little Elf and putting them on our website, we were trying to find a way for children to understand and talk about their experiences of living through a pandemic. Our metaphor for the pandemic was a large cloud, which offered scope for a gradual shining through of light as restrictions eased and darkened and eased again. These stories were well received nationally, and some school staff found creative ways to talk about the stories with the children, generating resources that were also shared on our website.

When the murder of George Floyd occurred and we began reflecting on the development of an antiracist resource, as described in Part 1 of this chapter, I wondered how we could use our learning from writing the Little Elf stories in our focus on antiracism. The passage of time during the pandemic seemed to offer a unique synergy of ideas stemming from our personal and professional lives. Personal relationships contributed to this work, and so I wrote the first very rough draft of the story with my niece. Those early conversations within the safety of my close relationship with her provided me with the confidence to propose this idea at work.

Initially, the interest group was made up of colleagues I approached because I knew of their interest and experience in story-writing and in the development of our antiracism work. We discussed how we wanted to create a story through which we can recognise our own privilege and have empathy for those whose lived experience is racism. With hindsight, however, the initial relationships that led to this group lacked the diversity we needed for wider perspectives and a richer understanding, a revelation of White naivety in itself that we could produce a narrative about White privilege without substantial challenge from those whose lived experience is racism. The journey of 'The Shimmer' is one of a service of educational psychologists grappling with, reflecting upon, critically thinking about, and ultimately, connecting with each other through a story that has seemed almost impossible to write and to end.

Our first draft provoked critical and emotive feedback when shared with our whole service. This first attempt encapsulated key characters as flowers, roses being representative of those privileged by a society valuing Whiteness, and the poppies reflecting those devalued and exploited within our racist society. The rose characters were revealed for their white saviourism, and the poppies lacked agency and voice, victimised. Connecting with this tension, the hurt, distress, and anger of colleagues as a result caused a raw exposure of us as a service that was hard to experience but seemed needed, and was given space, enabling exploration and reflection through the story metaphors and their limitations. For those of us in the group who had produced the story, it was incredibly difficult to hear this feedback, but it also provided an insightful critique that has since informed our subsequent joint and individual journeys with antiracism. It also helped us deepen and authenticate the discourses around the development of the story. It made us painfully aware of the fine line between reflecting and encouraging social divisions and hierarchies.

The support and supervision needed at this juncture should not be underestimated. This was provided by compassionate and empathic senior leaders as well as through less-formal peer supervision. There was pain, anger, and injustice felt, and a multitude of other emotions that I now realise I did not, and will never, feel. The journey of 'The Shimmer' has truly been a whole service journey, with colleagues bearing different types of load for it to continue, the rawest being for those whose lived experience is racism.

The momentum over three years to keep this story development alive has come predominantly from the relationship-based practice within our service, where nurture and authentic connections are valued and given space. Members of the team around the story have developed personal resonances to it and have been provided safe spaces (sometimes virtual, sometimes physical, sometimes metaphorical) to have these conversations. For example, our SPG and our solution-focused and narrative-based supervision have supported reflexive practice in relation to the development of the story as well as our personal antiracism journeys. We have found these conversations both supportive and challenging, shaping our individual and shared learning, consequently also shaping the story. This has shifted and changed based upon the learning taking place within and between us. The story bearers within the team have changed over the three years, passing on the baton. This has allowed for fresh ideas, but also emotional containment and a slowing down of processing around the story, which seemed essential, as it was promoting collaboration, and so it was important to hear all voices from within our service. We believe that hearing a range of voices about the story as it continues its journey will be equally essential before it enters the public domain. The story has taken so long to create because the process of writing it, based on relationships, has remained as valued, if not more valued, than the story itself. It is hoped that our reflective questions and activities in the pack accompanying the story will reflect our own learning, encouraging the story content to be processed in a slow and deliberate manner.

We hoped that our story would highlight social constructs of race, power, White privilege, inequity, and oppression within the relational safe space of metaphor and story. It is only with hindsight that I think we realised the enormity and fragility of the task we had set ourselves. We have wondered why this story continues to be so difficult to navigate and to write. We did not realise, perhaps naively, that to engage with this journey of story production would mean needing to go through a journey of growth individually and as a service. We have stretched our relationships, needing to openly discuss prejudice, privilege, and what this means for us together and individually, and the hurt, pain, and anger caused, within the room, rather than this remaining at a cognitive distance.

We continue to debate who is our audience and the intended outcome of the story, but ultimately, through metaphor, fantasy, and character, we have come to realise the power of discussing White privilege and antiracism within a predominantly White EPS and a local authority whose population is predominantly White.

This is a reflection from one EP involved in the writing of the first draft:

> *The first attempt of the story gave the notion of the poppies being helpless, there being victimhood and them needing validation by the roses. The group reflected on moving towards strength, resistance, and resilience as the central characteristics of the pop-pies, a story of courage. Questions posed included, 'Is there a way for us to centralise the experience of the poppies as opposed to the roses?' The poppies need respect and recognition from the roses and not care, as care gives the impression of white saviour and the need to rescue. There is also the significance of the beauty attributed to roses, and the hardiness of poppies, and on some level, the story may reinforce what plays out societally. The story felt important and that a story is needed, but we asked ourselves, 'What is the takeaway message, and how does the story leave those that identify with the poppies feeling?' The group was asked to think about the sovereignty of experience and whose experience we are emphasising in writing the story, acknowledging that the story could inadvertently reinforce 'supremacy' messages, that it's only a story!*

This quote illustrates the depth of discussion elicited from the first draft, which then aided our shared learning and connection in our movement forward, but at the cost of hurt and pain experienced by some colleagues. I wish to acknowledge that I can only try to empathise with this pain and anger and am in awe of my colleagues who persevere with the aim of trying to create change for future generations in a small way through this story.

The general feedback from the service at this time remained that the project to create a story was valuable, but we needed to go back to address the questions and critiques posed. As a result of this work and the wider work of the EPS, an internal BEEP (Black and Ethnic EPs) group was set up. There are four in the group, EPs and an assistant EP, who collectively report:

> *The internal BEEP group is powerful as it brings EPs that have shared experiences together and there's an energy to drive things forward. It's a place to discuss the impact of the antiracism work on us as those that have directly experienced racism in some form, to share perspectives, discuss how we feel and receive support.*

One EP shared, '[I]t leaves me feeling "lighter" rather than "heavy" about this work'.

The group reports that 'the challenge at times is to prioritise the group meetings amongst other priorities, but the group noted that it was important to make the time to meet'. Another member said that they feel able to express themselves, feel validated and there is a shared experience of those 'little feelings that you don't have to explain, especially how it feels when you are in spaces where you are the only non-White face in the room'.

The final phase?

Soon after this, the journey of the story was passed to the SPG focused on equity and inclu-sion, which had been tasked with our service's continuing professional development. This offered dedicated time and space for the further development of this project. A colleague who took up the story wrote about her hopes to have 'a story/narrative to open up the discussion in relation to the experience of racism, to account for both perspectives, those holding unconscious bias and those experiencing it'.

The story plot and characters were rewritten to involve the current characters, animals, based on follow-up work from the interest group, which had held lengthy emotional yet psychologically informed discussions reflective of feedback from the whole service. There was hope that the story could be enriched by the many views that were informing its development:

> I joined the SPG in September and was introduced to the animal story, never having read the poppy-and-roses story. We worked on developing the characters, hoping that the farm animals could reflect the different zones of the becoming antiracist concentric circles (fear, learning, growth, etc.). We also explored how the story could end, whether it should be quite open or with a direct action. In the end, after discussing as a group and based on service feedback, we decided to leave the ending open with the conversation between the animals.
>
> The biggest change in the story whilst I have been in the group is the introduction of 'the shimmer', which represents the farm animals' awareness (or lack of awareness) of their privilege, and how the system they live in benefits them but makes life harder for the woodland animals. The shimmer for the farm animals is around them, and when I picture it, it's also a lighter tone (maybe lilac), as it is something they have to actively choose to learn and acknowledge. Whereas for the woodland animals, I imagine the shimmer is a part of them, as it is their first-hand experience and a richer tone of purple.
>
> I have loved being a part of working on the story and having real time to reflect as a group. I think the woodland and farm animals represent the different groups well, and I was surprised that some people felt the woodland animals were the privileged ones, as they are truly free. In my eyes the woodland animals are disadvantaged by the system; therefore, even though they are free, they have less access to resources, and so life is automatically harder. I liked, however, that the characters of woodland animals and farm animals brought up this debate, as it opened up interesting conversations.
>
> As a group, we liked this visual representation of awareness of the unfair system and privilege. I also like how all the woodland animals behave differently and have their own independent approaches and thoughts, as even though they face the same hardships, it doesn't mean they will all respond in the same way.

At a recent service morning, our EPS revisited our story. The story became known as 'the story for change' following a discussion that members of our SPG had with tutors from the University of Sheffield who talked of the potential for change created by adopting stories in our work as psychologists. Prior to this, we had been unsure about how to describe our creation, which had begun from experience of writing therapeutic short stories.

Let me give you a flavour of the story as it was at that time and describe to you the feedback that came from this most recent sharing of our story for change. The story follows two different groups of animals, farm and woodland animals, as they meet and have conversations for the first time when disaster strikes and a tree falls, breaking the boundary between their two homes.

Following are extracts from the story for change (which has evolved into 'The Shimmer') as presented at the whole service day:

> *The farm animals were expectantly waiting for the farmer, Muddy Boots, to come round to top up their water troughs and give them their breakfast, as he did every morning. Pig was especially looking forward to having his back scratched by Muddy Boots as he said 'Good morning'. . ..*
>
> *In the nearby woods, fox and badger were relieved they didn't need to walk too far for their morning drink from the stream, which had plenty of water in for everyone for once. They decided today was going to be a good day as some days all the water was taken by Muddy Boots to make sure his farm animals had enough, which meant that in the woodland they had to go further upstream. Owl thought about this as he looked down from his tree and could feel his anger simmering up inside of him.*
>
> *The farm animals nervously approached the woods, led by squirrel, to find they were greeted by some familiar faces they had waved at many mornings. Pig, who was still worrying about his food, immediately asked where the food and water trough were. The woodland animals looked at each other and smiled knowingly. Badger explained that in the woods they have to find their own food and water from the resources available. . . .*
>
> *The animals settle down for the night. Goat and Sheep benefiting from the kindness of the woodland animals who take them in for the night. The woodland animals realise the farm animals are not quite ready to listen - not even goat or sheep. Badger reminds the other woodland animals how hard it has been for the farm animals to truly listen (or to see the shimmer yet) as they don't know how unfair life can be as their needs had always been met on the farm - but now they know more and have seen life in the woods, they need to listen to them, but not tonight.*

At the whole service morning, we had four groups of EPs who provided feedback on the latest version of the story. They all liked the metaphor of the 'shimmer' to indicate degrees of awareness of privilege, and one group wondered if the colours of this could correspond with the concentric circles mentioned earlier to indicate personal growth through, for example, fear and learning zones (Ibrahim, 2020).

Other positive comments included: '[W]e like the pride in the woodland animals and lifting the veil on the woodland experience', '[T]he animals work better than the flowers, as greater richness of varying perspectives can be explored', and '[W]e like the human character of Muddy Boots representing the system'.

It was reported that further development of the story is needed to bring about more depth of emotion and personality of characters. One group thought that Goat could think about what he might say to Muddy Boots to illustrate antiracist practice. Most thought that an ambiguous ending would work well for the reader to formulate their own thoughts.

We talked about how the finished story might be shared with schools/settings and other services. Everyone agreed that school staff using the story would require training to ensure understanding of their personal journeys and growth which underpin adopting this resource to enable raising awareness of privilege and antiracism in children. The training would also involve practising the reflective questions that are intended to accompany the story (yet to be finalised). Some thought that EPs trialling the use of the story first would be helpful, having focus-group feedback and perhaps sharing the story with emotional literacy support assistants (ELSAs) through our regular supervision sessions. Other colleagues wanted to see greater links to the *Equality – Everyone's Business* tool.

> I see the story being used with adults as part of CPD, for them to consider what the story evokes, for them to reflect on how they reconcile their own views/experiences; have they 'worked'/accounted for their own prejudice, unconscious bias, before they move forward with the story in their work with children?
>
> I would hope that training is delivered to staff first as part of antiracism training. Then those staff would be more skilled in delivering the story to pupils in schools. The age range could be primary and secondary schools.
>
> I hope the story can be part of a wider offer, where the story comes with training and time for reflection for staff planning on using it with students so that they understand the concepts and talking points. I then hope the story can be shared with students led by a trained adult who can facilitate open, reflective, and thoughtful conversations between, and with, students. Hopefully, by engaging with the story and conversations that follow, it will move people along the antiracist concentric circle zones, or at least encourage them to think how they can work on developing along the zones. I think the story can be used with a range of ages, but the reflective questions/prompts may need to be adapted depending on age group.

Taken from feedback from a member of the SPG 'equity and inclusion' working on the story at this time.

There was some discussion of intersectionality, including suggestions about 'more gender diversity' or to 'gender-neutralise characters', to demonstrate that the farm animals 'may be part of another disadvantaged group', and to consider having some endangered species involved, such as red squirrels. There was discussion of whether stereotypes of animals are useful for a story for children, in offering context, or whether these should be challenged in line with the themes being explored.

There were also conversations about whether the story, in fact, reflects power or privilege, and whether it should be described as a story of change around privilege or antiracism. A key area of continued debate is the categorising of the animals into farm and woodland. The metaphor being used here is of those who are favoured, recognised, and valued by the system and are offered resources, the farm animals, and those who are forgotten, not heeded to, disadvantaged, threatened, and exploited by the system, the woodland animals. But colleagues interpreted these groupings in varying ways, including seeing the farm animals as exploited and the woodland animals as free, and there was concern that the woodland animals may be seen as 'wild'.

There are no simple answers to the themes raised in these conversations, but we celebrate that, as a service, we are having the discussions, and that they have been made accessible and safer through the metaphor and characters of our story for change. We hope that the story will eventually provide a similar relational and learning space for adults and children in our schools/settings.

The story complete?

Most recently, the story has been back to a summer interest group, again with a mix of psychologists with varying levels of prior experience in its creation. It is hoped that after a polish and edit by the current SPG, the story will come back to the whole service in its completeness. Following feedback from this, our story, will hopefully be finalised, and reflective questions firmed up to accompany it to build a reflexive antiracism training package for school staff adopting the story.

Concluding thoughts

A relationship-based, collaborative systemic approach to our psychology (our ethos as a service) led to a working environment where this ambitious project incorporating the *Equality – Everyone's Business* tool and 'The Shimmer' story was possible. A synergy of people, ideas, trust, relationships, and time and an ambition to work truly collaboratively across our EPS and TETC team have led to this, which we have considered pioneering work. A belief in social constructionism, the hope for change, the appetite for personal journeys in recognising and exposing privilege, and a framework for reflecting on growth have been the foundations. There are many relationships, one to one and within groups and teams, that have led to the story being written and which continue to underpin the growth of this story and our wider antiracism agenda. The story project has been created through conversations and the sharing of personal and inspirational narratives and has highlighted the necessary focus on language needed for exploring and shifting embedded views.

The key premise of the suggestion for thinking about a story linked to our antiracism resource was the ambition for wanting people to connect through the story, to empathise with others' lived experience, and maybe to realise when listening is the only way to try to connect with another's experience. It was to also engage with the emotion, the resonance for individuals within their communities, and their personal and shared journeys with White privilege, inequality, oppression, power, and race. In line with our service values, we hoped that the psychological underpinnings offered by a narrative approach based on social constructionism, and the relationship-based approach linked to trauma as explored in the other Nottinghamshire EPS chapter in this book, would offer the grounding needed, recognising the experience of racism as trauma.

We are interpreting social constructionism as an explanation that truths are social in nature; what appears biologically or physically factual is interpreted differently across cultures and historical eras linked to the reasonings of those with social and political power. These social constructions are powerful social facts that impact in legal and cultural ways and on interpersonal relationships. Our *Equality – Everyone's Business* tool determines that '[r]ace needs to be understood not as a biological difference with biological consequences, but as a socially constructed categorisation of people, which has social consequences'.

In terms of the benefits of the metaphorical safe space for containing emotions, for exposing White fragility and White saviourism, for discussing micro-aggressions, allyship, and cultural competency, the journey with 'The Shimmer' has exceeded our expectations. It is difficult to express in print the richness of these conversations, the connection created, the bridge of words across understandings and lack of understandings, a peeling back of barriers in discussion, all voices being heard, everyone really listening. This work has revealed to us the power of developing and sharing a fictional story in order to connect with the lived experience of others and to critically reflect upon our own lived experience. This 'listening, learning, and growth' has shaped the story, created through our relational practice, and the story in equal measure has further aided our relational practice.

It is important to recognise that the relational support and shared learning (including SPG, interest groups, the BEEP, and in supervision) have made it possible for colleagues to be vulnerable and exposed, in different ways, over the last three years. This project has changed the thinking of everyone involved during the course of this journey. We had to slow it all down, and we had to learn that the end product was less important than the relationships involved. The commitment of the people sticking with it has been amazing, and the passing on of the baton and support for each other through changes of story bearers has aided our resilience and determination. This project could not have been achieved in isolation.

We can now acknowledge in the room which group of animals we identify with; we can hear challenge to our personal assumptions through discussion of the thoughts, feelings, experiences, and perspectives of the characters. We can hear voices through the characters to whom, in our daily lives, we may not make the time to listen. There remain limitations to hearing each other and frustrations and hurt, but when we reach such an impasse, we have navigated further than would have been possible without the story as a vehicle to authentically hear one another.

This has been, for us, a most fulfilling, complex, and relational piece of work towards creating change in our EPS and, hopefully, in the future, our schools/settings and services. We need to continue to be alongside one another, having open and compassionate conversations about how we relate with each other in a society that often seems slow to shift. Our best hopes are that the *Equality – Everyone's Business* tool and 'The Shimmer' can help all of us achieve this through the emotional connection brought about by experiencing the magic of fiction, and the links stories created between people, and in opening up conversations, especially the most difficult but essential of conversations. We hope that this can happen even in the most hostile of environments, paving out more compassionate outcomes for children.

We have thought at length about who is being offered the safe space through the metaphor of 'The Shimmer', and undoubtedly, it caters for those nervous of the use of language around racism. It potentially scaffolds the exposure of racism to those who turn away and do not listen ordinarily. Although we may critique whether or not this is necessary, I have been part of group conversations where this story has created a bridge, a tangible bridge of words, between those whose lived experience is racism and those who cannot emotionally feel racism. We wonder if our colonialised language does not provide words and phrases that, in any way, adequately reflect the feeling of racism, and maybe 'The Shimmer' might be a step in the right direction towards exposing this and providing some substitute language to begin more genuine conversations.

In writing this section of the chapter on behalf of myself and my colleagues, I have wondered, together with my supervisor, about my positionality. We concluded that it would be helpful to acknowledge how a White psychologist will never truly capture or understand the experience and feelings of racism. My roots and heritage are not the same as others', especially those of minoritised groups, and I have questioned my suitability to capture our service journey with 'The Shimmer' in light of my relative ignorance. We hope that our story will encourage those of all heritages to critique and to listen in recognising the entrenched nature of racism. 'I won't stop trying to be the person to listen' is the message I hope readers will take from our story.

On a final note, a few of us met recently with a colleague from the TETC team who had read 'The Shimmer' for us. The value of the story in shaping our conversation was quickly apparent, and so valued. We were immediately able to dive into complex, emotive themes through the use of the characters of the farm and woodland animals, and the metaphors such as the shimmer and woodland destruction. We reflected on how to bring optimism to the ending whilst recognising the entrenched misery of racism. The growth of the shimmer was thought to be the most helpful sliver of hope.

Summary box

In our chapter, we attempted to demonstrate how relationship-based practice under-pinned the creative work our service has done around antiracism, and how this would not have been otherwise possible. We hope this inspires others in their relationship-based working and encourages them to see the enormous benefits and how this can lead to the kinds of things we have done in Nottinghamshire. Being brave to stretch ourselves beyond our comfort zones has been important and only possible because we are doing it together. We also hope our chapter inspires others to engage in antiracist practice, both as part of personal journeys and within a team.

For further information, our website has information on both the *Equality – Everyone's Business* tool and the story for change 'The Shimmer', as well as the resources we used to support this work. The frameworks available reflect the approach taken by our service, which promotes connection, and were developed from the ground up, with all members of the service having the opportunity to contribute. This shows how we value giving EPs the time and space to be reflective together about our values and ideas. Our website can be accessed at this address: *https://em-edsupport.org.uk/Page/21130*.

We believe the *Equality – Everyone's Business* tool will be at its most influential when it is embedded in relational working in schools, as it is essential for staff to feel safe enough to have conversations with their colleagues and children on antiracism. In the same way, we intend that the 'story for change' be used through relationships where the adults sharing it feel safe enough to do so authentically and confidently and are prepared for children's responses.

References

Akala. (2018). *Natives: Race and class in the ruins of empire*. Two Roads.

Barnardo's. (2020). *How systemic racism affects young people in the UK*. Blog https://www.barnardos.org.uk/blog/how-systemic-racism-affects-young-people-uk

Brennan, N., Barnes, R., Calnan, M., Corrigan, O., Dieppe, P., & Entwistle, V. (2013). Trust in the healthcare provider – Patient relationship: A systematic mapping review of the evidence base. *International Journal for Quality in Health Care, 25*, 682–688.

Freeman, J., Epston, D., & Lobovits, D. (1997). *Playful approaches to serious problems narrative therapy with children and their families*. WW Norton.

Gaine, C. (2008). Race, Ethnicity and difference versus imagined homogeneity within the European Union. *European Educational Research Journal, 7*(1), 23–38. https://doi.org/10.2304/eerj.2008.7.1.23

Gillborn & Demack. (2018). *Exclusions review 2018.*

Hasson, U. (2016). *What happens in the brain when we hear stories?* Ted Talk https://blog.ted.com/what-happens-in-the-brain-when-we-hear-stories-uri-hasson-at-ted2016/

Hopkins, B. (2012). *The restorative classroom* (p. 44). Speechmark.

Ibrahim, A. M. (2020). Who do i want to be during COVID-19 chart (original author unknown).

Kendi, I. X. (2019). *How to be an antiracist*. One World.

Maslow, A. H. (1943). A theory of human motivation. *Psychological Review, 50*, 370–396.

Nottinghamshire County Council. (2021). *Equality – Everyone's Business – a tool to support the development of anti-racist practice in education settings.* file:///C:/Users/ed4cmw/Downloads/Equality%20-%20Everyone's%20Business%20Toolkit%20(FULL).pdf.

Runnymede Trust. (2020). *Race and racism in secondary schools.* https://www.runnymedetrust.org/publications/race-and-racism-in-secondary-schools

Sunderland, M. (2001). *Using storytelling as a therapeutic resource with children*. Routledge.

White, M., & Epston, D. (1990). *Narrative means to therapeutic ends*. WW Norton.

9 Exploring the relational power of appreciative inquiry

Drawing on previous experiences and diverse perspectives within an Educational Psychology Service to create new ways of working

Natalie Neal, Laura de Cabo Serón, Jayne Manning, Julie Connor, and Emily Williams

Introduction

This chapter is written by a group of educational psychologists (EPs) and aspiring EPs working in an Educational Psychology Service (EPS) covering a local area in the north of England. We work alongside schools, families, and other professionals across education, health, and social services to improve the learning and wellbeing of all children and young people (CYP). This chapter is relevant to anyone trying to work *with* others to instil change within systems and explore what change might feel like as a cooperative act that emerges from the collective participation of all those involved. We offer our experiences of bringing people together and reflect on what was inspiring, rewarding, and at times frustrating in this process. As this chapter will demonstrate, a relational approach can be used across a range of contexts and is applicable for any system/organisation that has strengths and is seeking to make changes.

Our journey started with reflecting together on our service values and the core constructs that we wanted to underpin our work with others. We were keen to work relationally within the process of change and growth, drawing on the idea that 'every interaction is an intervention' (Treisman, 2017). We wanted to engage with others in a way that promoted meaningful partnership and built community connection. To complement this, we wanted to work in a holistic way that moved beyond the individual and took account of the social context to facilitate change. Whereas in the past we might have been drawn to support learning and wellbeing by working individually with CYP, the rise in prevalence of CYP experiencing mental health difficulties means that systemic working can be more impactful.

Our endeavour to work in a more collaborative and contextual way led us to use an appreciative inquiry (AI) process with schools and education services. AI is described as 'the cooperative search for the best in people, their organisations, and the world around them' (MacCoy, 2014, p. 104). It is essentially a tool for facilitating change within a system but offers something different to the traditional problem-solving approach. Rather than focusing on identifying and 'fixing' problems, AI aims to build on the existing strengths of a system, to 'ride the wave' of success, by exploring what is already established and working well, and further developing the positives towards a preferred future. It does this through a five-step process (define, discover, dream, design, and destiny), outlined in Table 9.1.

DOI: 10.4324/9781003451907-9

Table 9.1 Outline of the appreciative inquiry process

Stage	Description
Define	Defining what it is the AI process is seeking to explore.
Discover	Identifying the 'best of' what is and looking at the organisation with the 'appreciative eye'.
Dream	Exploring what 'might be' and sharing information from the discover stage.
Design	Deciding and writing the direction of change. Possibility statements are written as a group as if they have been achieved, which are grounded in examples from the discovery phase.
Destiny	Assigning champions to each possibility statement so that it can continuously be planned to be met, revisited, and evaluated.

AI appealed to us because it offered a way to work with people that could validate their experiences, instil hope, and facilitate empowerment. As practitioners who often support in situations that are complex, where people may understandably experience feelings such as loss of hope and agency, this felt very important. It felt very 'human' in that AI assumes that the people involved are experts in their own contexts and have the capacity to implement change; for our service, we found it comforting to not be positioned as 'the expert' in the process. AI suggests that solutions can be arrived at through constructive and co-constructed conversations, and we liked that our role would be to facilitate change between others. AI emphasises the power of positive questioning to inspire, energise, reimagine, engage possibility, delight, intrigue, and build community (Browne, 2019). At the outset of our AI journey, we were very excited to develop our positive questioning skills, to discover how this might lead to a sense of collective capacity for creative thinking and new ways forward for systems/ organisations.

Throughout this chapter, we present three separate case studies which describe and evaluate how we have used AI across three different organisational contexts. Each case study includes the background context and rationale for using AI, a description of the process, and outcomes and reflections. Pulling these together, we offer broader reflections on using a relational approach, such as AI, to facilitate change. We present an honest account and detail potential barriers that from our experience can arise, and how these might be overcome. It is hoped that our accounts will provide realistic insight into how a relational, solution-focused approach can be adopted to bring about systemic change and ultimately improve outcomes for CYP.

Case study 1: A trainee educational psychologist's reflections on the AI process using Bion's ideas around working in groups as a framework

Background

A senior team member of an outreach team in the local authority, Jen, approached the EPS to do a piece of organisational work. The team included five primary colleagues and six secondary colleagues from the two senior members, an EP and a manager from the local authority.

The team was expanding, and there had been some tensions and a lack of cohesion within the original team in the previous academic year. It was also shared that during the COVID-19 pandemic and virtual working, the team members that worked for primary and secondary children had unintentionally split into two subteams (the team leader of the secondary team was Sarah), and the two subteams were not able to see each other's viewpoint, and this had led to disagreements.

In an initial discussion, Jen shared that she wanted to think about what was currently working well, improve team cohesion, and induct new staff. The team had recently received some positive feedback from an external agency, and this helped me decide that AI was the right approach, as the team had many strengths that could be built on.

Preparation

Emily felt it was important for Jen to decide how she would like the AI process to work. Jen shared she wanted the process to be as interactive as possible with the encouragement of the team working in different groups throughout the morning.

Table 9.2 provides a summary of what each stage of the process involves and how Emily planned to implement it. Timings were allocated to the different stages to ensure we completed the process within the time given (three hours).

Table 9.2 Plan of the AI process

Stage	Summary	How I would conduct this aspect of the model
Define	This part of the model looks at defining what it is the AI process is seeking to explore.	This will be done with Jen initially and then as part of a group discussion.
Discover – 30 minutes, 10-minute break	This is where the group identifies the 'best of' what is and looks at the organisation with the 'appreciative eye'.	I will share some ideas of sample questions that explore 'peak' experience and what the *best of* the organisation is. The group will then break into pairs and interview each other to explore 'peak experiences'. Pairs will then swap to ensure they have chance to speak to different team members. They will write their responses on Post-its (which can then be sorted in the next stage). There will then be a short break of 10 minutes, where I will sort ideas and quotes from interviews into themes.

(Continued)

Table 9.2 (Continued)

Stage	Summary	How I would conduct this aspect of the model
Dream - 20 minutes	This explores what 'might be' and shares the information from the discover stage.	Themes will then be shared with the group. The group will be asked to share what this information tells them about the values of the organisation. The group will consider what *could be* based on the experiences that they have shared. These ideas will be scribed onto a large flip chart paper. From this, the team will be asked to imagine what a new future could be. Visions and values will be shared, and a dream statement will be written as a group.
Design - 30 minutes	This is the stage where the direction of change is decided and directions are written. *Possibility statements* are written as a group as if they have been achieved. These need to be grounded in examples from the discovery phase. In this stage, it is hoped that there is *will in the group* to move towards the possibility statements.	Once the dream statement has been decided, the team will be asked what they need to do to achieve this. They will be asked to write their own possibility statements after sharing some examples. The statements need to be written as if they have been achieved to include some of the 'how' they will happen. The group will vote for what statements they wish to prioritise and plan for.
Destiny - 30 minutes	This part of the cycle allows champions to be assigned to each possibility statement so that it can continuously be planned to be met, revisited, and evaluated.	In this stage, possibility statements will be selected and then formed into an action plan, with an assigned champion and a set of actions that are time-bound.
Source: Adapted from Hammond (2013).		

The team were gathered in a room with a large rectangular table; interestingly, the primary colleagues sat at one side of the table, and the secondary colleagues at the other. During the session, the facilitators stood at the front and 'worked the room'. The mixing of the two subteams was also encouraged in different activities.

Post-it notes and large flip chart paper were used to record each stage of the process and to encourage the team to work interactively and to record their ideas. Each stage of the process had its own large sheet of paper, and this was then secured on the wall around the room so it was visible to be referred back to. At the end of the process, the flip chart paper was photographed and sent as a record to the team.

Reflections on the process

As we began to work through the process, I considered the work of Bion (1961) and his research around working in groups. I decided to use Bion's ideas as a framework to explore and reflect on how the group progressed through the AI process. This is because some aspects of the AI were very productive and positive, where others felt negative and stagnant.

The *work group mentality* is when a group is able to manage tensions and emotions and function effectively (Bion, 1961). By contrast, the *basic assumptions mentality* considers a group that is overcome by negative emotions and, because of this, loses its focus and purpose. This might lead to 'stagnation' (Bion, 1961).

The *discovery* aspect of the process seemed to go well. This is the point where the team were considering the best of what they were currently doing well and exploring examples of this. The room was 'buzzing', and people appeared to be energised and working well together. The group was very positive and productive and could be said to be working in the 'work group mentality'. Around the table, there were engagement, discussions, and positive body language. The team were able to select themes in their work around them being child advocates, working in a child-led way and making a difference to children.

However, as we moved into the *dream stage*, the team appeared to find it hard to identify a dream statement (what might be in the future). When trying to co-write the statement for their future vision, they shared that they were already at the dream stage as they were the best they could be. Because of how they perceived their team to be working, they decided to shift the focus of the dream statement to be around other teams in the local authority (LA). The dream statement was to share the best practise of their team with other teams in the LA. When writing the dream statement, the secondary team leader, Sarah, kept taking the discussion in other directions and away from the task, saying things like, 'We already know how to work in a child-centred way; it's other teams that need to change their ways'. This led the group to take a turn into the *basic assumptions mentality*. It felt as though Sarah had a different agenda and was trying, either consciously or unconsciously, to move the group away from its purpose and to shift the focus onto other teams. Productivity and positivity halted, and the AI process seemed to stop. The only person who was actively engaged at this stage was Sarah; all other team members were quiet, with their body language showing that they felt awkward or unsure.

It became very difficult at this stage to keep the discussion focused and get the AI back on track. I would have liked to be more direct to keep the team focused; however, I was conscious that perhaps it was not my role and that the team should be allowed to have a chance to share their views. I aimed to allow the team members time to share their views and used phrases such as 'I wonder how what you're saying can be linked to the dream' to gently steer them back to the focus.

Once the dream statement had been decided, the group then worked on the possibility statements. The team broke into smaller groups and again were highly productive and focused when writing these statements – they appeared to be back in the *work group mentality* mode, working in an animated way, smiling and chatting. The possibility statements centred on how they might work in a more joined-up way within the authority and encourage more child-centred practice. The group then voted to decide which statement they would create an action plan for as part of the *destiny* stage.

The groups were then given time to think about actions they could do to achieve the possibility statements; this would then form part of a time-bound action plan. In part of the discussion around how this would be achieved, Sarah chose to engage in a discussion with the manager around some frustrations of the outreach team, asking how other teams within the authority could adapt and improve their practice and how they would be held accountable for this. This change of direction took the group back into the *basic assumptions mentality*.

It appeared that Sarah found it hard to read the social cues in the room, and again, everyone became quiet and disengaged. The manager being questioned also appeared to be getting frustrated, and her responses were becoming increasingly short and succinct. Sarah appeared to have good relationships with her team, and I wondered if she saw her role in her team as the spokesperson who had the confidence to challenge the manager and change the focus of the discussions. I also considered if this had been something that had been decided on before the meeting.

We were not able to complete the action plan in the time given. I felt this left the session on less of a positive note due to the challenging nature of the discussions between Sarah and the manager. Furthermore, many of the team members were not involved at this point. I had wanted the team to come away with a set of actions and something tangible from the session. I reflected that I was outcome-focused and that perhaps having a tangible outcome at the end was only one aspect of the AI. It helped me to consider how the power of the AI is in the process and the staff discussion and reflection.

Drawing on my experiences of working in groups, I think most groups swing between being productive and positive and being diverted and negative. A large part of this can be due to the team dynamics. Perhaps having such a marked power imbalance in the staff who attended the AI (between the team and the manager) caused there to be an exaggeration of the *basic assumptions mentality* due to this being a rare opportunity to share views with a senior member of staff. Power dynamics and how they impact on group relationships is something that I will consider going forward into other organisational work. Marked power imbalances within groups may prevent people from saying what they think or using this as a rare opportunity to share frustrations with a more senior member of staff.

From this, I feel knowing team dynamics and taking them into consideration is an important part of the preparation before an AI. Furthermore, discussions around who should be part of the process may help a group stay more focused and productive.

Case study 2: Using AI to facilitate systemic change in the early years

Background

When working with a small early years setting, the manager explained that they wanted to improve how staff were meeting the needs of children who had received diagnoses of autism or who were on the assessment pathway for neurodevelopmental conditions. In discussion with the manager and early years area SENCo who works closely with the setting to support children with special educational needs, we recognised that staff in the setting were already using lots of strategies confidently and successfully in their practice but felt they needed further support to meet the diverse needs of neurodivergent children. We felt this presented a perfect opportunity to use AI to build the confidence of staff, by exploring what they were already doing and what was working well.

The AI took place with all staff who work in the setting at the end of the day during staff meeting time, facilitated by Natalie and the early years area SENCo. The process took just under one and a half hours. Around 40 staff members took part in the session, which brought with it several benefits and challenges. On one hand, the wide variety of experiences enabled a lot of helpful discussion during the session, and it ensured all staff had a good understanding of the changes that were being put in place following the session. On the other hand, it was tricky to facilitate the process, as everybody had such insightful and helpful contributions, making it difficult to make sure we stayed on track in the limited time we had. Despite this, staff embraced the opportunity to share how passionate they were about supporting children with special educational needs and draw on each other's strengths to further their practice.

Reflections on the process

At the beginning of the session, it appeared that the staff members did not seem fully aware of why we were there and were maybe caught off guard, as they were expecting a staff meeting. Maybe they felt uncertain about what to expect from the session and felt anxious about this? It may be that this way of working was unusual for staff, as the wider context of what is expected from early years staff may mean that they are less-involved in collaborative decision-making processes that are reflected in the AI process. We had decided not to explain the model and process of AI to staff before the session, as they may have prepared their answers in advance, potentially hindering meaningful discussion during the session. Instead, we relied on the manager to explain the purpose of the session to staff, which may have led to the misunderstanding. Would this be something to do differently when doing AIs in the future? Probably not, as the initial feelings of trepidation from staff were quickly replaced with in-depth discussion and sharing of experiences.

As we began the define stage, it became apparent that we needed to develop a shared understanding of the term *neurodiversity* before asking staff to discuss their practice related to this. It was here that we realised that only 2 of the 40 staff members had heard of the term and were able to share what they thought it meant. This led to a better understanding of staff members' prior knowledge and experience so the language being used during the process could be adapted to meet them where they were at.

When we moved into the discovery stage, staff worked in small groups of three or four to discuss a 'standout' moment from their practice when working with a neurodivergent child or a group of children. Everyone felt comfortable and safe to share their experiences. The room buzzed with energy as staff talked about their experiences, talking enthusiastically about the children they worked with and asking questions about each other's experiences. What was most surprising when sharing these back with the group was that everyone had different experiences and chose to share different aspects of their practice. Most experiences related to cases where they felt they had made a difference to the child's ability to access the setting's provision. There was a focus on increasing the wellbeing of the children, including examples of helping them build relationships with other children, feeling cared for, feeling accepted, and belonging. It was lovely to see how the relational nature of the AI approach brought staff members together over their shared passion for supporting the wellbeing of children.

A potential issue faced us in the dream stage, as the dream had already been defined by managers of the setting. How could we ensure buy-in of all staff members to make sure they felt included and wanted to take this journey of change alongside their managers? The dream needed to be elaborated and made concrete so staff felt it was achievable. By asking staff to imagine a film crew visiting their setting in a year's time and to describe what they would see/hear/feel that meant they were a neurodiversity-affirming setting, staff members were able to draw on what we had already discussed without prompting and come up with goals that were meaningful for them. Staff members commented that they felt everyone was on the same page about what they wanted to achieve together as a setting and felt closer as a staff team now that they were working towards clear shared goals.

The design stage was trickier; staff members wrote their ideas down but were at times reluctant to share these. The senior managers of the setting took a more leading role during this stage and fell back on things they had asked for previously (i.e. training) or vague things like, 'Get different resources'. We tried to overcome this by sticking peoples' ideas on flip chart paper and getting the group to vote for their priorities, which worked a little but still ended up aligning with what the senior managers had said. The dynamics of the group may have affected collaborative decision-making during this stage, as the people with the power to create change were present. This may be related to the context of the early years industry, where there are different levels of training for different members of staff, and those with what they perceived as 'lower qualifications' did not feel able to take part. I wonder if these perceived power differences in relationships affect the effectiveness of using an AI approach in some settings.

At the end of the session, we were able to create an action plan together that identified who was going to take action to make progress towards the goals we had co-created. Staff shared that they liked having a concrete outcome in the form of the action plan as it made the session meaningful, they knew what role they were going to play, and that things really were going to change.

Case study 3: Using AI to facilitate inclusion of the LGTBIQ+ community in a secondary school

Background

A senior team member and the school SENCo contacted the Educational Psychology Service because they felt they needed further support in meeting the diverse needs of their pupils. After a joint analysis of the common traits of the cases they had raised with the service during that academic year, LGTBIQ+ was identified as an area of support for the setting. The setting was already aware that there was a need for additional support in this topic and had run an LGTBIQ+ after-school club, where a member of staff facilitated projects and discussions around this theme.

It was agreed that including some pupils in this discussion would be important, as their voice needed to be central to our decisions. Therefore, appreciative inquiry was deemed as the right technique to structure the discussion and create a safe space for an open, shared, solution-focused reflection on how to move things forward.

Due to the pandemic, this appreciative inquiry session took place virtually. Each attendee was in a separate room. Two young people attended; one of them was at home, with their parent, and chose to have their camera off, while the other young person joined from school. It is likely that this set-up hindered our attempt to create a cohesive group and anticipate people's emotions, as the non-verbal communication input was reduced and the conversation fluency could feel, at times, paused by the features of video calls (e.g. putting hand up, muting and unmuting microphone, IT issues, etc.). However, these unexpected interruptions were embraced as opportunities to pause and reflect, to process what had been said before, and to prepare a well-reflected response. It is likely that this virtual set-up allowed us to have more control over the discussion and be able to facilitate it in a way that could offer more opportunities for participation from the two young people, as the chat function was available and used throughout the session.

It was a three-hour discussion where everyone had opportunities to contribute, to offer new ideas, to share their personal experiences, to share their hopes and wishes, and there was a real, authentic, and dynamic negotiation of shared meanings, values, and aspirations. I was impressed by how self-reflective school staff were in acknowledging what they did feel were areas for improvement, past mistakes, and opportunities for growth. The two young people felt comfortable enough to share their experiences, be critical with school, and talk about their fears and worries.

Reflections on the process

We started the session with setting ground rules, which we agreed on as to listen actively and with an aim to understand others' views, listen respectfully, allow everyone a chance to speak, work towards a shared understanding, and critique ideas, not people.

During the define stage, the participants agreed they wanted to develop an identity of an inclusive school culture where students feel happy and comfortable and able to share their problems, all staff and students are accepted, there is accessible support for students and staff of all identities and different backgrounds, and experiences of all community members are acknowledged and celebrated.

When we started the discovery stage, we had an open conversation about what progress the school community has made regarding this topic, what they are proud of, and what is currently working well. This discussion would often gravitate towards the school staff members, who seemed to find it easier to identify positives, things they had recently learned, developed, and things they were proud of. There was a strong focus on values, such as being open-minded, inclusive, diverse, and trusting. On reflection, it may be that we did not manage to keep the discussion grounded on actual strategies, tools, and opportunities, and the discussion became significantly abstract. In future AIs, we would potentially split the discussion into different groups and prompt them to structure their discussion by approaching the topic from different perspectives.

It was interesting to see how the dream stage was mostly led by the pupils; they were clear on what they wanted, what the school needed to change, and what they would like their school to look like in the future. This section perhaps sparkled the most interesting, dynamic, and reflecting discussions among the participants, as they were able to discuss how to meet the students' wishes; they were able to shape some of the dreams into aspirations that were specific and targeted, and there was an implicit recognition that there was a number of opportunities for change school could engage with. At this stage, our role was to make sure the discussion was kept on track, that there was a balance of contributions between participants and a general consensus.

When we reached the design stage, everyone was highly engaged in the discussion and positive in their contributions. Everyone seemed to feel safe to contribute and felt energised by the positivity from the previous section. However, it was hard to summarise the whole discussion into manageable, specific actions they could take. This section was heavily facilitated by us, and something that was extremely helpful was being able to go back to some of the key points from the previous sections. The fact that we used a PowerPoint and had shared screen meant that we could easily jump between sections and everything was recorded in a visual way.

As we started the destiny stage, we began to draft the action plan, which included school staff and any volunteering students to offer Q&A sessions to anyone at school, for school staff to access Stonewall training, and for the LGTBIQ+ club to create an information page online to raise awareness of who they are and what they do across school.

On reflection, this was an incredibly positive, valued experience by everyone involved, based on the feedback we received from all parties involved. It reinforced the relational approach schools take to support children, and it put personal connections, respect, and listening at the centre. However, one could argue the outcomes of the session were not suggesting actions transformative enough to meet some of the needs identified previously by school staff and the students involved. It could be argued that the process was probably influenced by everyone's own personal values and views as opposed to the shared values the school community had. To avoid this, in future AIs, we would hold a briefing session prior to implementing the AI, where we could make more explicit our shared values and expected outcomes of the session, including a discussion of what the school could aspire to become.

Conclusion

The three examples highlighted earlier provide recent examples of applying AI in a variety of educational contexts. Bringing these together, several aspects were felt to be prominent. These are detailed in the following.

Genuine strengths

Within each case study, there was a clear sense of hearing the viewpoints and experiences of the attendees. The AI approach provides a framework for sharing reflections and ideas within a group which, in these examples, was seen as a motivating and engaging process. Taking time to step away from the, at times, hectic environment of education settings and services can be hugely valuable not only for planning and team building but also mental wellbeing. This was especially prominent in the post-16 example, where a range of stakeholders was present. Here, being able to have an open and reflective conversation between pupils and staff members was hugely valuable.

Power dynamics

When working in a relational way with organisations, it is important to consider the relationships that exist/co-exist within them. In the examples shared, it was evident that such factors were at play. For instance, in the day nursery example, the management had the overarching say around how the AI approach was conducted, and this led to the rest of the participants being unaware about the process until they joined the activity. This, combined with the power imbalance between managers and employees, may have contributed to some of the difficulties experienced, such as reluctance to share ideas. This pattern could also be seen in the outreach team case study. Here, the voices of the minority, more senior team members took over the focus of session and led it in a particular direction. This power imbalance is perhaps unavoidable, but steps could be taken to minimise its impact. For example, explicitly talking about 'power' and reminding all participants that within the session they hold equal value, agreeing together ways to remain in this neutral state and how to tentatively challenge each other when someone is seen to be domineering. In addition, reflecting with individual members after the AI session about how they saw their role within a group context and gathering any views that they wish to share more widely but had not felt able to at that time could be helpful to ensure perspectives are heard as much as possible.

Context and environment

Environmental factors can also act to facilitate or inhibit the flow of the AI approach. In the post-16 example, the virtual nature of the session was beneficial in allowing a record of discussions and ease of participation; however, some of the non-verbal communication and experience of being physically together were lost. In this example, there were clear positives and drawbacks; therefore, it would be helpful to keep these in mind for planning future sessions, such as confidence in communicating, flexibility offered, and accessibility of the virtual vs. in-person approach. Ultimately, it would be advisable for attendees to choose the methods that best suits their individual needs and agreed aims.

It was reflected within the day nursery example that larger groups can be a challenge for the facilitators and is something to consider. However, within this example, by splitting into smaller groups for the discovery stage of the process, a chance for all to share their views was facilitated. Breaking into smaller groups was also a key success within the virtual school case study.

Contracting

The process of agreeing and contracting the AI approach is also important. From all the examples highlighted earlier, there was a clear rationale to build on what was already working well. However, there felt like a gap between agreeing on using the approach and taking part, to taking ownership of each stage, especially the 'design stage'. This is perhaps a more concrete stage, where possible action is agreed, and relates back to the power dynamics of who can have the final say. Within whose reach is the action, and what are the available options? In the post-16 example, it was reflected that possibilities can also be limited by wider societal views and what we believe and know to be possible. Helpful suggestions to ease these struggles include providing a workshop or training session prior to the main AI session to explore the target topic in more detail, highlighting important aspects to consider from what we already know and what might be possible. Secondly, sharing with the 'leaders' (those who initially contracted the AI approach) the benefits of creative thinking and for them to encourage attendees to be open to possibilities.

Next steps and key learning points

There were some key lessons that we took away from the preceding case studies that we will consider in the future when completing this kind of work.

- Offering pre-training sessions to explore the topic or the nature of the approach in more detail.
- Thinking about what the ground rules need to be, especially for 'leaders'.
- Consideration of the flexibility of the approach to suit the group, including the environment. What would suit all attendees best?
- Thinking about group sizes and practicalities around this.
- Planning for the future with the group. For instance, having a follow-up session several weeks or months later to consider the impact and how their agreed 'destiny' has developed.

Summary box

The experiences we had completing an AI approach led to largely open and reflective spaces for those involved. It was seen that participants were able to think and consider their strengths and possible ways to develop. As a team, we have identified our thoughts on next steps that could be taken to build on the approach when it is applied in our practice, and we encourage you to think about where this type of activity may fit within your current workplace.

You may find the following resources helpful for further information about the strategies described in this chapter:

Cooperider, D., & Whitney, D. (2005). *Appreciative inquiry: A positive revolution in change*. Barrett.

Cooperrider, D. L., Whitney, D. K., & Stavros, J. M. (2003). *Appreciative inquiry handbook: The first in a series of AI workbooks for leaders of change* (Vol. 1). Berrett-Koehler Publishers.

Gray, S., Treacy, J., & Hall, E. (2019). Re-engaging disengaged pupils in physical education: An appreciative inquiry perspective. *Sport, Education and Society, 24*(3), 241-255.

Lovallo, D., & Kahneman, D. (2003). Deluded by success: How optimism undermines executives' decisions. *Harvard Business Review, 51*(6), 56-63.

Preskill, H., & Catsambas, T. (2006). *Reframing evaluation through appreciative inquiry.* Sage Publications Inc.

Whitney, D., & Trosten-Bloom, A. (2003). *The power of appreciative inquiry: A practical guide to positive change.* Berrett-Koehler Publisher.

References

Bion, W. R. (1961). *Experiences in groups and other papers.* Tavistock Publications. [Reprinted London: Routledge, 1989; London: Brunner-Routledge 2001]

Browne, B. (2019, July 10). Bottled magic [Video]. *YouTube.* www.youtube.com/watch?v=1SbZhNw6fMg

Hammond, A. (2013). *The thin book of appreciative inquiry* (3rd ed.). Thin Book Publishing Co.

MacCoy, D. J. (2014). Appreciative inquiry and evaluation – Getting to what works. *Canadian Journal of Program Evaluation, 29*(2), 104-127. https://doi.org/10.3138/cjpe.29.2.104

Treisman, K. (2017). *Working with relational and developmental trauma in children and adolescents.* Routledge.

10 What works to create a supportive relational culture that enhances staff wellbeing?

An appreciative exploration of the organisational factors that enhance the wellbeing of staff working in a special education school

Amy Bamford

Introduction

The mental health agenda

Shortly after I began studying for my educational psychology doctorate in 2017, *Transforming children and young people's mental health provision: a green paper* was published (DoH & DfE, 2017). I was interested to see that 'early intervention' had been identified as playing a central role in reducing the current issues being experienced by children and young people, with schools indicated as key stakeholders.

Special educational needs (SENs), mental health, and wellbeing

I also came across research which suggested that children and young people with special educational needs and disabilities (SEND) are at an increased risk of academic failure, lower peer acceptance than their peers (Pinto et al., 2019), and more likelihood of experiencing mental health problems, such as depression and/or anxiety (Lindsay & Dockrell, 2012; Dickins, 2014). I recognised that this potentially introduced further issues for staff working with the children and young people with SEND, as they are even more likely to come across, and therefore play a role in, early intervention for their mental health needs.

Teacher readiness to support mental health

Due to the nature of their work, staff working in schools engage in regular and frequent (usually daily) interactions with children and young people, more so than most other practitioners, for example, those working in health or social care. Perhaps because of this, the green paper seemed to be affirming that schools were to play a pivotal role in mental health 'early intervention'. Even though I understood why this might make sense, it also struck me that school staff were being asked to play a key supportive role in the lives of children and young people in addition to their other responsibilities.

As I began to research this issue, I came across literature exploring the views of staff working in schools which suggested that they can feel burdened by children and young people's

DOI: 10.4324/9781003451907-10

mental health needs; for example, they experience a lack of confidence managing mental health-related needs within the classroom, have difficulty identifying pupils with mental health needs that may require intervention, and find it uncomfortable discussing mental or emotional health with students compared to other health topics (Kidger et al., 2009). In addition, there were concerns, raised particularly by teaching staff, with regard to the 'changing nature of their responsibilities' in relation to pupil mental health and worry about potentially negative implications for their sense of job satisfaction and their own wellbeing (Rothï et al., 2008, p. 1,227).

Staff mental health and wellbeing

Taking this into account, it was not surprising to read that as the pressures of the teaching role increase, in the academic year 2021, three-quarters of teaching staff reported experiences of stress, and just over three-quarters reportedly experienced mental health symptoms which they identified as being related to their work (Teacher Wellbeing Index, 2022). Similarly, a YouGov TeacherTrack survey (also carried out in 2021) indicated that one in two teachers reports having suffered at least one characteristic associated with work-related 'burnout', something which occurs as a result of sustained stress that never subsides. When defining *teacher burnout*, Maslach and Jackson (1981) identified three common features:

- *Emotional exhaustion*. When the teacher feels that they have no more left to give others on an emotional or psychological level.
- *Depersonalisation*. When the teacher experiences psychological detachment and social distancing from both their personal and professional lives.
- *Reduced personal accomplishment*. When the teacher feels that they are no longer effective in their professional responsibility.

It was indicated that just under half of teachers had experienced all the components associated with 'burnout' since the start of that academic year (2021).

Impact of burnout

Putting aside the physical and emotional impact of their role on teachers, research exploring the views of teachers in specialist SEND settings identified that those experiencing burnout often perceive themselves to be working for the benefit of the children and young people they are supporting (Farber, 2000). This seems to contrast with findings within the literature which indicate that generally when a teacher experiences burnout, students are more likely to be disruptive, struggle more socially and emotionally, and achieve their support plan targets less frequently (Jennings & Greenberg, 2009; Ruble & McGrew, 2013; Wong et al., 2017).

Perhaps even more worrying, within the Teacher Wellbeing Index (2022), it was suggested that over half the respondents have considered leaving the profession. In other words, the people being identified as playing a pivotal role in supporting the mental health of children and young people seem to be experiencing a mental health crisis themselves, to the point that they feel they are no longer able to carry out their job.

A shift in focus – from 'burnout' to 'wellbeing'

Whilst exploring the research in this area, I noted that 'wellbeing, or lack of it, is strongly related to work (dis)stress' (Bingham & Bubb, 2017, p. 175) and, subsequently, burnout. This made me wonder whether, instead of focusing on the stress, burnout, and the mental health issues of teaching staff, we should instead be exploring how we might better support their wellbeing.

Conceptualisation

Here is where I stumbled across difficulties, as conceptualising wellbeing was more difficult than anticipated. Eventually, I came across the following conceptualisation relating to schools:

> Wellbeing expresses a positive emotional state, which is the result of harmony between the sum of specific environmental factors on the one hand and the personal needs and expectations of teachers on the other hand.
>
> (Aelterman et al., 2007, p. 286)

As a trainee educational psychologist (TEP) thinking about my doctoral research, this conceptualisation felt fitting, as I was keen to explore the areas in which I felt I might be able to have the most influence within my role as a future educational psychologist. Whilst I may not be able to have much impact on factors outside of the school setting related to individual and/or personal circumstances, I might have more opportunity, hopefully, to influence systems within a school. Therefore, it seemed appropriate to explore how organisational factors within a school could be conducive to enhancing staff wellbeing, which prompted me to formulate the following research question:

> What organisational factors enhance the wellbeing of staff working in a special education school?

I particularly wanted to consider staff wellbeing in specialist settings because of the impact of the additional needs of the children and young people on their mental health and wellbeing and, therefore, the additional pressures that may be faced by staff working within these settings.

My aims

When planning the project, I decided that my aims were twofold:

1. To identify organisational factors that may enhance the wellbeing of staff working in a specialist school setting.
2. To facilitate a culture shift within the school to enhance staff wellbeing beyond the containment of the overarching project.

As well as carrying out my research project, I was keen to make an impact on those taking part.

Action research and appreciative inquiry

I hoped that an action research project, a research method that aims to simultaneously investigate and solve an issue, would both support the development of my findings as well as produce change within the setting.

At the time I decided to carry out my research, I was on placement in a local-authority Educational Psychology Service (EPS). When I discussed my project with some of my colleagues, I discovered that one special school in the area was taking part in a 'wellbeing award', with support from the service. It was suggested that this project may complement, and enhance, the work already taking place within the setting. Thankfully, in a meeting a few weeks later, the head teacher of the school agreed. After meeting with the head teacher to discuss the project facilitation within the school, I introduced the project to the whole staff team. On the basis of this discussion, ten members of staff consisting of both teachers and teaching assistant showed an interest in taking part.

I facilitated the project through a series of three focus groups involving the same people. The structure of each session was informed by appreciative inquiry (Hammond, 2013). I felt that appreciative inquiry would offer a way of considering organisational change by focusing on identifying, and reflecting on, doing more of what is already working. Appreciative inquiry would offer a hopeful and participative learning process in which the staff involved might engage in identifying, and thereby encourage, supportive practice across the setting (see Figure 10.1 for an outline of the process).

My intention was that by structuring the research through appreciative inquiry, I could address both aims of the project: generate findings as well as create the potential for organisational change. It would afford me the opportunity to encourage the group to focus on the core strengths of the organisation, then draw upon these to reshape the future for the setting.

This followed the process of appreciative inquiry (define, discover, dream, design, and deliver/destiny) as described by Hammond (2013). Please note, this was broken down into separate sessions due to the time limitations we had for each session. It could be completed across a series of full days.

Following my facilitation of these sessions, I decided to adapt my approach. For my written project, only the second focus group session was audio-recorded (and later transcribed), because it was the discussion within this session that focused on the organisational factors that may enhance the wellbeing of staff working within the setting, which encompassed my research question. The other focus group sessions moved on to how this information could be built upon within the setting to support staff wellbeing moving forwards.

Themes

As I was transcribing the second focus group discussion, I began to notice themes. Using a process of reflexive thematic analysis (Braun & Clarke, 2006, 2013), the following five themes were identified, and then developed:

- Leadership
- Having a shared goal and understanding
- Supportive structures being in place

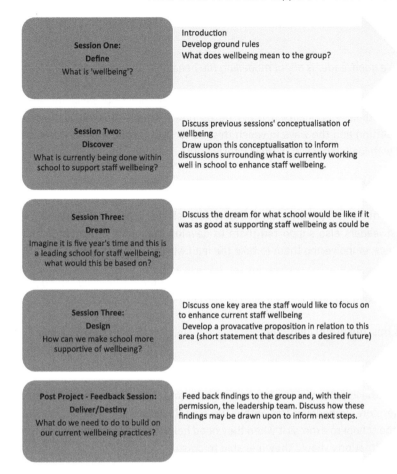

Figure 10.1 The appreciative inquiry process followed within my project.

- Staff feeling supported
- A person-centred approach

Each of these is explored in what follow.

Leadership

Within the group, it was discussed how school leaders play a pivotal role in creating a positive climate, conducive to staff wellbeing. The significant role of school leaders in defining and sustaining a school's culture was explored, with a central concept being that leadership was about influence rather than authority:

> *'It's the little things . . . yes, of course [they] have to lead . . . but they're also very willing.'*

Linked with this, making the values of the organisation visible to all staff whilst also showing how the wider vision may be realised and fulfilled was perceived to be a key role of leadership. In particular, the group identified the importance of modelling, which has also been suggested as a characteristic widely observed of leaders of 'great schools' (Brighouse, 2007):

> '[B]eing a good leader is about modelling the behaviour that you want your team to have.'

I perceived that another important element of the establishment of wellbeing amongst staff by leaders was their relationality. In other words, how relatable they felt to the staff working within that setting and the ways in which this led to staff feeling able to express and share their views with leadership within their interactions:

> 'I've never had any worries about going to either of them.'

An aspect of this was that the staff felt able to seek the support of leadership in difficult times, whilst leaders also supported them to develop their own competence and sense of self-confidence, empowering them to take the lead within such situations:

> 'I've said to SMT in the past . . . this works well with them [the child/young person], and they will take it on board.'

Building on this, the group identified:

> '[T]here's no room for ego in this kind of job.'

This indicates the importance of leaders demonstrating a relational approach within the setting and therefore embedding this within the overall culture and ethos. This enables staff working in the school to express it when they need help, whilst also empowering them to take a lead within situations should they feel able to do so.

Having a shared goal and understanding

> 'I don't think you can work here if you don't get it.'

Within the discussion, the group explained how everyone working within the setting appeared to have a shared goal and/or understanding of their roles. Whilst it is possible that this stemmed from the leadership team making the values of the organisation visible to all, it also seemed that the staff themselves felt that their own personal values were often key components. Interestingly, within the literature (see Emery & Vandenberg, 2010), it has been indicated that personal values are an essential component of overall job satisfaction, and therefore wellbeing.

Perhaps because of these shared values, one of the key sources of enjoyment and motivation for staff working in the school were the relationships they built with the children and young people they were working alongside:

> '[M]y high point really was just around the progress that she made . . . seeing the tiny little steps that she sort of made that were just fantastic.'

Garwood et al. (2018) highlighted that when staff in schools redefine 'student success', they are less likely to experience burnout but are more likely to experience wellbeing. Even more interesting for me was the clear focus within the groups on the impact upon staff of the relationships and connections that they had built with the children and young people they were working alongside, and the powerful difference that this has had on their own experiences within school:

> '[M]y goodness, I've made a difference to her, and she's made a difference to me. . . . [W]e'd made a connection.'

Supportive structures being in place

Formal structures

As the group members represented various roles within the setting, it was identified that formal structures, such as staff briefings, had been adapted to ensure that all staff within the school were able to access them within their contracted hours:

> '[I]t's nice to be included.'

This reflects the thoughts of Roffey (2012), who suggested that in order for staff to thrive in their roles, they need to feel, and be, included.

Alongside this, the staff shared how the day had been adapted so that they had been given time at both the start and end to engage in class meetings. The group suggested:

> '[T]hat was invaluable . . . the time.'

This enabled them to prepare themselves for the day, whilst also providing them with time and space for professional learning, within which the group shared that there was a

> 'collective pooling of knowledge and skill.'

This time supported the staff to discuss any problems or issues that had arisen within their practice, as well as giving them the chance to develop a sense of competency within their roles. They were able to problem-solve together within a space that had been specifically developed for this to happen. Overall, I thought that this appeared to help improve their work happiness, or wellbeing, as their feelings of self-efficacy were enhanced through their growth and development during discussions with others.

Informal structures

In addition to the formal structures enhancing relational culture and values within the school, boosting in the staff a sense of competency by providing agency and opportunities for personal growth, they also identified the importance of developing their own 'informal structures' for support. The group suggested that often, when they were experiencing challenges within their everyday roles, they would draw upon the knowledge and expertise of staff who were not necessarily working alongside them in their class or groups:

> *'[I]f you're struggling with something . . . go and ask somebody else and they've got a different look on it.'*

This enabled the staff to be open to, and access, an alternative viewpoint, for example, from someone who may have knowledge and expertise within a particular curriculum area or who may be able to offer an 'outsiders' view, thereby encouraging reflexivity. At the same time, I felt that this suggested the staff were supporting each other to experience feelings of personal accomplishment within their roles, which might, again, reduce feelings of burnout.

The group also spoke positively about their understanding of emotional literacy, which had initially been a focus to enhance the support offered to the children and young people, and how this had supported them too, as a wider staff team:

> *'[W]e're very good at noticing when each other becomes emotionally dysregulated . . . which really helps.'*

I perceived that this suggested that staff experiencing better wellbeing were also able to demonstrate higher levels of emotional intelligence, which enabled them to more effectively manage some of the demanding emotional situations that can arise when working closely with children and young people with additional needs in schools. This is supported by the literature, which indicates that when teachers feel supported by the school within which they work, the greater their feeling of personal accomplishment within their role, and therefore sense of wellbeing (Robinson et al., 2019).

Staff feeling supported

Within the group, it was apparent that feeling supported within the setting was a key component of wellbeing. In particular, they identified the lack of understanding of those who did not work within the setting:

> *'[I]f you speak to anyone outside of school . . . they're horrified.'*

Ultimately, this seemed to mean that professional working relationships with other staff members, as well as external practitioners, provided key networks of emotional support that both promoted and enhanced the wellbeing of the staff within the setting.

> *'[W]e've got others to lean on; we're not on our own.'*

Interestingly, Boujut et al. (2016) identified that these relationships are often pivotal to wellbeing, as staff identify that support from friends outside of the work environment is viewed as less important than support from practitioners within the organisation. The group also identified that during those times they were struggling, they had felt able to express themselves openly and honestly to other members of staff without judgement being made. Instead, support was offered:

> '[I]f you're sat in the corner, having a little cry or just a little rant . . . there's always that support.'

Sadly, in the Teacher Wellbeing Index (2022), it is reported that more than half of the teachers who responded lack the confidence to disclose unmanageable stress or mental health issues to their employer. However, as the problem persists, their mental health and wellbeing may well deteriorate further. It could be that creating an environment within which staff feel able to express themselves in this way helps promote a sense of positive mental health, as well as increase their sense of competency, as problem-solving is able to take place more quickly and supportively.

A person-centred approach

Webb et al. (2009) suggested that when head teachers describe themselves as 'people-centred' rather than 'task-centred', they are often focused upon both the wellbeing, development, and job satisfaction of staff working in the school, as well as the that of the pupils.

The group shared how within their own setting

> 'the way [they] talk to each other is nurturing, and the way [they] deal with people is nurturing.'

It appeared that this approach involved the development of a culture and ethos within the setting conducive to a high sense of care amongst all staff, both towards each other as well as towards parents and the children and young people in their care.

The group shared the importance of focusing on the wellbeing of individuals and of opportunities for reflection within their practice to ensure that they were able to do so effectively. Adopting these approaches made it apparent that the staff shared a central goal: providing the best support possible for the children and young people they were working alongside. This led to one suggestion that, following any difficulties with the young people, rather than focus on what went wrong, the staff would adopt the mindset of

> 'how can that be different . . . how can I change it . . . how can I make it better?'

In other words, how could they learn from and enhance their own practice to improve the overall outcomes for the young person? It was affirmed within the group that this was not just something that had magically happened within the setting but instead stemmed from the relational culture and ethos that had been established within the school, first by leadership, closely followed by the rest of the staff team:

> '[T]hat is a tone that is set from the top.'

Conclusion

Within the Teacher Wellbeing Index (2022), it is indicated that almost half the teachers who responded feel their organisations do not support employees well who have mental health and wellbeing problems. Sadly, this may lead to further implications across education for teaching staff who may feel unable to carry out their roles or leave the profession entirely to pursue alternative careers.

Despite this, I felt that my research provided a source of reflection, suggesting that the picture is not all bleak. Instead, through the implementation of simple, low- to no-cost relational approaches within settings, we may, in fact, be able to support, and even enhance, staff wellbeing across schools, resulting in better outcomes, not only for the staff, but also for the children and young people they are working alongside.

A common theme across my research was the importance of the role of leadership. Whilst I recognise that leadership was a theme of its own within this research, I think it is important to acknowledge the underpinnings of leadership across the other themes, both in terms of the establishment of a relational culture and ethos within the setting as well as the role played by the creation of specific systems and/or structures conducive to supporting staff wellbeing. Within this particular school, it was acknowledged by the group that leaders making small adaptations to the school day helped the staff feel valued and included as members of the team. In addition, there was recognition that this led to better communication, as all the staff were able to receive the same message first-hand rather than have to hear it from someone else. It was also apparent that the relational and trusting approach adopted by the leadership team across the school enabled the staff to have increased confidence within their roles, which, in turn, made individuals feel secure enough to be able to ask for help when needed and provided them with the agency to take responsibility for resolving issues if this was felt possible.

A further theme was the importance of the development of a supportive culture shared by staff across the school. This involved their ability to work collaboratively, openly, and honestly with each other. This included recognising when an individual might need further help and/or support, as well as providing empowering opportunities to engage in group problem-solving. By establishing this culture across the setting, it is apparent that when faced with a problem, staff working in the school felt able to reflect and explore their thoughts and feelings with other members of the wider team, increasing their sense of self-efficacy whilst also enabling them to develop and grow.

Although it has to be acknowledged that each of these themes was specific to this particular setting, my view is that they provide a source of reflection for all schools and settings about what might constitute a relationally based culture that is supportive of staff wellbeing and, in turn, the wellbeing of children and young people. I would recommend an appreciative inquiry approach being adopted by schools to enable staff participation in the identification of what is working well within the setting when it comes to staff wellbeing and how this might be built upon. As I found within my research, this simple approach not only generates rich findings but also provides the potential for staff agency, organisational activity, and growth, laying the foundation for an action plan to be co-developed and implemented across the whole school. Provocative propositions can be generated that can then be regularly reviewed by all the staff.

Linking back to the relational nature of this book, I find it fascinating that although focus of my research was exploring the organisational factors that enhance staff wellbeing, the themes identified were, in the main, relational. Wellbeing may not be something where it is possible to simply place a framework around. Rather, it is something we can seek to build within schools by creating the culture, space, and time for staff to feel valued, listened to, and heard within their relationships with each other, which is then modelled with the children and young people, affording the opportunity for shared problem-solving and resulting in a heightened sense of empowerment and confidence.

Summary

In this chapter, I discussed my doctoral research, which sought to explore the organisational factors which may enhance the wellbeing of staff working within a specialist educational setting.

Within the project, appreciative inquiry was drawn upon to both explore the organisational factors as well as facilitate change beyond the containment of the overarching project. Thematic analysis was then used to analyse the data, from which five factors were identified which contribute to enhancing staff wellbeing: leadership, shared understanding, supportive structures, feeling supported, and adopting a person-centred approach.

Finally, the interplay between these factors was explored, and suggestions made for how each factor might be drawn upon to support schools in moving towards a culture of wellbeing for staff and, as a result, the children and young people they work alongside.

References

Aelterman, A., Engels, N., Van Petegem, K., & Pierre Verhaeghe, J. (2007). The well-being of teachers in Flanders: The importance of a supportive school culture. *Educational Studies, 33*(3), 285–297. https://doi.org/10.1080/03055690701423085

Bingham, D. M., & Bubb, S. (2017). Leadership for wellbeing. In P. Earley & T. Greany (Eds.), *School leadership and education system reform*. Bloomsbury.

Boujut, E., Dean, A., Grouselle, A., & Cappe, E. (2016). Comparative study of teachers in regular schools and teachers in specialized schools in France, working with students with an autism spectrum disorder: Stress, social support, coping strategies and burnout. *Journal of Autism and Developmental Disorders, 46*(9), 2874–2889.

Braun, V., & Clarke, V. (2006). Using thematic analysis in psychology. *Qualitative Research in Psychology, 3*(2), 77–101.

Braun, V., & Clarke, V. (2013). *Successful qualitative research: A practical guide for beginners*. Sage.

Brighouse, T. (2007). *How successful headteachers survive and thrive: Four phases of headship, five uses of time, six essential tasks and seven ways to hold on to your sanity*. R M Education.

Department for Education. (2018). *Mental health in schools*. https://assets.publishing.service.gov.uk/media/625ee6148fa8f54a8bb65ba9/Mental_health_and_behaviour_in_schools.pdf

Department of Health and Social Care and Department for Education (DOF & DfE). (2017). *Transforming children and young people's mental health provision: A green paper*. www.gov.uk/government/consultations/transforming-children-and-young-peoples-mental-health-provision-a-green-paper

Dickins, M. (2014). *A to Z of inclusion in early childhood*. Open University Press.

Education Support. (2022). *Teacher wellbeing index*.

Emery, D. W., & Vandenberg, B. (2010). Special education teacher burnout and ACT. *International Journal of Special Education, 25*(3), 119-131.

Farber, B. A. (2000). Treatment strategies for different types of teacher burnout. *Journal of Clinical Psychology, 56*(5), 675-689.

Garwood, J. D., Werts, M. G., Varghese, C., & Gosey, L. (2018). Mixed-methods analysis of rural special educators' role stressors, behavior management, and burnout. *Rural Special Education Quarterly, 37*(1), 30-43. https://doi.org/10.1177/8756870517745270

Hammond, S. A. (2013). *The thin book of appreciative inquiry* (2nd ed.). Thin Book Publishing.

Jennings, P. A., & Greenberg, M. T. (2009). The prosocial classroom: Teacher social and emotional competence in relation to student and classroom outcomes. *Review of Educational Research, 79*(1), 491-525. https://doi.org/10.3102/0034654308325693

Kidger, J., Donovan, J. L., Biddle, L., Campbell, R., & Gunnell, D. (2009). Supporting adolescent emotional health in schools: A mixed methods study of student and staff views in England. *BMC Public Health, 9*, 403. https://doi.org/10.1186/1471-2458-9-403

Lindsay, G., & Dockrell, J. (2012). *The relationship between speech, language and communication needs (SLCN) and behavioural, emotional and social difficulties*. Department for Education.

Maslach, C., & Jackson, S. E. (1981). The measurement of experienced burnout. *Journal of Organizational Behavior, 2*(2), 99-113.

Pinto, C., Baines, E. M., & Bakopolou, I. (2019). The peer relations of pupils with special educational needs in mainstream primary schools: The importance of meaningful contact and interaction with peers. *British Journal of Educational Psychology, 89*, 818-837.

Robinson, O. P., Bridges, S. A., Rollins, L. H., & Schumacker, R. E. (2019). A study of the relation between special education burnout and job satisfaction. *Journal of Research in Special Educational Needs*. Advance online publication. https://doi.org/10.1111/1471-3802.12448

Roffey, S. (2012). *Positive relationships evidence based practice across the world*. Springer.

Rothï, D. M., Leavey, G., & Best, R. (2008). On the front-line: Teachers as active observers of pupils' mental health. *Teaching and Teacher Education, 24*(5), 1217-1231.

Ruble, L., & McGrew, J. (2013). Teacher and child predictors of achieving IEP goals of children with autism. *Journal of Autism and Developmental Disorders, 43*(12), 2748-2763. https://doi.org/10.1007/s10803013-1884-x

Webb, R., Vulliamy, G., Sarja, A., Hämäläinen, S., & Poikonen, P. L. (2009). Professional learning communities and teacher wellbeing? A comparative analysis of primary schools in England and Finland. *Oxford Review of Education, 35*(3), 405-422. https://doi.org/10.1080/03054980902935008

Wong, V. W., Ruble, L. A., Yu, Y., & McGrew, J. H. (2017). Too stressed to teach? Teaching quality, student engagement, and IEP outcomes. *Exceptional Children, 83*(4), 412-427. https://doi.org/10.1177/0014402917690729

11 'It's all about relationships'

Staff perceptions of Building Relational Schools (BRS)

Kate Taylor and Mary Scorer

Introduction

This chapter introduces Nottinghamshire's Building Relational Schools (BRS) project and reflects upon the relational-based practice that has been celebrated with our services, schools, and education settings.

The work draws upon what is essentially a relational act between local authority services, schools/settings, and ultimately, families, children, and communities. The golden threads woven throughout have been listening, reflection, learning, genuine collaboration, co-production, change, the power of language, and the importance and challenge of power redistribution (Suarez-Balcazar et al., 2019).

In constructing the chapter, we have become acutely aware of our own values of partnership-working and collaboration, which have penetrated throughout. The project has been about working with staff in education settings and exploring their strengths, their priorities, and how they think about relationships, whilst also experiencing these relationships within the sessions, with each other, and with educational psychologists (EPs).

In the spirit of collaboration, we have worked with those involved to think, as practitioners, how they would like the chapter to be organised so that it would be most helpful to staff in other education settings. The structure has honoured what they told us, and so the chapter is presented as themes, with illustrative quotes and the staff's key reflections and learning. We have also added our own personal reflections following each of the main themes.

Our shared hope is that the examples in this chapter are pertinent to, and practical for, other schools, education settings, and services. Our wish is that readers will reflect on their own good practice in these areas and potentially take away some of the learning to apply to their own contexts. We will therefore conclude the chapter with a series of reflective questions and signposts to resources.

Our story: Introducing our Building Relational Schools project

Increased interest in attachment theory (Bowlby, 1969) and the experiences of trauma and 'traumatic responses' (Asmussen et al., 2020) over the past decade have led to the development of a number of interventions in schools, alongside multiple publications (for example, Geddes, 200 6; Marvin et al., 2002; National Collaborating Centre for Mental Health (UK),

DOI: 10.4324/9781003451907-11

2015; Van Der Kolk, 2014). Many of these have focused on supporting adults to develop their knowledge and understanding of these concepts and come to a more attuned response to the children they work with (Bombèr, 2007; Bombèr et al., 2020; Bryson & Siegel, 2012; Hughes & Golding, 2012; Perry & Szalavitz, 2017; Treisman, 2017; Siegel, 2020).

Over the last five years, Nottinghamshire's Virtual School (VS), who work with education settings to meet the needs of children who are in care, were previously in care, and have a social worker, and the Educational Psychology Service (EPS) have worked in partnership with schools and education settings to develop the 'Building Relational Schools: Becoming Trauma Informed and Attachment Aware' (BRS) project. In this chapter, we will briefly describe BRS and present reflections from our schools and settings. We will also consider the profound journey that we, as individuals in our EPS, have been on, and continue to be on, as we work in collaboration alongside our schools/settings. What has become crystalised throughout our ongoing reflections is that the content of the project is inextricably linked to the experience of the relational interactions within the space created by the training sessions. We will return to these reflections throughout the chapter.

When we were looking to implement this project, our staff in schools were keen that we demystify the concepts and the psychology behind them. They wanted to ensure we make it accessible and translatable into the working world of education.

- What do we mean by *attachment* and *attachment awareness* in education?

The concept of 'attachment' was first conceived by Bowlby (1969) and has been used (Oshri et al., 2015; Parker et al., 2016; Verschueren & Koomen, 2012) and critiqued (Harlow, 2021; Thompson et al., 2022) as a framework within education (Bombèr, 2007; Geddes, 2017):

> Attachment is the emotional bond that forms between infant and caregiver, and it is the means by which the helpless infant gets primary needs met. It then becomes an engine of subsequent social, emotional, and cognitive development. The early social experience of the infant stimulates growth of the brain and can have an enduring influence on the ability to form stable relationships with others.
>
> (Psychology Today, 2023)

The first day of BRS training introduces the idea of attachment as the process by which new-born children begin, and continue to develop, a close bond with their carers and, in doing so, learn how to regulate their own feelings, relationships, and behaviour.

What has become clear in doing this work is that by reflecting on the concept of attachment and what this means in the classroom, staff are struck by the central importance of relationships in education. They begin to understand good relational-based practice grounded in attachment and how to respond to potentially unmet attachment needs (Attachment Lead Network, 2023).

- What do we mean by *trauma* and *trauma-informed practice* in education?

Trauma literally means 'to wound'. There are many definitions of *trauma* woven throughout the literature. The definition that that many educationalists (Gov, 2022) are agreeing on describes trauma as

[a]n event, series of events, or set of circumstances that is experienced by an individual as physically or emotionally harmful or threatening and that has lasting adverse effects on the individual's functioning and wellbeing.

(SAMHSA, 2019)

Trauma-informed practice has gained momentum over the last few years. It aims to increase staff awareness on the potential for trauma to negatively impact on individuals and communities in their ability to feel safe or develop trusting relationships. By understanding the concept of trauma, staff are able to reflect on how experiences of trauma and traumatic responses impact on children's, and adults', learning and behaviour (Scotland Gov, 2021).

The more healthy relationships a child has, the more likely they will recover from trauma and thrive. Relationships are the agents of change and the most powerful therapy is human love.

(Perry & Szalavitz, 2017, p. 85)

Education staff have told us that by understanding these concepts, they are able to think about how they might use this knowledge in the context of their individual settings. Many local authorities have engaged in different models of building attachment awareness and trauma-informed practice with their schools. They each aim to ameliorate the effects of trauma and unmet attachment needs for children through relationships, compassion, attunement, and the way they respond to children (Dingwall & Sebba, 2018; Fancourt & Sebba, 2018; Harrison, 2022; Hyde-Dryden et al., 2022; Parker, 2022; Rose et al., 2019b).

BRS recognises that investing in relationships is vital for adaptation and recovery from trauma and unmet attachment needs (Herman, 2015; Treisman, 2021). Relational-based practice is therefore central to this project. Nottinghamshire's development of BRS builds on the original work led by Bath Spa University and lessons learned through national research (Dingwall & Sebba, 2018; Fancourt & Sebba, 2018; Harrison, 2022; Hyde-Dryden et al., 2022; Parker, 2022; Rose et al., 2019a). This research highlighted a number of factors to support the successful implementation of relational-based practice, including whole-school approach (all staff aware of this work), continuity in engagement (the need for follow-up sessions), use of language and vocabulary (e.g. behaviour as distress), direct pupil involvement, trust in staff (the development of a safe and trusted adult in schools), support for staff (supervision models), and complementary approaches (emotional literacy, timeout, spaces). These elements were all incorporated into the training model of Nottinghamshire's BRS.

Nottinghamshire's current model of BRS has been through a series of iterations, following ongoing cycles of reflections and feedback with schools/settings. Previous training evaluations have highlighted that schools/settings were seeking:

1. Permission to prioritise relationships
2. Collaborative learning opportunities: reflection, discussion, shared knowledge
3. Time to reflect on behaviour policy paradigms
4. Consideration of implementation into individual school contexts

As a result, the content and style of delivery became co-produced by our schools/settings, for our schools/settings. At the time of writing this chapter, our BRS project consists of three days of training. On day 1, a rich picture methodology (Checkland, 1989) is employed to explore constructs of 'attachment' and 'trauma', which encourages open discussion and a shared understanding of these psychological concepts. The second day explores behaviour and distress and encourages the group to consider these though a trauma-informed and attachment-aware lens. The third day introduces action research (TES, 2023). The action research involves schools/settings applying their learning from the previous days of training and considering their reflections on their current practice to inform a plan to implement relational practice in the context of their individual school/setting (Structural Learning, 2021). This is followed by termly group supervision sessions with an EP.

What has become clear in this project is the conscious repositioning (Foucault, 1971) of the role of EPs as trainers, from experts giving information to collaborators, facilitators, and learners. One of our reflections as psychologists and trainers in this project is that this respectful, inclusive, and compassionate interaction itself is relational. It has forged even stronger connections between EPs and education staff and has enhanced the conversations that staff have felt safe to have, for example, talking about their own emotions, relationships, and vulnerabilities.

Staff from primary schools, secondary schools, special schools, alternative provisions, and post-16 colleges/providers across Nottinghamshire have all been involved in BRS and have contributed to the evaluation of the project, and hence the emerging themes. At the time of writing, we have been contacted by our early years settings to explore a similar project. The early years advisory teachers had heard about the BRS project through their interactions with staff in the Virtual School (VS). VS staff commented on the successes that they had witnessed in the schools they worked in when observing the responses of staff when supporting children in distress. They seemed able to respond calmly and safely. VS staff reflected on their belief that private and voluntary settings do not necessarily receive relational-based training and the staff do not always have frameworks for responding to children's emotions and behaviours. It felt worthwhile to invest in a relationship with early years settings and explore early relational-based support and intervention for children before they reach statutory school age.

Reflexivity: Recognising ourselves within this work

Throughout BRS, we have actively co-constructed and re-constructed the content and delivery of this project with the staff in schools/settings. It has felt important to us to value what is important to them and re-distribute power and expertise so we could authentically collaborate. However, we have never stood apart from this work in terms of the values and beliefs that we bring from our EPS and as individual EPs. We believe that we must make clear our investment in, and our human and potential emotional response to, the project. As such, it feels necessary to examine these beliefs, judgements, and practices so we can explore how they may have influenced BRS, and we can acknowledge and own any potential biases (Willig, 2013). We will address some of this in this section and follow up each of the main four themes with our personal EP reflections.

Nottinghamshire EPS arranges its ideas and ways of working into a framework of applied psychology, called collaborative educational psychology (CEP). This is a collaborative, consultative model of service delivery designed to put psychology into practice. This model of service delivery draws upon a number of psychological frameworks, including narrative psychology (White & Epston, 1990), personal construct psychology (Kelly, 1955), systems theory (Bronfenbrenner, 1979), symbolic interactionism (Mead, 1934), and positive psychology (Boniwell, 2006).

The EPS aligns with social constructionism (Berger & Luckmann, 1966), which holds the view that reality is constructed in interaction, through language. This is particularly relevant with respect to labelling and how this relates to the dominant perception about problems being located within child and the associated deficit discourse. Throughout BRS, the constructs of 'relationships,' 'attachment', and 'trauma' were defined and re-defined using psychological definitions alongside individuals' experiences and constructs.

As the education staff reflect on what has been important for them and what this means in practice, we will also offer EP reflections and grapple with our own reactions to these. Perhaps one of the fundamental reflections for us is that this has never been about imparting psychological knowledge onto education staff. As EPs, we have never stood outside of this project, and through the relationships, trust, care, intimacy, discussions, interactions, and shared knowledge, we have become part of it.

Reflections from our Nottinghamshire schools/settings

There are multiple-feedback mechanisms embedded in BRS, from training evaluations, audits, and evaluations to ongoing feedback and reflections in supervision. These have been important for continuously exploring the concepts, ideas, and cycles of learning implementation with the staff. It has been through this feedback that education staff have shaped the BRS project in both content and delivery.

We were keen to ask school/setting staff for feedback relevant to what they may wish to share for this book chapter. As a result, we re-issued questionnaires and invited those who wanted to have a chance to engage in a semi-structured interview. Twenty-two staff from the schools and settings responded to these additional questionnaires, and an additional four were interviewed in-depth. It is from each of these sources that we drew out recurring themes using reflexive thematic analysis methodology (Braun & Clarke, 201 2). Each of the themes is grounded in the voices of educational staff and have been checked back with them for their reflections. We have also included an 'EP reflection' section under each main theme. Throughout the construction of this chapter, we (as the authors) have had ongoing discussions about our own reflections and interpretations of the themes as they have emerged; therefore, we will incorporate our collective reflections talking in the voice of 'we'. We also interviewed one of the EP facilitators who has been heavily involved in BRS and will incorporate their views by inserting their words in quotations and referencing them as 'EP facilitator'.

Themes arising from these reflections

The recurring themes arising from the reflexive thematic analysis are depicted in the following figure (see Figure 11.1). The overarching theme is 'understanding behaviour and distress',

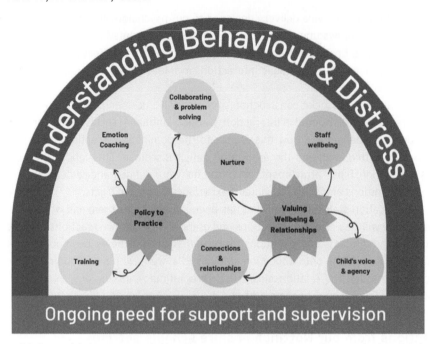

Figure 11.1 A model to represent the themes generated from the analysis of interview transcripts.

which encompasses two further themes: 'policy to practice' and 'valuing wellbeing and relationships'. Overall recognition for 'ongoing need for support and supervision' to do relational work well became our final, underlying, foundational theme. These themes are not mutually exclusive; they are all about relationships and involve an understanding of behaviour as a means to meet both children's and adults' needs. However, education staff suggested that we present each theme in turn visually to enable the reader to consider them clearly.

Overarching theme: Understanding behaviour and distress

It is perhaps unsurprising that 'understanding behaviour and distress' became the overarching theme reflected by staff when exploring relationships and the concepts of attachment, responses of trauma, and unmet needs. If we are able to understand what the behaviour is about, we can consider the most effective way to support it.

As illustrated in Figure 11.2, school/setting staff reflected that better understanding children's behaviour and distress empowered them to respond to it calmly and in a way that met the children's needs.

Staff reflections and learning

- Understanding children's behaviour and distress enables adults to respond to it with empathy, understanding, and compassion.

> 66 ————
> ...if he's really struggling in terms of being in continuous provision, they'll just take him away and just sit with him and just hold him and just give him that reassurance and love that he needs just to go back to baseline and kind of come back down from whatever's triggered his behaviour.
> Head Teacher; Primary School
> ———— 99

> 66 ————
> We all respond calmer now.
> Pastoral Support; College
> ———— 99

> 66 ————
> We also know that if they're not ready to learn, they're never going to achieve, because without that real bottom level stuff that you know, some children haven't been afforded that life of being able to have, you know they come from very chaotic backgrounds, they come into school, they've had no breakfast, you know, they're not ready to learn, they've not got the right uniform on and it's just all about us coming in...I think by having that and allowing the children the time to really reflect rather than just saying I'm sorry for doing something. And understanding them, knowing that, you know, perhaps before they walked in the door, they've just been told off. There's, you know, like say had no sleep, they're not even got their own beds. And in kind of really working on that empathy and curiosity around what's happened, you know, like, can you tell me a bit about why you think you're feeling like this?
> Pastoral Lead; Primary School
> ———— 99

> 66 ————
> Cause obviously behaviour is always a reflection of emotion, of how they're feeling.
> Head Teacher; Primary School
> ———— 99

> 66 ————
> The behaviour regulation plans are thought out nicely for each child. Exactly what works and what doesn't. So, if they're in this heightened state of emotion and this would work, or if not, then this would work, because obviously some children need an individual plan to be able to say when I'm overwhelmed, I can go and sit in the library. When I'm overwhelmed, the library might not be the best place for another child because they pull the books off the library shelves. So it's sort of like working out who can go where and what's best for them, really for all the children.
> Pastoral Lead; Primary School
> ———— 99

> 66 ————
> A few years ago I would have had that conversation and they would be saying things like he's being naughty, he's hitting out and what they were saying today were things like there's something in the day that he's not handling and we need to just find helping ways to regulate. And we don't know how to do that yet and we can brainstorm some ideas and just going down that. But it's the way staff talk about behaviours changed quite a lot in school and it's now that view of, OK, it is a communication tool. It's not just the child is just misbehaving or is a naughty child. And I think I would say that's one of the things I've really noticed in conversations with staff.
> SENCo & Assistant Head Teacher; Primary School
> ———— 99

Figure 11.2 Staff reflections: understanding behaviour and distress.

- By understanding how to respond to behaviours and distress, staff feel more equipped to respond calmly.
- Understanding emotions behind behaviours is central to supporting children and young people.
- Recognising that adults working with children also experience distress and sometimes display unhelpful behaviours when responding to children. It is important for the adults to check in with themselves and understand their own emotions and behaviours.
- There is a tension held between purist behavioural paradigms where reward/sanction are the responses to behaviour, which seem particularly favoured by some multi-academy trusts (MATs) and relational-based paradigms, where natural consequences and repairing relationships are the responses to behaviour.

EP reflections: Understanding behaviour and distress

As EPs exploring this key theme with staff, what really stuck us is that the staff were wanting to get a deep understanding of what behaviour was about. They were wanting to get underneath the external presentation of a behaviour and think about 'why' a child was behaving in a particular way.

There seemed to be a tangible shift from discussion about children's behaviours to reflecting on everyone's: their own and other adults in their school/setting. Some of the staff moved from the narrow lens of children to a wider one focusing on adults.

> '[A]dult's behaviour is really what it's all about. . . . [T]he teacher creates the emotional climate of the classroom.' (primary head teacher)

A psychodynamic perspective became a part of the reflections and training (Bion, 1961).

> 'The focus on what the adult brings to an interaction when responding to the distress of another feels so powerful. We can almost see people making that connection and realising that it's not a one-way street when it comes to the dynamics of that interaction – it's not just the child that experiences strong emotions in that moment. To support this, I try hard to provide a safe space for people to reconnect with their own relational experiences throughout their own lives. It can be emotionally demanding for people, and I admire how they are willing to do that during the training. It's such a privilege to have the opportunity to reflect so openly about how these relationships might have influenced values and practice. It appears to allow people to reconnect with themselves and think about how congruent they are being with their values when they reach out to another (this is equally the case for myself).' (EP facilitator)

From a personal perspective, what surprised us was that most people in the room were open to moving away from a purist behaviourist paradigm (Skinner, 1963) of behaviour management, considering this is the way teachers are often 'trained' to think about behaviour (Department for Education, 2019b). The current discourse around behaviour is strongly weighted towards external 'rewards and sanctions' heavily influenced by Tom Bennett's preferred paradigms (Bennett, 2010). Despite these influences, the staff were open and at times excited to look into other ways of thinking about behaviour. Maybe this is why these particular people were attracted to become part of this project – they are looking for something different.

Most people on this project aligned with the belief that responding to behaviour is about understanding it and not just praising it or punishing it. As EPs who often work around children where 'behaviour' is often an area of concern, I recognise how that felt hopeful.

The power of language became an important reflection for us. How children's situations were described and where there was a sense of agency felt key 'kind of came back down from whatever's triggered his behaviour'. '[Y]ou know, I nearly said choice of behaviour, but I didn't' (head teacher, primary).

> 'The shift in language that followed staff's better understanding of behaviour and distress, "behaviour" replaced "choice of behaviour" and within-child explanations, such as

"naughty", were replaced by adults seeing it as their role to support children to "regulate". This is hopeful, knowing the powerful influence language has on children's identities and their peers' perceptions of them.' (EP facilitator)

Becoming part of this work and reflecting throughout this project leaves us with a question: As EPs, how do our emotions, behaviour, and distress impact on the work we do?

Theme 1: Policy to practice

The theme of 'policy to practice' represents the requirement for policy to be something that is lived and acted upon, rather than simply a written document. There needs to be a shared understanding between staff for it to become part of everyday educational experiences and teaching practice. It needs to be written in collaboration with everyone it affects. It needs to be enacted and embodied in practice through the relational interactions between staff, families, children, and the wider community.

This theme is constructed of a number of subthemes.

Collaborating and problem-solving

The need for collaboration and collective problem solving was highlighted across the data [see Figure 11.3]. Through genuine collaboration, staff were challenging the power dynamics, validating everyone's views to enable more successful problem solving. There were reflections of problem solving 'with' others, rather than doing something 'to' or 'for' them.

(Wachtel, 2005)

Staff reflections and learning

- Whole-staff collaboration is essential to explore and rewrite meaningful behaviour policies.
- By collaborating and problem-solving, staff are able to better understand children's needs and respond to them in an attuned way.
- Working together as a staff team and having spaces to share practice enable barriers to be overcome.
- Regular check-ins around implementation of relational practice supported the sharing of good practice.
- Collaboration at its best ensures that children, families, and staff work 'with' one another.

Training (learning and reflections)

Training, learning, and the desire for continued professional development (CPD) in relational ways of working was a theme highlighted throughout the feedback and demonstrated in Figure 11.4. Education staff were keen that all colleagues received training to support their understanding of children's needs and their confidence to support children's distress. They wanted to ground this in psychological frameworks. The training

> 66 —————
>
> ...when I'd done the training, we came and had a look (at the behaviour policy)...it was more focused probably around negative behaviour, not the behaviours that you know that we're doing all the time to promote good behaviour, you know, healthy relationships, things like that. And so we looked at it as a whole school...we all got together in a staff meeting, looked at our policy and picked it apart a bit to have a look at...and really decided to do it more as a regulation policy, like behaviour regulation policy.
>
> SENCo; Primary School
> ————————— 99

> 66 —————
>
> We all got together in a staff meeting, looked at our policy and picked it apart a bit to have a look at what we thought was, you know, and that everybody's input into it. And then the SENCo she kind of like rewrote it. And from the training we used some of the other policies from other schools and picked out bits that we like that would fit our school community. And then all sort of agreed on it really. So that everybody knew what they were doing.
>
> Pastoral lead; Primary
> ————————— 99

> 66 —————
>
> What we want over the next 12 to 18 months to make sure that the vast majority of our staff have got that in place and that's kind of a real embedded expectation across that school.
>
> Head Teacher; Primary School
> ————————— 99

> 66 —————
>
> ...we held regular key stage meetings where staff brought where it worked well we did try and focus on staff who potentially were not necessarily the most natural and staff who would put those barriers up. And it was interesting how quickly they were saying, actually, no, I did. I was a bit against it in the staff meeting, but actually now I am beginning to see that and it was a really nice way to share practise.
>
> SENCo & Assistant Head Teacher; Primary School
> ————————— 99

> 66 —————
>
> We renew our behaviour policy each year and we decided to go down the behavioural relational route with our behaviour policy. So we initially changed it to really engage emotions coaching.
>
> SENCo & Assistant Head Teacher; Primary School
> ————————— 99

Figure 11.3 Staff reflections: collaboration and problem-solving.

sessions seemed to remind staff of the values they hold around children and education and gave them permission to align their practice with these. The training seemed to hold a space where staff could reflect on their values and the reasons they chose their profession. Relationships and child development were at the core of staff reflections.

Staff reflections and learning

- The BRS training has encouraged staff to extend and share aspects of this training with their wider school/setting communities.
- Whole staff training has led to increased confidence in supporting children.
- The BRS training has encouraged attendees to focus on providing specific staff members with specialised training that was in line with relational practice, for example, investing in emotional learning support assistant (ELSA) training to extend the support available to children.

Emotion coaching

Emotion coaching (Gottman et al., 1996), more recently popularised by Emotion Coaching UK (2019), has become a pivotal aspect of the BRS project and helpful in supporting staff to link

> " ————
> We are challenging our staff and other professionals in the way they deal with children and how to build positive relationships with all children particularly those who have been affected by trauma or who have insecure attachment.
> Head Teacher; Primary School
> ———— "

> " ————
> We have half termly teach meets and we expect staff to present kind of a piece of research or some kind of best practise as part of their subject so it's kind of ongoing CPD for them and ongoing CPD for everybody.
> Head Teacher; Primary School
> ———— "

> " ————
> I am in the process of completing ELSA training. I have implemented some of the skills learnt in my daily practise.
> Teaching Assistant; Primary School
> ———— "

> " ————
> From your training is giving it away to people. I think equally I'm a bit more confident in terms of talking and using technical vocabulary around it as well and bit more confident about fighting for what we believe in.
> Head Teacher; Primary
> ———— "

> " ————
> We have the new relationships and behaviour policy written and some training ready, more formal training ready for staff about PACE and our expectations in September and so also cause we're gonna have some new staff in September as well. We probably one or two new teaching staff, so it would be really useful to have that in place for them straight away.
> Head Teacher; Primary
> ———— "

> " ————
> He just needs to be on all the time. But I think kind of the course has helped us think in more different ways about how we can meet these needs because it certainly had less. And we've managed to train other members of staff, the certainly the staff that work with him treat him in a more kinder, accepting way.
> Head Teacher; Primary
> ———— "

Figure 11.4 Staff reflections: training.

theory to practical strategies. Staff in schools/settings were keen for tangible interventions to enable them to respond appropriately to children's distress, as exemplified in Figure 11.5. Emotion coaching provided them with a framework through which they could do this.

Reflections about how other relational interventions complement this work, like ELSA, were highlighted by the staff. BRS provided an umbrella for bringing together different approaches, for example, restorative practice (International Institute for Restorative Practices [IIRP], 2015; Wachtel, 2005). School/setting staff were keen to explore the collective frameworks for responding to children's behaviours and distress. Over the iterations of BRS and cycles of feedback, we developed the 'responding in the moment' model, which is based on Kim Golding's (2017) 'parenting in the moment'. This model draws from Golding's model with the first two steps recognising the role of the adult, noticing what is happening and acknowledging the potential impact of the behaviour on the adult. The next steps are about co-regulating, connecting, and supporting the child with their emotions. The final step is about supporting the repair and restoration of the relationship and brings in scripts from restorative practice (Wachtel, 2005).

> We have worked with staff on emotional coaching with students...it is now part of our vocabulary.
> Deputy Head Teacher; Secondary School

> All staff receive ongoing Emotion Coaching as this is the foundations of our Behaviour Regulation Policy. We changed our policy in line with the exemplars. We developed a Learning Mentor role to support pupils to regulate across school. We have termly trauma informed sessions with staff.
> SENCo & Assistant Head Teacher; Primary School

> Less movement around school of students who are dysregulated, they feel more supported by all teachers and less need to wander around to find their person.
> Designated Teacher; Secondary School

> I have begun to develop emotional resources to display in classrooms... supported by emotional coaching training the whole school completed, the best support the pupils in an emotional supportive way.
> Teaching Assistant; Primary School

> Children are supported in a more appropriate way to regulate...Staff use emotion coaching in day to day practice.
> Assistant Head Teacher; Primary School

> Emotion coaching was implemented across the whole school as a result of the training...now used as our 'go to' strategy for behaviour and emotional issues...also been integrated into the school behaviour policy.
> SENCo; Secondary School

Figure 11.5 Staff reflections: emotion coaching.

Staff reflections and learning

- Wider staff training on emotion coaching has led to a common vision for staff in many settings. Emotional understanding and emotional literacy have become encouraged and accessible in the school environment through visual displays and teacher lanyards.
- Through relational practices, including emotion coaching, staff are noticing that children are more able to talk about their emotions.
- Emotion coaching has enabled them to validate children's emotions. This has translated into adults supporting children's emotional needs across the school, rather than just responding to their behaviours.
- Using the 'responding in the moment' model, staff have become more attuned with their own emotions, ensuring to check in with themselves to see if they are in the right space to respond to children's distress.

- Utilising the reflective questions in the 'responding in the moment' model, staff can facilitate reflective conversations with children to support repair and natural consequences.

EP reflections: Policy to practice

As EPs and former teachers, we were unsurprised that existing behaviour policies and the idea of relationship-based practice presented opposing paradigms. We also understood some of the settings' reluctance to completely rewrite the way they respond to behaviour when that thinking is so embedded in education. What became apparent to us was that despite the policies, staff were looking at how relational connection and repair of relationships could be rooted into their policies. Some staff were also enjoying the challenge that this presented. An EP facilitator reflected on her experience of talking to a member of SLT in a secondary school: 'Ordinarily, she is very firmly in the punishment camp. By the end [of our chats], she said she felt more enlightened and had enjoyed challenging her thinking.'

All the education staff seemed to agree that relationships and the way we respond to distress are fundamental to this work. However, the challenge to recognise that they (the staff) are the intervention, and the key resource, took more convincing. We got the sense that staff were wanting an intervention or strategies, and it made us wonder how we have somehow deskilled our staff in education. They were looking to the EP as having the answers, and this felt fundamentally wrong to us. Talking through emotion coaching with the staff seemed to provide an effective 'strategy' to enable staff to feel empowered.

What struck us were the ripples of expertise within the group, from EP to and from the education staff. Everyone was learning. There was also movement from knowledge and policy to the importance of embodiment of relational responses.

> 'Relating to collaboration and problem-solving highlighted the importance of having a team. This training is hard to roll out whole-school without a team sharing your goal who can push the vision forward. Collaboration, problem-solving happened at its best when teachers made space for each other to discuss and share practice, challenges, and success. This collaboration and problem-solving as a team started in the discussion and reflective-based spaces carved out in all the training days and was continued in schools when staff returned with their relational action research plan that they shared with staff.' (EP facilitator)

It goes without saying that it takes time for policy to become practice. A helpful reflection came from our EP facilitator:

> 'There was a large range of time between when the schools interviewed had received training. Some had had 2 years to weave relational practice into their school culture; however, some had finished the training the previous term. This disparity highlighted that for sustained and consistent relational practice that is part of a school's ethos and engrained into their behavioural or regulation policy, it takes time. The importance of committing to the change and going through several cycles of action research for this change to be possible was important. It relates to research showing organisational change takes up to two years.'

Theme 2: Valuing wellbeing and relationships

The importance of wellbeing and its intrinsic connection with relationships was something that recurred throughout this evaluation and is present in other literature (Santini et al., 2020).

Valuing wellbeing and relationships as a theme is constructed of several subthemes.

Connections and relationships

Perhaps one of the most recurrent themes, undoubtedly impacted by the title and content of BRS, is the need for genuine, authentic, and unconditional connections and relationships, as illustrated in Figure 11.6. Peer relationships and their importance for the feeling of belonging to social networks were also highlighted.

> She was looked after herself when she was little and I didn't realise that when we recruited her, but she's built a really strong relationship with him. She kind of knows his triggers really well now, it doesn't always work, but 9 times out of 10... she's just really gentle with him and kind and you know he's horrible to her. She always makes sure that they sort it out before she goes. That kind of repair... it's about training our children, but also training our staff that that repair is really important.
> Head Teacher; Primary School

> For us it all links back to building really good relationships with our parents. And I think that's something we certainly have the benefit of our children. Absolutely because the kids we talk about, the kids sitting at the centre of what we do and yeah, that's kind of for all of us.
> Head Teacher; Primary School

> Just sit there. And when they say you hate me and you just sit there, go it's tough, I know it's really tough at the moment, but I'll sit here and I'll be with you. And that does seem to be something that does eventually get them to calm down... And I know it's a bit rubbish, but we're here and that that's not gonna change. And just giving that reassurance.
> Head Teacher; Primary School

> Because at the end of the day, that's what it's about really. About making sure our kids and our staff have decent relationships.
> Head Teacher; Primary School

> The priority next I think the work about playfulness for me [referring to PACE] ...I think it's about, you know, being accessible and being friendly and being kind and, you know, not necessarily playing trains or anything like that with a kid . So, it's about using your, you know empathy a bit better and about knowing the child.
> Head Teacher; Primary School

> The expectation is that they don't shout first, they actually kind of sit down and with the two children, whoever to listen to both sides, agree a way forward and how this can be avoided and then kind of mend the relationship.
> Head Teacher; Primary School

> Middays... Because their relationships with the kids are probably the least um, it's hard, isn't it? They're only here an hour a day here, an hour a day there. It kind of makes developing positive relationships tricky, but some of them are better than others.
> Head Teacher, Primary School

Figure 11.6 Staff reflections: connections and relationships.

Staff reflections and learning

- Relationships are key, and forming positive connections, with trust and consistency, is essential (child–teacher, child–child, child–family, or adult–adult).
- Forming a relationship with the parents/carers of children benefits the child and models ongoing positive relationships.
- Time and investment are needed to form positive relationships and connections with children and families.
- There are important cycles involved in relationships, including building, maintaining, and repairing them.
- Children/young people need support and sometimes explicit teaching about relationships and friendship.
- Social skill development is a skill for life and should be prioritised in the same way as academic subjects are.
- Having post-16 peer mentors enabled the promotion of positive peer relationships throughout college settings.

Staff wellbeing

Understanding the need for staff wellbeing has been one of the emerging themes throughout this project (see Figure 11.7). Staff reflected that in order for them to be able to respond in a positive way towards children's distress and behaviours, staff needed to be in a calm emotional space themselves.

Staff reflections and learning

- Staff notice and recognise the impact on themselves when supporting others in distress.
- Staff wellbeing needs to be prioritised and for staff to use each other as a supportive resource (team support) to open up conversations.
- Supervision is recognised as being important to enable honest, open conversations about wellbeing.

Nurture

Providing nurture (Boxall, 2002) became an important theme in BRS, as Figure 11.8 shows. Staff described the way the physical and social environment is enabled to respond to children and young people's needs.

Staff reflections and learning

The concept of nurture that setting staff reflected on included:

- Ensuring children's basic needs are met, for example, having the appropriate clothing (providing uniforms) and providing breakfast and snacks so that children are not hungry.
- Creating a place of belonging: having 'jobs' to do, ensuring children have 'time-in and not timeout', and gentle starts to the day (if feeling emotional).

> 66 ───────────
> It's about saying it in that moment when our emotions are running high too... in that moment, you're allowed to just go and have your moment too and come back down together kind of thing. And I think it's that sort of work that needed doing the most is like it's okay to say that you're tired and you're exhausted.
> Pastoral Lead; Primary School
> ─────────── 99

> 66 ───────────
> So we have formal termly meetings where we discuss anything they're struggling with, anything they want to develop further, anything they want to do next. But then we also did just bring two children that you are struggling with and that your still going to do the emotions coaching with cause your just frustrated with and let's come up with and we solution circled it and we got together and we do things like that. And we try and do that half termly and then we just try and do some informal things like particularly with TA team catch ups TA coffee afternoons. Sessions after school where we just get taken a drink and just try and have those moments where staff can talk if they want to or just come and spend a bit of time together.
> SENCo & Assistant Head Teacher; Primary School
> ─────────── 99

> 66 ───────────
> One of most helpful things is group supervision – time for staff to talk and reflect on barriers in a safe environment.
> Head Teacher; Primary School
> ─────────── 99

> 66 ───────────
> Greater understanding of staff wellbeing, more responsive to staff concerns, openness to helping and reciprocating.
> Deputy Head Teacher; Secondary School
> ─────────── 99

> 66 ───────────
> We worked with staff on window of tolerance, checking in with yourself before dealing with issues.
> Deputy Head Teacher; Secondary School
> ─────────── 99

> 66 ───────────
> You reflect on your own wellbeing before you go in.
> Deputy Designated Safety Lead & Behaviour Lead ;Special School
> ─────────── 99

Figure 11.7 Staff reflections: staff wellbeing.

- Having access to safe adults throughout the day to support regulation, to provide playful, accepting, curious, empathetic (PACE) responses (Hughes & Golding, 2012).
- Having bespoke sessions (post-16 mentors and ELSAs).

Child's voice and agency

Validation of children's voices and experiences seemed central, as illustrated in Figure 11.9. The importance of children experiencing a sense of agency and some control of their lives became a recurring theme throughout this project.

Staff reflections and learning

- Seeking children's voices and listening to what they have to say enables them to feel heard and validated and, in turn, strengthens relationships.
- Children enjoy having roles within school, such as being ambassadors, which supports their sense of agency and belonging.

> 66 —————————
> Allowing children to check in every day with staff which in turn will allow discussions to be had to ensure a positive start to the day.
> Head Teacher; Primary School
> ————————— 99

> 66 —————————
> Removal of time out passes, time in implemented instead.
> Designated Teacher; Secondary School
> ————————— 99

> 66 —————————
> Our Nurture currently it changes quite regularly really, but its a success through the whole school...But mostly it's year one to year six. So currently there are nine children that present with several different reasons as to why they go. So at the moment are mostly children that had early, you know, sort of ACEs they've had that there's ongoing concerns around low level neglect and things like that. So, food wise they have a snack when they're with us and table manners and all the things that are kind of missing those really early years experiences of play...so we focus on social skills, emotions and time spent with children and really child led play, so there will always be activities that are set out, but also then we'll get the small world out and the children can express how they're feeling kind of through the small world.
> Pastoral Lead; Primary School
> ————————— 99

> 66 —————————
> being able to do meet and greets in the morning for some children they really find it hard to come in and giving them some breakfast, settling them into class and checking up on them later really kind of helps them to, you know, and also they feel that they're part of our school community and some children have to have little jobs that they do because it just it's just easier to like and, you know, come in and feel settled.
> Pastoral Lead; Primary School
> ————————— 99

> 66 —————————
> if we're seeing patterns of behaviour, then the children, you know, will access other interventions... we use ELSA, we use drawing and talking. We use our nurture provision.
> Pastoral Lead; Primary School
> ————————— 99

> 66 —————————
> Our peer mentor has provided an additional opportunity for students with care experience to get support from someone they can connect with.
> Safeguarding Lead, Further Education College
> ————————— 99

> 66 —————————
> Staff are more aware of value of interactions with pupils and colleagues.
> SENCo; Primary School
> ————————— 99

Figure 11.8 Staff reflections: nurture.

- Hearing from children/young people ensures that their needs are met and they are getting the right support when required.

EP reflections: Valuing wellbeing and relationships

To us, 'valuing wellbeing and relationships' is at the core of this project. We do not think that relationships can be assumed; they take time, and prioritising, and their importance can get lost.

> *'It was refreshing to provide space where wellbeing and kind, trusting relationships are the priority, which contrasts with the usual demands on teachers and educational professionals, where results and academic performance are emphasised as the priority.' (EP facilitator)*

What struck us is that wellbeing for staff in education is not something that is always prioritised. This is a theme that has circulated educational literature for years (for example,

66 ——————
So kind of allowing the children to have that reflection time and see the impact of their actions and what's the regulation policy look like. Its about them, the children and their like emotions and reflecting on that.
Pastoral Lead; Primary School
—————————— 99

66 ——————
I would say children are more reflective of being able to say themselves 'Ohh And I'm not feeling great at the moment'. We've got one little boy who talked about bubbling bubbles in his belly and but it's because somebody spent the time to go through that with him. So he talks about. I'm getting bubbles now okay then what we're gonna do about it, let's go for a walk.
SENCo & Assistant Head Teacher; Primary School
—————————— 99

66 ——————
Children feel a higher degree of recognition- pupil discussion. Children enjoying role of ambassador- positive responses to seeing children being 'a good friend'.
Deputy Head Teacher; Primary School
—————————— 99

66 ——————
Students feel listened to and confident the support they are getting is helping them.
SENCo; Post 16 College
—————————— 99

66 ——————
Depends what the child wants and what they need and yeah, and we've got one little boy at the moment who comes upstairs purposefully for it [school sensory stations] and... he hasn't gone to sit in it, but he goes round for 10 minutes. Then he goes back to his class.
SENCo & Assistant Head Teacher; Primary School
—————————— 99

66 ——————
[school sensory stations]"there's a year six and year four boy who now they see it in each other and they'll say right shall we go and have a look come and sit with me and it's just that nice. Ohh we'll go and sit and do it together which is really really nice. And it is just somewhere and it's not led by us, which I think is quite nice. There's also emotions, books, there's music and there's entry lights.
SENCo & Assistant Head Teacher; Primary School
—————————— 99

66 ——————
Friendship group- children feel listened to and reduced instances involved in conflict in the playground.
Deputy Head Teacher; Primary School
—————————— 99

Figure 11.9 Staff reflections: child's voice and agency.

Department for Education, 2019a). This project has emphasised that more needs to be done to support the wellbeing of educational professionals. It made us wonder how EPs could be involved to support this.

> *'Refocusing on themselves/myself – reflecting and sharing around relationships, our attachments and trauma is a great equaliser. As a facilitator, I am not standing in front of people because I have experienced a 'picture-perfect' childhood. I don't stand outside of those experiences. What I ask them to do, I also ask of myself. The content applies as much to me as [to] anybody else in the room. I am 'human first' for every second of those sessions.' (EP facilitator)*
>
> *'In encouraging others to notice themselves, we notice ourselves. As a facilitator, it has encouraged me to think about not only my own wellbeing but also where my own setting sits in terms of being trauma-informed. At times this has felt uncomfortable, which*

has actually been really helpful, as it's this conflict that propels us towards changes that can lead to greater congruence with our values and practice. For example, reflecting on our team meetings and what we can introduce that we can to enable the experience to feel more trauma-informed.' (EP facilitator)

We often reflect that 'child voice and agency' is referred to in education settings. It makes us reflect on the authenticity of it and wonder about how it feels, what it means to a child, and how tokenistic this has the potential of being. In this project, it was heartening to hear about how children's experiences were listened to, and their 'embodied agency'. Children were playing roles within their education settings which had meaning and impact.

'We are trying to amplify the experiences of the children, not just by providing people with psychological frameworks, but also by sharing real-life voices. These are not always easy to hear, and again, it's that sense of safety that I think enables people to be present and really hear and see the child.' (EP facilitator)

Nurture as a concept was highlighted for children and staff and constructed of the way everyone got their physical and emotional needs met.

'I was really pleased the heart of the training was translated well to educational professionals. It's all about relationships.' (EP facilitator)

Underlying theme: Ongoing need for support and supervision

Figure 11.10 demonstrates the need for 'ongoing support and supervision', which became a theme that underpinned this project. Staff reflected that there is a need to support their own wellbeing and feel supported to facilitate changes in practice. There is an increasing recognition of the need for supervision in education settings in the literature (for example, Lawrence, 2020).

Staff reflections and learning

- Time together to think and reflect is essential to supporting change, especially when it feels difficult.
- Ongoing support allows staff to acknowledge and validate their difficult emotions and feelings about being relational in their practice.
- Supervision provides a safe space for staff, which supports their wellbeing.
- Support and supervision are not always readily available to staff in all settings.

EP reflections: Ongoing need for support and supervision

As EPs, we must realise how easy it is to take for granted the space that supervision provides us (Dunsmuir & Leadbetter, 2010). For the staff in this project, supervision held a space for the 'unspoken to be spoken' and for staff to explore in a way that they have not experienced before.

"

Group supervision has been really helpful....Allows time...Safe environment.
SENCo; Post 16 College

"

"

Almost like a network, just something where you could share ideas and just have those different perspectives, because again, I think we've become quite insular and I don't know now, but all our training was online. So as we did have conversations, it wasn't the same as being in a room and going Ohh God, today's been awful what to do and actually having that, and I do think that's something across the board. We were saying it in SENCo meetings and everything that just being face to face with people cause it isn't an easy place to be in and just having that human interaction to say, yeah, OK, it's a bit rubbish and actually just a break from the school just to go and actually have those conversations. And I I think that would be really useful. Is just something and I don't. Yeah, I don't know the reality of it, but just some sort of place where you could go and bounce ideas off and develop that practise wider.
SENCo & Assistant Head; Primary

"

"

I did like the supervision the other day cause that we know. Like when I went back and it's just nice to know that well it isn't nice, but people are struggling with the same thing which you know I mean that everybody was struggling with getting certain staff on board aren't they and doing it that way and that it takes time and just hearing it from other people especially that head teacher that says things and I'm like they're like how to approach different things and stuff.
Deputy Designated Safety Lead & Behaviour Lead ;Special School

"

"

it's nice to have those supervision sessions and kind of share with the people you have the training with.
Teacher; Primary School

"

Figure 11.10 Staff reflections: ongoing need for support and supervision.

> *'I noticed the shift in perception. Initially, people think it's [supervision] about monitoring and feel a sense of pressure and being judged. But pleased and proud that they changed their perception of supervision for educational professionals into a more positive thing they look forward to and, from responses, show they value. I hope this encourages them to advocate for this in their schools and settings.' (EP facilitator)*

It struck us that educational professionals value having time and space to be with other educational professionals to reflect, listen, and share ideas. They valued this interaction taking place in person rather than online, which suggested to me a need for 'authentic togetherness' and a safe space to do this.

> *'The BRS training journey resonates with humanistic values around unconditional positive regard and empathy. We take time to carefully encourage people from the start to be mindful of keeping themselves psychologically safe, but we also have to take responsibility for providing this safety for them too. We are asking people to reflect on some of their own life experiences, some of which might be very painful. This could feel too big an ask if people aren't supported to feel safe. Without a genuine authentic sense of care and safety from the facilitator, I wonder if people would connect to the training material in the same way.' (EP facilitator)*

The concept of community and the power of shared goals and values resonated for us:

'It generally appears that sharing psychological theories gives people a solid founda-tion to hang their experiences and skills on. It seems to give their values wings, and people really seem to fly in terms of their confidence when they hear a theory that enables them to practice in line with those values. The knowledge that there is an evidence base and a theory to support their practice seems incredibly validating.' (EP facilitator)

'Facilitating the training has been a humbling experience. There is such a remarkable wealth of expertise and experience in the room. At a basic level, I am simply providing what I hope is useful psychology to hang their impressive work from. I feel less expert, and Egan's [2013] skilled helper rings in my ears during the sessions. My sense is that I am applying psychology to support people to make sense of complex experiences and the emotional turmoil that we can find ourselves in when we reach out to support another, but I am also using that humanistic psychology [Rogers, 1959] to empower them to recognise their strengths and the practice that they already do that is trauma-informed.' (EP facilitator)

Implications for practitioners in schools/settings

Throughout the process of collaborating with schools/settings, hearing staff reflections, and in the construction of this chapter, we have identified a number of implications pertinent to staff working in schools/settings who are keen to adopt a relational-based approach in their contexts. There is a need for:

- Commitment and time to prioritise relational approaches at all levels. This therefore requires the involvement of leaders as well as the whole staff team – indeed, everyone who may interact with children/young people.
- Facilitation of, and access to, training or support to develop staff skills and knowledge so that they feel confident to deliver relational approaches and fully understand the ration-ale for relational practice so that they can confidently articulate it to others, for example, governors, parents/carers, and Ofsted.
- Acknowledgement of the central need to prioritise staff wellbeing and consider what should be in place to do this well, for example, supervision. Staff wellbeing is essential in responding to children's distress.
- Recognition and understanding that emotion coaching is fundamentally different to a behaviourist (reward/sanction) way of responding to children's distress and behaviour. Emotion coaching is about learning about emotions in the moment and experiencing an adult to calm strong emotions.
- Understanding that everyone (adults and children/young people) in the system has own-ership and responsibility for policy change and changes in practice. There is a need to embody the theory within practice by emphasising the importance of felt connection and that *everyone* plays a role; it is about how *everyone* responds to behaviour and distress.

Conclusion

The co-production of this chapter has led to the development of a number of themes and tangible areas of implementation for senior leaders to consider if they, too, are wanting to make their schools systems more relational.

The themes arising from staff reflections have shaped, and continue to shape, the development of Nottinghamshire's BRS project. The depiction of these themes evidences the need for training around 'understanding behaviour and distress', as this is about the way we all respond to both children's and adult's behaviour, distress, and emotions. It takes time to influence the culture of an educational setting, and they are never static; therefore, ongoing training is required around these areas to support the development of newer staff alongside providing ongoing support for the school/setting and its community. Staff were keen that policy is translated into practice through training and that staff embody these principles. The most tangible practice that was celebrated was in the development of emotion coaching. Staff reflected that in order to be able to carry out this work well, there was a need to collaborate and problem-solve within the contexts of their own schools and communities to implement this work.

The staff involved in BRS grappled with their previous understanding of behaviour management and their desire to support children relationally. This led to a further collaborative piece of work to develop a toolkit to support schools to implement this learning (Understanding Behaviour, East Midlands Education Support Service, 2022)

Staff recognised that doing relational work well requires 'ongoing support and supervision' to enable policy to reflect practice and enable the wellbeing of children and staff in schools/settings. Whilst this was celebrated through the project, there was recognition that staff in schools/settings are not always supported in this way, which can have a detrimental effect on their wellbeing and which is the foundation of relational-based practice.

As we constructed this chapter, 'Mental Health and Behaviour in Schools' (2023) was published. We were heartened that the staff's reflections and the themes constructed closely aligned with many of the messages throughout the paper. Particularly that

> [s]chool leaders should commission staff training around relational and restorative approaches to help make the necessary changes and build more inclusive and nurturing environments for all pupils.
>
> (Rainer et al., 2023, p. 11)

What we have learned from this project is that this is not about a one-off 'training' session. This work needs to become woven into the fabric of an education setting. It needs to be 'felt' by pupils, but also by the whole school community, including its staff.

Summary box

This chapter tells the story and the evaluation of Nottinghamshire's Building Relational Schools project. It describes how the Virtual School and Educational Psychology Service have worked in partnership with schools and other education settings to explore and implement relational-based practice. The chapter portrays the themes arising from these reflections, which have gone on to influence future iterations of this work. To some extent, the project has been shaped by education settings for other education settings. The role of EP as facilitator and active participant is highlighted throughout.

BRS consists of three days of training, discussion, and reflection, followed by action research and ongoing supervision. The psychological thinking that permeates the chapter is humanistic (Rogers, 1959) and interactional (Egan, 2013). The training days draw on the psychology and knowledge of attachment and trauma (Asmussen et al., 2020; Bombèr, 2007; Bowlby, 1969; Hughes & Golding, 2012; Treisman, 2017). The reflections highlight that the experience of being part of the project has been an essential component of its success and is in itself a relational act.

The chapter has been co-constructed with education staff who have been involved in this project. They were keen that it was accessible and purposeful for people working in education settings.

Throughout this project, it has been highlighted that relational practice is not something that is 'taught' but something that must be 'felt' through:

- Authentic connections
- Understanding and empathising with people's experiences, emotions, and distress (behaviour)
- Experiencing nurture, trust, and safety
- Genuine collaboration, valuing voices, and consideration of power imbalances

Consider collaboratively our reflective questions, depicted in Figure 11.11.

Recommended resources

Scaife, J. (2013). *Supervision in clinical practice: A practitioner's guide*. Routledge. 19 Dec 2013. Psychology.
   Attachment & Trauma Aware approaches in education | ARC (the-arc.org.uk)
   EPS Toolkits | The East Midlands Education Support Service (em-edsupport.org.uk)
   Our Virtual School Resources | The East Midlands Education Support Service (em-edsupport.org.uk)
   Understanding Behaviour in Schools | The East Midlands Education Support Service (em-edsupport.org.uk)

Thank-yous

This chapter has been co-produced with staff from the Nottinghamshire's Virtual School and the educational psychologists who have been involved in some of the delivery of these sessions. To everyone who has been part of Building Relational Schools and Ant-Racism Toolkit, but especially those who were interviewed and supported with this book chapter: Sutton Road Primary School, West Notts College, Dalestorth Primary and Nursery School, Lawrence View Primary, Fountaindale School, and Steph McGill, our head of the Virtual School and a particular EP who has been pivotal in facilitating many BRS sessions.

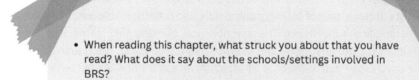

- When reading this chapter, what struck you about that you have read? What does it say about the schools/settings involved in BRS?

- How are relationships prioritised in your school/setting? How are they made, maintained and repaired when inevitable difficulties arise?

- How do you think about relationships with children, adults, families, communities?

- Who would know that relationships are important in your school/setting?

- How might you want to prioritise relationships further? What might you need to develop this further?

Figure 11.11 Reflective questions.

References

Asmussen, K., Fischer, F., Drayton, E., & McBride, T. (2020). *Adverse childhood experiences: What we know, what we don't know, and what should happen next*. Early Intervention Foundation.

Attachment Lead Network. (2023). *What is an attachment aware school*. Attachment Aware Schools Info and Attachment Lead Network.

Bennett, T. (2010). *The Behaviour Guru*. Bloomsbury Books.

Berger, P., & Luckmann, T. (1966). The reality of everyday life. In *The social construction of reality: A treatise in the sociology of knowledge* (pp. 33–42). Allen Lane.

Bion, W. R. (1961). Group dynamics. In *Experiences in groups and other papers* (pp. 141-191). Tavistock.

Bombèr, L. M. (2007). *Inside I'm hurting: Practical strategies for supporting children with attachment difficulties in schools*. Worth.

Bombèr, L. M., Golding, K. S., & Phillips, S. (2020). *Working with relational trauma in schools: An educator's guide to using dyadic developmental practice*. Jessica Kingsley Publishers.

Boniwell, I. (2006). *Positive psychology in a Nutshell: A balanced introduction to the science of optimal functioning* (p. 1). PWBC.

Bowlby, J. (1969). Disruption of affectional bonds and its effects on behavior. *Canada's Mental Health Supplement, 2*, 75-86.

Boxall, M. (2002). *Nurture groups in school: Principles & practice*. SAGE.

Braun, V., & Clarke, V. (2012). Thematic analysis. In H. Cooper, P. M. Camic, D. L. Long, A. T. Panter, D. Rind-skopf, & K. J. Sher (Eds.), *APA handbook of research methods in psychology, research designs* (vol. 2, pp. 57-71). American Psychological Association.

Bronfenbrenner, U. (1979). *The ecology of human development: Experiments by nature and design.* Harvard University Press.

Bryson, T. P., & Siegel, D. (2012). *The whole-brain child: 12 proven strategies to nurture your child's developing mind.* Hachette.

Checkland, P. B. (1989). Soft systems methodology. *Human Systems Management, 8*(4), 273-289.

Department for Education. (2019a). School and college staff wellbeing: Evidence from England, the UK and comparable sectors. (Research Report). publishing.service.gov.uk

Department for Education. (2019b). The trainee teacher behavioural toolkit: A summary (Guidance). *The Trainee Teacher Behavioural Toolkit: A Summary – GOV.UK.* www.gov.uk

Dingwall, N., & Sebba, J. (2018). *Evaluation of the attachment aware schools programme: Final Report.* Rees Centre, University of Oxford (pdf).

Dunsmuir, S., & Leadbetter, J. (2010). *Professional supervision: Guidelines for practice for educational psychologists.* British Psychological Society.

East Midlands Education Support Service. (2022). Understanding behaviour in schools A relationship based approach to inclusion. A practical toolkit for schools and educational settings. *Understanding Behaviour in Schools | The East Midlands Education Support Service.* em-edsupport.org.uk

Egan, G. (2013). *The skilled helper: A problem-management and opportunity-development approach to helping.* Cengage Learning.

Emotion Coaching UK. (2019). *Emotion coaching – United Kingdom.* emotioncoachinguk.com

Fancourt, N., & Sebba, J. (2018). *The Leicestershire virtual school's attachment aware schools programme: Evaluation report.* University of Oxford.

Foucault, M. (1971). Orders of discourse. *Social Science Information, 10*(2), 7-30.

Geddes, H. (2006). *Attachment in the classroom: The links between children's early experience, emotional wellbeing and performance in school.* Worth.

Geddes, H. (2017). Attachment behaviour and learning. In D. Colley & P. Cooper (Eds.), *Attachment and emotional development in the classroom: Theory and practice* (pp. 37-48). Jessica Kingsley.

Golding, K. S. (2017). *Everyday parenting with security and love: Using PACE to provide foundations for attachment.* Jessica Kingsley Publishers.

Gottman, J. M., Katz, L. F., & Hooven, C. (1996). Parental meta-emotion philosophy and the emotional life of families: Theoretical models and preliminary data. *Journal of Family Psychology, 10*(3), 243.

GOV. (2022). *Working definition of trauma-informed practice.* www.gov.uk/government/publications/working-definition-of-trauma-informed-practice/working-definition-of-trauma-informed-practice

Harlow, E. (2021). Attachment theory: Developments, debates and recent applications in social work, social care and education. *Journal of Social Work Practice, 35*(1), 79-91.

Harrison, N. (2022). *Attachment and trauma awareness training: Headteachers' perspectives on the impact on vulnerable children, staff and the school.* Rees Centre, University of Oxford

Herman, J. L. (2015). *Trauma and recovery: The aftermath of violence – from domestic abuse to political terror.* Hachette.

Hughes, D., & Golding, K. S. (2012). *Creating loving attachments: Parenting with PACE to nurture confidence and security in the troubled child.* Jessica Kingsley Publishers.

Hyde-Dryden, G., Brown, A., Trivedi, H., Tah, P., Sebba, J., & Harrision, N. (2022). *Attachment and trauma awareness training: Analysis of staff interviews and pupil focus groups in 26 case study schools.* Rees Centre, University of Oxford

International Institute for Restorative Practice. (2015). Restorative practice explained. The science of relationships and community. *Restorative Practices: Explained | Restorative Practices.* iirp.edu

Kelly, G. A. (1955). *The psychology of personal constructs. Vol. 1. A theory of personality. Vol. 2. Clinical diagnosis and psychotherapy.* W. W. Norton.

Lawrence, N. (2020). Supervision in education – healthier schools for all. *Barnado's Scotland report on the use of Professional or Reflective Supervision in Education. Supervision in Education – Healthier Schools for All – Main Report_0.pdf.* barnardos.org.uk

Marvin, R., Cooper, G., Hoffman, K., & Powell, B. (2002). The circle of security project: Attachment-based intervention with caregiver-pre-school child dyads. *Attachment & Human Development, 4*(1), 107-124.

Mead, G. H. (1934). *Mind, self, and society* (vol. 111). University of Chicago Press.

National Collaborating Centre for Mental Health (UK). (2015). *Children's attachment: Attachment in children and young people who are adopted from care, in care or at high risk of going into care.* National Collaborating Centre for Mental Health (UK).

Oshri, A., Sutton, T. E., Clay-Warner, J., & Miller, J. D. (2015). Child maltreatment types and risk behaviors: Associations with attachment style and emotion regulation dimensions. *Personality and Individual Differences, 73*, 127–133.

Parker, R. J. (2022). *Teacher perceptions of attachment aware approaches in schools-normative or transformative?* (Doctoral dissertation, Bath Spa University).

Parker, R. J., Rose, J., & Gilbert, L. (2016). Attachment aware schools: An alternative to behaviourism in supporting children's behaviour? In *The Palgrave international handbook of alternative education* (pp. 463–483).

Perry, B. D., & Szalavitz, M. (2017). *The boy who was raised as a dog: And other stories from a child psychiatrist's notebook – What traumatized children can teach us about loss, love, and healing.* Hachette.

Psychology Today. (2023). *Attachment.* www.psychologytoday.com/us/basics/attachment

Rainer, C., Le, H., & Abdinasir, K. (2023). Behaviour and mental health in schools. *Behaviour-and-Mental-Health-in-Schools-Full-Report.pdf.* cypmhc.org.uk

Rogers, C. (1959). A theory of therapy, personality and interpersonal relationships as developed in the client-centered framework. In S. Koch (Ed.), *Psychology: A study of a science. Vol. 3: Formulations of the person and the social context.* McGraw Hill.

Rose, J., McGuire-Snieckus, R., & Wood, F. (2019a). Impact evaluation of the attachment aware schools project for stoke and B&NES virtual schools: A pilot study. *Pastoral Care in Education, 37*(2), 162–184. https://doi.org/10.1080/02643944.2019.1625429

Rose, J., McGuire-Snieckus, R., Gilbert, L., & McInnes, K. (2019b). Attachment aware schools: The impact of a targeted and collaborative intervention. *Pastoral Care in Education, 37*(2), 162–184.

SAMHSA. (2019). Trauma and violence. *Substance Abuse and Mental Health Services Administration.* www.samhsa.gov/trauma-violence

Santini, Z. I., Stougaard, S., Koyanagi, A., Ersbⁱll, A. K., Nielsen, L., Hinrichsen, C., Madsen, K. R., Meilstrup, C., Stewart-Brown, S., & Koushede, V. (2020). Predictors of high and low mental wellbeing and common mental disorders: Findings from a Danish population-based study. *European Journal of Public Health, 30*(3), 503–509.

Scotland Gov. (2021). *Trauma informed practice: Toolkit.* www.gov.scot/publications/trauma-informed-practice-toolkit-scotland/documents/

Siegel, D. J. (2020). *The developing mind: How relationships and the brain interact to shape who we are.* The Guilford Press.

Skinner, B. F. (1963). Operant behavior. *American Psychologist, 18*(8), 503.

Structural Learning. (2021). Action research in the classroom: A teacher's guide. A teacher's guide to understanding your learners and improving student outcomes. *Classroom Practice. Action Research in the Classroom: A Teacher's Guide.* structural-learning.com

Suarez-Balcazar, Y., Francisco, V. T., & Jason, L. A. (2019). Behavioural community approaches. In *Introduction to community psychology.* Rebus.

Tes Magazine. (2023, March 3). *What is action research?.* www.tes.com/magazine/tes-explains/what-action-research

Thompson, R. A., Simpson, J. A., & Berlin, L. J. (2022). Taking perspective on attachment theory and research: Nine fundamental questions. *Attachment & Human Development, 24*(5), 543–560.

Treisman, K. (2017). *A therapeutic treasure box for working with children and adolescents with developmental trauma: Creative techniques and activities.* Jessica Kingsley Publishers.

Treisman, K. (2021). *A treasure box for creating trauma-informed organizations: A ready-to-use resource for trauma, adversity, and culturally informed, infused and responsive systems.* Jessica Kingsley Publishers.

Van der Kolk, B. (2014). *The body keeps the score: Mind, brain and body in the transformation of trauma.* Penguin.

Verschueren, K., & Koomen, H. M. (2012). Teacher – Child relationships from an attachment perspective. *Attachment & Human Development, 14*(3), 205–211.

Wachtel, T. (2005, November). The next step: Developing restorative communities. In *Seventh international conference on conferencing, circles and other restorative practices.* https://www.iirp.edu/news/the-next-step-developing-restorative-communities.

White, M., & Epston, D. (1990). *Narrative means to therapeutic ends.* WW Norton & Company.

Willig, C. (2013). *Introducing qualitative research in psychology.* McGraw-Hill Education.

12 Children in care proceedings

Trauma, commitment, and relational practice in schools

Tom Billington, Chris Davey, Jacqueline Hunter, Kelly Moran, and Sharon Richards

Introduction

Children who find themselves in the midst of family crises and breakdowns are frequently the most vulnerable in our school communities. While some young people can manage to contain the trauma and/or abuse they suffer, all too often, events in the home spill over into the school, nursery, or college. All aspects of the young person's life can be affected with adverse consequences upon their behaviour, their cognitive and emotional development, as well as their psychological and social functioning. Difficulties in any of these respects can have a serious impact, not only on the young person's educational prospects, but also on their future wellbeing and mental health across the whole life course.

Most situations will be managed or resolved, but there are occasions when the young person may have to be removed from the family home for a while or even permanently. Whether during any period of transition or uncertainty or following a more permanent resolution, it is our collective experiences that schools and education practitioners can provide vital sources of care, consistency, and stability when all else in the young person's life is in turmoil.

While some young people will need more obviously therapeutic interventions, it is our experience that individual members of school staff can and do often provide the emotional comfort and psychological sustenance necessary to protect the immediate but also the longer-term wellbeing of the child, although *'it's scary how our voice isn't heard'*. In this chapter, therefore, we acknowledge the importance of school culture and ethos, but we focus primarily on the commitments of individual members of staff to the day-to-day relationships they have, both with one another and also the young people in their schools, for *'it keeps coming back to the relationship. . . . [I]t's the relationships and the memories'*.

Origins of the chapter

Tom has worked in the Family Courts for roughly 25 years, providing psychological assessments of young people who have experienced many forms of disruption, disconnection, trauma (developmental, emotional, relational), and abuse (neglect, physical, sexual, emotional). The young person's distress invariably arises from issues in the home, such as parental mental ill health, alcohol and/or substance misuse, domestic violence, but sometimes abductions and even killings. The harm suffered by young people can occur during specific

DOI: 10.4324/9781003451907-12

incidents or else be endured through years of chaos and upheaval, and the situation can become subject to care proceedings. In England and Wales, child and family welfare is dealt with under the jurisdiction of the Family Division of the High Court, which can ultimately consider whether a child should be removed from the home, temporarily or even permanently.

During the early years of Tom's practice, the Family Court and the assessments required tended to focus solely on the child's place in a family, whether the birth family, foster care, or adoptive. The child could then find themselves not only being removed from their birth family but also taken away from familiar friends and communities, especially their schools. However, increasingly, Family Courts seem to be more aware of the significant role played, not only by friendship groups, community networks, and day-to-day activities, but also by some schools, in which many members of staff provide vital sources of care, continuity, and support in the young person's life. *'[I]f we don't stand up for the child, no one will.'*

Tom even locates much of his direct assessment work actually in schools, based on a premise that schools and nurseries are the location with which the young person is familiar. All too often, a school might be the only place in which the child can feel safe from harm, and while there are exceptions, for many young people, their nursery, school, or college can provide a sanctuary in which they come to know a more consistent and reliable source of care and nurture. *'[W]e have a sense of order. . . . [T]hey feel safe. . . . [I]f something's happened to you at night, you want a safe space.'*

Tom has come to pay ever closer attention to consultations with teachers and mentors. The data provided includes significant measures of punctuality, attendance, and educational attainments, but often, it is the more complex knowledge and understandings that school communities have accumulated about the child and their circumstances which can be so insightful. *'[W]e know the children.'* Listening to education-based practitioners has become an ever more important aspect of court assessments, with the teachers' own individual stories not only chronicling aspects of the young person's life but also frequently offering potential solutions or ways forward.

There are clearly occasions when the school or nursery is unable to manage the full extent of the young person's welfare needs and the child's situation deteriorates to the point of exclusion. However, this chapter draws on discussions between Tom and just a few of the many education practitioners whom he has known to have worked successfully with children who have suffered trauma and abuse.

Method

Following assessments of young people conducted by Tom in their schools, he subsequently contacted the fellow authors of this chapter to ask whether they would be prepared to discuss their work and potentially contribute to a book on relational practice. There could be no references to the original assessments, and we agreed to focus on experiences of safeguarding work in schools, in particular, with other children who have come to the attention of welfare services.

Tom provided a draft chapter proposal, the draft book proposal co-written by the editors, and we attended an initial meeting at the university for all potential book contributors. Following eventual confirmation of publisher contracts, separate sessions were then arranged in their respective schools in which the co-authors talked while Tom listened and made notes (many verbatim). However, much human communication takes non-verbal forms, and so he listened actively, not only to the words spoken, but also to the emotional content of their delivery, which was striking in its intensity. He then conducted a quasi-thematic analysis of the words spoken, mindful also of the qualitative emotional expressiveness that underpinned the various contributions.

Following analysis, Tom devised a chapter structure that accorded with the themes identified and with the emotional intensity communicated by staff. The initial chapter draft was sent to Chris, Jacqueline, Kelly, and Sharon, who were then invited to amend, remove, or supplement. Following a further meeting for all contributors in Sheffield, Tom completed the chapter in accordance with further contributions and guidance from the co-authors.

Taken overall, the accounts of the fellow contributors seemed to mirror the trauma being suffered by the child and family and that has been expressed so consistently to Tom by other educational practitioners over the years. *'[W]e're in a vulnerable position. . . . [W]e can feel helpless.'*

Child safeguarding

No child in care proceedings could be described as 'typical'. Any step towards such a position would be hostile to the best interests and wellbeing of the child, a leap taken away from a truly relational approach in which individuals are uniquely constituted in a particular constellation of time, space, and persons. That every single child matters can be no mere political slogan.

There are certain issues, however, that are common to the experience of children who come to the attention of the Family Court, and with a sickening regularity. These issues arise out of relational circumstances, in families and communities, that affect the child's experience of being parented. Following many notorious investigations into children's welfare services in England and Wales, the Children Act (1989) was a landmark legislation in which adult behaviours in four specific areas were identified as being so detrimental to a child's development and wellbeing that the state could instigate formal protocols for intervening in family lives.

Neglect refers to the material conditions within the family home or, else, the quality of daily care offered to the child by the parents. *Physical* and *sexual abuse* concern the potential or actual harm suffered by a child, for example, when experiencing aggression in the form of physical or sexual assaults. When the Act was first implemented, the fourth category, *emotional abuse*, could be more problematic due to uncertainties as to the kinds of evidence required or proposed, although emotional abuse is now commonly recognised as a feature of all childhood abuse. While there have been modifications and amendments to the Act, it is a tribute to all those involved in driving and developing the legislation that the underlying principle, that the child's best interests are 'paramount' above all other concerns, remains the cornerstone upon which child welfare and the Family Court should operate.

Education practitioners have specific responsibilities under the Act, and over the years, these have become codified by governments with bespoke roles established in the area of 'safeguarding', although the mandatory requirement to refer suspected abuse has since been extended to all citizens. Referrals to children's services are made by family members or people in the community, but often, it is health, police, and education staff who raise the alarm.

Some education practitioners have acquired considerable experience of working in child safeguarding and can be intensively involved with other agencies for weeks, months, and years. Their commitment can extend to child advocacy, for example, asking the child before a safeguarding meeting, *'[I]s there anything you'd like us to say for you?'* in their determination to protect a child and their best interests. *'[W]e're like a dog with a bone.'* Schools are also often best placed to reach out to families, and the relationship that education practitioners establish with parents can be key in achieving a hoped-for early resolution for the child. These relationships are far from straightforward and can raise tensions and conflicts. For example: *'[W]e have conflicting emotions because we know the parents. . . . [T]he hardest was when they were removed from mum.'* Sometimes, however, the difficulties being encountered by the family are difficult to contain, especially when *'some parents don't engage'* and *'some parents don't take responsibility'*.

For children who suffer *neglect*, it can be the actual material conditions in the family home that are problematic and might include lack of food or clothing, poor hygiene or sanitation, lack of attention to child healthcare issues, poor supervision, or even total parental absence. Breakfast clubs especially can provide insights into the stark realities faced by a child but can also provide an invaluable source of physical and psychological support. *'[T]he children would always say, "Can we have some more [food]?" . . . [E]ventually, the children became secure that the food wouldn't be taken off them.'*

Material conditions within the home encountered by some children can deteriorate to a level that would commonly be acknowledged as not only unacceptable but also, on certain occasions, as unbelievable. When health and childcare agencies become aware of such home conditions, they can intervene in order to provide support and attend to the material fabric. Despite the best efforts of all the agencies, however, some parents can continue to struggle; some will be experiencing acute levels of personal difficulty, for example, due to mental health issues or perhaps on account of their own childhood trauma. Education practitioners can reflect that, in some instances, *'our expectations of some parents are unrealistic'*, while there can be heartbreaking moments, for example, witnessing a mother's own realisation who *'held up her hand and said, "I can't do this"'*.

For other children, it is the level of alcohol and/or substance misuse that renders the parents incapable of maintaining home conditions or daily family routines, and there might be punctuality or school attendance issues due to the chaotic circumstances in the home. Without intervention, circumstances can again deteriorate to the extent that arguments and physical assaults erupt between family members, becoming even a regular occurrence within family life. In many of the aforementioned instances, the child can become invisible to the parents, who are either unaware of or are unable to see the damage their behaviours cause to their child's wellbeing and even development.

Most children know their parents far better than adults ever suspect and invariably become expert in understanding their parents' relational functioning. The child will become highly anxious and fearful as they come to predict those well-worn patterns of family life that they know will end, for example, in their mother (usually, but not always) suffering an assault. The sounds of distress from a loved one will be terrifying. Those moments of waiting and predicting the inevitable, realising that the person who is supposed to offer protection is unable to protect even themselves, are traumatic. The emotional and psychological impact of such events can be traumatic for all the family but will be absorbed by the child and taken into school, irrespective of whether the child has actually observed the incidents.

In some instances, the harm to the child involves a direct threat, and *physical* and/or *sexual abuse* are just that, incidents in which the child and their identity are punctured, physically and psychologically. Physical and sexual abuse leave deep scars on a young person's mental state, and the power relations acted out in such assaults distort the child's understanding of themselves and their place in the world. The chasm between those abusive (relational) conditions experienced and those promoted in school settings can be experienced as overwhelming for the child, psychologically and emotionally. *'[W]e deal with things in ways that can be foreign to a child . . . [but] we don't change our rules.'* The young person will endure many complex thoughts and feelings, and the trauma can destroy confidence in both themselves and others, making it more difficult for a child to accept or understand their own difference.

The child's confusions, distress, and trauma are likely to be communicated in a range of behavioural responses that challenge the resources of education staff on a daily basis, and the effects in schools are highly distressing for education practitioners. *'[W]e can't help but be affected by the trauma. . . . [I]t cuts deeply. . . . [W]e care about them.'* It is common for children who are the subject of abusive conditions in the home to *'protect the parents'*, but there are *'some parents [who] want a diagnosis'* as an explanation for their child's behaviours. The child can begin to seem the architect of their own destiny and functioning as attempts can be made to locate the blame on their behaviour or psychopathology. This strategy deflects attention away from either the family or the underlying trauma. Authors in this chapter are aware of more than one child who has become victim to a *'misdiagnosis.'* Family work demands that practitioners hold a delicate balance when contemplating parental and child need.

The co-authors from both schools in this chapter, despite being in different local authorities, each considers that they work in *'one of the most deprived [areas] in Europe'*. All too frequently, economic poverty is an underlying issue in the lives of many young people and families who come to the attention of school safeguarding teams, who are reporting increasing levels of parent need and use of foodbanks. We recognise the links between *'addiction and poverty'* in child safeguarding work, but it is important to note that the vast majority of families who are struggling to survive financially strive to protect their children in hugely stressful circumstances and will not recognise the abusive behaviours referred to in this chapter.

However, financial wellbeing does seem to offer an effective defence against the surveillance of childcare agencies, and there will be many children whose abuse and home circumstances go undetected due to the elevated social and economic status of their family. Abuse can afflict all families, irrespective of financial wealth, although the levels of surveillance do seem to be greatest in communities that suffer economic poverty.

Living and working with trauma in schools

There are many ways in which a young person can be affected by exposure to abusive conditions and individual children suffer a range of traumas, sometimes from their early years, but from birth, too, and even in utero. In this section, we articulate our position by suggesting three common kinds of trauma – *developmental*, *emotional*, and *relational*. However, all trauma, as with all human functioning, is experienced in a relational context of time, space, and other people.

We know from various strands of research (health, psychology, neuroscience) that intra-uterine environments are crucial to successful infant development. The mother's wellbeing is vital to her own physical health, but increasingly, we are becoming aware of the impact the mother's emotional state has upon the development of the unborn baby. Parents who are subject to care proceedings experience their own distress, and should the mother suffer either violence and/or drug- or alcohol-related issues during pregnancy, these can potentially have long-term repercussions for the development of her unborn child, physical and/or psychological.

There are many instances in which the child in family proceedings could be said to suffer different kinds of *developmental trauma*. The impact of foetal alcohol syndrome has clear physiological links to the development of the unborn child, but infant development is vulnerable to any kind of substance misuse or distress suffered by the mother. There are many situations known to the authors in which the infant's early development has been affected by both physical and psychological factors affecting the mother during pregnancy or in the first few months of life. In such instances, the age at which the infant begins to walk and/or talk can be delayed, while the development of other aspects of sensorimotor performance can be impeded. Trauma experienced during the early years can have knock-on effects across all aspects of functioning. For example, cognitive and social development can be affected in ways that demand the involvement of a range of early years professionals, from health visitors and paediatricians to hearing, occupational, and speech and language therapists, and can often lead to subsequent learning difficulties.

Our understanding of *emotional trauma* has increased significantly during the last 30 years or so. One of the initial difficulties in attempting to categorise a child as having suffered emotional abuse had been due to the unhelpful distinction between cognition and emotion. For much of the previous century, the attention of mainstream psychology had been drawn to either cognitive or behavioural analyses simply because the manifestation of these difficulties was supposedly easier to measure or quantify. During the last three decades, however, we have thankfully become more aware of the ways in which cognition, behaviour, and emotion are intertwined, sharing complex links. We now see that all forms of trauma invoke fear and distress but are psychological in its fullest sense, possessing a complexity that can potentially affect all aspects of a child's development and functioning, cognitive, behavioural, social, and indeed, relational.

In this chapter, we refer to *relational* trauma since it offers a more complex, comprehensive, but even more accurate scientific template than attachment theory for studying and analysing a parent–child relationship in adverse environmental circumstances. The deployment of attachment still has a tendency to focus narrowly on the relationship between an infant and the mother, and while clearly crucial to the infant's wellbeing and development, the attachment paradigm, in practice, can often continue to emphasise mother–infant interaction to the exclusion of other variables. Most children are subject to care proceedings for reasons that extend way beyond consideration, either of mother–child interaction or a psychopathology attributed to the individual child. Difficulties arise from very specific circumstances, which are psychological, but also *relational*, and even economic and cultural. One eminent neuroscientist concluded that '[human beings] swallow . . . human epistemology and ontology with their mother's milk' (Tallis, 2008, p. 140).

While Tallis here again focuses on the specific relationship between an infant and their mother as fundamental to future wellbeing, he suggests a far more complex template for understanding the development of the infant and their environmental 'conditions' (James, 1890/2010) than is routinely afforded by recourse to attachment, which often becomes reduced to simplistic concepts of 'disorder'. Affective, cultural, and critical neurosciences provide evidence that dyadic mother–infant relationships are not merely psychological or emotional but are the conduit via which the parent and child are embedded in a far wider economic, cultural, and indeed, relational fabric. It is in this sense that we suggest the *relational* as a more helpful concept that embraces the complexities of a child's experience and trauma, which was reflected in co-author accounts. For example: *'Aisha is in the middle of divorcing her parents.'*

It can be scientifically misleading, therefore, if we attribute a failure in childcare only to a mother, especially when it still seems to be mothers who, economically, politically, and culturally, cannot escape an abusive relationship or perhaps the chaotic circumstances of a drug-infused environment. While there are parents who are unable to fulfil their responsibilities in childcare proceedings, in many cases (but not all), it is the fathers who are able to elude the demands of full parental responsibilities. It is often mothers who are still deemed primarily responsible for care and protection of the child, although clearly, responsibility for the creation of conditions in which the child is protected from harm is far more complex.

For children who come to the attention of the Family Court, these complex conditions for successful early childhood development are unfortunately all too often permeated not only by parental violence, addiction, poverty, and chaos but also by the distress of the adults, which is transmitted to the infant in an intergenerational trauma. The impact on the child of the complex nature of the trauma or abuse, if un-remediated, can be lifelong and can be manifest not only in terms of a young person's wellbeing and mental health but also in all kinds of additional developmental needs, cognitive, behavioural, social, and learning. It is the impact of these circumstances from which education practitioners cannot escape in their daily work and for which the child needs support from outside the family.

Agency responses

The trauma circulating in childcare proceedings is extremely difficult, not only for the young person, but also for all practitioners and professionals working across the various agencies. Historically, social workers have been the experts in working with young people in the care system, and local-authority children's services continue to hold the primary legal responsibilities for child welfare. Children's social work is highly pressurised, however, and the demands on services seem continually to be increasing with perennial reports of under-funding. There is a sense in which education is being expected to fill this vacuum in childcare, and in this section, we share some perspectives from education practitioners who are always *'thinking how to plug that gap'*.

Some of the difficulties in childcare proceedings are linked to systemic issues since there are invariably a number of different agencies involved in the life of a single child. While children's services hold ultimate responsibility, social workers are routinely dependent on specialists from across a number of agencies, including health, the police, housing, probation services, foster care agencies, and education. Children's social work is complex and demanding, not least since each of the agencies involved has their own distinct set of responsibilities, protocols, and professional practices that do not always facilitate smooth inter-agency responses and partnerships. Systemic issues will impact on individual education practitioners who, like many social workers, no doubt, can become *'sick to death of picking up broken children'*.

The issue of *'communication'* between the agencies was a constant theme arising during the production of this chapter, and there was a perception that while schools might have *'a fantastic social worker'*, too often the system relies on *'admin teams [that] are not working for children'*. That is to say, it can be difficult for the various bureaucracies always to prioritise the needs of the individual child above all other requirements and across all areas of the organisation.

With the advent of safeguarding specialists and even safeguarding teams in schools and early years settings, it has become possible for education practitioners to articulate their contribution within child welfare processes, and there are opportunities for a better exchange and flow of information. School-based staff can attend many inter-agency meetings concerning individual children but can then have tricky decisions to make when dealing sometimes with highly sensitive or confidential information, for example, when deciding what information should be passed on to individual class teachers and other staff for, *'the class teacher has to work with the child every single day'*.

School-based staff find that they are *'the most consistent presence . . . at every meeting. . . . [S]ome people don't turn up'*. While another common concern is that *'social workers change'* with the consequence that school-based staff *'often provide the social worker with the background'*. It is our experience that social worker continuity is not only helpful during the child welfare processes, but given the turmoil and change experienced by the young person during care proceedings, maintaining practitioner continuity should also be seen as a more important priority that supports a child-centred approach.

The health agency which is most often associated with therapeutic childcare interventions is CAMHS (Child and Adolescent Mental Health Service). While many young people receive excellent support, there was again a perception that this service, too, has been under increasing pressure. *'CAMHS are overwhelmed.'* There were references in our accounts to *'long waiting lists'*, while there was also a view that *'there are too many hoops to jump through'*, that is, in order to obtain advice or achieve therapeutic support for young people. Staff reported that they *'are always contacting CAMHS. . . . [They] say they can't do anything until [the child is] safe'*. Schools also refer to Educational Psychology Services, although in some instances, there is an impression that while *'they write a lot of targets . . . [schools were] expected to pick things up'*.

Inter-agency working continues to throw up significant challenges for education practitioners, but the authors representing schools in this chapter have been gaining confidence in devising their own supportive networks. For example: *'[W]e've got a great [child safeguarding] team.'* There continue to be issues around *'funding and training'*, which is considered essential, as *'it can be dangerous if teachers don't know what they're doing [with a child]. . . .*

[W]e're not the specialists. . . . [W]e make it up as we go along'. There are also, perhaps, particular issues relating to *'teaching assistants [who] are doing a job they weren't trained for . . . [and can be especially vulnerable because] they live in the community'*.

Despite these important reservations, however, there is a growing awareness that education staff have access to a relational knowledge about a child and their family, and a realisation, too, that in some instances, they have *'become the specialists, doing it without funding or training. . . . [I]f [they] weren't there, things would be missed'*.

There continue to be challenges within the education sector, however, most of which seem to involve the competing demands between increasing child safeguarding responsibilities and more conventional educational aims and assessment measures. Ofsted was mentioned as a body whose measures do not always allow for the complex impact of intensive child welfare issues. There is a *'conflict with the curriculum'*, while at an individual level, *'a child can't do their SATS [standardised attainment tasks] because their head's full of what's going on at home'*. There are many occasions when *'we can't reach a child because of what's going on at home'*. The co-authors made clear links between childhood trauma and their educational performance and lamented, *'[W]e try to get through an education system that's still accountable to SATS.'* There was also a specific concern that *'when we get to the social and emotional stuff, there doesn't seem to be a pathway [of support]'*, and there was a plea for a clearer designated *'SEND [special educational needs] pathway for looked-after children'*.

In their efforts to access support, staff believe that they have *'a list of children with misdiagnoses'*, and very often, the schools still have to mobilise their own resources. In such circumstances, it is the network of relationships they manage to construct around the child that is crucial, although there is always a worry that *'if you do things too well, you'll lose the funding [i.e. additional resources for the child]'*.

The co-authors in this chapter were willingly taking on a massive responsibility in attempting to meet the needs of many children in their communities who are the subject of child welfare investigations, and in the process, *'we become exposed. . . . [W]e have anxieties about serious case reviews'*. It is the relationships staff engender in schools that enable them to provide support for one another in these situations whilst, in the process, enable them to support the individual child. Safeguarding staff in schools work with trauma on a daily basis and at many significant moments in the lives of the child. Educational practitioners are *'at flashpoints for a child they'll never forget'*.

Commitment and relational practice in trauma-informed schools

The presence of a young person who has suffered trauma or abuse can have a powerful impact on peer relationships, on the day-to-day functioning of a class, and on relationships between young people and all the adults in the school. During the sessions in preparation of this chapter, there was a constant theme that dominated the accounts of the educational practitioners who spoke consistently of their *commitment* to these vulnerable children. These commitments went beyond what could be expected of educational practitioners and demonstrated qualities, for example, that might elude the gaze and knowledge of an Ofsted inspection.

The co-author accounts not only evidenced personal emotional investments in the young people but also indicated an expertise in the establishing of relationships with the young people, colleagues, and parents that underpin successful work. In this concluding section, the co-authors' own remarks are represented mainly in their original form without comment in order to communicate something of the strength of their commitment. Their accounts are organised, firstly, into those from an individual perspective and, secondly, into comments that invoke the relational nature of the collegiality and teamwork support that is a vital aspect of the school culture and ethos.

Personal/relational commitments

'We invest in these children. They're ours.'
'It's a gut instinct [about a family].'
'We care when a child changes.'
'It's our problem.'
'It warms my heart, but it's upsetting.'
'It's a privilege. They work with us.'
'It's beyond a passion. It's the way you feel.'

There were instances when staff spoke of their relationships with individual young people whom they know to be distressed. For example, in respect of the needs and traumatised responses of one young person, I was told, *'Leyla needs a family for life. . . . [S]he would verbalise over and over again [i.e. the trauma].'*

The commitment to a relationship with individual young people was constantly evidenced. For example, the comment *'John, come here, what's going on?'* presents as a fairly commonplace kind of remark that is nevertheless permeated by the knowledge and understanding an educational practitioner might routinely possess about *'John'*, whose behaviour or circumstances were the cause of staff concern. There were other comments that demonstrated the reciprocal nature of these staff–pupil exchanges, and I was told that *'[because] we listen'*, the young person might sometimes offer seemingly spontaneous and misleadingly casual remarks about their home life. For example, *'Did I tell you? . . .'*

The approach constantly evidenced in co-author accounts was intrinsically *relational* and seemed indicative, too, of a broader school culture and ethos. The co-authors invariably used the first-person plural pronoun, and the constant use of *'we'* confirmed the *relational* understanding of the co-authors towards their work and one another, and of their contribution within the weft of the school community.

School/relational commitments

'There's a whole school ethos . . . approach to communication.'
'We've got a great team [i.e. "safeguarding"].'
'We don't really have behavioural difficulties in school.'
'There's lots of restorative work . . . emotional literacy.'
'We do it through respect, not fear.'
'We hold ourselves accountable.'
'We judge ourselves harshly.'

'We share moments of celebration.'

'We're brave and supportive of one another. . . . I hear her [a colleague] being brave [i.e. emotionally].'

'We share the same passion.'

The preceding commitments, whether personal or from the school, provide a template for relational practice in schools with young people who have suffered abuse or adverse childhood experiences (ACES).

Conclusion

Despite years of our working with young people, their trauma and distress, there was a positivity in the co-author accounts, and the communities they serve will be benefiting from their individual and collective endeavours. In particular, it is their commitment to individual young people which offers the young person hope by providing them with the consistency, trust, and individual emotional and psychological investment that they have lacked.

Young people in care proceedings have invariably encountered many significant adverse experiences, and the work that ensues is hugely difficult for all involved. The young persons have become accustomed to their needs going unmet and have, of necessity, become highly sensitised to all aspects of human relationships. While therapeutic interventions will be required for many young people, the first step towards recuperation and alleviation of a young person's distress can be taken by educational practitioners.

We believe that the emotional investments and psychological commitments can reap significant rewards, not only for the young person, but also for the practitioner. Many years ago, Tom posed 'five questions' that psychologists need to ask when working with young people:

How do we speak with children?
How do we speak of children?
How do we write about children?
How do we listen to children?
How do we listen to ourselves (when working with children)?

(Billington, 2006, p. 8)

In many respects, these questions have been answered by the co-authors in this chapter, who have both explicitly and implicitly addressed three key features of *relational* work in school with young people who have experienced trauma:

1. Availability
   'We listen.'
   'There's always someone there for them.'
2. Predictability
   'We're the consistency for the child.'
   'They trust us.'
3. Commitment
   'We love working with the children.'

Young people who have been traumatised develop acute sensitivities to the emotional and psychological presence or absence of their parents/primary carers, and their antennae remain sharp when in school, consciously or otherwise. When we work with children who are suffering distress, it is perfectly understandable that we defend ourselves or resist the trauma before us, not least since we can all too easily come to recognise our own fallibilities and vulnerabilities. Young people can know very quickly when a teacher or a psychologist, for example, is 'available' for a relationship, and should the practitioner be found lacking, the young person can object forcefully, acting out their trauma.

The dynamics of relationships between educational practitioners and traumatised young people can provide vital first steps in the young person's therapeutic journey. The educational practitioners in this chapter suggest that it can be rewarding work, that it is demanding work. It is, above all, a life's work.

Summary box

- Schools can be vital partners in the network of support for young people in care proceedings.
- Schools can be a source of protection, continuity, and stability during otherwise-chaotic or harmful home situations.
- School staff can become emotionally invested in young people and offer quasi-therapeutic relationships that can be an important step in managing the impact of trauma.

References

Billington, T. (2006). *Working with children: Assessment, representation and intervention*. SAGE

Department of Health. (1989). *The children act*. The Stationery Office.

James, W. (2010). *Principles of psychology* (Vols. 1 & 2). Dover Publications. (Original work published 1890)

Tallis, R. (2008). *The kingdom of infinite space: A fantastical journey around your head*. Atlantic Books.

13 Supporting neurodiverse LGBTQ+ students to thrive

Carol Fordham and Heather Paterson

Introduction

In this chapter, we will consider the experience of students with emerging or established neurodivergence combined with not identifying as cisgender or heterosexual. We do not assume that all LGBTQ+ students are neurodiverse, and vice versa. This chapter considers that particular cohort based on experience of working therapeutically with young people referred by SAYiT, a local charity supporting LGBTQ+ young people. The CEO of SAYiT has contributed specialist knowledge to the content of the chapter.

The themes of this chapter are based on the experiences young people shared of being in education. Being bullied and feeling lonely and isolated were common features, and sadly, not just by other children, but in several cases by staff.

> *'After coming out as transgender I experienced a lot of harassment and torment from staff and students. I gained no support or help.'*

Bullying was experienced consistently, and often without the knowledge or intervention of adults at home or at school.

> *'I hear "special", "autistic", and the R slur used regularly as insults. Students mock autism and imitate it.'*

Students fear that 'grassing' on bullying behaviour will only make it worse. When bullying was reported, the response from schools did not bring about the desired change, leaving students and parents frustrated and distressed. I heard several accounts of schools 'outing' LGBTQ+ students to parents without knowledge or consent and using 'dead names' or pronouns as punishment.

Some of the experiences of neurodiverse LGBTQ+ students referred for counselling support caused lasting psychological harm, which some young people have been able to overcome to form meaningful relationships and rewarding careers. Increasingly, students are identifying as non-binary in primary school and developing their identity in secondary school supported by key staff, with whom they have formed an attachment; the support of these adults has transformed their experience.

DOI: 10.4324/9781003451907-13

'Being LGBTQ+ at school is pretty alienating, unless you find others like you or a nice teacher.'

Some students have negotiated or been offered weekly check-ins with a staff member and feel empowered by the recognition of their needs. Others have been instrumental in the development of pride groups and peer education around diverse gender identity and sexuality.

There is some evidence of a correlation between neurodivergence and transgender young people. Although this is not always the case and may be an unhelpful assumption to make, I would argue that awareness and responsiveness may be life-transforming for this cohort of students. I have worked with adults who have had late diagnoses of autism spectrum and ADHD and have gained insight into their childhood experiences which they have processed in therapy. Understanding how their neurodiversity affected their relationships and behaviour, and the freedom to acknowledge their needs, has informed their experience, often bringing significant relief from depression and anxiety and improving their quality of life and relationships.

Many of the young people I have counselled have very supportive parents and families who respect and accept the process of their child/sibling/grandchild and want to influence change in the school environment to accommodate their needs. This is becoming an increasing priority at risk of being neglected, perhaps because of the cost of adapting buildings or the inconvenience of changing administration. More significantly, there exists an underlying resistance to transgender in particular, based on fear that can be expressed as anger and lead to oppressive policy and practice. The relevance of this chapter is to highlight the reality for a very vulnerable group, whose experience of education would be transformed by a relational approach that respects and responds to their needs.

Neurodiversity affects the sense of self; if children feel misunderstood, disliked, or unlovable, their self-acceptance will be compromised. Creating a culture in schools that embraces diversity and makes room for the extraordinary creativity of students whose needs are supported benefits the whole community. The distinction between neurodiverse and neurotypical seems increasingly redundant and is reminiscent of the notion of 'what is normal', We all have traits of neurodiversity in my experience, just as we are all emotionally unstable by definition; our moods change constantly, as do our cognitive and behavioural responses. So why do we continue to 'other' those whose difference attracts a diagnosis?

Political context

Schools generally want to do the best for all their students; however, in the current climate, we see increasing nervousness around how best to support LGBTQ+ and specifically trans and non-binary young people. Many currently working in schools may have themselves been educated under Section 28 or had little or no LGBTQ+ education or training so are trying to educate themselves on the issues impacting LGBTQ+ young people. They are uncertain of what they should or are allowed to do, and young people are increasingly aware of this. Previous government guidance for supporting trans young people in schools produced in conjunction with the LGBTQ+ charity organisation, Stonewall, was withdrawn following pressure from anti-trans campaign groups. At the time of writing, we are still awaiting long-delayed guidance from DfE, and in the meantime, political and media debates have moved from a position of how to support trans young people to how to deal with the problem of trans young people. We are yet to see what the final guidance will state, but the ongoing debates around this are again impacting young people's mental health and fuelling fears as to whether school will be a safe place for them, if indeed they consider it to be currently.

Cultural change

Creating safe spaces in schools for students facing the dual challenge of transgender and neurodivergence is essential during their formative developmental years. Adolescents are highly impressionable and remember the positive and negative influences from this stage for the rest of their lives. Wellbeing cafÈs in schools and colleges provide opportunities for students to come out in a supportive environment and experience connection with peers and adult facilitators. Students can be signposted or drop in to after-school or lunchtime sessions knowing they will be welcome, included, and free to participate or observe on their own terms. I often hear from autistic clients that they spend every lunchtime at school on their own because navigating social interactions and groups is too overwhelming or hostile.

Breakout space is typically a retreat from the pressures of the classroom, with negative connotations of not being able to cope.

> 'There are not enough spaces in school where people can simply just take time out; it always tends to be a busy area or just sat in an office.'

Having a pass out of class immediately draws attention to a student experiencing additional needs and can make the situation more uncomfortable for vulnerable young people. Having spaces where the culture is positive and open towards diversity is far more nurturing than going into an isolated environment with pastoral staff supervision, for example. Where staff and students are co-creators of a wellbeing cafe the agenda can be responsive, relevant, and relational. Having a choice of creative activities and discussion on agreed topics allows everyone to participate on their own terms; listening while crafting, or contributing to discussion, can accommodate their personal preferences and needs. Even limited experience of a supportive environment where students feel accepted can make a difficult experience of school more manageable, acting as an anchor in a storm.

Student-led education on LGBTQ+ and pride groups to support students can provide an essential sense of belonging to a cohort of students who are typically socially excluded or who isolate themselves for self-protection. Staff who accept that they can and need to learn from students experiencing different generational pressures and redefining boundaries around gender will facilitate enriching engagement. Asking about preferred names and pronouns, acknowledging when we get it wrong, and making an effort to get it right for students make a huge difference to their experience of acceptance or rejection.

> 'I had a teacher purposely misgender me multiple times behind my back, and I was told by the whole class that it had happened. . . . I was never asked how I felt about it.'

Schools provide breakfast for students to prepare them for their education, because hungry students cannot learn well. The same attention needs to be given to psychological needs. A lack of recognition and acknowledgement is a significant barrier to learning.

Environmental change

Gendered spaces are no longer relevant or even justifiable if we are to include non-binary children, when there is an alternative that is inclusive and respectful. Prioritising the creation of separate, gender-neutral facilities for changing and toilets will resolve a world of pain for self-conscious adolescents with body dysmorphia and gender dysphoria. Shared gendered changing areas and toilets are traditional bastions of bullying behaviour, and schools have a responsibility to update their facilities to meet the needs of students. Some of the young people taking part in SAYiT groups told me that they had not been allowed to use bathrooms in school because they are transgender; they were unable to eat or drink throughout the day as a result, adversely affecting their physical and mental health and ability to concentrate and learn. Other young people were asked to use the staff facilities.

> 'Directing me to staff bathrooms makes me feel like I am different from others, even if they are trying to help.'

Some local new build schools have ungendered facilities, and others are adapting existing facilities, but the vast majority persist with traditional outdated arrangements.

Moving education and services online during the COVID-19 pandemic has provided precedent for more flexibility in how schools deliver learning. Having time away from a highly stressful environment can be an adaptation that significantly helps sustain the health and wellbeing of neurodivergent LGBTQ+ students. Agreeing a reduced timetable or providing online learning to students at home provides respite from sensory overload and emotional overwhelm. It establishes a respectful acknowledgement and validation of the needs of individual students and could be included in an education healthcare plan.

Slowing down the pace and volume of movement in corridors and foyers through staggered start and finish times for classes and meals would also reduce stress for all students and create a more manageable environment for staff to supervise. Including neurodivergent and LGBTQ+ students on school councils and consulting their experience and knowledge on how to adapt the environment is likely to benefit all students and staff. Tapping into ASD students' special interests and harnessing ADHD-related hyperfixations can bring a wealth of resources and motivation to learning and enhance the confidence and sense of valued contribution amongst a vulnerable group of students. Having young people who love detailed research or are bigger-picture, outside-the-box, energetic thinkers and doers can transform the learning experience for the whole school. Aspirational schools recognise and maximise opportunities that diversity offers.

Ending the practice of isolation in response to challenging behaviour would be an important step towards a more trauma-informed approach to learning, and an easy win. Permission for students to take time out from the classroom is important as a choice that validates a need and should be within a comfortable, not punitive, space. In the same way staff sometimes need to manage behaviour by directing students to leave the classroom, disruptive behaviour will also respond better to a calm, supportive environment. Psychological distress can be expressed as anger or upset, and the child needs the same response whichever emotion is expressed. Abusive behaviour needs to be challenged and corrected within the understanding that we all lose control from time to time and need compassionate containment. An empathetic word and kind, practical response is more effective in the moment than punishment. The time for conversation and acknowledgement of consequences is when the heightened emotion has passed.

Relational change

'Having someone who will listen to you is really important to me and has helped me a lot.'

Students whose presentation attracts negative attention are often rejected, isolated, and abused. The quote is from a 14-year-old transgender boy with ASD and ADHD traits. School has not been a source of rewarding relationships for this student – daily bullying and spending breaks alone have been the norm. He is a highly intelligent, engaging, and proactive individual who has influenced change with straightforward support from responsive staff. Being listened to is important to every human; it does not require training, just a will to focus, observe, and respond to another person, then watch the revolution happen. Attachment is based on communication; eye contact; gentle, non-intrusive, and appropriate touch; tone of speech; and interpretation of body language. The presence of relaxed and friendly staff to receive and respond to distressed students is essential support and effective behaviour management.

When I first started working with this young person, he was miserable at school; the only space where he felt comfortable was isolated in the music room, where he spent his breaks and retreated to when the classroom environment became too overwhelming. His parents had suggested finding another school, but he thought it would be much the same experience and he would have to manage a stressful change when he was already struggling to cope and feeling suicidal.

Over time, the school began to embrace and respond to LGBTQ+ students, creating a pride group, which gave my client a sense of purpose and a place of belonging. He did not think the member of staff supporting the group was particularly responsive to the LGBTQ+ students but found another teacher who wore a pride flag and was open and supportive. This teacher offered my client daily check-ins, which transformed his experience of school. Gradually, he began to cultivate friendships and school no longer felt quite so hostile. He began to find witty, intelligent responses to 'roast' the bullies, gaining confidence and starting to feel that he could influence his environment.

Educational change

One of the key barriers to acceptance and support for LGBTQ+ and neurodivergent students is the fear of getting it wrong. Inevitably, students and staff will inadvertently mis-pronoun and misgender, responding to visual cues that can take time to adjust, but acknowledgement of mistakes reflects an understanding of the importance to respect the individual, expanding the window of tolerance for these mistakes. School staff are in a position of authority, and it is uncomfortable to be wrong-footed. If the culture supports curiosity, openness, and owning errors, it is far easier to navigate unfamiliar territory.

A relational approach to education cultivates openness to learning and change on an individual and collective basis. LGBTQ+ and neurodiverse students have much to teach staff and their peers about their reality and experiences, which encourages mutual respect and may highlight individual, organisational, and political oppression. Cisgender neurotypical students and staff need to be gentle with themselves in responding to differences and acknowledge their discomfort in adapting to emerging and growing cultural change. It feels new to those who have not experienced gender or sexual fluidity, and they may want to ignore or even resist the experience of others to defend their own sense of self. When transgender students are experimenting and redefining chosen names, perhaps multiple times, it may feel difficult to remember to use the preferred name, and embarrassing to get it wrong. It is like learning a new skill; it takes practice and patience, and we go on making mistakes, which needs to be accepted.

Guidance for schools

Several studies show that neurodiverse people are more likely to be LGBTQ+, and vice versa, with some groups weaponising this. While it may be the case that there is a greater overlap between these two groups, this is only an issue if you perceive being neurodiverse and/or being LGBTQ+ as a negative outcome. Some groups have focused on trying to find a cause of this coincidence, which can be both ableist and anti-LGBTQ+, much like the 1980's attempts to find the 'gay gene' to 'cure' homosexuality. Neurodiverse LGBTQ+ young people are being presented as having something 'wrong' with them that needs to be fixed, negatively impacting their mental health. It is, however, more likely that neurodiverse people who have a non-neurotypical understanding of the world also have a different understanding of heteronormative and cisnormative views of sexuality and gender.

Both LGBTQ+ and neurodiverse people are viewed in a framework of deviating from a norm. However, in both cases, that 'norm' is socially constructed and has varied over time and across geographies and cultures. All generations break ground within their cultural constraints, and whilst some social and political persuasions resist the challenge of accepting and adjusting to reality, change is inevitable, can be inconvenient, and may be unwelcome. If we can step back from how we think and feel about the perceived threat and remember to show respect to all those affected, we are taking a relational approach which develops understanding and finds a way forward that includes the whole community, which is better for wellbeing and educational outcomes.

Your Legitimate Rights as an Individual may be a useful benchmark to apply in the education setting for staff and students:

1. You have a right to need things from others.
2. You have a right to put yourself first sometimes.
3. You have a right to feel and express your emotions and your pain.
4. You have the right to be the final judge of your beliefs and accept them as legitimate.
5. You have the right to your opinions and convictions, *and the right to change them*.*
6. You have the right to your experience – even if it's different from that of other people.

7. You have the right to protest any treatment or criticism that feels bad to you.
8. You have the right to negotiate for change.
9. You have the right to ask for help, emotional support, or anything else you need (even though you may not always get it).
10. You have a right to say no; saying no doesn't make you bad or selfish.
11. You have a right not to justify yourself to others.
12. You have a right not to take responsibility for someone else's problem.
13. You have a right to choose not to respond to a situation.
14. You have a right, *sometimes*, to inconvenience or disappoint others.

(*text in italics added by author)

'Nobody ever taught me about LGBT+ in school, so I was stuck wondering why I felt uncomfortable with my body and why schools brushed [off] my discomfort with changing in classrooms with other children. . . . [P]eople didn't know how to deal with my needs and told me to get over it.'

One young adult participating in a group at SAYiT made a plea that staff in schools are trained to reach out to the 'outliers'; she was the first transgender student in her school with undiagnosed autism. She was facing educational, social, and emotional barriers that made life extremely difficult. One teacher took an interest and noticed that she was a bright student who had difficulties expressing her ideas in written communication and arranged a scribe for an exam. This was the first exam the student passed at school, which transformed her experience; she became aware of her capability and had hope.

One young person was distressed by a PSHE lesson called 'the trans debate', which they found very transphobic.

'If queer culture is taught or if neurodivergence is taught, we should be asked . . . about how to go about it and what might be helpful to teach – we know what it's like to be treated the way we are, so ask us.'

Another young person observed that:

'[P]eers, tutors, etc. do not understand or respect asexuality or being trans.'

Involving students with lived experience in developing and delivering education alongside supportive staff would influence cultural, environmental, relational, and educational change to the benefit of the whole school.

Summary box

Staff in schools have skills and experience in supporting the emotional wellbeing of children and young people and ability to adapt practices to be inclusive and validating for all students, with support. Having a space to share experiences and reflect on how to develop the environment and culture relationally is essential for all roles supporting young people. Accessing staff training and support through local specialist services is recommended, but equally important is an open and curious approach that will allow for connection and recognition, inviting young people to share their experiences and express their needs. Creating spaces that are welcoming and supportive is key, and introducing wellbeing cafes and ending the practice of isolation transforms the school environment. Treating LGBTQ+ neurodivergent students with the same respect and concern as other students is a reasonable and achievable expectation. Supporting them to thrive, contribute, and shape the school environment is enriching for everyone.

14 Emerging adulthood and working with uncertainty

A multi-agency perspective

Tom Mullen

Introduction

EMERGE Leeds is an NHS-led multi-agency service which seeks to work with young adults, aged 18–25 years old, who are believed to have complex emotional needs which may at times be described as emerging personality disorder. In this chapter, I will describe how a group of diverse professionals, including psychological, creative, and occupational therapists, work in partnership with colleagues from a range of third sector organisations incorporating youth work, housing support, and peer support services to work alongside young people as they navigate and manage the transition from youth to adulthood.

The young people we work with have earlier lives in which trauma has significantly shaped their developmental trajectory and impacted upon their sense of self and their understanding of and trust in relationships with others. They have frequently developed means of coping with distress which could be considered maladaptive, are often self-defeating, and would be viewed as high-risk. This often involves self-harming by cutting or deliberately overdosing or placing themselves in situations which seriously compromise their safety and/or the safety of others, for example, standing on railway tracks, threatening to jump from bridges, etc.

In this chapter, I will describe how we seek to form a collaborative relationship with the young person and work to develop a shared sense of their life story and narrative. I will explore the inherent dangers in pathologising behaviour, which could be viewed as experimentally age-appropriate. I will explore the belief that young people cannot and should not be defined by the trauma they have experienced as they frequently are by services tasked with responding to their expressed distress. I will argue that practitioners must commit to a relational stance to both best support the young people we work with and to sustain themselves in their practice.

EMERGE Leeds

In 2001, we worked on a citywide review of policy, service provision, and working arrangements across Leeds for those people believed to attract the label of personality disorder. This approach involved bringing together a multi-agency steering group which included people who had used services and was prompted by widespread acknowledgement that all services were struggling to provide a helpful response to meet the needs of this population; worse

DOI: 10.4324/9781003451907-14

still, at times, services were seen to be hostile, stigmatising, and excluding. The review led to a proposal to establish a citywide managed clinical network (MCN) as a dedicated resource to improve our understanding and practice and to develop new ways of engaging and working with individuals who had spent many years ricocheting around agencies and services.

In 2004, the Leeds Personality Disorder Managed Clinical Network was funded by the Department of Health to be 1 of 11 national pilot sites. MCNs are noted to be a practical means of agencies working together to resolve challenges and difficulties that no one organisation can resolve on their own. In effect, they are concerned with anticipating the range of needs a population may present with and centrally funding and managing a shared resource. In this instance, the Leeds MCN included staff from health, social care, housing, probation, and third sector services coming together to embark on a journey of learning and collaboration.

In the first years of working, the average age of those who used the service was 36 years old; however, by 2018, the average age of those using the service was 21years old, and in 2020, we were supported to become a dedicated service for 18- to 25-year-olds with complex emotional needs, and a focus group of young adults who used services decided upon the name EMERGE Leeds.

We retained the MCN structure, but partners have altered and evolved over the years, particularly with a wish to be young person-centred and in response to learning and promising evidence of what works. At any given time, we can work with up to 100 young adults for up to one year. We have a team of care coordinators who have a caseload of up to 15 young people, and they work alongside their EMERGE Leeds colleagues in any combination which may best support the individual wants and needs of the young person.

The work

At its core, the work is viewed as relational. Our understanding of relational practice will be explored further in this chapter, but it is grounded in acknowledging that the young people we see come to us having had a life of significant and often challenging relationships with family, peers, education providers, health and social care professionals, and countless others. Relationships which are often characterised by mistrust, fear, and vulnerability. They have developed a range of helpful and unhelpful coping strategies to manage their emotional distress, and they are between the age of 18 and 25 years old, which is developmentally significant as they seek to make sense of their own evolving identity and sense of self.

It is in this context that we seek to get alongside the young person, to create a safe and containing space in which we can hear and understand their story and develop a shared formulation which may help make sense of some of the challenges they consistently face in daily living. The challenge of this task should not be underestimated, as it invariably involves navigating both practical and personal difficulties and working to foster trust and an understanding of our offer of work. We will meet the young person in any environment or space which will work for them; this may be at a traditional office base but could as easily be at their home or in a local park, and we will agree a frequency of meeting and explore together who else may be helpfully involved in their care.

Whilst the individual care coordinator works through this introductory and exploratory stage of relationship building, they are supported by what we describe as a 'team around the young person' (TAYP), which will involve a senior clinician and other colleagues coming together on a regular basis to support the thinking and practice. This is a vital structure for our work as it is a mechanism of ensuring we remain committed to reflecting as a team, and it supports the care coordinator to feel safe and contained in their practice in order to have the greatest likelihood of supporting the young person to equally feel safe and contained when working with us. It is often the case that during this early exploratory phase of relationship building, we will see the young person engage in a range of behaviours which compromise their safety and wellbeing and may result in them coming into contact with other services, including crisis services, accident and emergency teams, the police, and so on. It is common for the young people we work with to have formal safeguarding concerns, most commonly in regards their ongoing vulnerability, and this will require our service to be involved in working with colleagues as a part of the multi-agency safeguarding process. The TAYP affords a space in which we can consider the young person and the range of risk behaviours whilst maintaining a curious and non-judgemental stance as we seek to develop a planned and thoughtful approach to the work without being drawn into an unhelpful reactive response. It also gives us time to consider how the young person interacts with other services and how this range of other services responds to the young person, which will be important when we seek to work alongside wider services to support a formulation-led, considered, and consistent response.

We will seek to introduce wider EMERGE Leeds colleagues to the work with the young person as required, based upon an understanding of what may be most helpful. The following is a brief overview of the EMERGE Leeds partners and the role they play and, it is hoped, will offer a sense of a collective team approach in which interventions and support are layered but unified in embracing an approach which is compassionate, considered, and consistent.

Partners in practice

A frequent consideration in the work is seeking to ensure that the young person is residing in accommodation which is safe and affords a relatively secure base. The 'home' environment can vary enormously. Some young people may continue to live in a family home, where the dynamics within are significant contributors to their ongoing mental health difficulties; others may be 'sofa surfing' – relying upon friends and acquaintances to provide a space on a temporary basis. Others, again, may be living alone and can be struggling to cope with the requirements of maintaining a property and their own safety within. Having dedicated housing support workers within the EMERGE Leeds team is a real asset and has proved incredibly helpful over the years. The housing workers are seconded from Community Links, a leading third sector organisation in the city. They can assess the current housing situation for the young person and explore with them a range of realistic possibilities to either support them in their existing environment or to actively seek alternative accommodation and to navigate the often-complex processes which this entails. The housing support workers are fully integrated members of the team who access the same training and supervisory provision as all other team members and, as such, are able to approach their defined role in a psychologically informed way which is consistent with the principles of the service.

As a specialist service, we offer what would be considered to be a high level of contact with those whom we support, but we are always mindful of the reality that this remains a relatively small amount of time in the life of a young person. A few hours of direct contact per week pales in comparison to the vast time periods the young person seeks to fill in the course of a day or week. As staff members, we are aware that large chunks of our time are scheduled and governed by diary appointments and meetings and our often-busy family and social lives. We may complain of having little or no time. This could not be further from the lived experience of many of the young people we work with, who can often find themselves lacking in occupational structure and friendship/family groups and instead are left with the daunting prospect of managing recurring anxieties, thoughts, and ruminations on a regular basis. We are fortunate to have a dedicated occupational therapy (OT) team as part of our EMERGE Leeds service, and it is the role of our OT colleagues to help us better understand the young people as occupational beings and to gain a coherent sense of what this means for them. In practice, this may involve occupational assessments and working alongside young people to understand their interest and competence in relation to life tasks and hobbies/pursuits. It may involve exposing the young people to a range of occupational experiences to better appreciate their strengths and challenges, and it is often about us seeking to engage the young person as an occupational being in order to gain a better appreciation of how their time may be constructively filled with activity which is appropriate to their wishes and skills. This point is hugely important, as a failure to understand the interests or strengths of a young person can often lead to well-intentioned professionals setting up a range of activities for young people which they simply fail to engage with as it is often something which is unfortunately pitched at the wrong level or may be considered too anxiety-provoking or simply never have really been of interest to the young person. Our OTs are also interested in understanding any sensory issues which the young person may present with and to supporting environmental adaptations which may improve the likelihood of them being able to stick with a task or an exercise.

When young people are referred to EMERGE Leeds and we commence an assessment, we often find ourselves considering whether their struggles and presenting behaviours should be viewed in the context of someone requiring support and intervention from secondary mental health services or viewed as developmentally appropriate, given the adjustments and adaptations required to manage the transition from youth to adulthood. Within the EMERGE Leeds service, we employ dedicated youth workers, seconded from the Market Place, a leading youth work organisation in the city, and they seek to improve the wider team's understanding of age-appropriate interventions and activity which is commensurate with the developmental stage of the young people we see. The youth workers offer an alternative engagement with the young person, introducing them to both individual and group work experiences, where they will have an opportunity to connect with other young people and a wider range of services and support options which are young person–centred. They will also walk alongside the young person, supporting them in various social settings and connecting with the young people on their own terms.

Whilst we would regard all interventions offered as therapeutic, some of the young people we see will be ready to engage in a formal therapy either on an individual or group basis, and this work is delivered by our psychological and creative therapists. Our talking therapies include a range of modalities, including cognitive analytical therapy (CAT), mentalisation-based therapy (MBT), dialectical behaviour therapy (DBT), and require a significant commitment from young people to regularly and consistently attend sessions and to manage the processing of learning and discovery which will inevitably occur as a consequence of the work. For many of the young people we see, it may be difficult to talk about their trauma and troubles, and it could be that other means of therapeutically engaging them would be of greater benefit. To this end, we also have creative therapists, who can offer both music and drama therapy as an alternative to the more frequently deployed talking therapies.

Within the EMERGE Leeds service, we also employ peer support workers (PSW). Seconded from Touchstone, another leading third sector organisation, the PSWs are experts by experience, having lived with many of the challenges that our young service users experience, including having navigated and negotiated a way through care services. The PSWs offer a peer-to-peer relationship, and it is hoped that their sharing of their own learning and experience alongside an offer of genuine support can be of great benefit both to the wider staff team and those we work with.

As previously stated, we can work with the young people for up to one year, and we may, in exceptional circumstances, extend this for a longer period. Given the numbers of young people we work with, the multiple services we liaise and foster relationships with, and the range of complex needs and risk issues which we seek to understand and mitigate, it is essential that we commit to ensuring that we have in place supportive structures and mechanisms which can ensure that all staff remain open and reflective in their practice and we all continue to capture learning, the good and not so good, which will enable us individually and collectively to evolve and adapt to make the best offer and effort we can to the young people we are working with.

We have a senior team of clinicians and service managers who are actively involved in the clinical work and ensure that each member of staff has regular clinical supervision. There are weekly clinical review meetings attended by all staff, where we consider the care of a number of young people and our understanding of their presenting needs, their communication, and we seek to test our own thinking and practice. We also have regular clinical governance meetings, which bring together all partner organisations to share learning from research and evaluation activity, learning from service user and partner feedback, learning from incidents, and to review our work against quality measures and standards.

We have recently worked with young people to produce a people involvement and participation strategy. This involves young people and staff coming together in groups and meetings to consider the issues that matter to those who use the service and to work on ways of continually being responsive to observations and feedback. It involves young people being actively involved on recruitment panels, being consulted with on policy matters and issues which impact upon wider delivery of the service, co-delivering training to staff and other teams, developing and delivering peer support groups, and generating ideas for new involvement opportunities and initiatives.

Working with the wider system

For many years, those in health and social care have struggled to work with individuals they believe to present with characteristics which could be defined as 'personality disorder'. Within our service, we have always regarded it as vital that we not only work directly with service users and their families but also work with wider system providers to develop their knowledge and understanding of people whom they can all too easily label in any number of pejorative ways. This experience is familiar to a large number of the young people we encounter, with there being a frequently held view that they are not deserving of mental health service interventions by virtue of *'knowing what they are doing'* or, as has been often stated by any number of practitioners in any number of teams, *'we only make them worse when we get involved'*. Both statements in italics are, of course, for the most part, true; unfortunately, though, they are used with a desire to exclude people from services rather than to be curious about why an individual with clear capacity and awareness would choose to deliberately and repeatedly harm themselves and then present themselves repeatedly to apparently caring services which consistently proceed to act in ways which lead to an escalation of their distress. It would be a reasonable assertion to believe that many within the wider services, on encountering the young people we work with, firstly simply fail to see them as 'young people' and, secondly, are unable to adopt a relational stance. This is highly problematic, not least because we know that young peoples' expectations of services will be shaped by how they experience services, but arguably of greater concern is that each encounter results in the perpetuation of an invalidating response to the young person's clear communication of pain and distress, which likely led them to be help-seeking.

This inability to firstly recognise a 'young person' is, in all likelihood, the consequence of a mental health and social care system which decides that, on reaching the chronological age of 18 years old, you are now an adult, the same as any other adult, be they 28, 38, or 48 years old, and you will all be treated in the same way and receive exactly the same service as adults. This is arguably one of the greatest travesties of our current system, this complete failure to acknowledge how developmentally important this 18- to 25-year-old time period is and to respond in an informed way with due care and sensitivity. There is now, more than ever, an acknowledgement that this period, sometimes referred to as 'emerging adulthood', is unique and critical in human development. Some of the noted characteristics include 'instability' with frequent changes of plans, partners, jobs; 'identity exploration' involving attempts to work out who you are and who you might be; 'self-focused' exercising freedoms and independence whilst delaying significant adult responsibilities; and 'increased risk-taking', be that with drug experimentation or a failure to fully consider consequences. There are other cited aspects of this developmental stage, but suffice it to say that it warrants greater consideration than it is currently afforded by policymakers and those who seek to shape the future of our caring services.

The inability to hold a relational stance is a practice concern which is, in part, explained by an overwhelmed and under-resourced mental health system which can appear to function by processing people and numbers rather than considering people as relational beings. Our EMERGE Leeds understanding of relational practice is developed and honed with ongoing training and development. We have to hold in mind the impact of trauma upon young people and how this affects their relationships with themselves and others, and we need to maintain a relational awareness in our day-to-day work, including an awareness that some relational impacts may be unconscious, as aspects of self can be unprocessed and may be too painful, confusing, or difficult to acknowledge. It is only through the development of a safe and containing therapeutic relationship that we can begin to explore with curiosity and openness what may be driving an individual's behaviour and actions and leading to challenges and repeated patterns in relationship-forming. Many young adults, including those we work with, have what we might describe as a less-than-coherent sense of self. They can have multiple, often contradictory, presentations of self in the space of hours, depending upon the social space and circumstance they may find themselves in. This can be equally perplexing for them and for those who seek to work with them. However, time and again, we must return to the task of sustaining and growing a helpful therapeutic relationship in which we are non-judgemental, curious, compassionate, and kind.

Within EMERGE Leeds, we have consistently offered training and consultation to all other services and for individual practitioners and teams. There is a great uptake of this offer across the city and beyond, and there are no doubt benefits which are realised as a result of this supportive activity. It is, however, the case that despite our concerted citywide efforts to improve the general service response to people labelled as suffering from 'personality disorder', we still all too frequently encounter the same unhelpful and damaging attitudes which prompted us to undertake this journey of work over 20 years ago. Some of this can be, at times, explained by staff changes, team and system alterations, and memory being lost in relation to prior learning. However, it appears much more likely that, despite our best efforts, a culture has prevailed across the mental health system in which those service users who are considered too difficult, too demanding, and too confusing are 'othered' and excluded from access to all manner of services and opportunities. It is therefore important that, as a service, we are able to make use of our relational stance to assist us to make sense of the wider system and its response to this work. Again, we return to the conscious and unconscious processes at play – we can, if you like, observe the system to have a mind, which is susceptible to the same logical errors of understanding which arise in each of us. A simple example of this would be when we hear talk of young people causing 'splitting' in teams and services and ostensibly being blamed for services and teams being unable to find a shared coherent view or approach. Of course, we know that young people in this instance are not the creators of this split; we know that it is a truth that teams split teams, but the convenience of locating the problem in the behaviour of the young person all too often appears irresistible. The group mind proceeds to buy into this belief, and for example, when the young person as previously described proceeds to display developmentally appropriate contrasting representations of 'self', this is used as further evidence of their attempts to deceive and split.

In the same way which we approach the clinical work with young adults, we must approach the work with system partners. It is unhelpful to be overtly critical and judging of the clearly unhelpful actions we frequently witness or hear of. Instead, we must return once more to the relational stance, to seek to gain a healthy, therapeutic relationship with wider colleagues based upon compassion and kindness, curiosity, and non-judgement, consistency, and validation and the holding of hope. Our commitment to relational work must be shown in how we work with our service users, our colleagues within our team, and those across the wider system if we are to realise an ambition of consistently creating spaces in which we can have healthy and helpful dialogue and work collaboratively to mutually learn the means of resolving the many challenges we face in pursuit of a good life.

Conclusion

We are privileged to be afforded time in the lives of those young adults we work with, and whilst this endeavour is relatively new, we must do all we can to bring together key learning and share this for the consideration of wider interested stakeholders.

The term *personality disorder* has always been considered contentious and/or offensive and arguably has little clinical utility. Young adults from the service were consulted on this term and settled on a preference for *complex emotional needs* as a descriptor term, albeit with acknowledgement of how poorly defined this may be and noting the power of language to sometimes unhelpfully shape perception. What we have discovered is that those referred to our service are commonly described by others as having any combination of or all of the following: disordered eating, being autistic/neurodiverse, suffering from anxiety and depression, having gender identity issues, misusing illegal substances and alcohol . . . and possibly an emerging personality disorder!

What we have observed is that the young people are so much more than any diagnostic label. They are interesting, funny, creative, and curious about themselves and the world(s) that they inhabit. They are also, often with good reason, fearful, mistrusting, and uncertain. It is perhaps this uncertainty that can lead them to seek a diagnosis, possibly as a means of bringing some certainty into what are very confusing times. We must relentlessly work to remain objective and mindful of the continuing impact which significant and serious life traumas have had upon the thinking, development, and relationships of the young adults and relentlessly strive to support and nurture their further growth and development and be forgiving of the mistakes that they and we make along the way.

Summary box

Key learning points

The time between 18 and 25 years old, sometimes referred to as 'emerging adulthood', is a unique and critical period of human development and can be confusing and troubling for both the young individual and those who seek to work with them.

A cohesive, coordinated multi-agency response which is relationally focused can afford an opportunity to collaboratively work with young adults to better understand their life narratives and positively inform their future growth and development.

It is essential to compassionately work with and understand the wider system which the young adult encounters and to support the system players to work with the challenge of uncertainty in practice.

15 *REFLECT*

A collaborative and reflective relational approach that empowers adults to better understand and nurture, and children and young people to flourish

Claire-Marie Whiting

Acknowledgements: Joanne Askew, Rachel Crosby, Karen Davies, Scott Johnson, Lisa Morris, Carol Taylor, Kathryn Thorn, and Jemma Wilkinson. Current and former members of Rotherham Educational Psychology Service who collaborated to create *REFLECT*.

Introduction

In part, *REFLECT* was generated in resistance to the suggestion that we create a model for schools based upon 'age-related expectations' for social and emotional skills. It was suggested that doing so would help track progression and trajectories for achieving predicted outcomes, similar to those adopted within the academic curriculum. Whilst adopting language such as 'working towards', 'achieving', and 'exceeding' age-related expectations might arguably work for literacy skills or maths and generate workable data that might satisfy external bodies seeking to measure and compare children and young people, and schools, we felt that when applied to social and emotional development, a discourse is implied that would position some children and young people as 'behind', emotionally, perhaps needing an intervention to help them 'catch up'. If the emotional 'gap' between them and their peers is significant, this could warrant a referral via a diagnostic pathway to specialists and, ultimately, the allocation of a label to explain what is 'wrong' with them.

As a group of psychologists, we preferred to work from the relational premise that how we communicate our emotions is associated with a tapestry of complex interactions with others that will have occurred throughout our lives, the contexts within which we exist, and significant life events. We rejected the idea of a discourse that pathologises a child or young person for what might be a very understandable emotional response. We also recognised that, as human beings, any of us might communicate distress or excitement through behaviour that could be categorised as developmentally 'younger' than our chronological age. At these times, we require others to provide a relational response that matches our needs rather than be in receipt of judgement, an intervention, or a label.

Psychological understandings implicit within *REFLECT*

We began to collaborate to develop a model which would avoid the notion of a straight-forward linear trajectory, instead enabling a more holistic understanding of children and

DOI: 10.4324/9781003451907-15

young people's social and emotional development. We also wanted the model to be helpful for schools and settings. However, as an eclectic group of educational psychologists, each of us potentially championing our own psychological position and long-held constructs, coming together to co-create an agreed way of understanding social and emotional development proved to be an enriching and dynamic experience. It became important for us to listen to each other, reflect on the ideas colleagues were introducing, and work out an approach that would avoid individuals feeling undermined, or their ideas rejected. Without being explicit about it, we modelled what became the *REFLECT* approach through our interactions and the safe, relational context that was created, and that we tried to replicate again when we began to discuss our thinking with wider partners. In this way, we came to an agreement about the psychological approaches we felt had been important in evolving our shared understanding.

Child development

We began thinking about traditional models of child development in education, starting with Piaget. These models tended to describe growth milestones in a linear way, for example, in cognition, language, and physical development, and identify the typical ages or stages at which they occur following a chronological trajectory, such as birth to infancy, to pre-school, to school-age, to adolescence, and to adulthood. We did not wish to dismiss outright this way of conceptualising child development. We agreed that understanding a child or young person's capacity to learn is valuable in thinking about the degree of challenge with which they are expected to cope. However, we also wanted to incorporate other ways of thinking about development to enable a more fluid and less-constrained perception of how children and young people grow emotionally. We found it helpful to acknowledge that the social and environmental context is not ignored even within traditional theories prior to Vygotsky's theory of sociocultural development (DeVries, 1997).

Attachment and psychodynamic theory

We agreed on the importance of attachment theory, which draws upon psychodynamic perspectives by emphasising the impact of early relational development on all that happens afterwards for a child or young person, for example, their relationships with others, cognition, language, social skills, and physical growth. The nurturing relationship between the infant and primary caregiver is understood to provide the blueprint for the way children and young people form emotional connections or attachments with others and the way they view and relate to the world. John Bowlby, commonly understood to be the first attachment theorist, defined this as '[a] deep and enduring emotional bond that connects one person to another across time and space' (Bowlby, 1969).

It is suggested that if a child or young person experiences attachments that feel secure, mental processes will develop that help them regulate their emotions, reduce their anxiety, have some insight, and 'attune' to others (Sroufe & Siegel, 2011). These are concepts underpinning relatively new developments in schools, such as attachment-aware and trauma-informed practice. Cubeddu and MacKay (2017), writing about nurture groups in schools, explain the importance of *attunement*, which is defined as 'how responsive an individual is to another's emotional needs . . . marked by language and behaviour which reflect awareness of the individual's emotional state' (p. 264). When we experience attunement from others, we are therefore more likely to reciprocate and demonstrate the same skills in our own relationships.

We were interested in this idea of adults tuning into the emotional context of the child or young person alongside containment, which refers to a relational ability to 'hold' whatever the other person needs emotionally to create a sense of being emotionally safe. We also considered the wider application of attachment theory in the potential for schools to feel like safe relational spaces. Stephen Hyman (2012) introduced the metaphor of a 'holding' environment as one that fosters the natural development of the full potential of each child or young person. In this kind of environment, security is bolstered, and learning optimised (Hyman, 2012).

Drawing upon the work of Winnicott (1965), Hymen suggests that adults in schools need to:

- Empathetically attune to the needs of the children and young people in their care
- Be flexible enough to contain or suspend their own needs in order to soothe, support, and facilitate children and young people's emotional needs
- Read the child or young person's non-verbal signals and respond accordingly, soothing as needed

Hymen asks adults in schools to understand that children and young people see themselves through their eyes. Geddes (2006) also stresses that school learning is profoundly influenced by the security and stability of the student–teacher relationship. A holding environment is therefore one that fosters responding to children and young people in ways that are attuned and contain their emotional needs.

We therefore recognised the potential for schools to provide safe, containing contexts generated through attuned relationships between adults and children or young people, nurturing opportunities for emotional growth.

Social constructionism

Connected to these ideas, social constructionist thinking also featured in our discussions, prompting us to take account of the power relationships involved in interactions between a child or young person and others, particularly adults, and how their self-understanding, beliefs, and assumptions are constructed through language which is, in turn, situated in the wider discourses they experience:

> It is through the daily interactions between people in the course of social life that our versions of knowledge become fabricated. Therefore, social interaction of all kinds, especially language, is of great interest. . . . [T]he goings-on between people in the course of their everyday lives are seen as the practices during which our shared versions of knowledge are constructed.
>
> (Burr, 2015, p. 5)

In thinking about social and emotional development, it might be argued that some of the constructs generated about, and laden upon, children and young people are not only limiting but also potentially damaging. The social constructionist lens begs us to reflect upon the importance of *every* interaction we might have with, or about, a child or young person, the language we use, and the power we have to influence the way they think about themselves and therefore interact with others (Billington, 2006b). Wider social structures like schools and the (political) discourses they cultivate impact our own constructs, which contribute to the constructs children and young people hold about themselves, others, and the world around them, shaping their identity. However, adopting this position also introduces the possibility of change. It is possible to reconstruct realities by using different language about children and young people, creating a relational space for greater agency and participation and richer, more complex discourses and narratives. The idea of alternative identities is thereby made possible. Tom Billington's five questions remind practitioners to keep this in mind:

> How do we speak with children?
> How do we speak of children [to others]?
> How do we write of children?
> How do we listen to children?
> How do we listen to ourselves [when working with children]?
>
> Billington (2006a, p. 8)

Ecological systems theory

It was therefore evident to us that it is important to understand the systems within which children and young people exist, including structural inequalities playing out in their lives, and experiences of marginalisation which inevitably contribute to their social and emotional wellbeing. In thinking about opportunities and limitations for children and young people's social and emotional development, theorists such as Bronfenbrenner (1994) beg us to better understand the child or young person in the context of their family, school, and powerful socio-political systems.

Systemic practice and collaboration

Drawing upon family therapy, *systemic practice* is a generic term given to working with families and individuals mindful of, and working within, the relationships between people, across the generations, and in the context of all the human systems within which people live. This way of working encourages practitioners to help dismantle some of the constraining, pathologising, and limiting narratives that submerge individuals and which can saturate conversations about children and young people identified with social and emotional needs. Instead, more collaborative approaches are encouraged. This makes it possible to consider how we might work together to facilitate alternative stories that involve growth, voice, and the empowerment of children, young people, and their families. Collaboration and co-production, which necessarily involve a partnership approach, rely upon practitioners becoming more self-aware, reflective, and reflexive, mindful of constructs and prejudices they may be taking with them into a conversation. This way of working requires reflecting 'in' the midst of dialogue as well as 'on' it afterwards (Schön, 1983). It involves circularity and flexibility rather than fixed or linear ways of thinking, allowing scope for 'not knowing', remaining curious, and being open to different perspectives (Anderson, 2005, 2006). As a result, systemic, relational approaches provide an alternative to blame, and 'within child or young person', pathological explanations can be avoided. More flexible 'both and' explanations replace 'either . . . or' because it is understood that children and young people have had different experiences within their own ecological systems, and that lives and relationships are often messy. They do not fit neatly or easily into linear models of social and emotional progression.

REFLECT

The *REFLECT* alternative we developed attempts to unite developmental, social constructionist, psychodynamic, and systemic perspectives. In so doing, a genuinely collaborative and reflective approach is advocated.

The *REFLECT* model consists of five *phases* of emotional development: 'Here I am!', 'This is me', 'Me and you', 'Who am I?' and 'Learning to be' (see Figure 15.1). The relationship between the phases is understood to be cyclical and, at the same time, dynamic and flexible, in that it is accepted a child, young person, or adult might move between any of the phases at any point in their lifetime. There is a foundational understanding that children and young people have a need to experience attunement and nurture, which, in turn, enables reciprocity (the give-and-take that occurs in relationships). Ideally, these experiences will begin in the home and continue to be embedded through interactions and relationships at school and within other contexts encountered. The educational context has an important role to play.

Pilot studies involving schools demonstrated that *REFLECT* is a flexible tool that can be used in a variety of ways. It has proved useful in consultations related to individual children and young people and their families but was also adopted by one school to introduce a whole-school approach that promoted a culture supporting emotional wellbeing and inclusion. In Rotherham, *REFLECT* and the complementary four cornerstones of co-production and inclusive practice (see the related chapter in this book) promote whole-school relational approaches designed to generate inclusive and co-productive cultures. The cornerstones are 'welcome and

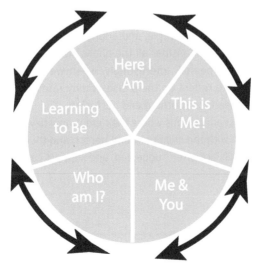

Figure 15.1 Dynamic, cyclical nature of the REFLECT model and the five phases.

care', 'value and include', 'communicate and partnership', and at their heart is 'trust'. Similarly, *REFLECT* is asking for individuals representing a range of systems and holding different degrees of power and interests to come together, in trust, as partners. The intention is to create a safe relational and reflective space where individuals can speak openly, listen to each other, and work collaboratively to change what often feel like painful and distress-laden experiences for everybody concerned. It is hoped that next steps, because they are collaboratively constructed, should encourage a greater sense of empowerment, agency, and ownership.

The dream is that using the *REFLECT* model will feel generative, enabling richer understanding of the fluid nature of social and emotional needs children and young people might experience, resisting the temptation to pathologise when very human emotions are being communicated, thus avoiding blame. When the model was discussed with our parent carer forum, it was received with relief. Parent carers suggested that the model liberated them, and their children and young people, from experiencing what they considered to be blame-laden discourses, even when these were heavily disguised. One parent reflected that it made her realise her child's situation was not her fault, and she could see how she might apply the same approach at home. This was also voiced by a parent carer group we met in a school.

The five phases and *REFLECT* model in action

The model is based on an interactive, dynamic understanding of emotional development. The approach involves identifying needs, setting collaborative goals, and celebrating progress. The fluid and cyclical nature of the model reinforces that emotional needs can develop and change over time and in response to different experiences and events. *REFLECT* is not cyclical in a one-directional sense, but the circle demonstrates how we might all be engaged in a to-ing and fro-ing when it comes to our social and emotional needs and skills. A child or young person's emotional presentation may seem typical of one phase, but it is accepted that we all experience situations differently, bringing with us our past and current experiences of relationships, environments and systems, and the constructs that have been generated. We might therefore simultaneously demonstrate emotions and related needs across phases. For example, although 'Here I am' illustrates the emotional needs expected of an infant, there are times older children and young people, and adults, may also find aspects of themselves here, which is why it is helpful to consider all the phases when understanding the emotional context for a child or young person. Interestingly, when we deliver training based on the model and ask school staff to reflect on the phases, many refer to those occasions they slip into 'Here I am' and their need for soothing and nurturing.

For some, it may at first seem obvious where their emotional development broadly lies. However, through collaboration with the child or young person and their family, reflecting on what is taking place, helpful details are often suggested, and support can be tailored accordingly.

The phases

'Here I am'

The model is set out here with the 'Here I am' phase outlined first; it is proposed that this is used as a starting point.

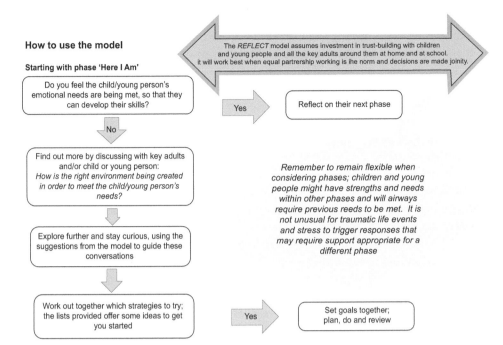

Figure 15.2 How to use the *REFLECT* model.

Figure 15.3 Here I am – establishing trust.

Based upon attachment theory and Maslow's hierarchy (1943), 'Here I am' outlines our foundational needs for healthy social and emotional wellbeing, starting in infancy. Addressing these needs is fundamental to enabling the other phases, so that as human beings, we can function. They are the roots of our human relationships.

Despite discourses compelling us to measure progress against age-related norms or stages, *REFLECT* illustrates how we may all return to phases that might be expected of an infant, for example, during times of trauma or loss. It is demonstrated that in response to these experiences, we require attuned and containing responses from others around us (nurturance) that will support us to cope.

The model sets out questions that might be explored within consultations for children and young people for whom 'Here I am' could offer insight, for example, by asking whether a child or young person's basic needs are being met, and whether they are generally happy and contented (do they laugh and smile?).

Feedback from school staff indicated that it would be helpful to know what to do for a child or young person that needs a 'Here I am' response. Although we resisted putting together a menu of strategies, mindful of every child or young person's unique experience, we made some suggestions focusing on creating the relational and contextual conditions that would offer soothing to an infant, child, young person, or adult, no matter their age.

A set of additional questions was also generated, to be introduced when reviewing the implementation of any agreed approaches and generating next steps.

'This is me!'

As the phases develop, it is possible to see how they lead toward the goal of being able to understand our own behaviour and emotions, and how these impact on other people. 'This is me' is about coming to an awareness that there is a world out there, and an appreciation by the child or young person of their place within it, and impact upon it. Following 'Here I am' and the establishment of basic trust and attunement with other people comes the development of sensory awareness of yourself and your environment.

This is Me!

Exploring the World

I need to:
Begin to share my experiences with others
Be curious and show interest in new things
Get things wrong, make a mess, use my physical skills
Occupy myself with self-chosen activities as well as follow instructions from others
Explore the world around me, safely and with consideration
Play with others; seek out opportunities, offer ideas or suggestions
Make simple choices
Manage some of my feelings on my own
Recognise and communicate my likes and dislikes
Recognise and know how to talk about some feelings
Concentrate on task and stay focussed for short periods
Take my turn and manage some waiting
Have a sense of my body limits, body shape and size and be aware of others when I am active

Figure 15.4 This is me – exploring the world.

For an individual perceived to be demonstrating this phase, adults need to set boundaries without also introducing too many limitations or causing harm. Behaviours relevant to this phase may typically be seen in a nursery, but that is not to say that they are exclusive to children of this age. It is not only toddlers who throw tantrums! Because cognitive thought is not always linked to behaviour communicating emotions, the introduction of consequences may not work for children and young people felt to be experiencing this phase. The same is true for adults thinking irrationally at times of stress. It is a very egocentric phase in which to be, because it is all about 'I WANT!' with little comprehension of what this means for anyone else.

So how do adults respond in the face of such challenge? It is important to think about the behaviour in context. By considering a child or young person's social and emotional needs, there may have to be acceptance that, at times, there will be an unavoidable lack of control. Some behaviours will not be a conscious choice. It is a 3-year-old's prerogative to exert their right to be a 3-year-old. This is far easier to understand and accept than when a 13-year-old responds in exactly the same way. At these times, it is important to challenge our expectations and assumptions and tailor our response accordingly.

Again, the model sets out questions that might be explored within collaborative consultations for children and young people for whom 'I am me!' could offer insight, such as whether they can seek out adults to meet their needs, and are they able to approach different or new experiences with interest?

Suggested approaches focus on school staff creating relational and contextual conditions that might support a child or young person whose behaviour might be consistent with 'This is me!' whatever their age. They include trying to attune to the child or young person's experiences and wellbeing, to be 'with them'. As in the previous phase, a set of additional questions has been generated to be introduced when reviewing the implementation of any agreed approaches and generating next steps.

'Me and you'

I need to:
Feel that I belong
Be accepted for who I am
See how I fit into the thoughts and lives of others
Be curious about other people
Want to initiate play with others
Have opportunities to socialise
Have role models who show empathy, care and acceptance
Understand that people are different
And they might have different views to me
Accept praise and help when it is offered
Learn how to develop a tolerance towards other people

Figure 15.5 You and me – becoming relational.

The child or young person in this phase is becoming more socially aware and developing an appreciation of others around them. They are gaining recognition that all people are different, and this has an impact on relationships. Developing an awareness of others' needs and being supported to learn how to respond will foster their emerging empathy. This will help them be less egocentric. This phase also involves learning skills of negotiation and turn-taking and becoming more independent in related activities. There will be a growing realisation that there should be give and take (reciprocity) and, at times, a certain amount of backing down in order to get along harmoniously.

The environmental context is really important to consider in enabling social relationships and groups to thrive. The model relies on people who know that child or young person well in different contexts being invited to offer their insight.

Questions that might be explored within collaborative consultations for children and young people who seem to be functioning within 'Me and you' might include whether the child or young person is developing friendships (becoming relational) and recognising emotions in other people. Suggested approaches focus on school staff modelling appropriate play skills and expressing genuine concern for others, providing opportunities for over-learning of skills, such as turn-taking, and allowing for the exploration of thoughts. As in the previous phases, a set of additional questions has been generated to be introduced when reviewing the implementation of any agreed approaches, and in generating next steps.

'Who am I?'

This phase might involve consideration of how a child or young person might respond differently within different social groups. Multiple factors can influence where an individual is

I need to:
Feel happy with my own self image
Feel confident to be able to give my opinion and contribute to discussions
Recognise how I am special and unique
Have a realistic view of my strengths and areas of need
Appreciate my gifts and recognise my own unique contribution
Accept differences in others
Identify with others; family/carers/friends, to develop a sense of belonging
Accept praise and help offered

Figure 15.6 Who am I? – developing identities.

within this phase, for example, their perceived cognitive ability or limitation of experiences related to deprivation, isolation, or family circumstances. When using *REFLECT*, it is important to appreciate that setting timescales to move on to the 'next phase' is not appropriate, and that for some individuals, there may need to be considerable investment in thinking about support for other phases before there can be an expectation that some of these needs can be realised, ensuring that everybody is involved in conversations about what might constitute realistic expectations and goals. It is important to avoid the disappointment of agreed milestones not being achieved.

Questions that might be explored within collaborative consultations for children and young people who seem to be functioning within 'Who am I?' might include whether the child or young person has their own interests and hobbies, is able to ask for help, can take responsibility for their actions, is managing being different to others, and can accept others being different. It would be expected that the child or young person has a strong voice in these conversations.

Suggested approaches include providing opportunities for self-expression through creative means, such as art, writing, drama, and enabling space for personal belongings, somewhere private and personal. As in the previous phases, a set of additional questions has been generated for use when reviewing any agreed next steps.

'Learning to be'

This final phase highlights how we are all within the *REFLECT* model somewhere, our needs sometimes spanning across different phases, at times on the same day! Most of the needs in this phase may be actualised in adulthood, and some may never be fully addressed. The dynamic nature of 'learning to be' implies that this is not really about self-actualisation, but rather, within humanhood, there is a continuous process of learning and exploration. It is expected that as young people, and adults, our needs will fluctuate and ebb in and out of the phase, depending on circumstances and experiences that impact on our emotional wellbeing.

I need to:
Make decisions and manage my affairs independently
Engage confidently in social interactions with a range of people in different contexts
Change my responses depending on social expectations
Tune in to the emotional mood of others, and adapt my responses accordingly
Reflect on, and show insight into, my own feelings and how they affect my behaviour
Take responsibility for looking after my own wellbeing by learning, and using, strategies that are helpful for my physical and emotional health
Enjoy and participate in reciprocal relationships
Accept and undertake growing and changing social responsibility for others over time, e.g. friends, family members, partner, children, work colleagues, parents and wider society
Be reflexive and able to consider questions of meaning and morality related to life and death, relationships, and society, from own and others' perspectives, demonstrating sensitivity and insight

Figure 15.7 Learning to be – reflecting through life.

The phase emphasises the multiple identities we take on as we socialise in different circles, or operate in different systems, and how we try to behave according to the social expectations and demands placed upon us, and the roles we adopt with different people and in different groups. These can also change over time and depend on other factors, such as our relationships or worries related to other parts of our lives.

This phase also introduces questions about the meaning of life. It is to be expected that our understanding of the world, and ourselves, may develop over time, through our interactions with multiple others, the systems we function within, and our experiences, for example, places to which we travel, further learning, and the families we ourselves constitute.

Questions that might be explored within collaborative consultations for children and young people who seem to be entering 'learning to be' might include whether the young person is able to reflect on how they are feeling and take action to support themselves when needed, engage in activities that help them stay physically and emotionally healthy, collaborate with relevant others to solve problems, and reflect constructively on issues of identity, life, and personal and social meaning.

Suggested approaches include modelling positive relationships and consistently giving positive feedback, metacognition work, and providing opportunities for small-group reflection.

As in the previous phases, a set of additional questions has been generated to be introduced when reviewing the implementation of agreed approaches and generating any next steps.

Conclusion

When we considered our aspirations for *REFLECT*, we were hopeful that the model would enable the voice of the child or young person communicating emotional responses to the relationships, contexts, and systems around them to be more meaningfully heard. We wanted to support collaboration between schools, families, and external agencies, in doing so empowering and containing everybody by introducing a relational structure through which constructive, reflective conversations could take place. We felt that understanding, skills, and confidence might be strengthened so that emotionally charged and potentially distressing situations might be more contained. At a whole-school or setting system level, we were optimistic that use of the model might bring increased attunement and fulfilment in all relationships, supporting us collectively to be more mindful of the language we use when we talk about, and write about, children and young people, thus bringing greater reflexivity to our practice. Keeping in mind 'learning to be', by reflecting together in this way, our own emotional wellbeing would also, hopefully, improve, and a culture of relational practice and inclusion would be cultivated.

The principles and relational psychology behind the *REFLECT* model have been implicit in our practice, and much-needed, during and after the COVID pandemic. At the same time, there seems to have been a flurry of research and national guidance for schools published related to emotional health and wellbeing, and behaviour.

Public Health England in partnership with the Department of Education (DfE) (Public Health England and DfE, 2021) issued updated guidance on promoting and supporting student mental health and wellbeing in schools and colleges by adopting whole-school approaches, for example, through social and relationship education (SRE), staff training, the continuation of mental health practitioners in schools, and mental health support teams (MHSTs). A holistic approach to boosting wellbeing as opposed to pathologising or diagnosing is suggested.

Arguably conversely, advice on behaviour in schools for head teachers and school staff (DfE, 2022) indicates that it is for individual schools to develop best practice for behaviour. Once again, a whole-school culture of positive behaviour is promoted. It is advocated that creating a culture with high expectations of behaviour will benefit both staff and pupils, establishing calm, safe, and supportive environments conducive to learning. A behaviour policy should provide details on how staff will consistently support students to meet expectations and help create a predictable environment. However, included in the strategies suggested for students who are persistently disruptive are a range of sanctions, such as school detentions, searching, screening and confiscation, suspensions, and permanent exclusion. Section 24 provides examples of adjustments for children and young people with special educational needs and disabilities (SEND), for example, adjusting uniform for children and young people with severe eczema and offering staff training on autism.

The potential for supporting children with social and emotional needs, the kind of needs highlighted in the *REFLECT* model, is not explored.

We hope that *REFLECT*, by offering an alternative, relational, and psychologically based understanding of social and emotional development and the communication of emotional needs that we all experience, will provide a helpful narrative and structure for schools, in collaboration with families and services, that will prevent the separation, loss, and exclusion of children and young people from our schools and systems (Billington, 2000).

Summary box

- *REFLECT* is a model created by Rotherham Educational Psychology Service to support collaborative reflection that enables greater mutual understanding of the relational and contextual conditions that will help children and young people grow emotionally.
- It provides a fluid and flexible psychosocial narrative for conceptualising behaviour and mental health space and encourages partners to come together to consider what they can do to support positive change.
- It is an alternative to purely behaviourist approaches to understanding social, emotional, and mental health and offers resistance to limited linear conceptualisations that reduce complex systemic interactions to simplistic measurement and individualised pathologisation.
- The model could be used as part of a graduated response to social and emotional need, but it is not intended to provide an exhaustive list of strategies; the focus, rather, is on partners coming together to reflect upon the relationships, environmental contexts, and life events that might be impacting upon the potential of children and young people to flourish

- We hope that at a whole-school or setting system level, the model might bring increased attunement and fulfilment in all relationships (an alternative way of expressing this would be to consider how love can be made more tangible within school contexts and within the lives of the children and young people to whom we are responding – see Sahaja Timothy Davis's chapter in this book).

If you are interested in *REFLECT* and would like more information, please do contact us: *Homepage – Rotherham Educational Psychology Services.*

References

Anderson, H. (2005). Myths about 'not-knowing'. *Family Process, 44*(4), 497–504

Anderson, H. (2006). *Collaborative therapy: Relationships and conversations that make a difference.* Routledge.

Billington, T. (2000). *Separating, losing and excluding children.* Routledge/Falmer.

Billington, T. (2006a). *Working with children.* SAGE.

Billington, T. (2006b) Psychodynamic theories and the 'science of relationships' (Bion): A rich resource for professional practice in children's services. *Educational and Child Psychology, 23*(4), 72–79.

Bowlby J. (1969). *Attachment. Attachment and loss: Vol. 1. Loss.* Basic Books.

Bronfenbrenner, U. (1994). Ecological models of human development. *Readings on the Development of Children, 2*(1), 37–43.

Burr, V. (2015). *Social constructionism* (3rd ed.). Routledge.

Cubeddu, D., & Mackay, T. (2017). The attunement principles: A comparison of nurture group and mainstream settings. *Emotional and Behavioural Difficulties, 22*(3), 261–274. https://doi.org/10.1080/13632752.2017.133198

Department for Education (DfE). (2022). *Behaviour in schools.* https://assets.publishing.service.gov.uk/government/uploads/system/uploads/attachment_data/file/1101597/Behaviour_in_schools_guidance_sept_22.pdf.

DeVries, R. (1997). Piaget's social theory. *Educational Researcher, 26*(2), 4–17.

Hyman, S. (2012). The School as a Holding Environment, *Journal of Infant, Child, and Adolescent Psychotherapy, 11*(3), 205–216.

Geddes, H. (2006). *Attachment in the classroom.* Worth Publishing.

Public Health England and DfE. (2021). *Promoting children and young people's mental health and wellbeing.* https://assets.publishing.service.gov.uk/government/uploads/system/uploads/attachment_data/file/1020249/Promoting_children_and_young_people_s_mental_health_and_wellbeing.pdf.

Schön, D. (1983). *The reflective practitioner.* Basic Books.

Sroufe, A., & Siegel, D. (2011). *The verdict is in: The case for attachment theory.* www.drdansiegel.com/uploads/1271-the-verdict-is-in.pdf

Winnicott, D. W. (1965). *The maturational processes and the facilitating environment: Studies in the theory of emotional development.* International Universities Press.

16 The role of intersubjective processes and the impact they have on relationships in educational settings

Emily Forde

Introduction

Relationships in educational settings are crucially impacted by intersubjective processes that allow young people to produce meaning through their interactions with their teachers. Intersubjective processes shape dynamics between teachers and students in educational settings, and the significance of relationships in schools is acknowledged by a large body of theory and research. Amidst a surge in the mental health needs of young people, escalating exclusions, and a policy landscape lacking emphasis on relationships, the pivotal role of STR has become increasingly crucial in addressing the multifaceted challenges faced by students today. Therefore, the significance of STRs cannot be overstated, because they fundamentally impact the educational experience (Cornelius-White, 2007) and have a bearing on the academic and personal growth of students. Thus, nurturing strong STRs should be a top priority for educators.

Relationships between students and teachers have the potential to significantly shape and transform lives. Like the sturdy roots of a tree nourishing its branches, these connections foster growth, learning, and empowerment. In the realm of education, teachers act as guiding lights, igniting curiosity and excitement within their students. They possess a remarkable ability to recognise the unique potential that lies within each individual and help them uncover their talents. By building genuine connections, teachers create safe and supportive spaces where students can flourish.

This chapter is meant to serve as a source of motivation and reflection for educators who wish to place a greater emphasis on building positive, lasting connections with their students. It will include a range of theories relating to STR and provide concrete examples to demonstrate each theory, offering different lenses through which to view STR. This chapter will explore research related to STR and the impact of these relationships on young people. I will also focus on the research I conducted with six young people and their lived experience of STR. By placing these experiences at the forefront, the chapter aims to establish a meaningful connection between research findings and reflection for practitioners, offering valuable insights for those engaged in the field of education.

Theory

Theories relating to STRs delve into the multifaceted dynamics and impacts of these connections on the educational experience. These theories recognise the pivotal role that

DOI: 10.4324/9781003451907-16

relationships play in fostering student learning, engagement, and overall wellbeing. They explore the reciprocal nature of these relationships, emphasising the influence of both teachers and students in shaping the educational process. By examining various theoretical perspectives, educators gain insights into how to establish supportive, empowering, and transformative STRs that promote optimal educational outcomes. Understanding these theories is useful because they provide a conceptual framework that goes beyond day-to-day interactions, offering a deeper understanding of the dynamics at play and empowering those who work in education to create a supportive and enriching educational experience for their students. The significance of the connections between teachers and students is important to learning, development, and emotional wellbeing and has been elucidated through a range of theories, research endeavours, and philosophical viewpoints. In the interest of this chapter, several crucial theories and research findings will be summarised.

Bringing the theories to life

Examining these theories through a vignette, we delve into the relationship between Naz, a reserved year 9 student in a UK high school, and his English teacher, Mr Anderson. Despite Naz's quiet demeanour and struggles with self-esteem, he exhibits a passion for graphic novels and certain types of poetry. In English class, he refrains from participation, sitting with a lowered head and reluctance to seek support. Mr Anderson, aware of Naz's preference for avoiding attention, navigates this situation carefully. This vignette serves as a lens to apply theoretical frameworks, illustrating the formation of an STR as a foundation for Naz in different ways.

Attachment theory

Bowlby's attachment theory, which is extensively discussed in other sections of this book, will be briefly overviewed here to provide context.

Many of you will be familiar with attachment theory developed by John Bowlby (Bowlby, 1988), focusing on the emotional ties that develop between individuals, including parent–child relationships. Other partnerships, like those between students and teachers, can be viewed through this lens. Attachment theory, as developed by John Bowlby, underscores the importance of emotional connections in relationships, including those between students and teachers. It posits that a secure attachment, characterised by trust and responsiveness, is crucial for emotional wellbeing and academic success. While attachment theory has faced criticism for its empirical validity and cultural applicability, its insights remain valuable in educational settings.

We can use the vignette as a way to view attachment theory in practice. This vignette serves as a real-world illustration of how attachment theory principles can be put into practice within an educational setting. In an English classroom, Mr Anderson applies attachment theory to support Naz, who exhibits hesitancy in initiating learning tasks. Recognising the potential need for a secure attachment, Mr Anderson creates a safe and supportive environment, gradually building trust and becoming a secure base for Naz. This approach fosters a positive student-teacher relationship, enabling Naz to feel emotionally secure, engage in learning, and gain confidence over time. Mr Anderson reinforces this bond by incorporating Naz's interests, such as graphic novels, into the classroom routine, providing encouragement, and offering gentle guidance during challenges. As a result, Naz develops a strong attachment to Mr Anderson, forming a foundation for emotional wellbeing and active participation in classroom activities. Through this vignette, Mr Anderson exemplifies the practical application of attachment theory in promoting positive STR and supporting students' emotional and academic growth.

Sociocultural theory

The sociocultural perspective in educational theory, championed by Vygotsky and Cole (1978), underscores the inherent link between social interaction and learning. This perspective challenges behaviourist approaches like Skinner's operant conditioning by emphasising the importance of social context, language, and cultural factors in cognitive development. Vygotsky's zone of proximal development (ZPD) highlights the role of social scaffolding in learning, emphasising collaboration between students and teachers.

In the scenario with Naz struggling to engage in a learning task, Mr Anderson applies Vygotsky's sociocultural theory by recognising Naz's ZPD and the significance of social interaction. Acknowledging Naz's interest in poetry, Mr Anderson employs collaborative learning strategies rooted in sociocultural theory. Instead of pressuring Naz individually, Mr Anderson integrates collaborative elements into the learning environment, assigning projects that involve collective analysis and interpretation of poems. This approach creates a social context for learning, allowing Naz to engage with peers and contribute meaningfully within his ZPD.

During class discussions, Mr Anderson actively encourages Naz to express his thoughts, providing scaffolding to boost his confidence. When Naz encounters challenges, Mr Anderson uses probing questions to stimulate critical thinking and involves him in the problem-solving process. Through purposeful social interactions, Naz's understanding deepens, and he gains the confidence to participate actively. Mr Anderson's application of sociocultural theory involves leveraging collaborative projects and encouraging social interactions to support Naz in overcoming challenges and actively engaging in the learning task. This aligns with Vygotsky's principle that learning is a social process occurring through interaction and collaboration with others, demonstrating the practical application of sociocultural theory in fostering a supportive learning environment.

Humanist principles

Humanistic psychology, championed by Carl Rogers, emphasises the pivotal role of relationships between teachers and students. Rogers advocates for a person-centred approach, urging teachers to nurture a caring environment with empathy, understanding, warmth, and sincerity. The humanistic dimensions of teacher–student interactions, characterised by honesty, justice, care, and respect, are crucial for facilitating students' adjustment to their educational environment, especially those at risk. Prioritising interpersonal connections aligns with a humanistic perspective, as emphasised by Loe (2017) and supported by research on STR by Carroll and Hurry (2018).

Mr Anderson, applying a humanistic approach, understands Naz's preference for avoiding attention and fosters a supportive environment valuing each student's unique qualities. Recognising Naz's literary interest, he encourages the exploration of preferences and interpretations, creating a positive, supportive environment that emphasises self-awareness and personal responsibility for learning. In Mr Anderson's class, Naz experiences a genuine sense of belonging, where his unique identity is recognised and respected. The classroom culture promotes not only academic engagement but also emotional connections among students and with the material, fostering a positive and inclusive learning experience. Mr Anderson's collaborative approach, providing constructive feedback and emphasising strengths, aligns with humanistic principles, creating an environment where Naz feels recognised, valued, and supported in his journey of learning and self-discovery.

Relational theory

Gergen's (2009) relational theory, which is extensively discussed in other sections of this book, will be briefly overviewed here to provide context.

Gergen's (2009) relational theory views STR as dynamic, co-constructed through ongoing interactions and rejecting fixed roles. In the classroom, a dialogical approach fosters open communication, collaboration, and mutual understanding, with roles negotiated based on context and needs. Gergen's theory underscores that STRs are shaped by shared experiences, communication, and cultural context, challenging the one-sided transmission of knowledge and promoting a cooperative approach. This perspective asserts the centrality of relational processes to human existence, advocating for education that prioritises connections over solely developing the mind.

Let us explore the STR between Mr Anderson and Naz through the lens of Gergen's relational theory, emphasising the co-creation of meaning and the dynamic nature of their interaction.

Mr Anderson recognises the significance of building a relational connection for meaningful learning experiences. He initiates open dialogues with Naz, encouraging him to share personal interpretations of literary works. Rather than positioning himself as the sole authority, Mr Anderson creates an atmosphere where both teacher and student actively contribute to the construction of knowledge. For example, during a literature discussion, Mr Anderson invites Naz to share his unique perspectives on a novel they are studying, valuing and incorporating his viewpoint into the broader class discourse. This collaborative approach allows Naz to perceive himself as an integral part of the learning community, contributing to the shared understanding of the subject matter.

As their relationship evolves, Mr Anderson and Naz engage in reciprocal exchanges, where both teacher and student influence each other's perspectives. The classroom becomes a relational space where meaning is co-constructed through ongoing dialogue and interaction. Gergen's relational theory underscores the importance of these shared moments in shaping the learning environment, emphasising the dynamic, interconnected nature of the STR in high school.

Mr Anderson, applying Gergen's theory, recognises the significance of building a relational connection for meaningful learning experiences. He initiates open dialogues with

Naz, encouraging collaborative knowledge construction. As their relationship evolves, Mr Anderson and Naz engage in reciprocal exchanges, turning the classroom into a relational space where meaning is co-constructed through ongoing dialogue, emphasising the dynamic, interconnected nature of the STR in high school.

In conclusion, it is important to remember that while these theories offer frameworks for comprehending STRs, individual experiences may vary depending on a variety of variables, such as the cultural context, a person's personality, and the particular dynamics of the classroom and school.

Research on STRs

Relationships between students and teachers can significantly impact students' academic, social, and emotional growth. Research consistently demonstrates that positive relationships between teachers and students enhance learning outcomes, classroom behaviour, student engagement, and the overall learning environment. In this exploration, we will delve into key areas of research supporting these positive effects.

Student voice and STR

It is well-known that positive STRs contribute to successful outcomes for both teachers and students (Williford et al., 2017). Student-centred research can provide insights into the types of interactions students enjoy, the value of those connections, and the consequences of those ties.

According to Cefai and Cooper (2010), students tend to have more respect for teachers who exhibit empathy, friendliness, reliability, consistency, and support. In their complex lives, students seek authentic connections (Sapiro & Ward, 2020) and prefer teachers who maintain consistency in their interactions (Lloyd-Jones et al., 2010). Power-balanced interactions are preferred by students as they enhance the sense of community and lead to more positive interactions among peers, ultimately resulting in better academic outcomes. Cefai and Cooper's (2010) study indicates that students believe teachers can help achieve power parity by showing appreciation for their ideas and valuing their input.

Research also identifies students' desire to be treated with dignity and fairness and to have a voice in addressing perceived unfair treatment (Jahnukainen, 2001). Additionally, students want teachers who believe in their talents and treat them with respect (Cefai & Cooper, 2010; Jahnukainen, 2001).

Factors of positive STR

Researchers have identified several variables that impact the effectiveness of STRs. Strong interactions between students and teachers, as indicated by Fredriksen and Rhodes (2004), are characterised by minimal conflict and heightened levels of closeness. These factors foster children's curiosity and enhance their ability to regulate emotional, cognitive, and social capacities.

The study suggests that teachers' ability to strike a balance between the necessity for classroom structure and the students' need for independence can predict whether students will take ownership of their education, exhibit a motivation to succeed, and perceive themselves as competent. Fredriksen and Rhodes (2004) assert that educators can effectively address the social and academic needs of children by creating an environment conducive to encouragement and inclusivity.

Importance and impact of STR

The literature suggests that positive STR can be associated with favourable outcomes for both educators and learners (Claessens et al., 2017). The dyadic nature of the STR is such that it is relied upon, responded to, and essential for favourable outcomes in various domains, including academics, social interactions, emotional wellbeing, and behavioural patterns, as noted by Williford et al. (2017). Cornelius-White (2007) conducted a meta-analysis of research investigating the effectiveness of learner-centred relationships within educational institutions. The findings revealed that students experienced multiple benefits, including heightened engagement, refined analytical skills, elevated levels of contentment, better academic performance, improved attendance, reduced disruptive behaviour, heightened motivation, improved social connections, and increased self-esteem (Cornelius-White, 2007). According to Cornelius-White's research, the utilisation of humanistic and person-centred approaches, including empathy, warmth, and collaboration, can result in advantageous STR.

Academic outcomes

An increasing body of empirical research suggests that cultivating strong relationships between pupils and teachers can yield a variety of advantages in the educational milieu. Bergin and Bergin (2009) found that when the STR creates a sense of security and motivation, it can help increase academic achievement. Additionally, research has demonstrated that fostering interpersonal relationships within schools can positively impact academic performance (Peterson & Bonell, 2018). According to the findings of Roorda et al. (2017), there is a positive correlation between STRs characterised by positivity and enhanced academic achievement and student involvement. This leads us to think about how this can be achieved. According to Hernandez et al. (2017), various research studies have demonstrated a correlation between perceived teacher closeness and academic achievement.

Impact of STR on social, emotional, and psychological adjustment

Prior studies have underscored the significance of positive teacher–student interactions in promoting the social and emotional development of students. Roorda et al. (2011) described the affective, or emotional, components of STRs as emphasising the importance of warmth and empathy, as these traits are linked to social competence. Interpersonal connections within the school environment can facilitate the restructuring of relationships and foster resilience. This underscores the significance of social relationships beyond the domestic setting, particularly in educational institutions, where engagements with social peers and educators can promote positive adaptive conduct as well as academic and affective wellness (Tayler, 2015).

Further support from Kennedy and Kennedy (2004) suggests that the STR can develop into a bond that bears resemblance to that of a primary carer and a child, owing to the emotional and physical proximity between them. The establishment of this bond possesses the capability to furnish children with a sense of assurance and safeguard them from psychological strain. Moreover, positive STRs have also been linked to improved emotional and social adjustment in young people (Breeman et al., 2015), enhanced resilience (Yu et al., 2018), and positive subjective wellbeing (Moore et al., 2018).

The aforementioned studies indicate that implementing relational strategies can cultivate a favourable educational atmosphere, underscoring the significance of positive interpersonal exchanges in advancing social and emotional development and thereby enhancing academic performance. Furthermore, empirical studies have indicated that the establishment of high-quality relationships can alleviate the impact of risk factors on students, resulting in favourable outcomes for those with social, emotional, and psychological needs (Sabol & Pianta, 2012). These results support the idea that interactions and relationships between adults and children are crucial proximal processes that add up to shape development across time (Bronfenbrenner & Morris, 2006). Therefore, it is crucial for all of us working in education to place a high priority on fostering healthy interactions with students in order to support their general wellbeing and social-emotional growth.

Listening to the experiences of young people

I conducted a study to explore the perceptions of students in years 9 and 10 regarding their interactions with teachers. The goal was to address a gap in existing research by providing young voices a platform to share their experiences in mainstream secondary high schools. Through interviews and interpretive phenomenological analysis, the study delved into the students' perspectives, aiming to deepen our understanding of how relationships in education impact their learning journey. The focus was on uncovering the meaning-making and experiences of students as they interact with teachers, shedding light on the significance of these relationships in their educational experiences.

All names used in the study have been anonymised for confidentiality, and I express gratitude to the young participants for openly sharing their experiences. Among the themes that emerged from the research, two struck me as particularly important for understanding the breadth and depth of their experiences. This section features quotes from the students, blending their voices with my interpretations to bring their experiences to the forefront. These insights aim to enrich understanding for those in educational settings, providing tangible examples that bridge theory with real-world scenarios. The quotes enable readers to visualise how discussed theories manifest in students' experiences, enhancing the content's applicability and relatability. The next section will present research findings on STR in mainstream secondary high schools.

The specialness of the relationship

I use the term 'special' because, from the conversations, it is clear that these relationships are more than ordinary but genuinely special and highly significant. Participants described enduring connections built on closeness, reliability, and genuine affection. These relationships go beyond companionship; they offer emotional support, understanding, and acceptance. 'Special' aptly captures their experiences, creating something remarkable beyond the ordinary. This is represented in the quotes:

> *She means the world to me.*

> *Sarah*

This description illustrates the significance of the relationship as immeasurable and that she holds the relationship as of central importance. I interpreted that the relationship is special and unique, as such a statement would not encompass all relationships. The feeling of uniqueness is further reinforced by Sarah's remarks:

> *There isn't another person like her.*

> *Sarah*

The comment illustrates that she feels the relationship is rare and irreplaceable, which, in turn, means that it is special and unlike others she has experienced at school. It signifies that this connection is exceptional and incomparable to others' experiences, particularly within the school setting. Implicitly, it draws a comparison to other teachers. Another comment only reinforces this idea:

> *I'd say Ms Black stands out to me the most because she just knows more, which makes it feel separate to others.*

> *Ben*

This comment highlights how the relationship feels different and distinct from that of other teachers in the school. By using the term 'stands out', Ben is implicitly comparing his experience of this relationship to others. The unique nature of this relationship is described through the teacher's deeper understanding of him compared to other teachers, which sets it apart. His description of their relationship suggests that 'Ms Black' has a deeper understanding of him compared to other teachers, making their connection unique. A similar sense of the relationship's significance emerges when discussing the level of care shown towards John. This sense of care is not something he experiences with other teachers. This notion is further reinforced by the following quotes:

> *It seems like they care about you even when nobody else does.*

> *John*

> *No one really listened to me about it except Ms Black.*

> *John*

Through these statements, the student makes a comparison between this relationship and others by expressing how he feels 'heard' when he is with Ms Black, an experience distinct from that with other teachers at school. This level of comparison towards other teachers is also reflected in another comment:

Well, it made me feel like I had somebody in school and that I wasn't alone. And like she was really supportive.

Jess

The quote highlights the relationship's uniqueness, making Jess feel less isolated and emphasising emotional support and connectedness. It suggests that this connection differs from other STRs, providing companionship and understanding. Overall, the comment underscores the importance of supportive relationships in academic settings for enhancing student wellbeing. This emotional connectedness aligns with research, such as the National Research Council (2004), stating, 'A youth's emotional connection with adults is the single most essential component in supporting positive development.' Studies by Breeman et al. (2015) suggest positive STRs are linked to improved emotional and social adjustment in young people. These sentiments reflect students' appreciation for the exceptional nature of their relationship with Ms. Black, recognising her as a truly unique teacher in their school experience. Other comments similarly express how students felt emotionally supported during challenging times:

She was the one I could go to when things were hard.

John

I feel this comment expresses the importance this teacher had to John during a challenging time. The teacher stood out as a 'beacon' of support, whom he could rely on and seek help from during difficult times. This description conveys a profound emotional bond between him and the teacher, highlighting the protective factors that have formed as part of their relationship. Furthermore, the specialness of the relationship was evident through descriptions that imply a psychological connection between the student and the teacher. One student expressed that there was a shared and reciprocal emotional bond between them, as they stated:

Like she cares about me. Like I care about her, and she cares about me. We've got like a . . . like a string bond . . . tied together, so we trust each other.

JJ

The student uses the term 'string bond', which illustrates their deep connection to the teacher. I infer this to mean that the connection feels strong and enduring, as they feel connected even when they are not together. The metaphor JJ used implies they have an unbreakable connection, which holds great significance and feels special to him. This description also highlights that caring is reciprocated within the relationship, acknowledging the student's role in the connection and the mutual feelings of care. This representation of a special feel to the relationship is also reflected by another student, who states:

[S]he's done a lot for me, yeah. I wouldn't want to be at school if she left or wasn't here. It's like she knows me, and my troubles and I feel like she's doing it cos she wants to.

John

This quote suggests they feel a strong connection with the teacher. Their experiences imply that they value this person's presence in their lives and feel that they understand him on a deeper level. I infer that they feel the interactions with this teacher are genuine because they 'want' to be available to support him, rather than being the role or duty of a teacher. I interpret the experience that they have with this person as being incredibly meaningful to them, which acts as a 'pull factor' (Thambirajah et al., 2008) towards school, as he states they 'wouldn't want to be at school if she left or wasn't here'. John recognises how much the teacher has helped him and how important their presence is in their life. Another student also acknowledges the unique nature of the relationship, stating:

> *Everyone needs that person in school, like I have her.*
>
> *Rebecca*

Rebecca uses the word 'need' when they talk about having that special and unique person in their life at school. The word 'need' implies that it is essential and part of what supports her in school. Although Rebecca identifies that the person at school is special to her, she also recognises that all young people need a person in school who enables them to have a special relationship. This points to the recognition that these relationships are important, as reflected in the following quote:

> *She means a lot to me, and it means a lot to have her here for me at school.*
>
> *John*

This comment illustrates the level of importance they place on the relationship. Using the term 'have her here for me at school' points to an experience of trust and reliability in the relationship. He recognises that the teacher 'means a lot' to him, which signifies they value the relationship they have with the teacher beyond just being a student. The importance of one STR is apparent through the quote by JJ:

> *She is the one that stands out and you admit to like your friends and you show everyone.*
>
> *JJ*

I interpret this to mean that they have a sense of pride in the relationship he has with the teacher because he is happy to 'show off' the relationship to his peers. Another quote noted how they feel prioritised by the teacher:

> *She's really nice and like knows if you need help. She puts me first like I'm the only one there.*
>
> *JJ*

This comment reflects that students feel acknowledged and prioritised in the teacher's company, creating a shared sense of importance and reinforcing that their presence is valued. The phrase 'knows if you need help' suggests an intuitive connection between the teacher and the student. The use of 'only one there' indicates a genuine and connected interaction, fostering a sense of importance. The concept of 'presence', as proposed by Rodgers and Raider-Roth (2006), suggests that a genuine and open teacher can better understand and respond to the needs of students, fostering a stronger connection.

The metaphor 'you click' and 'clicked' was used by the young people, which I feel demonstrates the natural and effortless feeling of the relationship, which enabled a bond between themselves and the teacher to form:

> *You click. . . . [Y]ou just get along with them. Or they use it to talk to you and have a laugh with them and everything.*

> *Sarah*

> *But then when I started talking, I don't know, I just, like, the bond clicked. And then I just, like, I've been open with her ever since.*
>
> *Ben*

This natural and effortless feel to the relationship with one teacher is also shown in further statements:

> *So just, like, I feel like I've got, you know, the right fit for me, like the right teacher to speak to. I feel like she understands my needs and everything.*

> *Jess*

When they use the term 'the right fit for me', I interpret that to mean that she can be herself and the teacher is accepting of her needs unconditionally. I feel that by using the term 'the right fit', she is signifying that she recognises their relationship is the right fit in both directions, thus meaning it feels special. Jess spoke about how the teacher had left the school, which meant she had lost that key relationship; this is represented in the following quote:

> *She left about two weeks ago. So she was kind of like my main, like, help teacher, and she was there if I ever needed her. I still feel like we will always be close.*

> *Jess*

Despite Jess's sadness that the teacher is no longer at the school, they formed an exceptional relationship that allows her to feel an ongoing sense of connection, representing an enduring closeness despite the distance. When she comments that 'she was always there if I ever needed her', it represents the sense of reliability and trust she had developed in the relationship, which is what made the relationship feel distinctive. The degree of closeness in the relationship was also evident in the following remarks:

> *I'm really close with her at the minute, and like, she just helped me so much, and I know that she's a teacher that I can just go to and talk to whenever I want.*

> *Rebecca*

This recognition of closeness is also present in previous research by Fredriksen and Rhodes (2004), who define *closeness* as one of the indicators of a 'strong' STR.

Power and STRs

In contrast to the impactful 'special' relationships mentioned earlier, students also expressed a sense of unfairness and disempowerment in relationships. There are power imbalances between teachers and students in educational settings due to the presence of power dynamics. These power dynamics may be strengthened or weakened by intersubjective processes. In the provided quote, Sarah candidly reveals the emotions she experienced during her interactions with her teacher. Her expressed feelings of embarrassment, humiliation, and heightened anxiousness shed light on the power dynamics within their STR:

> *Like, if I didn't understand the work, he would be like, 'Oh, well, Sarah has not done her work or listened', and he would, like, announce it to the whole class. I just wanted to run away. I just wanted to get out.*

> Sarah

By publicly highlighting Sarah's lack of understanding, the teacher not only exhibits a disregard for her feelings but also reinforces a hierarchical dynamic wherein the teacher's power is asserted at the expense of Sarah's self-esteem and dignity. Consequently, Sarah is left feeling disempowered in her relationship with the teacher. Sarah adds to the comment:

> *It's like I'm already anxious and they are then shouting on top. Or like they know that you've got, like, the problems but they still, like, pick on you.*

> Sarah

Sarah's statement conveys a sense of heightened anxiety and frustration stemming from a perceived lack of understanding and empathy from her teacher. Despite Sarah's existing anxious state, she feels as though her teacher intensifies her distress by consistently singling her out for criticism. This reveals a level of frustration with the teacher's apparent failure to recognise her struggles or offer support. It suggests that Sarah desires a teacher who can empathise with her challenges and respond more compassionately. Such an environment, where Sarah's needs are not adequately acknowledged or addressed, contributes to a continued sense of powerlessness.

> *I was having a panic attack that two Fridays ago, and the teacher said they didn't want to be here either. And I was like, 'You get paid.' I, like, it annoys me when I say it, because I don't want to be here. I have a really valid reason not wanting to be here, not on your reasons just because you're tired.*

> Sarah

Sarah's comment reveals a perceived power imbalance within the STR. She feels that her feelings are not being acknowledged or understood by the teacher. Sarah's interpretation of the situation highlights her frustration at not being listened to and the lack of empathy displayed by the teacher.

> *Sometimes they treat you like you're thick if you don't understand it. Stuff like that.*

> John

I interpret that this experience diminishes John's confidence and invalidates his knowledge and perspective, which may have a significant impact on John's self-esteem and engagement in the learning process. Feeling belittled and invalidated, John may become disheartened, leading to decreased motivation and a reluctance to participate actively in the classroom.

> *She's always had a thing against my brother too. I don't know if it's just a thing. I think it's because I'm not, like, good at French and everything. So she just expects me to be, like, something I'm not.*
>
> Sarah

Sarah's comment reveals a profound sense of unfair judgement and a lack of control over the situation. She believes the teacher harbours negative feelings towards her older brother, suspecting that this bias extends to her. Sarah links this perceived prejudice to struggles in French, feeling the teacher expects certain qualities from her. This poignant statement showcases Sarah's perception of being judged based on factors beyond her control. The teacher's preconceived notions, influenced by the knowledge of Sarah's brother, create a perceived gap between expectations and Sarah's capabilities, leaving her feeling insecure and burdened.

> *I don't like it, because it feels like I'm being singled out because I haven't been in lessons because of my anxiety and everything, or because I don't understand it. And because I'm just anxious in the moment and I feel like I have been singled out because of it.*
>
> Rebecca

> *It's like she's taking it personally. It's not [that] we don't get along. We just have, like, we just clash. So she takes it personally that I don't go to her lessons and everything. But it's not. It kind of is, but it's kind of not – do you know what I mean?*
>
> Rebecca

> *Like, if you do the one thing wrong, like, I could be sat there, like, just not doing anything, like, looking out the window for two minutes. And I'd get screamed at, like, well, that's your comment.*
>
> Jess

These quotes highlight a power imbalance in the STR, with the teacher exercising authority through disciplinary measures. Jess feels the imposed sanctions are disproportionate, fostering a sense of injustice. The teacher's actions seem to prioritise control and discipline over understanding the underlying reasons for behaviour. This reflects a traditional STR approach, marked by a communal and involuntary dynamic with evident power disparities (Lodge & Lynch, 2004). This dynamic reinforces the teacher's authority, diminishing student agency and fostering an atmosphere of fear or intimidation.

> *I've always been told, treat people how you want to be treated, so I act all nice for them, but they just act all mean to me.*
>
> JJ

JJ's statement reveals a profound awareness of the contrast between his values and the treatment he receives from some teachers. This comment demonstrates JJ's genuine desire for reciprocal treatment aligned with his values. He values the idea of being treated with kindness, empathy, and fairness. Yet he experiences a disconnect between his expectations and the reality of how others treat him.

> *When I've done stuff and it's my fault, yeah, fair enough, I can take a comment about . . . but just when I haven't and everyone else is doing it, he singles me out.*
>
> *John*

John feels targeted by the teacher and feels a sense of unfairness that the teacher 'singles him out'. John's experience suggests a power dynamic within the STR where the teacher exercises their authority in a way that targets and blames him disproportionately. This unequal treatment may undermine John's confidence, create a sense of resentment, and diminish his trust in the fairness of the educational environment. He adds:

> *Yeah, I'm not that badder student, I don't think, but it just seems that he sees me like that. . . . [H]e's an absolute wanker [sighs].*
>
> *John*

In John's statement, he expresses his perception that his teacher views him in a negative light, which results in a sense of unfairness. Despite not considering himself a particularly bad student, John feels that the teacher sees him in a different, unfavourable way. This comment conveys John's disappointment and longing for the teacher to hold a more positive opinion of him. This discrepancy between his self-perception and the teacher's perception contributes to a disheartening experience for John, where he wishes for a more favourable view from the teacher.

Future directions

The research underscores the vital need to cultivate positive and secure STR in education. A notable revelation is the extensive range and depth of experiences shared by students, emphasising the pivotal role these relationships play in their lives. The theme 'the specialness of the relationship' highlights the profound importance of these connections, serving as a crucial protective factor amid challenges. Exploring the theme of 'power in STR' unveils students' perceptions of unjust actions, leading to feelings of disempowerment and influencing their emotional experiences.

This research illuminates that prevailing theory and research on STR may fall short of recognising the intricate complexity and profound depth inherent in these relationships. It successfully captures these dimensions, underscoring the unique and multi-dimensional nature of student-teacher experiences. This contributes to a richer understanding of the dynamic interplay within these significant educational relationships.

In conclusion, student-teacher interactions are integral to young people's educational experiences. Prioritising young individuals' experiences and narratives about STRs can empower them to be agents of change in education. By placing their stories at the centre, educators can facilitate positive transformations in this domain.

Summary box

Checklist of successful strategies

- *Invest in genuine connections*. Prioritise authentic interactions to foster trust and rapport with students.
- *Apply theoretical frameworks*. Utilise theories on STRs to understand dynamics and enhance teaching practices.
- *Encourage reflective practices*. Engage in regular self-reflection to assess and improve personal interactions with students.
- *Utilise real-life examples*. Learn from practical vignettes, like the 'Naz and Mr Anderson' case, to apply theories in educational settings.
- *Promote student voice*. Provide opportunities for students to express their identities and share their unique perspectives in class.
- *Establish inclusive classroom norms*. Collaborate with students to co-create inclusive norms that promote respect and understanding.

Additional references

Roorda, D. L., Koomen, H. M., Spilt, J. L., & Oort, F. J. (2011). The influence of affective teacher – student relationships on students' school engagement and achievement: A meta-analytic approach. *Review of educational research, 81*(4), 493–529.

References

Bergin, C., & Bergin, D. (2009). Attachment in the classroom. *Educational Psychology Review, 21*, 141–170.

Bowlby, J. (1988). Developmental psychiatry comes of age. *The American Journal of Psychiatry, 145*(1), 1–10.

Breeman, L.D., Wubbels, T., van Lier, P. A., Verhulst, F. C., van der Ende, J., Maras, A., Hopman, J. A., & Tick, N. T. (2015). Teacher characteristics, social classroom relationships, and children's social, emotional, and behavioral classroom adjustment in special education. *Journal of School Psychology, 53*(1), 87–103.

Bronfenbrenner, U., & Morris, P. (2006). The bioecoloigical model of human development. In *Theorectical models of human development* (pp. 793–828). Wiley.

Carroll, C., & Hurry, J. (2018). Supporting pupils in school with social, emotional, and mental health needs: A scoping review of the literature. *Emotional and Behavioural Difficulties, 23*(3), 310–325.

Cefai, C., & Cooper, P. (2010). Students without voices: The unheard accounts of secondary school students with social, emotional and behaviour difficulties. *European Journal of Special Needs Education, 25*(2), 183–198

Claessens, L. C., van Tartwijk, J., van der Want, A. C., Pennings, H. J., Verloop, N., den Brok, P. J., & Wubbels, T. (2017). Positive teacher – student relationships go beyond the classroom, problematic ones stay inside. *The Journal of Educational Research, 110*(5), 478–493.

Cornelius-White, J. (2007). Learner-centered teacher-student relationships are effective: A meta-analysis. *Review of Educational Research, 77*(1), 113–143.

Diaz, A., Eisenberg, N., Valiente, C., VanSchyndel, S., Spinrad, T. L., Berger, R., Hernandez, M. M., Silva, K. M., & Southworth, J. (2017). Relations of positive and negative expressivity and effortful control to kindergarteners' student – teacher relationship, academic engagement, and externalizing problems at school. *Journal of Research in Personality, 67*, 3–14.

Doyle, C., & Cicchetti, D. (2017). From the cradle to the grave: The effect of adverse caregiving environments on attachment and relationships throughout the lifespan. *Clinical Psychology: Science and Practice, 24*(2), 203.

Fredriksen, K., & Rhodes, J. (2004). The role of teacher relationships in the lives of students. *New Directions for Youth Development, 2004*(103), 45–54.

Gergen, K. J. (2009). *Relational being: Beyond self and community*. Oxford University Press.

Jahnukainen, M., 2001. Experiencing special education: Former students of classes for the emotionally and behaviorally disordered talk about their schooling. *Emotional and Behavioural Difficulties, 6*(3), 150–166.

Kennedy, J. H., & Kennedy, C. E. (2004). Attachment theory: Implications for school psychology. *Psychology in the Schools, 41*(2), 247–259.

Lloyd-Jones, S., Bowen, R., Holtom, D., Griffin, T., & Sims, J. (2010). *A qualitative research study to explore young people's disengagement from learning*. Welsh Assembly Government Social Research.

Lodge, A., & Lynch, K. (2004). *Diversity at school*. Institute of Public Administration for the Equality Authority.

Loe, R. (2017). Relational schools. In *Paradoxes in education* (pp. 259–272). Sense Publishers.

Moore, G. F., Cox, R., Evans, R. E., Hallingberg, B., Hawkins, J., Littlecott, H. J., Long, S. J., & Murphy, S. (2018). School, peer and family relationships and adolescent substance use, subjective wellbeing and mental health symptoms in Wales: A cross sectional study. *Child Indicators Research, 11*, 1951–1965.

National Research Council. (2004). *Children's health, the nation's wealth: Assessing and improving child health*. National Research Council

Peterson, A. J., & Bonell, C. (2018). School experiences and young women's pregnancy and parenthood decisions: A systematic review and synthesis of qualitative research. *Health & Place, 53,*

Rodgers, C. R., & Raider-Roth, M. B. (2006). Presence in teaching. *Teachers and Teaching: Theory and Practice, 12*(3), 265–287.

Roorda, D. L., Jak, S., Zee, M., Oort, F. J., & Koomen, H. M. (2017). Affective teacher – student relationships and students' engagement and achievement: A meta-analytic update and test of the mediating role of engagement. *School Psychology Review, 46*(3), 239–261.

Sabol, T. J., & Pianta, R. C. (2012). Recent trends in research on teacher – child relationships. *Attachment & Human Development, 14*(3), 213–231.

Sapiro, B., & Ward, A. (2020). Marginalized youth, mental health, and connection with others: A review of the literature. *Child and Adolescent Social Work Journal, 37*, 343–357.

Tayler, C. (2015). Learning in early childhood: Experiences, relationships and 'learning to be'. *European Journal of Education, 50*(2), 160–174.

Thambirajah, M. S., Grandison, K. J., & De-Hayes, L. (2008). *Understanding school refusal: A handbook for professionals in education, health and social care*. Jessica Kingsley Publishers.

Vygotsky, L. S., & Cole, M. (1978). *Mind in society: Development of higher psychological processes*. Harvard university press.

Williford, A., LoCasale-Crouch, J., Whittaker, J., DeCoster, J., Hartz, K., et al. (2017). Changing teacher-child dyadic interactions to improve preschool children's externalising behaviors. *Child Development, 88*, 1544–1553.

Yu, M. V. B., Johnson, H. E., Deutsch, N. L., & Varga, S. M. (2018). "She calls me by my last name": Exploring adolescent perceptions of positive teacher-student relationships. *Journal of Adolescent Research, 33*(3), 332–362.

17 Special time

An intervention to support the building of teacher-pupil relationships to promote belonging, trust, and development of positive attachments with school staff

Rachel Cooper, Laura Griffiths, Lucy Hatton, and Angela Wright

Behaviourism: A meaningful deterrent?

Within England, government guidance for schools indicates that 'good behaviour in schools is central to a good education' (DfE, 2022b, p. 5), with all schools required to have a behaviour policy to clearly outline the expectations around behaviour in the school setting. Traditionally, a behaviourist approach is used within schools to manage behaviour and set out clear rules and expectations. Originating in the early 1900s through the work of Watson, Pavlov, and Skinner, the practice of behaviourism can be understood as reinforcing or deterring responses to a stimuli through a process known as conditioning.

In the present day, school behaviour policies typically outline a tiered response to student behaviour, in which rewards (such as praise, stickers, or house points) are used to encourage compliance and conformity, whilst consequences and sanctions are used in an attempt to discourage rule breaches. Isolation, detention, and suspension (fixed-term exclusion), or even permanent exclusion from school, are all frequently issued to deter undesirable behaviours. This approach is promoted by DFE guidance (2022b, p. 10), which states 'behaviour should be taught to all pupils, so that they understand what behaviour is expected and encouraged and what is prohibited. This then requires positive reinforcement when expectations are met, while sanctions are required where rules are broken'. This approach to behaviour management in school is frequently endorsed in government guidance (e.g. DfE, 2013, 2022a, 2022b) and referenced in educational literature and research (e.g. Rogers, 2000).

However, despite government endorsement, it would seem to us that over-reliance on punitive approaches as a means of behaviour modification is flawed. Firstly, the behaviourist perspective has received criticism for not taking account of a person's individual context, their emotions or thought processes (Whitaker, 2021), and the multitude of other factors that can impact and influence a pupil's presentation and functioning in school, as will be discussed within this chapter. Secondly, it is reasonable to suggest that when implemented well, the chosen system of behaviour management should achieve the goal of improving the behaviour of students (through a desire to avoid consequences and gain rewards). However, government figures indicate that school exclusions consistently rise each academic year (other than the year 2020 due to the COVID-19 pandemic); in the academic year 2021/2022, there were 2,200 permanent exclusions in England during the spring term (DfE, 2023). Data shows that the number of suspensions has also increased, with persistent disruptive behaviour most frequently listed as the reason.

DOI: 10.4324/9781003451907-17

Might we, therefore, suggest that, in the whole, school behaviour policies underpinned by behaviourist approaches are not the most effective way of engaging pupils and managing behaviour? Perhaps we need to be reminded that *discipline*, in its truest sense, is not 'the practice of training people to obey the rules' (as defined by the *Oxford Dictionary*) but instead means an opportunity to teach, guide, and lead by example (Siegel & Bryson, 2012; Knost, 2013).

Relational approach: A powerful alternative

We argue that a behaviourist approach is too narrow in perspective, is reactive and overly focused on consequences and short-term compliance. Whilst punishment may act as a deterrent for some (Baker & Simpson, 2020), the data proves it is not effective for all. It does not take into account a pupil's thoughts and feelings, their needs, or the past experiences that impact upon their actions in the school environment. As such, it is not equitable to treat pupils the same without consideration of individual differences and needs. All pupils are not the same; a blanket approach will not always work, especially for those children who might be viewed as 'complex', such as those identified as being vulnerable or having a special educational need. Our experience as educational psychologists (EPs) in understanding the functions of behaviour is consistently focused on looking beyond the behaviour. As such, in sustaining behaviour change for an individual pupil, as well as at a wider whole school, we advocate for a shift towards a more person-centred approach, which focuses on relationships rather than compliance. As Perry (2019, p. 177) highlights:

> *When we behave well, it's rarely because we want a reward or because we fear a punishment, it's because behaving with consideration towards other people comes naturally to us.*

As EPs, we recognise the power of relationships and the potential they cultivate. Taking a relational perspective enables a way of interacting with others that embodies values we hold at the core of working with children and young people: respect, empathy, collaboration, honesty, compassion, safety, and growth. A relational approach is not just a more 'human' approach but one we professionally advocate to be more effective for all involved.

Research offers an optimistic perspective that focusing on relationships between teachers and pupils has wide-reaching implications, offering the potential to:

- Support development of a positive emotional climate (Rucinski et al., 2018)
- Increase positive behaviours, as well as behaviour for learning (Driscoll & Pianta, 2010; Lei et al., 2016)
- Result in positive changes in emotional regulation, social competence, and resilience to academic challenge, leading to increased academic achievement (Bergin & Bergin, 2009; Roorda et al., 2017)
- Enhance a pupil's sense of school belonging (Allen et al., 2018)
- Increase wellbeing for teachers and staff involved (Spilt et al., 2011)

Understanding the intersubjective relationship

Embracing a more relational orientation involves shifting away from individualism, where the child is regarded as solely responsible for their own actions and choices and their behaviours are viewed in isolation from their context and environment. In contrast, what is required is a position which sees the child as a social being, influenced and shaped through interaction with those around them. In understanding the importance of this perspective, we can look to the influential psychology of Colwyn Trevarthen (1998, 2001) in his work on attachment and the concept of the intersubjective relationship. This is a relationship in which experience is shared, and through attuned interaction, new and shared meaning is co-constructed. He posits that through shared experiences, an individual learns about themselves (primary intersubjectivity) and that they also learn about others and the world around them (secondary intersubjectivity). Through the reciprocal experiences of the relationship, each person in the relationship is open to influencing the other and being influenced by them.

Parent-child relationships

The quality of the relationship and interactions a child has with their primary caregiver(s) has long since been recognised in parenting literature. The importance of attuned, empathetic parent-child interactions was first recognised by Ginott (1965), whilst attachment theory, proposed by Bowlby (1969), focused on the 'lasting connectedness between human beings'. Over time, our understanding has shifted from attachment 'types' to the impact of early parent-child relationships on brain development (Sunderland, 2016) and the protective features these relationships offer in the face of adversity and trauma (Golding, 2017; Golding et al., 2020; Garner & Yogman, 2021). Despite this shift, the key focus on attuned, consistent, empathetic, and responsive interactions between a child and their caregiver has remained.

Special time in parenting

Parenting approaches consistently highlight the benefits of play and, more specifically, 'special time' spent interacting together through uninterrupted child-led activities in which the adult responds sensitively and with unconditional positive regard. Whilst play fundamentally provides a platform for the growth of skills essential for healthy development (e.g. speech and language skills, thinking skills, and those required for emotional regulation and resilience), 'special time' brings additional benefits that other types of parent-child interaction do not offer, creating circumstances in which:

- High emotional connection can occur without distraction through 'high-intensity positive relational moments' (Sunderland, 2016, p. 100)
- Parents can engage in interactions based not on reaction or correction, but rather reciprocation and trust
- Key adults can become attuned to a child's signals whilst also providing a means of promoting emotional regulation (James, 2010)
- A 'bank of positive feelings and experiences' can be established and subsequently 'drawn upon at times of conflict' (Webster Stratton, 2005, p. 29)

'Special time' offers an opportunity to experience reciprocity through intersubjective relationships, in which a child learns 'who they are, what they can do and how to relate to the world around them' (Webster-Stratton, 2005). This holds particular value for young people who are thought to have missed out on consistent and attuned responses from a primary caregiver, or where early childhood adversity has disrupted experiences crucial for healthy development or adversely affected the picture they have come to form of themselves and others as a result of this (Golding et al., 2020). In acknowledging the influence of one person to another within a reciprocal relationship, we are opened up to the potential of interactions and the dialogic space that they offer as the foundational tool for change. Through shared experiences, we can effect positive changes through building relational trust and opening and sharing in conversations and interactions to explore new ways of being (Vasillic, 2022).

So what are the features of 'special time' that provide a quality interaction in which the parent–child intersubjective relationship can grow? Ginott (1965) suggested the key aspects of empathetic parent–child interactions as hearing both a child's words and their emotions, showing genuine respect for their feelings, empathising by feeling what the child is feeling, mutually respectful communication, and setting limits on actions, but not emotions and desires, providing a safe forum for emotions to be expressed. 'Attuned emotional responsiveness', within the context of parenting, refers to a parent's capacity to accurately and empathically read their child's signals, whilst also utilising the principles of PACE: playfulness, acceptance, curiosity, and empathy (Golding & Hughes, 2012). This method of communication requires a level of self-awareness on the part of the adult to ensure messages are reflected back to the child in a helpful manner (e.g. using a calm and gentle voice and playful manner) (James, 2010; Sunderland, 2016).

Special time in the educational setting

Trevarthen (2001) may have been focusing on early parent–child relationships and interactions, but application into the school setting holds strong rationale. From the perspective of primary intersubjectivity, when the dominant experience of a child in school is of being told off and sanctioned for their behaviour, with adult reactions guided by a linear, behaviourist perspective, what they may learn about themselves is that they are a failure, they are inconsequential, and their needs are not worth being attended to. From the perspective of intersubjectivity, the interactions that may occur within a school when following a behaviourist approach are unlikely to be influencing the meaning that each person takes from the situation about themselves, the other person, and the world around them in a way that will allow positive change (particularly for the young person) to occur.

Helen Cockerill, a speech and language therapist, introduced the idea of non-directive communication therapy through 'special time', in the classroom, as an approach to supporting children with profound and multiple/complex learning difficulties (PMLD) to 'make sense of their world and move forward towards emergent interpersonal communicative behaviours' through 'face to-face, human-to-human interactions' (Cockerill, 1991, as cited by Jones & Maltby, 2002, p. 22). Rooted in play therapy and client-centred counselling, non-directive communication provides a way for adults to 'be' alongside children by 'following their interest and attention' (Jones & Maltby, 2002).

'Special time' draws some parallels with non-directive play therapy and mirrors many of the known benefits, for example, using playtime to gain insights, explore emotions, redirect inappropriate behaviours, and develop empathy for others. Special time implemented within a school setting mirrors the benefits that occur when used by parents within the home, whilst also establishing the many values that underpin relational practice, for example, trust between both parties, authenticity within the relationship, and the creation of a safe time and space for containment and collaboration.

Implementing special time in school

Special time, delivered as an integrated intervention approach, is one-to-one time with an adult, where there are no other distractions for the duration. The adult **must** be able to give the child their undivided attention for the allocated time, with no interruptions (such as other staff asking them questions or asking them to do another task). Special time is led by the child, with an adult following their lead, unless there are concerns about their safety. This may include playing a game of their choice, reading a book, crawling under the table, being outdoors etc., as long as the adult is giving the child positive attention.

The key principles of special time, as a school-based intervention, are as follows:

- Time is set aside for special time. The frequency and duration of this is child-dependent and must be decided collectively.
- The session is entirely child-led, with no demands made of the child during this time. However, to keep the child safe, there must be obvious limits on what can happen during this time. Often, settings find it helpful to have motivational resources available for the child to choose from, especially for those who become overwhelmed by or experience difficulty making choices.
- Ensure that the parameters of the sessions are clear for the child. They must know when the session will start and end, as well as how often they can expect to have special time, daily.
- It must be undertaken on an individual basis with the child and key adult. The number of adults may be negotiated, but the rationale of developing safe and trusting relationships lends itself to fewer adults being involved, to promote and enable these relationships to flourish.
- Provide a commentary on the child's play by using language adapted to their developmental needs to describe their actions in the here and now. This enables the child to feel that the adult is interested in and attuned to them.
- Provide language linked to where the child's attention is focused. This makes it more likely that the child will process and receive this.
- Resist the urge to evaluate, ask questions, and direct play.
- Respond to the child's attempts to make social contact. For example, receiving by returning eye contact and smiles, copying actions and gestures, and providing a commentary.
- Decide what language to use to respond to danger, for example, saying, 'I'm sorry I can't let you do that because . . .', rather than simply 'no', and remembering the importance of PACE in how these messages are delivered.
- Special time is not intended to be used as a reward (behaviourist approach) but rather time to develop a sense of connection with adults, and as such, it should take place regardless of other factors (or incidents/difficulties) occurring throughout the school day.

Ultimately, special time allows for a child to have regular positive experiences with others, promoting a sense of belonging. It also enables the child to think, to cooperate, to feel good about themselves and the people around them, allowing them to be safe, settled, and able to cognitively attend to learning. Special time creates the conditions for authenticity and collaboration to occur within a shared experience that is centred on the child's needs and wants.

Individual case study

The following is an account of my experience (Rachel) in creating, implementing, and reviewing special time in a primary school to support Jack*.

A referral to the Educational Psychology Service (EPS) was made for Jack when he was in year 3. Jack was reported to have been relatively settled in school until year 2, where 'low-level behaviours', such as fidgeting, talking, and distracting others, were observed by staff. Following his transition to year 3, Jack presented as being highly dysregulated, daily. This led to him, at times, hurting and lashing out at staff, running out of class, as well as sitting and hiding under tables, with Jack presenting as being 'in crisis' throughout the day. He was described as 'being at risk of permanent exclusion', which the head teacher did not want to do. At times, Jack would appear settled but would then quickly experience 'fight-and-flight' behaviours. This high level of unpredictability made it difficult for staff to proactively support him.

At the time of EPS involvement, there were several teaching assistants (TAs) working with Jack over the course of the week, due to the level of support that he required and the emotional impact that his needs had for them (which highlights the presence of secondary stress). They were understandably upset and frustrated with highly emotional situations experienced daily. This made them present as being wary of Jack and ultimately impacted their relationship and interactions with him, which were often focused on de-escalation, providing explanation and instructions to keep him and others safe.

Having observed Jack, and with the information provided by staff, I explained to the SENCO, head teacher, and Jack's mother my view that he was not feeling safe and regulated, and that any cognitive demands placed on him were simply too much. It was apparent he needed opportunity to regulate at multiple points throughout the day and needed time to develop safe and trusting relationships with key adults. As such, special time was recommended to facilitate this and work towards enabling him to experience a sense of physical and emotional safety, necessary to achieve a secure sense of belonging (Riley, 2023). Once agreed, I then spent time with the TAs to explain this approach, the research, and the theory behind it.

Initially, we considered what a personalised special time timetable would need to look like for Jack. It was felt, collectively, that he could manage roughly 15 minutes in the classroom before needing a break and time to regulate. As such, we started the timetable with a routine of 15 minutes in the classroom and then 15 minutes' special time, which was repeated throughout the duration of the day. It was determined that if, on arrival to school, it was evident Jack was already hyper-aroused, he would have special time first. It was also made clear Jack must have his special time, irrespective of what he did in the classroom (i.e. if he sat under the table and/or did not feel able to undertake any work).

Staff were informed Jack could choose the activities he wanted to do during special time, within reason (as long as the activities were safe, then they were to be allowed) and that the adult with him at these times would not place any form of demand on him, other than reinforcing the routine and supporting the transition back to the classroom. A timer was used alongside verbal preparation (countdowns) for the transitions.

During the initial fortnight, Jack experienced difficulty returning to the classroom from special time, as he had not yet begun to fully trust the adults when they reinforced the routine and was not reassured that he would have special time again. However, it was evident that during special time, relationships were quickly developing. Jack and the key adults supporting him were increasingly comfortable within each other's company and were experiencing playful (key component of PACE) and positive interactions, strengthening their connection. It was wonderful for everyone to hear Jack and adults laughing together and enjoying being with one another.

Despite expected teething problems and days whereby the approach did not seem to be working, staff persisted and maintained consistency with regards to the routine, until this became embedded for Jack, enabling him to calmly move from special time to adult-led and unpreferred activities. Within a half term, we were able to reduce the number of support staff working with Jack and also gradually increased his time in the classroom to 20 minutes, followed by 20 minutes' special time, repeated throughout the day. This meant he was in the classroom for 40 minutes of a one-hour lesson and, with the adults that he was developing a safe relationship with, attempting aspects of the curriculum. Over the course of the academic year, his time in class was gradually increased so that he only received and required formal special time at the end of the day. Changes to the timetable were determined collectively in conjunction with Jack's mother, school staff, and me; decisions made were based on regular review meetings.

Towards the end of the academic year, Jack was supported by one key adult, who then moved into year 4 with him. When in year 4, Jack did not require formal special time and had started to accept and engage with learning, as he felt safe and regulated enough to be able to manage academic demands, with the support from trusted adults. However, staff continued to utilise PACE principles during all interactions with him.

The benefits of this approach were vast, in that Jack observably became and felt safe in school. He started to develop trust in the wider staff team, with his key adults as his 'secure base'. It was clear that Jack did not feel threatened by staff, and vice versa, with interactions being much more social, with an observable ease between them. Importantly, staff shared with me that they had been given opportunity to get to know Jack, understand what his interests were, learn about his strengths and motivators, and reported that they enjoyed spending time with him. This had a big impact for them and their emotional wellbeing.

Considerations for practice

In our experience, special time is referred to as both a concept and an intervention. 'Special time' as a concept is a wide one, and as such, settings may suggest that they have tried this approach; however, the key principles of the special time intervention are often not adhered to. It is therefore essential that practitioners ask what special time currently looks like when this is being considered, so that it remains authentic and congruent with the principles and psychological underpinnings of the approach.

When reflecting on the individual case study, a key factor was the full support the head teacher, support staff, as well as Jack's mother gave me. Special time was not a widely used or well-documented school-based intervention (at that time), and therefore, they trusted me to try something creative and novel in developing a timetable and personalised intervention for Jack. The support at senior management level was crucial, as, justifiably, some staff members were dubious and hesitant when asked to implement the approach. On the days I was not in school, senior management reinforced the need to maintain the routine and supported staff to continue to implement the strategies, allowing for consistency. Additionally, they identified spaces for Jack to go and ensured he had access to resources they knew that he liked. For example, they allocated a computer in the ICT suite for him so that he could still use this during ICT lessons.

It was understood by all involved that there was no definite timescale and that any adaptations to his personalised timetable would be informed by his progress. As such, staff were incredibly patient with him and the process, understanding that the focus had to be on emotional regulation, wellbeing, and relationships, meaning, that 'learning' would be impacted by this until a time whereby he could participate.

Why does special time work? Essentially, play is a great arena for teaching communication skills, valuing a child's contribution, exploring likes and dislikes, growing confidence, and building trust. Webster-Stratton (2005) suggests that children are 'likely to become more involved, interested and creative' when an adult follows their lead. Adults become attuned to and accepting and empathic to their needs, which are fundamentals of a relational approach (Whitaker, 2021), enabling the child to feel that they really matter and are important.

Special time provided Jack with protected time and relational interactions, in which he could feel safe, learn more about himself and others around him, and develop a sense of acceptance and belonging within his school community. At the same time, the adults working with him developed their understanding of Jack, as well as how the experience of school felt for him and how he could best be supported, subsequently changing the way in which they interacted with him. Reduction in episodes of dysregulation provided a very visible measure of the positive impact of special time and, more specifically, the experiences of intersubjectivity (shared and attuned interactions allowing for positive, safe, and trusting reciprocal relationships to be shaped between Jack and staff) that this approach encompasses. As Treisman (2018, p. 237) emphasised, '[t]he magic is in the relationships and the meaningful connections'. Special time created the conditions for authenticity in the relationships between Jack and key adults in school, facilitating a sense of collaboration, shared understanding, and mutual respect.

Limitations

Whilst the benefits are clear and many, there are a number of implications that require consideration, especially for those thinking about this approach. There is no denying that special time is time-demanding and adult-dependent. However, it is essential to recognise that when a child is dysregulated, adults are often required to support them to co-regulate and keep them and others safe. As such, the level of support and intervention required is often extensive, but with special time, this is reframed and develops to become proactive and positive, maintaining connections and relationships, to sustain feelings of safety and a sense of belonging. Ensuring a sense of belonging, with a sense of safety as pre-requisite, has a positive effect on emotional wellbeing and academic outcomes (Popoola & Sivers, 2023).

Additionally, it is essential that staff 'buy into' the approach and become less attached to traditional behaviourist methods of behaviour management, reinforced through policies and government guidance, such as Behaviour in Schools Guidance (Department for Education, 2022b). When the idea of special time was initially broached to the staff supporting Jack, significant time was invested in explaining the psychology behind the intervention and why a relational approach was vital for him, to challenge the narrative held by some that we were suggesting we 'reward' Jack for his behaviours. Those who could not consider an alternative narrative other than 'he's choosing to behave like this' were not identified as being appropriate adults to support him. However, when the successful impact of the intervention became evident, the feedback from the wider staff team was very positive, and the benefits and advantages of a relationally based supportive approach were recognised.

Some important aspects of parent–child play and interaction cannot easily be transferred into a school setting. Sunderland (2016) highlights the importance of warm physical contact through cuddling and physical-social play, so thought may need to be given to how this aspect of interaction can be accounted for in line with safeguarding guidelines. Whitaker (2021) emphasised the importance of relational approaches as part of the culture of the whole school, where every interaction is understood as intervention. It is essential that special time sit within the values of a relational approach embedded within the ethos, policies, and practices of the setting.

Conclusion

Whilst it may not feel comfortable for some within education for 'learning' to take a back seat, it is vital to refer to and understand the wealth of research that explains how the brain develops and functions, including how children must be safe and settled in school to access the cognitive domains that enable learning to happen and children to flourish in all aspects of their development. By prioritising and reinforcing cognitive demand over the emotional and safety needs of children, we will never resolve the status quo. The long-term impact on the emotional wellbeing of children and of staff must be prioritised to enable holistic, healthy development, including enabling academic achievements.

Shifting away from behaviourism, embracing, paying attention to, and valuing relationships are not new within educational psychology. In encouraging staff within schools to feel confident and empowered in implementing a relationally congruent approach to supporting young people, special time undoubtedly offers a specific practical approach to enable a relational lens to be added to the toolbox of staff in schools. Leo (2007, p. 87) communicates this clearly in saying, 'Either we spend time meeting the children's emotional needs by filling their love cup or we will spend time dealing with behaviours caused by their unmet needs. Either way, we spend the time.'

References

Allen, K., Kern, M. L., Vella-Brodrick, D., Hattie, J., & Waters, L. (2018). What schools need to know about fostering school belonging: A meta-analysis. *Educational Psychology Review, 30*(1), 1-34.
Baker, S., & Simpson, M. (2020). *A school without sanctions: A new approach to behaviour management.* Bloomsbury.

Bergin, C., & Bergin, D. (2009). Attachment in the classroom. *Educational Psychology Review, 21*(2), 141-170.

Bowlby, J. (1969). *Attachment. Attachment and loss: Vol. 1. Loss.* Basic Books.

Cockerill, H. (1991, October 21-22). *Using non-directive communication therapy techniques with young AAC users.* 3rd National Conference Proceedings Communication Matters Workshop, Portland Training College, Mansfield, Notts. F:\- Archives - Important Folders\CM archive\Master Artwork\Cm Vol (communicationmatters.org.uk)

Department for Education. (2013). *Behaviour and discipline in schools: Guide for governing bodies.* www.gov.uk/government/publications/behaviour-and-discipline-in-schools-guidance-for-governing-bodies

Department for Education. (2022a). *Revised behaviour in school guidance and suspension and permanent exclusion guidance: Government response to consultation.* www.gov.uk/government/publications/school-exclusion

Department for Education. (2022b). *Behaviour in schools: Advice for headteachers and school staff.* www.gov.uk/government/publications/behaviour-in-schools-2

Department for Education. (2023). *Permanent exclusions and suspensions in England 2021-2022.* www.gov.uk/government/statistics/permanent-exclusions-and-suspensions-in-england-spring-term-2021-to-2022

Driscoll, K. C., & Pianta, R. C. (2010). Banking time in head start: Early efficacy of an intervention designed to promote supportive teacher-child relationships. *Early Education and Development, 21*(1), 38-64.

Garner, A., & Yogman, M. (2021). Preventing childhood toxic stress: Partnering with families and communities to promote relational health. *Pediatrics, 148*(2)

Ginott, G. (1965). *Between parent and child.* Macmillan

Golding, K. S. (2017). *Everyday parenting with security and love: Using PACE to provide foundations for attachment.* Jessica Kingsley Publishers.

Golding, K. S., & Hughes, D. A. (2012). *Creating loving attachments with PACE to nurture confidence and security in the troubled child.* Jessica Kingsley Publishers.

Golding, K. S., Phillips, S., & Bombèr, L. M., (2020). *Working with relational trauma in schools: An educator's guide to using dyadic developmental practice.* Jessica Kingsley Publishers.

James, O. (2010). *How not to F*** them up.* Vermillion.

Jones, T., & Maltby, M. (2002). Switching to communication. *International Society for Augmentative and Alternative Communication, 17*(1) 22-27.

Knost, L. R. (2013). *The gentle parent: Positive, practical, effective discipline.* Little Hearts Books

Lei, H., Cui, Y., & Chiu, M. M. (2016). Affective teacher - student relationships and students' externalizing behavior problems: A meta-analysis. *Frontiers in Psychology, 7*, 1- 12.

Leo, P. (2007). *Connection parenting: Parenting through connection instead of coercion, through love instead of fear.* Wyatt-Mackenzie Publishing.

Perry, P. (2019). *The book you wish your parents had read (and your children will be glad that you did)* (pp. 177). Penguin Life.

Popoola, M., & Sivers, S. (2023). Maslow, relationships and square pegs. In *Square Pegs: Inclusivity, compassion and fitting in; A guide for schools.* Fran Morgan, Ellie **Costello** and Crown House Publishing. Independent Thinking Press.

Riley, K. (2023). Three key questions about belonging. In *Square Pegs: Inclusivity, compassion and fitting in; A guide for schools.* Fran Morgan, Ellie Costello and Crown House Publishing. Independent Thinking Press.

Rogers, B. (2000). *A whole school approach to behaviour management.* Paul Chapman Publishing Ltd.

Roorda, D. L., Jak, S., Zee, M., Oort, F. J., & Koomen, H. M. Y. (2017). Affective teacher - student relationships and students' engagement and achievement: A meta-analytic update and test of the mediating role of engagement. *School Psychology Review, 46*, 1- 23.

Rucinski, C., Brown, J., & Downer, J. (2018). Teacher-child relationships, classroom climate, and children's social-emotional and academic development. *Journal of Educational Psychology, 110*(7), 992-1004.

Siegel, D. J., & Bryson, T. P. (2012). *The whole-brain child.* Random House.

Spilt, J. L., Koomen, H. M. Y., & Thijs, J. T. (2011). Teacher wellbeing: The importance of teacher - student relationships. *Educational Psychology Review, 23*, 457-477.

Sunderland, M. (2016). *The science of parenting* (2nd ed., p. 100). DK Publishing.

Treisman, K. (2018). *A therapeutic treasure box for working with children and adolescents with developmental trauma.* Jessica Kingsley Publishers.

Trevarthen, C. (1998). The concept and foundations of infant intersubjectivity. In S. Braten (Ed.), *Intersubjective communication and emotion in early ontogeny* (pp. 15-46). Cambridge: University Press.

Trevarthen, C. (2001). Intrinsic motives for companionship in understanding: Their origin, development, and significance for infant mental health. *Infant Mental Health Journal, 22*, 95-131.

Vasillic, B. (2022). Behaviour as relational process: Linking theory to practice. *Educational Psychology in Practice, 38*(4), 379-391.

Webster-Stratton, C. (2005). *The incredible years*. Incredible Years.

Whitaker, D. (2021). *The kindness principle: Making relational behaviour management work in schools*. Independent Thinking Press.

18 Beads of life for transition to high school

Educational and child psychologists' retelling their embodied narrative practice with young people, staff, and families

Catherine Beal and Helen Waters

Introduction

This chapter offers retellings and reflections on our work as an experience of embodied practice. Our relationships with narrative, with others, and with each other (two educational and child psychologists, EP) enabled us to invite people to take a position of agency, in authoring their own stories of self. An act which we hoped would make it possible to reclaim spaces for the expression of preferred identities and stories, about what mattered to these young people, staff, and family members.

'Beads of life' is a narrative practice developed by Portnoy et al. (2016). We were influenced by practices and ideas embedded within this approach and offered them as a response to young people transitioning to high school whose school lives and files were populated with dominant accounts of their identities being 'challenging' and 'vulnerable to exclusion'. Through discussions over time with primary school special educational needs disability coordinators (SENDCos), we identified young people who needed their stories to be known (Bombèr, 2020), as an alternative to early permanent exclusion, displacement, or absenteeism from their high school experience (Billington, 2000). We facilitated a two-day beads of life intervention within the young people's current schools and the high schools in their local communities that they were likely to transition to. Day 1 involved preparing primary schools to select a key adult who would accompany the young person for a morning group session with us. This adult was invited to take an outsider witness position (Walther & Fox, 2012). An outsider witness is positioned to experience the beads of life from a curious perspective alongside the young person whilst paying continuous close attention (Vasilic, 2022) to the stories they tell. This morning session was informed by Portnoy et al. (2016) beads of life methodology. Young people, with their key adult sitting alongside them, used beads to explore stories of their 'daily lives', 'skills and abilities', 'important people and their gifts', 'where I come from', and 'hopes, wishes and dreams' (Portnoy & Ireland, 2019). The young people, in turn, then shared their stories, to be witnessed and acknowledged by the group as a whole (including staff, young people, and ourselves). We facilitated an individual therapeutic session with each young person, within a private, quiet space in their primary school. Finally, they returned to the high school venue for an afternoon session, where a definitional ceremony (Myerhoff, 2007) took place, involving their key school adult, family members, and high school staff identified to support the transition (Walther & Fox, 2012). Definitional

DOI: 10.4324/9781003451907-18

ceremonies are places where people come together to share their stories about place, community, and self with an audience that witness and acknowledge these accounts as a performance of identity (Myerhoff, 2007).

We offered the beads of life experience as part of our resistance towards the status quo, or ritual dance (Cubbedu & MacKay, 2017), of adults' constructions of children and young people, using the discourses (Potter & Wetherell, 1987; Burr, 1995; Parker, 1992, 2012) available to them (e.g. school reports, how they are spoken about, media representations, etc.). This included language attempting to describe and advocate for the needs and challenges faced by young people, formally recorded as demonstrating social emotional mental health (SEMH) needs, on their special educational needs and disability (SEND) registers. These habitual dances, or acts of oppression, are embedded within our typical processes, systems, and service delivery models for practice. We also experienced beads of life as a stance against poverty, oppression, and social injustices in the communities we responded to (Reynolds, 2021).

We noticed that this way of practicing gave space for curiosity and demanded that we step deeply into a place of listening, exploring, and acts of patience. Young people, too, stepped into acts of patience, respect, and nurture in ways that staff had not previously had the privilege to witness (Walther & Fox, 2012).

This experience of EP work was a performance of our preferred professional identity. This offered alternative narratives to the dominant accounts of EP as 'problem-solver', 'local authority officer', 'statutory advice giver', and 'expert'. In reclaiming EP identity as multi-storied, we took an active stance to make this practice visible (Winslade, 2002) and, in doing so, 'thickened' narratives which speak to relational identity (Shotter & Gergen, 1989) and emotion as knowledge. As a stance against 'thin' descriptions or a compartmentalising of EP role as 'doing direct work with children' or 'assessment' or 'planning meetings', or 'consultation', or 'supervision'. Finding ourselves seeking accounts of identity outside the known and familiar (White, 2007) educational context, we invited this practice from clinical psychology and therapy into being and with us as part of our work as applied psychologists connected to narrative practices.

This chapter retells our embodied practices as follows:

1. Relational identity
2. Safe space to stand: space as agency
3. Relationships and emotional knowledge as practice
4. A call to action in response to the social and political landscape for education
5. Future directions

Retelling our embodied practices: Relational identity

Portnoy et al. (2016) were drawn to the narrative underpinnings implicit within the tree of life (Ncube, 2006), recipes of life, etc., as these offered a collective space to tell, and retell, rich multi-storied accounts of people's experiences and identities (Denborough, 2008). Portnoy et al. (2016) narrative response was prompted by her reflection that, once a cancer diagnosis was given, 'cancer' became the dominant account for a person's identity and what was possible in their lives. Individuals experienced reductive descriptions of themselves as 'young people with cancer' that replaced multi-storied tellings and acknowledgement of their particular identities and relationships. These tellings then influenced the stories they were expected to voice and perform, in their daily lives, inside and outside of the hospital (Portnoy et al., 2016). This resonated with our experiences of interacting with dominant accounts of young people as 'vulnerable to exclusion', and our typical roles in understanding their needs and describing provision for transition. In our work, we were audience to, and part of, the tell-ing of accounts which categorised and marginalised these young people and silenced their stories: of selves, what mattered to them, and what was important to them. Their stories were obscured by what professionals had been positioned to listen to so that they 'knew what they needed to do' (Marston et al., 2017). We worked with the young people, schools, and pro-fessionals in our communities to take an active and embodied stance against these practices of transition. Working with communities, we created space for families and staff to listen to and experience the stories that these young people needed to tell (White, 2005).

Our act to resist the status quo, and the ritual dance associated with 'transition planning', began through conversations with staff. We listened out for descriptions of young people who would benefit from a relational response to their needs, including therapeutic time and space with an EP.

Dominant discourses about these young people and their families dictated that they would experience exclusion, crime, and unemployment (Buckley & Decter, 2006). We were drawn to the beads of life (Portnoy et al., 2016) as a way of positioning the audience as outsider witnesses (Walther & Fox, 2012), to suspend their judgement and listen with curiosity to the stories young people told. Listening to the young person was prioritised over existing transi-tion practices, where adults meet to tell their story about the young person in order to inform high school provision. We selected this transition as a key point of intervention, informed by our understanding of the role of transitions as 'autobiographical turning points' (Bruner, 2004, p. 120) that encourage and legitimise changes in identity stories. We understood this space for performance of identity as a more ethical way to consider transition.

Giving time and attention to these narratives, as told by the young people themselves, directly informed the ways the primary and high school staff related to young people, within and following this intervention. By acting as advocates for their hopes, wishes, and aspira-tions, the staff built trusting relationships with the young people they accompanied. The beads of life (Portnoy et al., 2016) became our relational space to invite multiple accounts of identity and ways of being, for young people, schools, and their families.

Our beads of life-inspired approach offered people an opportunity to be listened to and to listen with curiosity in order to honour the children's multi-storied accounts of strengths, knowledges, skills, and values (White, 2007). This meant actively positioning staff (and our-selves) as outsider witnesses, which enabled us to respond in a decentred and influential way, as part of our call to action through listening. Within the definitional ceremonies (Myerhoff, 2007), we experienced transformative relational identity (Shotter & Gergen, 1989; Zimmer-man, 2001) with each other, with staff, with family members, with and between the young people, which offered an experience of resonance and belonging (Reynolds, 2002). This gave space for continued reflection around the multiple stories told about the young people we had the privilege of becoming involved with. We experienced this space as a 'coming home' to narrative therapeutic territories, grounded in our shared narrative diploma teachings, talking with people in the spaces they live their lives in (Myerhoff, 2007). We worked together to become a solidarity team (Reynolds, 2011), to support, protect, and hold each other accountable in order to resist our familiar stomping ground, involving fast-paced conversations in response to service demands (Reynolds, 2013).

As a solidarity team (Reynolds, 2021), we used reflexive practice to support each other to engage with the beads of life, as an embodied and felt experience. This shared position made it possible for us to be active in reclaiming the space for expression of preferred identities/stories about what mattered to these young people. We embraced the beads of life as decentred yet influential practice and worked to enable families and school staff to enter into this experience as outsider witnesses, with permission to listen with curiosity and respond with authenticity to what they heard that resonated with them. This event became a safe place from which to stand (Ncube, 2006), to honour stories of young people, their strengths, skills, and knowledges, and the histories of these. During the sessions, the young people and audience developed relationships with the stories they heard and told. This offered a collective acknowledgement that helped individual stories be transported with them as they embarked on the transition to high school.

In contrast to repeated 'performances' of dominant identities that dictate the 'shoulds' of who we can be in our roles around transition for young people (Marsten et al., 2016), the beads of life became a space to explore what our identities 'could' be in relation to each other. During this reflection, we recognised that we were continuing to be influenced by the dominant accounts of EP role, by anticipating how we would be positioned by others. As EPs, we embodied our preferred accounts of identity as experiential explorers of the knowledges, skills, and values of young people, families, and staff. This performance of identity was a stance against dominant accounts of EP as 'expert', 'giver of knowledge', 'LA officer', and 'assessor of need'.

Embodying this preferred identity involved several risks. First, it meant taking the risk of making new ways of knowing and being EP possible and visible. We risked young people, families, and staff disengaging from our established role of expertise, and of resisting these practices on the basis that they were 'too therapeutic' and 'not what we were expecting'. We also risked our service critiquing this offer as an allocation of 'too much resource' to individual young people and schools (Reynolds, 2013). Staff shared worries with us about these particular young people being in a space together. Their concerns centred on the lived experiences of families, staff, and agencies of challenges they had endured as part of their daily lessons, interactions, and interventions. We noticed ourselves responding to these concerns with 'traditional' and 'familiar' strategies, including a space to separate and regulate, options for leaving if the space was too challenging, adding structure and further scaffolding to beading if needed. We reflected in action (Schon, 1983) as the young people embraced and thrived through our continued responses of acceptance and curiosity, and when positioning the audience to actively listen. Our confidence in being alongside young people as they explored this way of being with us, and with each other, was critical. For example, we sat alongside young people as they took time to explore the resources and develop the confidence to speak. We stood alongside them as they climbed on and threw resources, before stepping into the space to sit and be listened to, observing as young people actively listened to each other's stories with curiosity and acknowledgement.

As we had anticipated having to protect our safe space to stand in order to offer this work, we smiled as we discovered that children, young people, families, and staff were willing to explore this new territory with us. Using this approach, we witnessed resonance between young people, families, and staff that connected them to shared hopes and dreams, taking space to replace or sit alongside previous stories of challenge. We understood that it may be us as EPs that needed to reclaim self-authorship of our role and identities, creating agency for our practice moving forward (Moore, 2005; Osgood, 2010; Winslade, 2002).

Retelling our embodied practices: Safe space to stand, space as agency

Within narrative therapy, we talk about adopting a riverbank position to sit alongside the young people, families, and professionals we work with to centre their expertise in narrating their lived experience and its effects (White, 1997). Within this, when people face challenges, adversities, or oppressions, we imagine them as if they were in the river. This river has rapids, and the particular challenges become visible as rocks, tree trunks, crocodiles, waves, etc. In practice, it is tempting to jump in to save them, to build boats or bridges as expected routes out of the river. However, in narrative practice, we centre their journey and their relationship with this journey of life. We work to invite them to a safe space to stand on the riverbank. We are alongside them as we listen to them with curiosity and provide space for them to explore their relationships with the challenges they face, and to see the landscape of alternative actions and ways of being. This space supports their agency in exploring what is possible for them. This is a therapeutic endeavour, as healing occurs within the context of relationships (Cherry, 2021), through the sharing of valued histories and witnessing preferred accounts of identity (Denborough, 2008, 2014).

Creating this space for listening allowed these young people to make their preferred identities visible, in a context where they were recognised and acknowledged. The young people were then able to perform their preferred identities, not only in the context of the beads of life intervention, but also, later, in other areas of their lives. By making it possible for young people to contribute actively to how they would like to be seen and understood, new possibilities for action and identity were created. Through the act of listening, we were able to learn how young people relate to their communities, family, and friends. This, in turn, can offer an insight into their ways of relating to and being in the world and what they give value to. This can then inform our understanding as practitioners as to how best to guide, advocate, and help them feel safe and connected to their school community (Freeman et al., 1997; Todd, 2000).

Our professional history of practicing together provided a safe place for *us* to stand, from which we could embrace decentred practices. The trust between us, and the way we are attuned to one another, made it possible to immerse ourselves in the experience and be present, enabling us to listen in an outsider witness position to the stories told within this space. Our embodied experience of the beads of life was one in which we were both central and decentred. We were central, as our narrative practices created and facilitated this embodied experience for, and with, adults and young people (White, 1997). We supported each other through supervision to remain within this territory of practice, resisting interruptions from dominant accounts of EP role that called us to perform assessment of needs, guided problem-solving, or creation of next steps within the interaction.

Trusting in the experience, and each other as colleagues, appeared to offer containment for the participating adults. Subsequently, the young people's behaviours indicated that they felt 'held' by the way we, as EPs, related to each other. This holding was embodied throughout our interactions, our volume and tone of voice, how we moved, how we organised the physical environment, and how we used resources from family life (e.g. food, drink, tablecloths) to create this safe space to stand (Ncube, 2006). Our aim was to communicate messages such as 'This is a space for you', 'You are welcome here', through a combination of the 'look' of the environment and, most importantly, the 'feel' of the space. We worked closely with our community of primary and high schools to plan how to enable staff and families to have the space and time to truly listen, to relate and to sit alongside these young people.

We ensured that it was understood and expected that the role of staff was to listen and be part of the experience (Walther & Fox, 2012). They were not responsible for the content or performance of the young person, as this was held by us and by the group experience. This was a powerful demonstration for us all that when young people, families, and staff are invited into safe spaces to stand, they will connect, relate, and explore identity together. With commitment to relational practices, group dynamics did not have to be managed or manufactured; they were organic and authentic. The engagement and accounts shared by the young people, staff, and families evidenced that they experienced the space as one where they felt comfortable to share stories about their lives.

During the session, some adults needed reassurance that this was a space for them to perform identities, rather than needing to have rehearsed a script in response to the young people's stories. We explained that whatever they shared within the moment would be 'good enough' and okay for us and them. In turn, the young people experienced that stories could change and whatever they chose to tell would be honoured and valued. This was an example of our narrative practice and its transformative effect on these young people, as they were given space to re-author their preferred identities, through retellings of their histories of family, friends, and schooling, as well as impacting the adults positioned as witnesses, listening curiously, intentionally, and compassionately (Edwards et al., 2012; Cherry, 2021).

Retelling our embodied practices: Relationships and emotional knowledge as practice

Catherine and Helen: Our relationship with each other, our community for practice, and relational practices of narrative working

The social and relational context for our relationship with EP practices and each other was explored through years of joint work and narrative study. Following the doctorate, our training at the Institute of Narrative Therapy was informed by a relational pedagogy, which demanded that we actively immerse ourselves in the experience of listening, exploring narrative practices, and responding therapeutically to what we heard. This took place in a safe space to stand with ongoing guidance and supervision from a narrative therapist. During the course, mistakes, questions, and critical reflections were all scaffolded on the path to embodying decentred practice. Relationships between students (psychologists, therapists, researchers, nurses, doctors, etc.) as part of each module were nurtured both within the 'classroom' and outside of it. Narrative therapy between clients and therapists can be transformative and 'life shaping' (White, 2004, p. 130), not only for the people seeking help, but also for the practitioners engaged in working with individuals, groups, and communities. Taking this perspective can reorientate the practitioner towards what matters, through resonance with their values and accounts of practice (Denborough, 2008).

Planned reflective supervision made it possible for us to explore alternative ways of responding to our work and role, allowing us to have agency in our relationship with professional 'shoulds' for practice (Moore, 2005). We focused our attention on developing experience, skills, and knowledge of how the beads of life could make a difference in the world of educational psychology and strengthen narrative-informed community practices between staff, young people, and their families.

Our profession of educational psychology is an institutionalised role of privilege, expertise, and power, which has a history of being drawn on to marginalise and pathologise. Our engagement with narrative practices required an investment of time to explore what each of us gives value to. Our histories of practice and shared stories about what matters to us across our experiences as EPs, and working with communities of young people, their families, and the staff supporting them. This made shared values visible, which, when threaded together, narrated an aspirational and passionate account to advocate for others in ways that honour the knowledge and expertise they bring to understanding and constructing ways of being. Our shared values include ways of relating to identity, relationships, and experiences of education, facilitating safe spaces to stand, advocating for adults to sit alongside young people as they explore future possibilities for their lives, and sustaining connections with what matters to them. Crucially, we share a commitment to working in ways which are underpinned by principles of social justice and informed by community practices and wisdom (Buckley & Decter, 2006; Denborough, 2008; Reynolds, 2002).

EP as emotional worker: The value of emotion in our work

History, context, and dominant paradigms connected with ways of working determine the value that emotions in professional practice are afforded at a given time (Yanay & Shahar, 1998; Damasio, 2000; Bergner, 2003). The story of therapists as emotional workers, and the effect of client–therapist relationships, as critical for positive change has long been established (Bergner, 2003; Cherry, 2021). EPs need to further contribute to shaping the narrative of 'EP as emotional worker' as part of the shift towards relational ways of working in educational contexts. EPs must continue to participate in research and practice debates about 'relational practice', especially when seeking to connect and respond to the communities we work with (Gergen, 2009; Reynolds, 2013). Permission to explore alternative professional ways of being is fundamental to professional growth, learning, and care-taking of oneself and others, as well as teaching that vulnerability and curiosity are essential for professional development, if we are to keep pace with the changing educational, political, social, and technological landscape.

We have been drawn to narratives which value emotion as knowledge and as practice (Armstrong et al., 2012), in addition to arguments articulating the contribution and impact of 'the relationship' (Osgood, 2010; Doucet & Mauthner, 2012; Hughes, 2012). These narratives sit alongside dominant accounts of the 'shoulds' of being professional outside of therapeutic disciplines.

Some professional narratives, and wider discourses relating to ways of being 'professional', posit 'emotion' and 'professionalism' as existing in opposition. These narratives and discourses are often embodied within guidelines and regulatory processes designed to ensure practitioners adhere to ethical standards. Alongside these processes, practitioners need opportunities to re-negotiate, re-author, and re-construct what these labels mean for practice and the effects of practices on role (Winslade, 2002). Such opportunities enable practitioners to make active and informed decisions about the positions they adopt, the relationships they have with their 'professional' status, and what this means for their identity and practice. This includes engaging with narratives that are concerned with 'leaning into the unknown', the importance of spaces to 'be playful to create and innovate', and 'taking informed and managed risks'. Multi-storied accounts of professionality are vital for innovative advances in practice, which take a stand against social injustices and oppressive political acts.

Retelling our embodied practices: A call to action in response to the social and political landscape for education

Working with many children, young people, families, and staff, we have witnessed the huge efforts being made to care-take, provide support, and identify ways of helping individuals, groups, and communities who are experiencing adversity and challenge. These adversities and challenges are often the effects of trauma, poverty, housing crises, needing to seek asylum, and the impact of systemic, political, and institutional ways of 'solving problems'. Historically, this has compounded marginalisation, stigma, and division as barriers to diversity and cohesion. Building from Benjamin Perks's conversation with Lisa Cherry about his UNICEF work (Cherry, 2021), we set out in our practice to resource families to have space, time, and support to play together and to build early relationships. The goal of this practice was underpinned by a commitment to creating trauma-informed schools and communities capable of preventing intergenerational transmission of adverse childhood experiences at a universal level across society.

Our schools show us that they need relationships between staff, young people, and families, but policies, funding, and diktats for the purpose of education remove space, time, and resources for relating. This is occurring in a context where the creative arts, relationships, and having your basic needs met (e.g. having enough food, clean clothes, heating the home, etc.) have been positioned as privileges, for those that can afford them, instead of a human right for all. Against this backdrop, the beads of life presented us with hope, in the form of an intervention, founded on responding respectfully and impactfully to the relational needs of the young people we were working with at that time.

Our reflexive practice within our narrative training, work in local authorities, peer supervision, and friendship gave space for shared resonance around valuing work with communities constructed by other professionals as 'hard to reach' (Chilokoa & McKie, 2007), 'dangerous', 'notorious', 'antisocial', and 'deprived' (Buckley & Decter, 2006). These communities were talked about and identified through the reductionist lens of statistics and reputation. These statistics and headline judgements acted as dominant accounts, with the effect of 'othering', separating, and excluding people who were, in fact, responding to experiences of poverty, trauma, environmental, educational, and economic marginalisation. Subsequently, professionals were being positioned in role to 'fix', 'rescue', 'save', or 'prosecute'. This made alternative accounts of these communities as 'loving families', 'resourceful', 'resilient', 'inspirational', 'tough', and 'talented' invisible to professionals and less visible to communities themselves. 'Professional truths and expert knowledge' (Marsten et al., 2016, p. 165) over-crowded the space intended for community narratives about how they live their lives and, in particular, how young people are constructing their knowledge of school: what it means to 'be a learner', to be labelled as 'being at risk of exclusion', or 'having SEMH needs', when transitioning from primary to high school.

Future directions

'Narrative, restorative and systemic practices are examples of relationally attentive ways of working' (Vasilic, 2022, p. 386). Narrative therapy offers principles and values which can guide and orientate the practitioner to serve the multi-dimensional dynamic that is involved in meaning-making between each other and the world around us. This invites us to attend to, and illuminate, the narratives and wider discourses in which we are continuously interwoven. This also enables us to make visible social, political, environmental, and cultural acts of power that seek to oppress and maintain marginalised communities, as well as possibilities for action.

There is a need to negotiate and re-negotiate EP role and identity within the ever-changing cultural and political context in which EPs practice (Winslade, 2002). This provides opportunities for growth, understanding, and the deconstruction and reconstruction of knowledge. We can then draw on this knowledge to navigate our work, guided by values, intentions, and evidence-based practice that is reflective of the historical landscape.

Professionals implementing relational practice are called to consider what this means for their everyday interactions. This includes their communications, sharing of intentions, space given to explicit knowledge construction with others, and performance of preferred professional identities. An unrelenting commitment to relating, within a safe place to stand (Ncube, 2006), is essential for growth in regards to ourselves as people, our roles, and our ways of being in the world as practitioners (Reynolds, 2021).

Summary box

We invite the reader to reflect on the following questions, which we have asked ourselves:

- Where has this chapter left you?
- What relationship would you like with relational practices?
- If you had space to hold what matters to you close to you in your work, what would this have you doing? Have you saying? Have you feeling?
- Where, when, and with whom do you find your safe spaces to stand to author your identity? Your practice? Your relationships?

- How do you create safe spaces to stand to share accounts of identity with your staff, young people, and families?
- If you feel drawn to the beads of life, who will you recruit into your solidarity team (Reynolds, 2011, 2014), to support and challenge you as you explore these narrative practices with others? Who would you like to witness and acknowledge your work?
- Who do you tell your preferred account of professional identity to?
- If you wrote the story of relational practice, what might it say about what you give value to and what matters to you in your work life?
- If you've been drawn to the beads of life, what does this mean for the training and supervision you need your organisation to commit to for you?

Strategies

1. Make spaces and times for young people, staff, and families to relate and listen to each other's stories.
2. Connect with your solidarity team for relational practice (Reynolds, 2011).
3. Engage with narrative training for the beads of life (www.ticketsource.co.uk/whats-on/england/seven-dials-club-covent-garden-community-centre/narrative-training-tree-of-life-beads-of-life-workshops-apr-2024).
4. Secure your supervision for ethical relational practice.

References

Armstrong, A., Green, K., & Sangiacomo, A. (2012). *Spinoza and relational autonomy: Being with others.* Edinburgh University Press Ltd.

Bergner, R. (2003). Emotions: A relational view and its clinical applications. *American Journal of Psychotherapy, 57, 4.*

Billington, T. (2000). *Separating, losing and excluding children: Narratives of difference.* Routledge.

Bombèr, L. M. (2020). *Know me to teach me: Differentiated discipline for those recovering from adverse childhood experiences.* Worth Publishing Ltd.

Bruner, J. (2004). The narrative creation of the self. In L. Angus & J. McLeod (Eds.), *The handbook of narrative and psychotherapy: Theory, practice and research.* SAGE.

Burr, V (1995). *An introduction to social constructionism.* London: Routledge.

Buckley, E., & Decter, P. (2006). From isolation to community: Collaborating with children and families in times of crisis. *The International Journal of Narrative Therapy and Community Work, 2,* 3-12.

Cherry, L. (2021). *Conversations that make a difference for children and young people: Relationship-focused practice from the frontline.* Routledge.

Chilokoa, M., & McKie, J. (2007). Whose Voice is it Anyway. In K. J. Pomerantz, M. Hughes, & D. Thompson (Eds.), *How to reach 'hard to reach' children. Improving access, participation and outcomes.* John Wiley & Sons Ltd.

Cubbedu, D., & MacKay, T. (2017). The attunement principles: A comparison of nurture group and mainstream settings. *Emotional and Behavioural Difficulties, 22*(3), 261-274

Damasio, A. (2000). *The feeling of what happens. Body and emotion in the making of consciousness.* Penguin Random House.

Denborough, D. (2008). *Collective narrative practice: Responding to individuals, groups and communities who have experienced trauma.* Dulwich Centre Publications.

Denborough, D. (2014). *Retelling the stories of our lives: Everyday narrative therapy to draw inspiration and transform experience.* W.W. Norton & Company, Inc.

Doucet, A., & Mauthner, N. S. (2012). Emotions In/and Knowing. In D. Spencer, K. Walby, & A. Hunt (Eds.), *Emotions Matter: A relational approach to emotions*. University of Toronto Press.

Edwards, C., Gandini, L., & Forman, G. (2012). *The hundred languages of children: The Reggio Emilia experience*.

Freeman, J. C., Epston, D., & Lobovits, D. (1997). *Playful approaches to serious problems: Narrative therapy with children and their families*. New York: W.W. Norton & Company, Inc.

Gergen, K. J. (2009). *Relational being: Beyond self and community*. Oxford University Press.

Hughes, J, N. (2012). Teacher-student relationships and school adjustment: Progress and remaining challenges. *Attachment and Human Development, 14*(3), 319-327.

Marsten, D., Epston, D. & Markham, L. (2016). *Narrative Therapy in Wonderland: Connecting with Children's Imaginative Know-how*. New York City: W.W. Norton & Company, Inc.

Moore, J. (2005). Recognising and questioning the epistemological basis of educational psychology practice. *Educational Psychology in Practice, 21*(2), 103-116.

Myerhoff, B. (2007). *Stories as equipment for living: Last talks and tales of Barbara Myerhoff*. The University of Michigan Press.

Ncube, N. (2006). The tree of life project using narrative ideas in work with vulnerable children in Southern Africa by Ncazelo Ncube. *The International Journal of Narrative Therapy and Community, 1*.

Osgood, J. (2010). Reconstructing professionalism in ECEC: The case for the 'critically reflective emotional professional'. *Journal of Early Years, 30*, 119-133.

Parker, I. (1992). *Discourse dynamics* (Critical Analysis for Social and Individual Psychology). Routledge.

Parker, I. (2012). Discursive psychology now. *British Journal of Social Psychology, 51*, 471-477.

Portnoy, S., Girling, I., & Fredman, G. (2016). Supporting young people with cancer to tell their stories in ways that make them stronger: The beads of life approach. *Clinical Child Psychology and Psychiatry, 21*(2), 255-267.

Portnoy, S., & Ireland, L. (2019). The "Beads of Life" approach adapted for young people with acquired brain injury. In J. Jim & E. Cole (Eds.), *Psychological therapy for paediatric acquired brain injury*. Routledge

Potter, J., & Wetherell, M. (1987). *Discourse and social psychology: Beyond attitudes and behaviour*. SAGE.

Reynolds, V. (2002). Weaving threads of belonging: Cultural witnessing groups. *Journal of Child and Youth Care, 15*(3), 89-105.

Reynolds, V. (2011). *Supervision of solidarity practices: Solidarity teams and people-ing-the-room (Context)* (pp. 4-7). Association for Family and Systemic Therapy.

Reynolds, V. (2013). "Leaning in" as imperfect allies in community work. *Narrative and Conflict: Explorations in Theory and Practice, 1*(1), 53-75.

Reynolds, V. (2014). Centering ethics in therapeutic supervision: Fostering cultures of critique and structuring safety. *The International Journal of Narrative Therapy and Community Work, 1*, 1-13.

Reynolds, V. (2021). *Justice-doing at the intersections of power*. Dulwich Centre Publications.

Schon, D. (1983). *The reflective practitioner: How professionals think in action*. Basic Books.

Shotter, J., & Gergen, K. (1989). *Texts of identity*. London: Sage.

Todd, L. (2000). Letting the voice of the child challenge the narrative of professional practice. *Dulwich Centre Journal, 1-2*, 72-79.

Vasilic, B. (2022). Behaviour as relational process: Linking theory to practice. *Educational Psychology in Practice, 38*, 379-391.

Walther, S., & Carey, M. (2009). Narrative therapy, difference and possibility: Inviting new becomings. *Context*, 3-8.

Walther, S., & Fox, H. (2012). Narrative therapy and outsider witness practice: Teachers as a community of acknowledgement. *Educational and Child Psychology, 29*(2), 8-17.

White, M. (1997). *Narratives of therapists' lives*. Dulwich Centre Publications.

White, M. (2004). *Narrative practice and exotic lives: Resurrecting diversity in everyday life*. Dulwich Centre Publications.

White, M. (2005). Children, trauma and subordinate story development. *The International Journal of Narrative Therapy and Community Work, 3-4*, 10-21.

White, M. (2007). *Maps of narrative practice*. W.W. Norton & Company, Inc.

Winslade, J. (2002). Storying professional identity. *The International Journal of Narrative Therapy and Community Work, 4*, 33-38.

Yanay, N., & Shahar, G. (1998). Professional feelings as emotional labour. *Journal of Contemporary Ethnography, 27*(3), 346-347.

Zimmerman, J. (2001). The discourses of our lives: A theoretical introduction to narrative work in schools. *Journal of Systemic Therapies, 20*(3), 1-9.

19 Winnicott: (Chinese) parents at play and relational being

Changjie Meng

Winnicott's relational wisdom: Playing in the space between

Transitional space

Winnicott (2005) believes that playing unfolds within a transitional space that exists between our inner world and the interconnected world outside – the intermediate area of experience. He describes this space as follows:

> [T]he third part of the life of a human being . . . inner reality and external life both contribute. It is an area that is not challenged, because no claim is made on its behalf except that it shall exist as a resting-place for the individual engaged in the perpetual human task of keeping inner and outer reality separate yet interrelated.
>
> Winnicott (2005, p. 3)

To Winnicott, the infant's experience is negotiated in this transitional space, and what he proposes regarding children at play could also be applicable to adults. His evocative suggestions on transitional space served as an important focal point in my doctoral research.

Transitional space can be conceptualised in terms of what he terms *transitional objects* and *transitional phenomena* (Winnicott, 2005). Accordingly, in Winnicott's study of infants, he suggests that transitional objects, as a baby's initial 'not-me' possession, represent and internalise the breast or the mother. As such, transitional objects have symbolic value for infants. The true quality of the transitional object relies on the fact that it can become 'more important than the mother' and is 'an almost inseparable part of infant' (Winnicott, 2005, p. 9). The transitional object, as Winnicott suggests, 'gives room for the process of becoming able to accept difference and similarity' (2005, p. 8). Transitional phenomena, according to Winnicott, are an intermediate area between the inner world and external life. Significantly, the transitional space is regarded as a journey of progress towards experiencing throughout life. His writing beautifully illustrates this tendency and takes on an aesthetic sense:

> Its fate is to be gradually allowed to be decathected, so that in the course of years it becomes not so much forgotten as relegated to limbo. By this I mean that in health the transitional object does not 'go inside' nor does the feeling about it necessarily undergo repression. It is not forgotten and it is not mourned. It loses meaning, and this is because the transitional phenomena have become diffused, have become spread out over the

DOI: 10.4324/9781003451907-19

whole intermediate territory between 'inner psychic reality' and 'the external world as perceived by two persons in common', that is to say, over the whole cultural field.

Winnicott (2005, p. 7)

This evocative piece of writing provides us with clues for exploring how a person gradually widens into the experience that may belong to play, art, religion, imaginative living, etc. To an adult also, the personal intermediate area can bring extraordinary joy and may involve a degree of overlap. A degree of overlap here, according to Winnicott, can be viewed as a shared experience that can bridge the realms of culture, art, religion, philosophy, imaginative living, etc. Since a person's transitional object is gradually decathected, the intermediate area of experience continues to evolve, and cultural interests develop throughout life. Through this process, we launch into a journey of progress towards experiencing and potential change, that is, in relation to others.

In Winnicott's theory of transitional objects and transitional phenomena, both positive and negative factors are negotiated, for example, from love and hate to illusion-disillusionment. Winnicott values the transitional space as necessary 'for an infant to proceed from the pleasure principle to the reality principle or towards and beyond primary identification' (2005, p. 13). If 'all goes well', the mother can be internalised as 'good-enough' (2005, p. 14). The good-enough 'mother' functions as one who makes an active adaptation to an infant's needs, a gradually lessening adaptation in accordance with an infant's 'growing ability to account for failure of adaptation and to tolerate the results of frustration' (2005, p. 14). This approach explains the ways in which parents can encourage independence in the child while, at the same time, nurturing and supporting them. From this perspective, there is an acknowledgment that the (psychological) commitment of parents plays a crucial role in shaping success in infant progress and development.

The role of the good-enough mother holds practical significance, too, in the nurturing of a good-enough adaptive environment. In the context of my doctoral research, a parallel concern arose: whether a parent capable of providing adequate care can access a correspondingly good-enough environment that can harmonise with their parental role and provide support in navigating other life circumstances.

The illusion, in Winnicott's theory of transitional space (2005, p. 16), is that 'there is an external reality that corresponds to the infant's own capacity to create', that is, if the mother's adaptation to the infant's needs is good enough. The transitional space offers a neutral area for experience, offering a space in which a healthy disillusionment can progress from the task of weaning, for example, and can eventually transform in years to come as a space that can be filled by both parents and educators. Importantly, according to Winnicott, the illusion (for example, of omnipotence), while belonging inherently to the individual, cannot be solved in isolation and is resolved in negotiation with others. By undergoing the process of embracing the letting go of the illusion in the intermediate area, an individual can discover a soothing release from the strain of seeking to impose their will upon others, that is, by entering the space in which relationships can develop (Winnicott, 2005).

The processes of disillusionment can involve feelings of sadness, loss, and disappointment that lie at the core of depressive tendencies. Winnicott views depression as a mood that functions in three main areas in his work. Firstly, he perceives depression as a developmental shift from relating to using objects, indicating a healthy object survival. Secondly, he considers the ways in which depression can also arise from early emotional blockages due to environmental failure. Finally, he suggests that our (psychological) defences can be necessary to avoid the experiential pain of the sadness or loss felt within the depression. Winnicott's use of the term 'depression' can be understood, therefore, as being both healthy and pathological.

We can discern the happy fate of depression in Winnicott's work: a person becoming depressed or feeling sad can itself be a sign of health, signifying that an individual has the capacity to sense 'their own awfulness' (Winnicott, 2006, p. 75). This self-awareness, in turn, can lead to a sense of responsibility in respect of recognising oneself and also the other. He believes that sadness can be valuable, as it helps individuals process loss, which is crucial for navigating disillusionment. Given that, to Winnicott, the term 'depression' can be considered as emotionally healthy or normal, his theory of emotional development is crucial as it grows under the operation of the maturational process (Davis & Wallbridge, 2018). Winnicott's 'self' is not only subjective, continuous, and developmental but also relational.

Play in the space between

Winnicott (1969) suggests that the capacity to play is associated with using an object, which is developed from his theory of the transitional object and the transitional phenomena. Based on his study, it is possible for individuals to gradually develop the capacity to play and to 'find' and 'use' external objects with their own 'independence and autonomy' (Winnicott, 1969, p. 711). There is a process of developing from object-relating to object-usage, in which 'playing' becomes possible (Winnicott, 1969, p. 711).

Object-relating is regarded as an experience in which the subject 'allows certain alterations in the self to take place' (Winnicott, 1969, p. 712). In object-relating, the subject, whilst, to some extent, depleted, is enriched by feelings that something of themselves as subject is found in the object via what Winnicott would regard as operational projections and identifications (Winnicott, 1969). In this way, the object becomes meaningful for the subject. According to Winnicott, 'the object, if it is to be used, must necessarily be real in the sense of being part of shared reality, not a bundle of projection' (1969, p. 712). The clinical terms used in Winnicott's theory can help us understand object-relating and object-usage better:

> [T]wo babies are feeding at the breast; one is feeding on the self in the form of projections, and the other is feeding on (using) milk from a woman's breast. Mothers, like analysts, can be good or not good enough; some can and some cannot carry the baby over from relating to usage.
>
> Winnicott (1969, p. 712)

However, changes from relating to usage cannot happen automatically. He emphasises the importance of m/other (i.e. relational) figures but notes that 'the baby creates the object, but the object was there waiting to be created and to become a cathected object' (Winnicott, 2005, p. 119). It seems that the mother figure's realness and capacity for love are being tested, to see whether the object can tolerate being created and wait to be encountered, as real (i.e. the m/other).

According to Winnicott (2005), play then starts from the m/other figure feeling sufficiently confident in operating somewhere between the object that the baby has the ability to observe and being herself waiting to be observed, that is, in the transitional space. Play can begin with the child (subject) repudiating the object, re-accepting the object, and perceiving the object as an external phenomenon. The playground in the relationship as a potential space emerges and implies a mutual, relational trust (Winnicott, 2005). It is worth noting that for the child at play, the excitement can be immense:

> It is exciting not primarily because the instincts are involved. . . . The thing about playing is always the precariousness of the interplay of personal psychic reality and the experience of control of actual objects. This is the precariousness of magic itself, magic that arises in intimacy, in a relationship that is being found to be reliable.
>
> Winnicott (2005, p. 64)

Upon tracing this excitement, it seems that the destructiveness in changes from relating to usage may not always be scary for the subject; instead, it is oriented towards potentials. Throughout this transformative process, rather than an actual separation, it is only the perceived threat of separation (Abram & Hjulmand, 2018). Overcoming this threat of separation (separating the *not-me* in *me*) can lead an individual to progress from dependence towards autonomy, from isolated being towards relational being (Abram & Hjulmand, 2018). Transitional phenomena, which carry such excitement, develop through individual play and then progress to shared play, gradually extending into broader cultural experiences. Here, through the art of playing, self's stories are woven, relationally, and our essence is shared, face-to-face.

Playing in the intermediate area of experience, according to Winnicott, is synonymous with self-experiencing and creative living (Abram & Hjulmand, 2018). A sense of self is formed through experiences of relaxation, rooted in states of trust, and expressed through physical, mental, and creative activities, as observed in playing (Winnicott, 2005). The sense of true self tends to be spontaneous and creative, and I propose that the concept of a sense of self here aligns with the notion of an authentic self. In the less-purposeful or structured experiences associated with play, our authentic self can emerge more naturally.

The existence of 'me' comes out of questioning, representing a crucial moment when becoming aware of a sense of self amid formlessness (Abram & Hjulmand, 2018), and in a neutral zone (the third area). Winnicott (2005) suggests that within this state, everything can take on a creative dimension. In this way, Winnicott's theory of a relational creativity is deeply rooted at the very beginning of life (Abram & Hjulmand, 2018), building from an infant's illusory feelings of omnipotence into the infant's ability for creative activity.

Winnicott underscores primary psychic creativity as a drive towards health (Abram & Hjulmand, 2018). The infant who creates the imaginary breast over and over again is involved in a kind of remembering which comes to internalise/symbolise not only the object but also cultural experiences, embedding them in our subjective experiences of 'remembering'. Such subjective experiences of 'remembering' become an internal resource and thus lead to creative living. Winnicott posits that creativity, in this context, as universal, as a fundamental aspect of being alive or to engaging with external phenomena (Winnicott, 2005). Therefore, he emphasises the importance of developing the capacity for creative living and seeking the possibilities of hidden creativity:

> The creativity impulse is therefore something that can be looked at as a thing in itself. . . . [A]n artist is to produce a work of art, but also as something that is present when any-one-baby, child, adolescent, adult, old man or woman-looks in a healthy way at anything or does anything deliberately.
>
> Winnicott (2005, p. 92)

It is worth noting that creativity in Winnicott's theory is referred to as creative living, in which no special talent is needed (Winnicott, 1990). It was possible in my doctoral research, therefore, to approach parents' narratives from Winnicott's interpretive stance, in which there is a focus on ideas of a relational creativity (Winnicott, 2005).

Winnicott also emphasises the importance of a supportive environment for an individual's creativity and freedom to explore. As we stay mindful of the intermediate space between the infant and the mother, this kind of in-between space may potentially emerge through the adult's own confidence in the reliability of others or things (Abram & Hjulmand, 2018). Drawing on Winnicott's relational perspective, the subsequent section will allow a parent's narratives about play to emerge and unfold.

Embodied innocence: When parents embrace play

In this section, extracts are taken from an interview with 'Mathew', a (Chinese) parent with whom I worked as part of my doctoral research. You are invited as reader to imagine how the relational permeates Mathew's accounts of play with his children and the ways in which it becomes part of the relational fabric within his experience of family life.

A brief portrait of Mathew in words

Mathew was one of the six Chinese participants in my doctoral research. He was a husband to Jasmine and father to their two children. He was the youngest child in his family who, after graduating from a technical school at 20, worked in a local factory for a year and then joined his father's company. At his 23rd year, Mathew and Jasmine were married. He told me that while they had a very happy time together before marriage, after marriage, he underwent a transformation of identity and a great change. He admitted that such a huge life change was both exciting and scary to him, especially when they had their firstborn, Alex. Over time, he gradually tried to learn how to play with his children, with the support of his wife. His narratives illuminated something of the deep beauty of change, growth, and the simple yet fervent melody of family bonds woven through play.

'I felt refreshed': Playing together with children as a transitional space for a parent.

Mathew described his time with the children as limited, but his preferred activities include engaging in outdoor games with them, like badminton, jump rope, sandbags tossing, and biking, often playing together in the spacious court near his company.

He also shared how he engages with his children daily. Often, they can spend less time together because he feels tired after work and prefers to relax with his phone; meanwhile, the two children do their homework. From Jasmine's perspective, Mathew may not seem as involved in the activities with their two children. When I asked, *'How do you spend most of your time?'* he recalled:

> *I mainly work during the daytime, and I'm tired at night. Perhaps my wife would say, 'You come back home and then just say you are tired.' She told me that I didn't have an aware-ness of spending time with the kids. I just watch my phone all the time. . . . I am indeed a little tired when I come back. I spend little time with them because they also have home-work, and their grandparents accompany them on weekends. We often interact and play together when we go to friends' houses and have dinner with friends.*

Mathew then gave a detailed example of playing blindfold games. Unlike the constrained and impatient manner in which Mathew interacts with his children in their daily lives, the ways he engages with his children in play seemed mutually enjoyable and beneficial:

> *A while ago, I found myself immersed in blindfolded games with them. This is a certain game I cherish playing with them. When hide-and-seek isn't the chosen game, this is the one I naturally gravitate towards.*

Then I asked, *'Are there any memorable moments?'* He told me:

> *The blindfold game was very interesting. I really enjoyed it. I felt refreshed when playing with them. Tossing sandbag, jumping rope, engaging in blindfold adventures . . . [t]hese are the games that I come up with. I taught my kids, as well as their little friends. They felt very happy when they saw sandbags. As for jumping rope, they hadn't played before. They felt very happy when they played this game. And I played the blindfold games with them. Sometimes, they would say they wanted to play these games with me. I also cher-ished the moments we spent playing together.*

I asked, *'How do you feel when playing with them?'* He answered:

> *I'm really into it. I take it very seriously. They basically can't find me. Like playing blindfold games, I hide very well. As a parent, I feel very happy when I see my children are very happy. I'm happy when they are healthy. I'm very happy to see their smile. But I'm also very angry when they are naughty, particularly when my daughter struggles to control her temper. I'm not fond of that. She can be a bit too stubborn at times. Sometimes my temper flares up, so we can't teach them properly.*

In his portrayal, Mathew positions himself as a selector of games, as a guide during play. He represents himself as refreshing in the moments shared with children through playing.

Winnicott's idea of transitional space (2005) suggests that playing can create a transi-tional space wherein self-expression and rich potentials can flourish beyond the boundaries of ordinary, everyday life. Play is situated between the inner self and external world, offering a resting place where an individual cannot be challenged. This enables individuals to experience themselves not easily surfaced in their daily lives. Then what is experienced in playing may potentially integrate into the ways Mathew engages with his children in their everyday lives. In the example of playing blindfold games, a similar transitional space seemed to arise for Mathew.

In their daily life, Jasmine seemed to play a dominant role, while Mathew seemed to struggle to seize the initiative which is reflected in their respective narratives. For instance, Jasmine told Mathew not to discipline their children when he was impatient. While Jasmine relies on Mathew for support, she does not fully trust his abilities as a father and does not encourage his involvement. Despite Mathew's wanting to contribute to their children's education, his voice can be underestimated by Jasmine. In addition, concerning the relationships between Mathew and his parents, he said:

> My hope is that my children can be in good health. I also hope them to become self-reliant and financially independent, without the pressure to excel academically. Don't follow in my footsteps. I grew up living with my sister under my parents' roof. Our education ideas are different. They gave us life plans, leaving us with no personal aspirations. I once excitedly shared my plans with them, only to be met with discouragement. It was [a] struggle for me to do something when I was young. I needed to ask my parents for their permission.

Mathew sees his own parents as dominant and more powerful than him, viewing himself as reliant and obliged to follow their lead. However, he emphasises that he holds different ideas on education.

As Mathew played with his children, he donned the director's hat, choosing games and teaching children how to play. This could have been Mathew's wish to seize the initiative and take charge of his own life, and this energy enables him to represent himself as feeling 'refreshed' when playing with children. Drawing upon Winnicott's idea of transitional space (2005), when playing, Mathew stepped onto a bridge between his daily life and inner world, where he could weave his own script. Amidst these refreshing and playful moments, Mathew discovered himself in specific ways and experienced initiative in his connections with his children, which was elusive in 'everyday' life.

Mathew often smiled as he recounted these episodes and seemed to enjoy this version of himself while playing with children. I think that Mathew's play is not just a foray into different games; it is an adventure back to his childlike self. For example, in the blindfold game, his descriptions suggest that he is really involved in the play, values it, for it is in this unchallenged resting place that the anxiety and depression clouding his everyday life simply fade away.

Mathew's description of play evokes his reflections on relationships with his children in everyday life. He expresses happiness when his children are joyful and healthy. Their smiles bring him joy. On the other side, he admits his frustration and anger when his children misbehave or show stubbornness. He acknowledges that his own temper might sometimes hinder effective guidance for the children.

It is suggested that if Mathew could have a deeper understanding of his own behaviour in play and his playful side, he could become more patient and open in his interactions with his children. This might lead to him taking more active roles in his relationships with his family members. By embracing playfulness, Mathew could improve his ability to engage positively with his environment. I think that when Mathew engages in playful activities with children and shares stories of his playtime, he is creating beautiful opportunities for himself to grow, reflect, and develop a more playful interaction with his surroundings.

As Mathew had attempted to navigate the sadness of earlier times, he was deeply immersed in his own emotions and could not fully embody the spirit of play. Yet such feelings can simultaneously provide a precious opportunity to play with our own life experience. Parents who are able to craft a mindful space for their personal experiences can use such emotions to unlock the capacity to embrace the promise of relational play with their children.

Discussion

The psychoanalyst Mitchell proposes that relationality is viewed as 'universal and fundamental', and goes on to suggest thus:

> Mind has increasingly been understood most fundamentally and directly in terms of self-other configurations, intrapsychically and interpersonally, present and past, in actuality and in fantasy.

Mitchell (2014, p. xiii)

Winnicott was an intrinsically relational thinker and offered creative play as a healthy means of self-expression and of being in the world. With parents and their everyday lives at the core, play not only embodies joy shared with children but also emphasises experiential and growth-oriented aspect in cultivating relationships. When seen through the lens of the 'relational', practical avenues unfold for parents to discover and engage, thereby enriching the expanse of play. For example, in Mathew's case, the exploration of play is unveiled through two aspects: engaging in playful activities with his children and adopting a playful approach as a means of navigating sadness.

Constructing Mathew's play with his children through the lens of Winnicott's ideas of transitional space enables us to uncover nuanced layers, revealing the importance of play for parents. While playing, a parent can become a director, scripting their own story and grasping a version of their child's being that often remains elusive in their daily life. Immersed in play, the emotional burdens that cloud one's everyday life may simply fade away. The happiness shared by parent and child naturally nurtures their bond. Play is an adventure back to one's childlike innocence.

In our interview, Mathew said, *'We need to make some changes and find the right balance.'* His reflective perspective enabled him to reflect on play and its potential uncertainty to make a wider impact on the relational life of the family.

Summary

In the making of this current chapter, play has been observed and constructed in relation to others, and in the process, we can ourselves playfully shift our attention from focusing on 'the cared-for-in-themselves to a focus on the cared-for-in-relation to others' (Todres et al., 2014, p. 9). The mindful choices we can make are cultivated and embodied in the play. The in-between world of play can be viewed as a conscious, transitional space in which our creative responses are allowed to unfold softly, even in the face of challenging situations. In the intermediate area of experience, the attitudes towards ourselves and others are better observed and cultivated; negative thoughts are weakened, and stable attitudes with kindness towards others are gradually formulated. The playful attempts can then shift our attention back to daily life with kindness and allow self-other relationships to flow.

There is a huge value in incorporating play into a parent's life. Discovering the art of embracing play becomes a gift for parents. The challenge lies in skilfully cultivating this gift to create safe relational spaces. It becomes paramount for parents to carve out secure spaces in relation to themselves and their children and to embark upon exploring bonds with trustworthy others. In the realm of play, 'others' becomes a possibility, an opportunity for healthy and beautiful meaning arising in a parent's (relational) consciousness.

Box summary

- Play is an important part of a child's emotional development.
- Play provides spaces, transitional/relational, for creativity and the processing of emotion, both for the child and the parent.
- Play provides opportunities for parents whose own potential for growth can be *'refreshed'* in the playful relational spaces they enjoy with their children.

References

Abram, J., & Hjulmand, K. (2018). *The language of Winnicott: A dictionary of Winnicott's use of words* (2nd ed.). Routledge.

Davis, M., & Wallbridge, D. (2018). *Boundary and space: An introduction to the work of DW Winnincott*. Routledge.

Mitchell, S. A. (2014). *Relationality: From attachment to intersubjectivity*. Psychology Press.

Todres, L., Galvin, K. T., & Dahlberg, K. (2014). "Caring for insiderness": Phenomenologically informed insights that can guide practice. *International Journal of Qualitative Studies on Health and Wellbeing, 9*(1), 21421.

Winnicott, D. W. (1969). The use of an object. *International Journal of Psycho-Analysis, 50*, 711-716.

Winnicott, D. W. (1990). *Home is where we start from: Essays by a psychoanalyst*. W.W. Norton & Company.

Winnicott, D. W. (2005). *Playing and reality*. Routledge.(Original work published 1971)

Winnicott, D. W. (2006). *The family and individual development*. Routledge.

20 Final thoughts from our authors

As one of the book's editors, it has been a privilege to have had the opportunity to continue working with people and ideas that have been part of my life for many years. **(Tom Billington)**

Participating in this project allowed me to collaborate with colleagues, exchanging insights around a shared value: the understanding that knowledge resides within our community. I hope this book inspires others to do the same, recognising that effective communication and active listening foster collaboration and shared success. **(Natalie Neal, Laura de Cabo SerÛn)**

The longer that I have worked in, and with, education settings, the more I have reflected that safe and trusted relationships and human connection are the only things that really matter. Building Relational Schools is about working with the relationships in the community to support inclusion and a sense of belonging. **(Dr Kate Taylor)**

Despite my initial tentative steps, my courage grew as I became more immersed in the welcoming and supportive community through which this book has evolved. Warm reflections have been embodied in our encounters. Spaces were created that encouraged each of us, editors and authors, to be honest in voicing our fears and vulnerabilities. Through a sense of connected fragility as a network of people working in a range of challenging educational contexts, a shared strength and conviction were generated. This book is important and needs to make a difference. For me, the relational creation of the book has mirrored the content. This has not been a clinical process, rather a very human one. **(Claire-Marie Whiting)**

While what I have to add to the cannon might not be 'new' in terms of ideas that have ever been thought, I do feel that I am part of something that is unique via its connection to the University of Sheffield's work in critical educational psychology. **(Tim Corcoran)**

This project, which embraces relational theory and practice, offers a much-needed breath of fresh air to our educational endeavours. It helps us understand the mental health and wellbeing challenges many students and teachers face, by shifting the focus from the individual student or teacher to the dominant discourse of the educational institution itself. This alternative, I believe, can reignite the original purpose of education: to engage learners in contributing to the creation of liveable communities by becoming aware of their civic and relational responsibilities. **(Sheila McNamee)**

DOI: 10.4324/9781003451907-20

It is hoped that readers develop an awareness, curiosity, and understanding of the application and effectiveness of a special time intervention, by allowing others to develop practical ways of nurturing relationships and prioritising these in their daily interactions with children. **(Dr Rachel Cooper, Dr Laura Griffiths, Dr Lucy Hatton, Dr Angela Wright)**

Being involved in this project has brought me in contact with lots of wonderful people and ideas that have inspired me to practice what I truly believe and embolden me to live these beliefs more fully and openly. **(Sahaja Timothy Davis)**

More than ever, schools are in the centre of children in crisis; we are expected to not only identify, report on, and attend to needs but to also maintain strong relationships and provide the stability that these children often lack. **(Sharon Richards)**

Confidence in the power of our voice, and story, standing alongside accounts from professionals we admire, respect, and seek to engage with, as part of our solidarity teams for practice. A shift in being positioned by systems, to accepting agency in values-led relationships with systems, over time. **(Dr Catherine Beal, Dr Helen Waters)**

The process of writing our chapter led us to deconstruct what we mean by relational working in Nottinghamshire and how this is evident in our practice. We now have a deeper understanding of relational practice, to see that we are actually relational, and this has the power to bring about lasting change. **(Pauline Clarke, Dr Jo Marriott)**

We have been supported by the feeling of solidarity between us, and the recognition that, on a very fundamental level, we share a worldview and important values which are central to who we are. Our hopes are that our ideas will find points of connection for the reader and will prompt further thinking. Ultimately, we hope that this will lead to more open discussion about the relationship between our personal and professional lives within the field of educational psychology and other professional domains. **(Mary Chilokoa, Emily Jackson)**

The writing of this book has been a privilege, an insight, and hopefully transformational in developing our school practice yet further. **(Chris Davey)**

Being part of the relational project feels like being where I'm meant to be. **(Changjie Meng)**

Index

Note: Page numbers in *italics* indicate figures, and page numbers in **bold** indicate tables in the text